# Pass the PMP® Exam

## Tools, Tips and Tricks to Succeed

### Second Edition

Sean Whitaker

Apress®

*Pass the PMP® Exam: Tools, Tips and Tricks to Succeed, Second Edition*

Sean Whitaker
ChristChurch, Canterbury, New Zealand

ISBN-13 (pbk): 978-1-4842-2073-3          ISBN-13 (electronic): 978-1-4842-2074-0
DOI 10.1007/978-1-4842-2074-0

Library of Congress Control Number: 2016944183

Managing Director: Welmoed Spahr
Lead Editor: Steve Anglin
Technical Reviewer: Mike Roberts
Editorial Board: Steve Anglin, Pramila Balan, Louise Corrigan, Jonathan Gennick,
    Robert Hutchinson, Celestin Suresh John, James Markham, Susan McDermott,
    Matthew Moodie, Ben Renow-Clarke, Gwenan Spearing
Coordinating Editor: Mark Powers
Copy Editor: Tiffany Taylor
Compositor: SPi Global
Indexer: SPi Global
Artist: SPi Global

Distributed to the book trade worldwide by Springer Science+Business Media New York, 233 Spring Street, 6th Floor, New York, NY 10013. Phone 1-800-SPRINGER, fax (201) 348-4505, e-mail orders-ny@springer-sbm.com, or visit www.springeronline.com. Apress Media, LLC is a California LLC and the sole member (owner) is Springer Science + Business Media Finance Inc (SSBM Finance Inc). SSBM Finance Inc is a **Delaware** corporation.

For information on translations, please e-mail rights@apress.com, or visit www.apress.com.

Apress and friends of ED books may be purchased in bulk for academic, corporate, or promotional use. eBook versions and licenses are also available for most titles. For more information, reference our Special Bulk Sales–eBook Licensing web page at www.apress.com/bulk-sales.

Any source code or other supplementary materials referenced by the author in this text are available to readers at www.apress.com/9781484220733. For detailed information about how to locate your book's source code, go to www.apress.com/source-code/. Readers can also access source code at SpringerLink in the Supplementary Material section for each chapter.

Printed on acid-free paper

*This book is dedicated to you for choosing to commit to your own ongoing professional development.*

*No form of education is ever wasted, and without doubt the greatest investment you can ever make is in your own development.*

*noli cedere cognoscere*

# Contents at a Glance

About the Author ............................................................. xli

About the Technical Reviewer ....................................... xliii

How to Use This Book ..................................................... xlv

■Chapter 1: Foundational Concepts of Project Management ........... 1

■Chapter 2: Integration Management ............................................. 35

■Chapter 3: Scope Management ...................................... 91

■Chapter 4: Time Management ................................................. 133

■Chapter 5: Cost Management ...................................... 199

■Chapter 6: Quality Management .................................... 241

■Chapter 7: Human Resource Management ..................... 279

■Chapter 8: Communications Management ...................... 327

■Chapter 9: Risk Management ...................................... 353

■Chapter 10: Procurement Management............................. 405

■Chapter 11: Stakeholder Management ............................ 445

■Chapter 12: Ethics and Professional Conduct ................. 475

■Chapter 13: Eligibility, Study, and Exam-Taking Tips ................. 495

■Chapter 14: Blank Mind Maps ..................................... 499

▓**Chapter 15: Formulas to Remember**............................................ **503**

▓**Chapter 16: PMP® Examination Tasks Puzzle Game**................... **505**

▓**Chapter 17: PMP® Examination Role-Delineation Domain Tasks** ............................................................................. **511**

**Glossary of Key Terms** .................................................................. **513**

**Index**............................................................................................. **533**

# Contents

About the Author ............................................................. xli

About the Technical Reviewer ....................................... xliii

How to Use This Book ..................................................... xlv

■Chapter 1: Foundational Concepts of Project Management ........... 1

Objectives ......................................................................... 1

The Purpose of the PMBOK Guide ...................................... 2

What Is a Project, a Program, and a Portfolio? ..................... 4

What Is Project Management? ............................................. 8

Project Management, Operations Management, and
Organizational Strategy ................................................... 11

Organizational Influences on Project Management ............... 13

The Project Life Cycle ...................................................... 15

Chapter Summary ........................................................... 21

Exercises ....................................................................... 22

Review Questions ........................................................... 23

Answers ......................................................................... 26

Exercises .................................................................. 26

Review Questions ....................................................... 30

■Chapter 2: Integration Management ................................... 35

What Is Project Integration Management? ........................... 35

Develop Project Charter ................................................... 37

Inputs ............................................................................ 41

Project Statement of Work...................................................................................42

Business Case ......................................................................................................42

Agreements ..........................................................................................................43

Enterprise Environmental Factors .......................................................................44

Organizational Process Assets.............................................................................44

**Tools and Techniques** .....................................................................................**45**

Expert Judgment ..................................................................................................45

Facilitation Techniques ........................................................................................45

**Outputs**.............................................................................................................**46**

Project Charter......................................................................................................46

**Develop Project Management Plan** ................................................................**47**

**Inputs** ................................................................................................................**48**

Project Charter......................................................................................................49

Outputs from Other Processes..............................................................................49

Enterprise Environmental Factors .......................................................................50

Organizational Process Assets.............................................................................50

**Tools and Techniques** .....................................................................................**51**

Expert Judgment ..................................................................................................51

Facilitation Techniques ........................................................................................52

**Outputs**.............................................................................................................**52**

Project Management Plan .....................................................................................53

**Direct and Manage Project Work**....................................................................**55**

**Inputs** ................................................................................................................**56**

Project Management Plan .....................................................................................57

Approved Change Requests..................................................................................57

Enterprise Environmental Factors .......................................................................57

Organizational Process Assets.............................................................................57

**Tools and Techniques** ............................................................ 58

    Expert Judgment ............................................................................. 58

    Project Management Information System ....................................... 58

    Meetings .......................................................................................... 58

**Outputs** ................................................................................ 59

    Deliverables .................................................................................... 59

    Work Performance Data .................................................................. 59

    Change Requests ............................................................................ 60

    Project Management Plan Updates ................................................ 60

    Project Document Updates ............................................................. 60

**Monitor and Control Project Work** ................................... 61

**Inputs** ................................................................................... 63

    Project Management Plan ............................................................... 63

    Schedule Forecasts ........................................................................ 63

    Cost Forecasts ................................................................................ 63

    Validated Changes .......................................................................... 63

    Work Performance Information ....................................................... 64

    Enterprise Environmental Factors ................................................. 65

    Organizational Process Assets ....................................................... 65

**Tools and Techniques** ............................................................ 65

    Expert Judgment ............................................................................. 65

    Analytical Techniques ..................................................................... 65

    Project Management Information System ....................................... 67

    Meetings .......................................................................................... 67

**Outputs** ................................................................................ 67

    Change Requests ............................................................................ 67

    Work Performance Reports ............................................................ 68

    Project Management Plan Updates ................................................ 68

    Project Document Updates ............................................................. 68

Perform Integrated Change Control...........................................................69

Inputs ......................................................................................................71

    Project Management Plan ...............................................................................71

    Work Performance Reports ..............................................................................71

    Change Requests...........................................................................................72

    Enterprise Environmental Factors ....................................................................72

    Organizational Process Assets..........................................................................72

Tools and Techniques ...............................................................................72

    Expert Judgment ...........................................................................................72

    Meetings......................................................................................................73

    Change-Control Tools.....................................................................................73

Outputs....................................................................................................73

    Approved Change Requests..............................................................................73

    Change Log..................................................................................................73

    Project Management Plan Updates ...................................................................74

    Project Document Updates ..............................................................................74

Close Project or Phase ............................................................................75

Inputs ......................................................................................................77

    Project Management Plan ...............................................................................77

    Accepted Deliverables ...................................................................................77

    Organizational Process Assets..........................................................................77

Tools and Techniques ...............................................................................78

    Expert Judgment ...........................................................................................78

    Analytical Techniques ....................................................................................78

    Meetings......................................................................................................78

Outputs....................................................................................................78

    Final Product, Service, or Result Transition .......................................................78

    Organizational Process Asset Updates ..............................................................79

Chapter Summary ......................................................................... 80

Exercises ...................................................................................... 81

Review Questions ....................................................................... 82

Answers ....................................................................................... 85

    Exercises .......................................................................................... 85

    Review Questions ........................................................................... 86

**Chapter 3: Scope Management** ...................................... 91

What Is Project Scope Management? ....................................... 92

Plan Scope Management ........................................................... 94

Inputs .......................................................................................... 95

    Project Management Plan ............................................................. 95

    Project Charter ............................................................................... 95

    Enterprise Environmental Factors ............................................... 96

    Organizational Process Assets ..................................................... 96

Tools and Techniques ................................................................ 96

    Expert Judgment ............................................................................ 96

    Meetings .......................................................................................... 96

Outputs ........................................................................................ 97

    Scope Management Plan ................................................................ 97

    Requirements Management Plan .................................................. 98

Collect Requirements ................................................................ 98

Inputs ........................................................................................ 100

    Scope Management Plan .............................................................. 100

    Requirements Management Plan ................................................ 100

    Stakeholder Management Plan .................................................... 100

    Project Charter ............................................................................. 100

    Stakeholder Register ................................................................... 100

### Tools and Techniques ................................................................. 101
Interviews...................................................................................... 101

Focus Groups................................................................................ 101

Facilitated Workshops .................................................................. 101

Group Creativity Techniques ........................................................ 101

Group Decision-Making Techniques ............................................ 101

Questionnaires and Surveys......................................................... 102

Observations................................................................................. 102

Prototypes .................................................................................... 102

Benchmarking ............................................................................... 103

Context Diagrams ......................................................................... 103

Document Analysis ....................................................................... 103

### Outputs.......................................................................................... 103
Requirements Documentation ...................................................... 103

Requirements Traceability Matrix ................................................ 104

### Define Scope ................................................................................. 105

### Inputs ............................................................................................ 106
Scope Management Plan............................................................... 106

Project Charter.............................................................................. 106

Requirements Documentation ...................................................... 106

Organizational Process Assets..................................................... 106

### Tools and Techniques ................................................................. 107
Expert Judgment ........................................................................... 107

Product Analysis ........................................................................... 107

Alternatives Generation ................................................................ 107

Facilitated Workshops .................................................................. 107

### Outputs.......................................................................................... 107
Project Scope Statement.............................................................. 107

Project Document Updates ........................................................... 108

## Create WBS ................................................................................................. 109

## Inputs ....................................................................................................... 110

### Scope Management Plan ................................................................... 110

### Project Scope Statement .................................................................. 110

### Requirements Documentation .......................................................... 111

### Enterprise Environmental Factors .................................................... 111

### Organizational Process Assets .......................................................... 111

## Tools and Techniques ............................................................................ 111

### Decomposition ................................................................................... 111

### Expert Judgment ............................................................................... 112

## Outputs .................................................................................................. 112

### Scope Baseline .................................................................................. 112

### Project Document updates ............................................................... 114

## Validate Scope ...................................................................................... 115

## Inputs ..................................................................................................... 115

### Project Management Plan ................................................................. 116

### Requirements Documentation .......................................................... 116

### Requirements Traceability Matrix ..................................................... 116

### Verified Deliverables ........................................................................ 116

### Work Performance Data .................................................................... 117

## Tools and Techniques ............................................................................ 117

### Inspection .......................................................................................... 117

### Group Decision-Making Techniques ................................................. 117

## Outputs .................................................................................................. 117

### Accepted Deliverables ...................................................................... 117

### Change Requests .............................................................................. 117

### Work Performance Information ......................................................... 118

### Project Document Updates ............................................................... 118

Control Scope .................................................................. 119

Inputs ............................................................................ 119

    Project Management Plan ............................................................ 119

    Requirements Documentation ...................................................... 120

    Requirements Traceability Matrix .................................................. 120

    Work Performance Data .............................................................. 120

    Organizational Process Assets...................................................... 120

Tools and Techniques .................................................... 120

    Variance Analysis...................................................................... 120

Outputs .......................................................................... 121

    Work Performance Information ...................................................... 121

    Change Requests...................................................................... 121

    Project Management Plan Updates ................................................ 121

    Project Document Updates .......................................................... 121

    Organizational Process Assets Updates .......................................... 121

Chapter Summary .......................................................... 122

Exercises ....................................................................... 123

Review Questions............................................................ 124

Answers ......................................................................... 127

    Exercises ............................................................................... 127

    Review Questions ..................................................................... 128

▓Chapter 4: Time Management ..................................... 133

What Is Project Time Management?................................. 133

Plan Schedule Management............................................ 134

Inputs ............................................................................ 135

    Project Management Plan ............................................................ 135

    Project Charter......................................................................... 135

Enterprise Environmental Factors .................................................................. 136

Organizational Process Assets....................................................................... 136

## Tools and Techniques ................................................................. 136

Expert Judgment ............................................................................................ 136

Analytical Techniques .................................................................................... 137

Meetings........................................................................................................ 137

## Outputs......................................................................................... 137

Schedule Management Plan............................................................................ 137

## Define Activities........................................................................... 138

## Inputs ........................................................................................... 139

Schedule Management Plan............................................................................ 139

Scope Baseline .............................................................................................. 140

Enterprise Environmental Factors .................................................................. 140

Organizational Process Assets....................................................................... 140

## Tools and Techniques ................................................................. 140

Decomposition................................................................................................ 140

Rolling-Wave Planning.................................................................................... 141

Expert Judgment ............................................................................................ 141

## Outputs......................................................................................... 141

Activity List.................................................................................................... 141

Activity Attributes .......................................................................................... 142

Milestone List ................................................................................................ 142

## Sequence Activities...................................................................... 143

## Inputs ........................................................................................... 144

Schedule Management Plan............................................................................ 144

Activity List.................................................................................................... 144

Activity Attributes .......................................................................................... 144

Milestone List ................................................................................................ 144

Project Scope Statement................................................................................ 144

Enterprise Environmental Factors ............................................................. 145

Organizational Process Assets .................................................................. 145

## Tools and Techniques ................................................................. 145

Precedence Diagramming Method (PDM) .................................................. 145

Dependency Determination ...................................................................... 147

Applying Leads and Lags .......................................................................... 148

## Outputs .................................................................................... 149

Project Schedule Network Diagrams ........................................................ 149

Project Document Updates ....................................................................... 150

## Estimate Activity Resources ..................................................... 151

## Inputs ...................................................................................... 152

Schedule Management Plan ...................................................................... 152

Activity List .............................................................................................. 152

Activity Attributes .................................................................................... 152

Resource Calendars .................................................................................. 152

Risk Register ............................................................................................ 152

Activity Cost Estimates ............................................................................ 153

Enterprise Environmental Factors ............................................................ 153

Organizational Process Assets .................................................................. 153

## Tools and Techniques ................................................................. 153

Expert Judgment ...................................................................................... 153

Alternative Analysis ................................................................................. 153

Published Estimating Data ....................................................................... 153

Bottom-Up Estimating .............................................................................. 154

Project Management Software .................................................................. 154

## Outputs .................................................................................... 154

Activity Resource Requirements ............................................................... 154

Resource Breakdown Structure ................................................................ 154

Project Document Updates ....................................................................... 155

## Estimate Activity Durations ...... 156

## Inputs ...... 157

Schedule Management Plan ...... 157

Activity List ...... 157

Activity Attributes ...... 157

Activity Resource Requirements ...... 157

Resource Calendars ...... 157

Project Scope Statement ...... 158

Risk Register ...... 158

Resource Breakdown Structure ...... 158

Enterprise Environmental Factors ...... 158

Organizational Process Assets ...... 158

## Tools and Techniques ...... 159

Expert Judgment ...... 159

Analogous Estimating ...... 159

Parametric Estimating ...... 159

Three-Point Estimating ...... 160

Group Decision-Making Techniques ...... 162

Reserve Analysis ...... 163

## Outputs ...... 164

Activity Duration Estimates ...... 164

Project Document Updates ...... 164

## Develop Schedule ...... 165

## Inputs ...... 167

Schedule Management Plan ...... 167

Activity List ...... 167

Activity Attributes ...... 167

Project Schedule Network Diagrams ...... 167

Activity Resource Requirements ...... 167

Resource Calendars.................................................................................167

Activity Duration Estimates.....................................................................168

Project Scope Statement.........................................................................168

Risk Register .........................................................................................168

Project Staff Assignments .......................................................................168

Resource Breakdown Structure.................................................................168

Enterprise Environmental Factors .............................................................168

Organizational Process Assets.................................................................169

Tools and Techniques ........................................................... 169

Schedule Network Analysis .....................................................................169

Critical Path Method ...............................................................................169

Critical Chain Method .............................................................................173

Resource Optimization Techniques............................................................173

Modeling Techniques ..............................................................................174

Leads and Lags.....................................................................................175

Schedule Compression ...........................................................................175

Scheduling Tool.....................................................................................175

Outputs ............................................................................... 175

Schedule Baseline .................................................................................175

Project Schedule....................................................................................176

Schedule Data ......................................................................................177

Project Calendars ..................................................................................177

Project Management Plan Updates ............................................................177

Project Document Updates ......................................................................177

Control Schedule ................................................................... 178

Inputs ................................................................................. 179

Project Management Plan ........................................................................179

Project Schedule....................................................................................179

Work Performance Data ..........................................................................179

Project Calendars ...................................................................................... 180

Schedule Data .......................................................................................... 180

Organizational Process Assets.................................................................. 180

## Tools and Techniques ................................................................ 180

Performance Reviews................................................................................. 180

Project Management Software .................................................................. 181

Resource Optimization Techniques.......................................................... 181

Modeling Techniques................................................................................. 181

Leads and Lags......................................................................................... 182

Schedule Compression.............................................................................. 182

Scheduling Tool......................................................................................... 182

## Outputs ................................................................................... 183

Work Performance Information ................................................................. 183

Schedule Forecasts ................................................................................. 183

Change Requests....................................................................................... 184

Project Management Plan Updates ........................................................... 184

Project Document Updates........................................................................ 185

Organizational Process Asset Updates ..................................................... 185

## Chapter Summary ..................................................................... 185

## Exercises ................................................................................. 187

## Review Questions...................................................................... 188

## Answers ................................................................................... 191

Exercises .................................................................................................. 191

## Review Questions...................................................................... 193

## ▓Chapter 5: Cost Management ................................................... 199

## What Is Project Cost Management? ............................................. 199

## Plan Cost Management .............................................................. 200

## Inputs .................................................................................... 201

Project Management Plan ........................................................................... 201

Project Charter............................................................................................ 201

Enterprise Environmental Factors ............................................................. 202

Organizational Process Assets.................................................................... 202

## Tools and Techniques ................................................................. 202

Expert Judgment ......................................................................................... 203

Analytical Techniques ................................................................................. 203

Meetings...................................................................................................... 203

## Outputs........................................................................................ 204

Cost Management Plan................................................................................ 204

## Estimate Costs ........................................................................... 205

## Inputs ......................................................................................... 207

Cost Management Plan................................................................................ 207

Human Resource Management Plan ........................................................... 207

Scope Baseline ........................................................................................... 207

Project Schedule.......................................................................................... 208

Risk Register ............................................................................................... 208

Enterprise Environmental Factors ............................................................. 208

Organizational Process Assets.................................................................... 208

## Tools and Techniques ................................................................. 208

Expert Judgment ......................................................................................... 209

Analogous Estimating.................................................................................. 209

Parametric Estimating ................................................................................ 209

Bottom-Up Estimating ................................................................................ 209

Three-Point Estimating................................................................................ 209

Reserve Analysis ........................................................................................ 211

Cost of Quality ............................................................................................ 212

Project Management Software .................................................................... 212

Vendor Bid Analysis ................................................................................ 212

Group Decision-Making Techniques ......................................................... 212

## Outputs .................................................................................................. 212

Activity Cost Estimates ........................................................................... 212

Basis of Estimates .................................................................................. 212

Project Document Updates ...................................................................... 213

## Determine Budget ................................................................................. 214

## Inputs .................................................................................................... 214

Cost Management Plan ............................................................................ 214

Scope Baseline ....................................................................................... 215

Activity Cost Estimates ........................................................................... 215

Basis of Estimates .................................................................................. 215

Project Schedule .................................................................................... 215

Resource Calendars ................................................................................ 215

Risk Register .......................................................................................... 215

Agreements ............................................................................................ 216

Organizational Process Assets ................................................................. 216

## Tools and Techniques ........................................................................... 216

Cost Aggregation .................................................................................... 216

Reserve Analysis .................................................................................... 217

Expert Judgment ..................................................................................... 217

Historical Relationships ........................................................................... 217

Funding Limit Reconciliation .................................................................... 217

## Outputs .................................................................................................. 218

Cost Baseline ......................................................................................... 218

Project Funding Requirements ................................................................. 219

Project Document Updates ...................................................................... 219

Control Costs .................................................................................. 220

Inputs ............................................................................................. 220

    Project Management Plan ................................................................. 221

    Project Funding Requirements ......................................................... 221

    Work Performance Data .................................................................. 221

    Organizational Process Assets......................................................... 221

Tools and Techniques ..................................................................... 221

    Earned Value Management................................................................ 221

    Forecasting...................................................................................... 225

    To-Complete Performance Index (TCPI)........................................... 227

    Performance Reviews...................................................................... 228

    Project Management Software ......................................................... 228

    Reserve Analysis ............................................................................ 228

Outputs........................................................................................... 228

    Work Performance Information ........................................................ 228

    Cost Forecasts................................................................................ 228

    Change Requests............................................................................ 229

    Project Management Plan Updates .................................................. 229

    Project Document Updates.............................................................. 229

    Organizational Process Asset Updates ............................................ 229

Chapter Summary ........................................................................... 230

Exercises ........................................................................................ 231

Review Questions............................................................................ 232

Answers .......................................................................................... 234

    Exercises ........................................................................................ 234

    Chapter Review .............................................................................. 237

▓**Chapter 6: Quality Management** ............................................... **241**

What Is Project Quality Management? ............................................. 241

Plan Quality Management ................................................................ 243

Inputs ............................................................................................. 244

    Project Management Plan ..................................................................... 244

    Stakeholder Register ............................................................................ 245

    Risk Register ....................................................................................... 245

    Requirements Documentation ............................................................... 245

    Enterprise Environmental Factors ........................................................ 245

    Organizational Process Assets.............................................................. 246

Tools and Techniques .................................................................... 246

    Cost-Benefit Analysis........................................................................... 246

    Cost of Quality .................................................................................... 246

    Seven Basic Quality Tools .................................................................... 246

    Benchmarking ..................................................................................... 252

    Design of Experiments.......................................................................... 252

    Statistical Sampling............................................................................. 252

    Additional Quality Planning Tools......................................................... 252

    Meetings.............................................................................................. 252

Outputs........................................................................................... 253

    Quality Management Plan..................................................................... 253

    Process Improvement Plan.................................................................... 253

    Quality Metrics.................................................................................... 254

    Quality Checklists ............................................................................... 254

    Project Document Updates ................................................................... 254

Perform Quality Assurance............................................................. 255

Inputs ............................................................................................. 256

    Quality Management Plan..................................................................... 256

    Process Improvement Plan.................................................................... 256

Quality Metrics.................................................................................256

Quality Control Measurements ...........................................256

Project Documents .................................................................257

Tools and Techniques ...............................................................257

Quality Management and Control Tools ...........................257

Quality Audits.........................................................................261

Process Analysis ....................................................................261

Outputs .........................................................................................261

Change Requests....................................................................262

Project Management Plan Updates ...................................262

Project Document Updates....................................................262

Organizational Process Asset Updates .............................262

Control Quality.........................................................................263

Inputs ............................................................................................263

Quality Management Plan.....................................................263

Quality Metrics.......................................................................264

Quality Checklists .................................................................264

Work Performance Data .......................................................264

Approved Change Requests..................................................264

Deliverables ...........................................................................264

Project Documents ................................................................264

Organizational Process Assets............................................264

Tools and Techniques ...............................................................265

Seven Basic Quality Tools....................................................265

Statistical Sampling..............................................................265

Inspection ...............................................................................265

Approved Change Request Review.......................................265

Outputs .........................................................................................266

Quality Control Measurements ................................................................. 266

Validated Changes ................................................................................... 266

Verified Deliverables ............................................................................... 267

Work Performance Information ............................................................... 267

Change Requests ..................................................................................... 267

Project Management Plan Updates ........................................................ 267

Project Document Updates ..................................................................... 267

Organizational Process Asset Updates ................................................. 267

Chapter Summary ............................................................................. 268

Exercise ............................................................................................. 269

Review Questions .............................................................................. 270

Answers .............................................................................................. 273

Exercises ................................................................................................. 273

Review Questions .............................................................................. 274

Chapter 7: Human Resource Management ...................................... 279

What Is Project Human Resource Management? ............................. 280

Plan Human Resource Management ................................................. 280

Inputs ................................................................................................. 281

Project Management Plan ....................................................................... 281

Activity Resource Requirements ............................................................. 281

Enterprise Environmental Factors ......................................................... 281

Organizational Process Assets ............................................................... 282

Tools and Techniques ........................................................................ 282

Organizational Charts and Position Descriptions ................................. 282

Networking ............................................................................................... 287

Organizational Theory ............................................................................. 287

Expert Judgment ..................................................................................... 291

Meetings ................................................................................................... 291

**Outputs** ............................................................................ 291

    Human Resource Management Plan ............................................ 291

**Acquire Project Team** ...................................................... 292

**Inputs** ............................................................................. 293

    Human Resource Management Plan ............................................ 293

    Enterprise Environmental Factors ............................................... 293

    Organizational Process Assets .................................................... 293

**Tools and Techniques** ...................................................... 293

    Preassignment ........................................................................ 294

    Negotiation ............................................................................ 294

    Acquisition ............................................................................. 294

    Virtual Teams ......................................................................... 294

    Multicriteria Decision Analysis .................................................. 295

**Outputs** ............................................................................ 295

    Project Staff Assignments ........................................................ 295

    Resource Calendars ................................................................. 295

    Project Management Plan Updates ............................................. 296

**Develop Project Team** ..................................................... 296

**Inputs** ............................................................................. 297

    Human Resource Management Plan ............................................ 297

    Project Staff Assignments ........................................................ 297

    Resource Calendars ................................................................. 298

**Tools and Techniques** ...................................................... 298

    Interpersonal Skills ................................................................. 298

    Training ................................................................................. 304

    Team-Building Activities ........................................................... 305

    Ground Rules .......................................................................... 307

    Co-location ............................................................................. 307

Recognition and Rewards.................................................................307

Personnel Assessment Tools ...........................................................308

## Outputs ..........................................................................308

Team Performance Assessments .....................................................308

Enterprise Environmental Factor Updates........................................309

## Manage Project Team..................................................310

## Inputs ............................................................................310

Human Resource Management Plan ................................................311

Project Staff Assignments ..............................................................311

Team Performance Assessments .....................................................311

Issue Log .....................................................................................311

Work Performance Reports .............................................................311

Organizational Process Assets.........................................................312

## Tools and Techniques ....................................................312

Observation and Conversation.........................................................312

Project Performance Appraisals ......................................................312

Conflict Management .....................................................................312

Interpersonal Skills........................................................................313

## Outputs ..........................................................................314

Change Requests...........................................................................314

Project Management Plan Updates ..................................................314

Project Document Updates..............................................................314

Enterprise Environmental Factor Updates........................................314

Organizational Process Asset Updates .............................................314

## Chapter Summary .........................................................315

## Exercises ......................................................................316

## Review Questions..........................................................317

**Answers** ....................................................................... 320

   Exercises ................................................................ 320

   Chapter Review ........................................................ 322

**▓Chapter 8: Communications Management** ................... 327

**What Is Project Communications Management?** ............ 327

**Plan Communications Management** ............................. 328

**Inputs** ............................................................................ 329

   Project Management Plan ............................................ 329

   Stakeholder Register .................................................. 329

   Enterprise Environmental Factors ............................... 330

   Organizational Process Assets .................................... 330

**Tools and Techniques** .................................................. 330

   Communications Requirements Analysis ...................... 330

   Communications Technology ....................................... 331

   Communications Models ............................................. 331

   Communications Methods ........................................... 333

   Meetings ................................................................... 334

**Outputs** ........................................................................ 334

   Communications Management Plan .............................. 334

   Project Document Updates .......................................... 335

**Manage Communications** ............................................. 336

**Inputs** ............................................................................ 336

   Communications Management Plan .............................. 336

   Work Performance Reports .......................................... 337

   Enterprise Environmental Factors ............................... 337

   Organizational Process Assets .................................... 337

**Tools and Techniques** ........................................................... 337

    Communications Technology .............................................. 337

    Communications Models ................................................... 338

    Communications Methods .................................................. 338

    Information Management Systems ......................................... 338

    Performance Reporting .................................................... 338

**Outputs** ........................................................................ 338

    Project Communications ................................................... 339

    Project Document Updates ................................................. 339

    Project Management Plan Updates ......................................... 339

    Organizational Process Asset Updates ..................................... 339

**Control Communications** ....................................................... 340

**Inputs** ......................................................................... 341

    Project Management Plan .................................................. 341

    Project Communications ................................................... 341

    Issue Log ................................................................. 341

    Work Performance Data .................................................... 342

    Organizational Process Assets ............................................. 342

**Tools and Techniques** ........................................................... 342

    Reporting Systems ........................................................ 342

    Expert Judgment .......................................................... 342

    Meetings .................................................................. 343

**Outputs** ........................................................................ 343

    Work Performance Information .............................................. 343

    Change Requests .......................................................... 343

    Project Management Plan Updates ......................................... 343

    Project Document Updates ................................................. 343

    Organizational Process Asset Updates ..................................... 344

Chapter Summary .......................................................................... 344

Exercises ..................................................................................... 345

Review Questions........................................................................ 346

Answers ...................................................................................... 348

    Exercises ................................................................................... 348

    Chapter Review ......................................................................... 349

**Chapter 9: Risk Management ...................................... 353**

What Is Project Risk Management? ............................................. 353

Plan Risk Management ............................................................... 355

Inputs ......................................................................................... 356

    Project Management Plan .......................................................... 356

    Project Charter........................................................................... 356

    Stakeholder Register ................................................................. 356

    Enterprise Environmental Factors ............................................. 356

    Organizational Process Assets................................................... 356

Tools and Techniques ................................................................. 357

    Analytical Techniques ............................................................... 357

    Expert Judgment ....................................................................... 357

    Meetings.................................................................................... 357

Outputs ...................................................................................... 358

    Risk Management Plan.............................................................. 358

Identify Risks.............................................................................. 361

Inputs ......................................................................................... 362

    Risk Management Plan.............................................................. 362

    Cost Management Plan.............................................................. 362

    Schedule Management Plan....................................................... 363

    Quality Management Plan.......................................................... 363

    Human Resource Management Plan ........................................... 363

Scope Baseline ................................................................................... 363

Activity Cost Estimates ..................................................................... 363

Activity Duration Estimates............................................................... 364

Stakeholder Register ........................................................................ 364

Project Documents ........................................................................... 364

Procurement Documents................................................................... 364

Enterprise Environmental Factors .................................................... 364

Organizational Process Assets.......................................................... 364

Tools and Techniques ............................................................. 365

Documentation Reviews.................................................................... 365

Information-Gathering Techniques .................................................... 365

Checklist Analysis............................................................................. 366

Assumption Analysis......................................................................... 366

Diagramming Techniques ................................................................. 366

SWOT Analysis ................................................................................. 367

Expert Judgment .............................................................................. 367

Outputs................................................................................... 367

Risk Register .................................................................................... 367

Perform Qualitative Risk Analysis ........................................ 369

Inputs ..................................................................................... 370

Risk Management Plan...................................................................... 370

Scope Baseline ................................................................................. 370

Risk Register .................................................................................... 370

Enterprise Environmental Factors .................................................... 371

Organizational Process Assets.......................................................... 371

Tools and Techniques ............................................................. 371

Risk Probability and Impact Assessment.......................................... 371

Probability and Impact Matrix........................................................... 372

Risk Data Quality Assessment .......................................................... 372

Risk Categorization.............................................................................372

Risk Urgency Assessment ...............................................................372

Expert Judgment ...............................................................................373

## Outputs........................................................................................ 373

Project Document Updates..............................................................373

## Perform Quantitative Risk Analysis ....................................... 374

## Inputs ............................................................................................ 375

Risk Management Plan.....................................................................375

Cost Management Plan.....................................................................375

Schedule Management Plan.............................................................375

Risk Register ....................................................................................375

Enterprise Environmental Factors ..................................................376

Organizational Process Assets.........................................................376

## Tools and Techniques ................................................................. 376

Data Gathering and Representation Techniques.............................376

Quantitative Risk Analysis and Modeling Techniques.....................377

Expert Judgment ..............................................................................379

## Outputs........................................................................................ 380

Project Document Updates..............................................................380

## Plan Risk Responses ................................................................. 381

## Inputs ............................................................................................ 381

Risk Management Plan.....................................................................381

Risk Register ....................................................................................382

## Tools and Techniques ................................................................. 382

Strategies for Dealing with Negative Risks or Threats...................382

Strategies for Dealing with Positive Risks or Opportunities...............383

Contingent Response Strategies .....................................................383

Expert Judgment ..............................................................................384

**Outputs** ............................................................................... 384

    Project Management Plan Updates ................................................. 384

    Project Document Updates ........................................................... 384

**Control Risks** ........................................................................ 385

**Inputs** ................................................................................. 386

    Project Management Plan ............................................................. 386

    Risk Register ............................................................................ 386

    Work Performance Data ............................................................... 386

    Work Performance Reports ........................................................... 386

**Tools and Techniques** ............................................................ 387

    Risk Reassessment .................................................................... 387

    Risk Audits .............................................................................. 387

    Variance and Trend Analysis ......................................................... 387

    Technical Performance Measurement ............................................... 387

    Reserve Analysis ....................................................................... 388

    Status Meetings ........................................................................ 388

**Outputs** ............................................................................... 388

    Work Performance Information ...................................................... 388

    Change Requests ....................................................................... 389

    Project Management Plan Updates ................................................. 389

    Project Document Updates ........................................................... 389

    Organizational Process Asset Updates ............................................. 389

**Chapter Summary** ................................................................. 390

**Exercises** ............................................................................ 391

**Review Questions** ................................................................. 393

**Answers** ............................................................................. 397

    Exercises ................................................................................ 397

    Chapter Review ........................................................................ 400

# Chapter 10: Procurement Management..................................... 405

## What Is Project Procurement Management?....................................... 405

## Plan Procurement Management........................................................ 406

## Inputs ............................................................................................ 407

Project Management Plan ............................................................................. 407

Requirements Documentation ....................................................................... 408

Risk Register ................................................................................................ 408

Activity Resource Requirements.................................................................... 408

Project Schedule........................................................................................... 408

Activity Cost Estimates ................................................................................. 408

Stakeholder Register .................................................................................... 408

Enterprise Environmental Factors ................................................................. 409

Organizational Process Assets....................................................................... 409

## Tools and Techniques ..................................................................... 410

Make-or-Buy Analysis................................................................................... 410

Expert Judgment .......................................................................................... 411

Market Research ........................................................................................... 411

Meetings....................................................................................................... 411

## Outputs........................................................................................... 412

Procurement Management Plan..................................................................... 412

Procurement Statement of Work ................................................................... 412

Procurement Documents............................................................................... 412

Source-Selection Criteria ............................................................................. 413

Make-or-Buy Decisions ................................................................................ 413

Change Requests.......................................................................................... 414

Project Document Updates ........................................................................... 414

## Conduct Procurements.................................................................... 415

## Inputs ............................................................................................ 415

Procurement Management Plan ........................................................................ 415

Procurement Documents ................................................................................ 416

Source-Selection Criteria ............................................................................... 416

Seller Proposals ............................................................................................. 416

Project Documents ......................................................................................... 416

Make-or-Buy Decisions ................................................................................. 416

Procurement Statement of Work .................................................................... 416

Organizational Process Assets ....................................................................... 417

## Tools and Techniques ................................................................. 417

Bidder Conference ......................................................................................... 417

Proposal Evaluation Techniques .................................................................... 418

Independent Estimates ................................................................................... 418

Expert Judgment ............................................................................................ 418

Advertising ..................................................................................................... 418

Analytical Techniques .................................................................................... 419

Procurement Negotiations .............................................................................. 419

## Outputs ..................................................................................... 419

Selected Sellers ............................................................................................. 419

Agreements .................................................................................................... 419

Resource Calendars ....................................................................................... 422

Change Requests ........................................................................................... 422

Project Management Plan Updates ................................................................ 422

Project Document Updates ............................................................................. 423

## Control Procurements ............................................................... 424

## Inputs ....................................................................................... 425

Project Management Plan .............................................................................. 425

Procurement Documents ................................................................................ 425

Agreements .................................................................................................... 425

Approved Change Requests ........................................................................... 425

Work Performance Reports ............................................................... 426

Work Performance Data .................................................................. 426

## Tools and Techniques ................................................... 426

Contract Change-Control System ..................................................... 426

Procurement Performance Reviews ................................................... 426

Inspections and Audits .................................................................. 427

Performance Reporting .................................................................. 427

Payment Systems ........................................................................ 427

Claims Administration .................................................................... 427

Records Management System ......................................................... 428

## Outputs .................................................................... 428

Work Performance Information ......................................................... 428

Change Requests ........................................................................ 429

Project Management Plan Updates ................................................... 429

Project Document Updates ............................................................. 429

Organizational Process Assets Updates ............................................ 429

## Close Procurements ..................................................... 430

## Inputs ...................................................................... 431

Project Management Plan ............................................................... 431

Procurement Documents ................................................................ 431

## Tools and Techniques ................................................... 431

Procurement Audits ...................................................................... 431

Procurement Negotiations .............................................................. 432

Records Management System ......................................................... 432

## Outputs .................................................................... 433

Closed Procurements .................................................................... 433

Organizational Process Assets Updates ............................................ 433

## Chapter Summary ....................................................... 434

Exercises ................................................................................ 435

Review Questions .................................................................. 435

Answers ................................................................................ 438

    Exercises ................................................................................ 438

    Chapter Review ......................................................................... 439

▓**Chapter 11: Stakeholder Management ........................... 445**

What Is Project Stakeholder Management? ...................... 445

Identify Stakeholders ........................................................ 446

Inputs ................................................................................ 447

    Project Charter........................................................................ 447

    Procurement Documents............................................................ 447

    Enterprise Environmental Factors ............................................. 447

    Organizational Process Assets................................................... 448

Tools and Techniques ....................................................... 448

    Stakeholder Analysis ............................................................... 448

    Expert Judgment ..................................................................... 449

    Meetings................................................................................. 450

Outputs............................................................................... 450

    Stakeholder Register ............................................................... 450

Plan Stakeholder Management ......................................... 452

Inputs ................................................................................ 453

    Project Management Plan ......................................................... 453

    Stakeholder Register ............................................................... 453

    Enterprise Environmental Factors ............................................. 453

    Organizational Process Assets................................................... 453

## Tools and Techniques ........................................................ 453
### Expert Judgment ........................................................... 454
### Meetings ................................................................... 454
### Analytical Techniques ...................................................... 454

## Outputs ..................................................................... 455
### Stakeholder Management Plan ................................................ 455
### Project Document Updates ................................................... 455

## Manage Stakeholder Engagement .............................................. 456

## Inputs ...................................................................... 457
### Stakeholder Management Plan ................................................ 457
### Communications Management Plan ............................................. 457
### Change Log ................................................................. 458
### Organizational Process Assets .............................................. 458

## Tools and Techniques ........................................................ 458
### Communications Methods ..................................................... 458
### Interpersonal Skills ....................................................... 459
### Management Skills .......................................................... 459

## Outputs ..................................................................... 459
### Issue Log .................................................................. 459
### Change Requests ............................................................ 460
### Project Management Plan Updates ............................................ 460
### Project Document Updates ................................................... 460
### Organizational Process Asset Updates ....................................... 460

## Control Stakeholder Engagement ............................................. 461

## Inputs ...................................................................... 462
### Project Management Plan .................................................... 462
### Issue Log .................................................................. 462
### Work Performance Data ...................................................... 462
### Project Documents .......................................................... 462

Tools and Techniques ............................................................. 463

    Information Management Systems ............................................. 463

    Expert Judgment ............................................................. 463

    Meetings .................................................................... 464

Outputs ............................................................................ 464

    Work Performance Information ................................................ 464

    Change Requests ............................................................ 464

    Project Management Plan Updates .......................................... 464

    Project Document Updates .................................................. 464

    Organizational Process Asset Updates ...................................... 464

Chapter Summary .............................................................. 465

Exercises ........................................................................ 466

Review Questions .............................................................. 467

Answers .......................................................................... 469

    Exercises ................................................................... 469

Chapter Review ................................................................ 470

▨Chapter 12: Ethics and Professional Conduct ........................ 475

Responsibility, Respect, Fairness, and Honesty ........................ 476

Responsibility .................................................................. 476

Respect .......................................................................... 478

Fairness .......................................................................... 480

Honesty .......................................................................... 481

Chapter Summary .............................................................. 483

Exercise .......................................................................... 483

Review Questions .............................................................. 484

Answers .......................................................................... 489

    Exercise .................................................................... 489

    Review Questions .......................................................... 490

▓**Chapter 13: Eligibility, Study, and Exam-Taking Tips** ................. **495**

Eligibility ............................................................................................... 495

   PMP Prerequisites ............................................................................................. 495

Study Tips .......................................................................................... 495

Exam-Taking Tips ............................................................................... 496

Question-Answering Tips ................................................................... 497

▓**Chapter 14: Blank Mind Maps** ..................................................... **499**

▓**Chapter 15: Formulas to Remember** ............................................. **503**

▓**Chapter 16: PMP® Examination Tasks Puzzle Game** ................... **505**

Instructions ....................................................................................... 505

▓**Chapter 17: PMP® Examination Role-Delineation
Domain Tasks** ................................................................................. **511**

**Glossary of Key Terms** ................................................................... **513**

**Index** ............................................................................................... **533**

# About the Author

**Sean Whitaker, BA, MSc, MBA, PMP** has a diverse project management background, having successfully managed complex projects in the construction, telecommunications, and IT industries. He brings this diversity of experience into sharp focus with his emphasis on professional project management.

In addition to this book, Sean is the author of many books on project management, including

*PMP Training Kit*, Microsoft Press/O'Reilly Publishing, 2013

*PMP Rapid Review*, Microsoft Press/O'Reilly Publishing, 2013

*The Professional Project Manager*, CreateSpace Independent Publishing Platform, 2014

*The Practically Perfect Project Manager*, CreateSpace Independent Publishing Platform, 2012

Sean regularly trains, coaches, teaches, and speaks about professional project management around the globe. He has been a volunteer with the Project Management Institute since 2005. When not teaching, speaking, or writing about project management, Sean is a keen and accomplished musician.

Please visit his web site at http://seanwhitaker.com.

# About the Technical Reviewer

**Mike Roberts** is a New Zealand–based project management professional and trainer. Mike offers project management services across the IT sector and has experience delivering projects through both traditional and agile techniques.

Mike is the principal trainer and partner at Falcon Training. He has been facilitating project management training for number of years. He has a reputation for his ability to connect with students and his commitment to learning. He is always happy to discuss the application of the wide variety of approaches available across all industries: IT, construction, health, retail, government, and more!

Mike is also an active volunteer with the New Zealand chapter of the Project Management Institute. He was recently awarded the PMINZ Volunteer of the Year award to recognize and honor his significant contribution to the PMI and the project management profession.

# How to Use This Book

Congratulations on committing to studying to take the Project Management Professional (PMP) credential.

This book contains all the information you need to pass the PMP examination. I have taken my time to be sure to include all the information necessary to pass the exam as well as some extra information about the profession of project management.

Here is a guide to all the extra bits and pieces in the book:

- *Words in Italics:* These are key terms, and you should try to memorize and understand all of them. Each is included in the Glossary of Key Terms at the rear of the book.

- *Exam tips:* These highlighted pieces of text give you direct tips for the exam.

- *Real World:* These highlighted sections of the book provide examples of the theory in action from my own experience. They are intended to add to your understanding of the concept being explained and also to share with you some of the lessons I have learned throughout my career.

- *Notes:* These provide slightly more information about the topic being discussed that is not always directly related to the exam but is usually very interesting.

- *More Info:* Most sections start with a brief indication of where you can go in the PMBOK Guide for more information about that particular topic.

- *Quick Check:* The Quick Check questions and answers at the end of each section are intended to give you the opportunity to quickly review the material you have just read with some simple questions.

- *Review questions:* At the end of each chapter are multiple choice questions that test your knowledge and understanding of the topics just covered.

- *Exercises:* Each chapter concludes with exercises to test how well you understand the topics just covered.

- *Study aids:* At the rear of this book, you will find some valuable study aids such as mind maps and a puzzle game to help you study.

Take your time as you go through this book, and complete all the exercises and questions. This way, you will be prepared to pass the PMP exam.

This book is designed to be used with the bank of more than 400 practice exam questions I have written. You can find them online at any good book retailer simply by searching for my name.

If you need extra assistance, I have also recorded a complete online PMP study course for Lecturio, which you can sign up for and view at your leisure. Simply search for PMP and my name at www.lecturio.com.

Finally, think of me as your personal PMP coach. Not only do you have access to the contents of this book, but you can also e-mail me at any time with questions, and I will answer.

Good luck!

Sean Whitaker
sean@seanwhitaker.com
P.S. If you wish to use this book as the foundational text for any PMP exam preparation courses you want to run, please e-mail me for a complimentary set of slides to help you out.

## CHAPTER 1

▧ ▧ ▧

# Foundational Concepts of Project Management

This chapter describes foundational concepts of the PMBOK˙ Guide. It introduces you to the purpose and content of the PMBOK Guide and provides definitions of projects, project management, program management, portfolio management, organizational project management, operations management, organizational strategy, business value, and the project life cycle. All of these foundational concepts are important to ensure that you understand the terminology used by the PMBOK Guide, which also appears in the PMP˙ exam. It is important that you take time to fully understand these concepts, because they underpin many of the processes, tools, and techniques that come later in the book.

---

▧ **Exam Tip**    Remember that the PMP exam tests a lot of elements, including your understanding of the PMBOK Guide terminology and concepts. You may come across a question that has an answer that is what you would actually call something in real life but is *not* how the PMBOK Guide would refer to it. In this instance, always answer according to the PMBOK Guide. Also, pay close attention not only to the terms but also to the various inputs and outputs.

---

## Objectives

- To introduce and outline the key foundational terms, purpose, and contents of the PMBOK Guide

- To understand the differences and interrelationships between project, program, and portfolio management

- To understand the relationships between organizational project management, operations management, and organizational strategy

© Sean Whitaker 2016
S. Whitaker, *Pass the PMP® Exam*, DOI 10.1007/978-1-4842-2074-0_1

- To understand the role that business value and strategic planning have in project management

- To define organizational process assets and their benefit to project management

- To define enterprise environmental factors and the ways in which they can assist and constrain a project

- To define and understand the characteristics of the project life cycle, including project phases

# The Purpose of the PMBOK Guide

---

▓ **More Info**    *The PMBOK Guide*

You can read more about the purpose of the PMBOK Guide, 5th edition, in the guide itself, in Chapter 1, section 1.1.

---

The full title of the PMBOK Guide is *A Guide to the Project Management Body of Knowledge*. If you break that down into its component parts, you can get an understanding of what sort of document it is.

First of all, it is a guide. This means it is not a prescriptive instruction manual that must be followed to the letter, and individuals and organizations can, and do, choose to implement only appropriate portions of the PMBOK Guide. It presents the information as a guide for you to use when and if it is useful. Obviously, it is a guide to the profession of project management. Because the profession of project management is both relatively young and also very wide in its application, any book purporting to be about it is necessarily both iterative and also broad in the information it contains.

This is the 5th edition of the PMBOK Guide and represents a major change from previous versions: it includes an extra knowledge area and more in-depth coverage of foundation topics. The development and updating of the PMBOK Guide is an ongoing process; an updated edition is released every three to four years. Make sure you have access to the latest copy of the PMBOK Guide. It is also aligned with ISO 21500:2012 Guidance on Project Management.

---

▓ **Exam Tip**    ISO 21500:2012 is an international standard for project management developed by the International Organization for Standardization. (The initials ISO come from the French way of saying this.) It provides guidance and a high-level description of concepts and processes that are considered to form good or best practice in the profession of project management.

---

Finally, as a body of knowledge, it contains what is considered to be a fairly complete set of knowledge about the profession of project management. Many professions, including civil engineering, software engineering, contracting, and even massage therapy have bodies of knowledge associated with them. Overall, the PMBOK Guide presents what is generally recognized to be good practice in the profession of project management. This means the processes, tools, and techniques that it presents are useful to most projects most of the time. It is up to the organization or the project management team to determine which, if any, of the processes, tools, or techniques are useful for any project they are working on. This process of selecting only those processes, tools, and techniques that actually provide benefit when managing your projects is called *tailoring*.

## REAL WORLD

The PMBOK Guide is not a project management methodology. It is a framework document containing the collection of what is considered good project management practice for projects of any size, complexity, and industry. In order to build a project management methodology, you are directed to take from the PMBOK Guide only those processes, tools, and techniques that are appropriate and add value to your project via the process of tailoring.

In addition to representing a robust body of knowledge, the PMBOK Guide also presents standardized terminology. This means there is generally a single word or phrase to define and describe each element of project management. It allows project managers and project team members in the same organization, and between organizations, to communicate effectively.

## REAL WORLD

The benefit of a standardized terminology cannot be overestimated. I have been in many situations with people from different organizations who made simple mistakes because they used different words for the same thing. I once asked a contract manager on my team for the project schedule, and he sent me the schedule of materials. After three requests and increasing confusion on both sides, we finally figured out that I was requesting what he referred to as the project timeframe. On another occasion, I was assisting a firm that was growing rapidly and recruiting project managers every week. The biggest challenge they faced was the different terminology all these experienced project managers used. We worked on developing a common organization-wide project management vocabulary to improve communication between all the project managers and project team members.

Of course, your main interest in the PMBOK Guide is that it is a very useful text on which to base your study for the Project Management Professional (PMP) certification. Passing the PMP exam requires knowledge of the entire contents of the PMBOK Guide, as well as knowing the "Project Management Institute Code of Ethics and Professional Conduct."

---

■ **Exam Tip**   Even if you had a photographic memory and could remember every page of the PMBOK Guide, you would not necessarily score 100% on the PMP exam, because the exam is based on the results of a role-delineation study about what professional attributes a project manager should have. The PMBOK Guide is a very useful text on which to base your study, because its contents are built on the knowledge of many disciplines, and often a single phrase or sentence in the PMBOK Guide can refer to an entire other subject area. That is why simply studying the PMBOK Guide is not the best approach to preparing to sit the PMP exam. This book not only introduces you to the entire contents of the PMBOK Guide but also presents a lot of other information so you are prepared to pass the exam.

---

### Quick Check

1. How should you use the PMBOK Guide in your projects?

2. Apart from offering a collection of good practices in project management, what other main benefit does the PMBOK Guide provide?

### Quick Check Answers

1. By selecting from it only those processes, tools, and techniques that are appropriate for your projects based on size, complexity, and industry.

2. It provides a standardized terminology, or lexicon, for the profession of project management.

# What Is a Project, a Program, and a Portfolio?

---

■ **More Info**   Project, Program, Portfolio

You can read more about the definition of a project, a program, and a portfolio in the PMBOK Guide, 5th edition, in Chapter 1, section 1.2.

---

It may seem straightforward to define exactly what a *project* is, but it is important that you know how the PMBOK Guide defines one. Several key elements separate project work from ongoing or operational work.

The first and most important element of a project is that it has a defined start and end, making it a temporary endeavor. On the other hand, operational, or ongoing, work is ongoing and repetitive.

A project also delivers something unique—something that hasn't been done before. Ongoing work is repetitive and delivers the same thing every day or every year.

Finally, a project delivers a product, service, or result. This allows projects to be used to deliver a range of deliverables in many industries, whether they are based on goods or services.

---

▓ **Exam Tip**   There are only two types of work in the world, according to the PMBOK Guide. All work is either operational work or project work. If it is operational work, then it is repetitive and ongoing. If it is project work, then it has a defined start, middle, and end and delivers a product, service, or result.

---

## REAL WORLD

You may find a degree of overlap between project work and operational work. There are certainly some projects that bear a striking resemblance to each other and perhaps could be construed as ongoing work. It is the unique aspect of each—and that it is done slightly differently, in a different location, to produce a slightly different product, service, or result—that makes it a project.

A portfolio of projects includes all the projects, whether interdependent or not, that an organization is undertaking. They are connected only by their common goal of delivering the organization's strategic goals.

A *program* of projects describes projects that have some sort of interdependency between them. They may all be part of a larger deliverable; for example, you could have several projects, each of which makes a different part of a new aircraft, but the final deliverable depends on managing the projects together as a program. The projects may also share a common goal, and the program manager needs to monitor and resolve any actual or potential conflicts in the pursuit of those goals.

A project can be part of a program and part of a portfolio. Figure 1-1 shows that all programs are part of a portfolio, but that projects can be either directly part of a portfolio or part of a program.

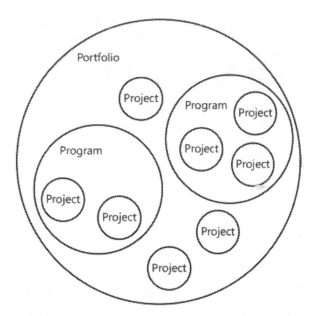

***Figure 1-1.*** *The relationship between portfolios, programs, and projects in an organization*

Project, program, and portfolio management are separate yet interrelated elements of the profession of project management. The combination of the project management, program management, and portfolio management disciplines is seen as integral and necessary to deliver the organizational strategy; and, therefore, any action undertaken in any of the three elements should always align with the organization's strategy.

Portfolio management ensures that all projects selected to be completed by the organization align with the organizational strategy. Portfolio management has an organizational scope that reflects the organizational strategy. Often projects or programs are grouped together into a single portfolio that reflects a specific strategy.

---

▓ **Exam Tip**    The PMBOK Guide places a great deal of emphasis on the alignment of organizational strategy and the profession of project management as a strategic enabler for delivering the strategy. Always assume that the default position in a question is that an organization has a strategy and is using project management to achieve that strategy.

---

Program management focuses on managing interdependencies within projects with a common goal or capability. Program managers are skilled at forecasting, anticipating, and dealing with real or perceived conflict between projects in the same program. All programs have projects, but not all projects are part of programs.

▩ **Exam Tip**   An interesting distinction made by the PMBOK Guide is that if the relationship between separate projects is based on having a shared client or seller, or shared technology or resources, then the projects should be managed as a portfolio rather than a program.

The *project management office* (PMO) is the part of the organization responsible for project management excellence. It provides support for the project manager, which can mean many things, depending on the level of organizational project management maturity. A PMO can simply be a place where a project management methodology is developed and stored; or, at the other end of the spectrum, it can be where all the project managers are located, which provides common reporting, manages shared resources, and is responsible for portfolio, program, and project management across the entire organization.

The PMBOK Guide defines three main types of PMO, differentiated by the level of control and influence they have, as shown in Figure 1-2. The *supportive* PMO provides templates and basic processes and captures lesson learned. The *controlling* PMO may take responsibility for development and implementation of a project management methodology and provide project governance as well. The *directive* PMO takes direct control of management of projects in the organization.

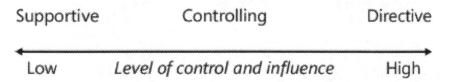

*Figure 1-2. The types of project management office (PMO), from supportive to directive*

The type of PMO an organization should have also depends on the level of organizational project management maturity the organization has attained. *Organizational project management maturity* is a way of assessing where an organization is currently with its level of sophistication and maturity around project management processes, tools, templates, and methodology, and then assessing where they should be. Organizations handling large and complex projects should be at a higher level of project management maturity than organizations managing small and simple projects. Organizations with a high level of project management maturity should have a more directive PMO.

▩ **Exam Tip**   If you see a reference to OPM3 in the exam, it is referring to the Organizational Project Management Maturity Model, which is a tool from the Project Management Institute (PMI) for assessing an organization's level of portfolio, program, and project management maturity.

**Quick Check**

1. What are the three key elements that distinguish project work from ongoing work?

2. What are the key differences between a program and a portfolio of projects?

3. How would you describe the main differences between project, program, and portfolio management?

4. What function would a project management office play in an organization with a high level of project management maturity?

**Quick Check Answers**

1. First, a project has a temporal element defining a start and an end, making it temporary rather than ongoing. Second, it delivers something unique and never done before. Finally, it involves delivery of a product, service, or result.

2. In a program of projects, the projects share an interdependency, whereas in a portfolio of projects, the projects are united only by the fact that they are all being completed by the same organization.

3. Portfolio management is the top-level selection process of projects to ensure that they deliver the organization's strategy. A program of projects contains projects that share a common goal or capability, and individual projects are focused on delivering a product, service, or result that will contribute to achievement of the organizational strategy. Remember that all programs have projects, but not all projects are part of programs.

4. An organization with a high level of project management maturity will use a directive project management office to take control of the way in which all projects are selected, managed, reported on, and communicated about in the organization.

# What Is Project Management?

---

▦ **More Info**   Project Management

You can read more about the definition of project management in the PMBOK Guide, 5th edition, in Chapter 1, section 1.3.

---

*Project management* takes the tools, techniques, and skills contained in the PMBOK Guide and applies them to the project to deliver the product, service, or result. It is a proactive, rather than a reactive, discipline.

---

▓ **Exam Tip** Being proactive is a key point about professional project management. If a question on the exam gives you the option to be proactive, it is probably the correct answer.

---

The PMBOK Guide, 5th edition, contains a description of 47 project management process in 10 knowledge areas. These 47 processes are placed in 5 process groups—initiating, planning, executing, monitoring and controlling, and closing—to describe the stage in the project in which they are best used. Managing a project means taking the appropriate process and the tools and techniques associated with it and applying them appropriately to the work that needs to be done. Project management, then, is simply the application of any of the PMBOK Guide knowledge areas with the goal of delivering a product, service, or result.

One of the tasks of project management is the balancing of competing constraints on a project. These constraints can be scope, quality, schedule, budget or cost, resources, and risk. If any one of these constraints changes, it will likely place additional pressure on one or more of the other constraints. For example, if you have to deliver a project in a shorter time period, you may need additional budget to complete the work, and your known risks may increase while quality decreases.

---

▓ **Exam Tip** You should know that one important aspect of project management is recognizing and navigating your way through competing constraints on a project. This is evident in planning a project and also when considering a request for a change to a project, where a request for more time may impact schedule, risk, or quality.

---

An important aspect of project management is that, generally speaking, you cannot know everything there is to know about a project at the outset, and, thus, project management is highly iterative. This means you may be able to define the work to be done for the next few weeks accurately, but beyond that you can't plan as well because there is more uncertainty; so you plan in an iterative manner, meaning you plan many times, each time with more information. *Progressive* elaboration is an iterative process that acknowledges that you will know more, the more you do. For example, at the beginning of a software project you may know the general expected outcome and the first steps on the path to delivering it, but as you move along in the project you become more aware of the magnitude of the work and can plan the project schedule, budget, and risks better. *Rolling-wave planning* is another type of iterative planning where you plan in detail the next appropriate time period; as you keep progressing throughout a project, you keep planning that same length of time in detail.

▓ **Exam Tip** If you see the term *progressive elaboration* or *rolling-wave planning* on the exam, it is referring to the concept of knowing more about the project, the more work you do.

---

## REAL WORLD

It is important to let your project stakeholders know that projects are generally iterative and subject to progressive elaboration, to counter the expectation that you can plan everything at the beginning of a project.

### Quick Check

1. How would project management differ from managing an ongoing business activity?

2. How does iterative planning differ from progressive elaboration of a project?

### Quick Check Answers

1. Project management uses the process, tools, and techniques of the PMBOK Guide, is subject to multiple interdependent constraints, and is subject to iterations and progressive elaboration. It is also a temporary endeavor with a defined end. An ongoing operational business activity may or may not be subject to interdependent constraints, and it does not have a defined end.

2. You can deliberately choose to plan iteratively even with a known scope of work. You can decide to focus your detailed planning activities on the immediate future and revisit the planning stages as the project progresses. Progressive elaboration, or rolling-wave planning, implies that not everything is known about a project and more will become known as the project moves along.

# Project Management, Operations Management, and Organizational Strategy

---

▓ **More Info**    Project Management, Operations Management, and Organizational Strategy

You can read more about project management, operations management, and organizational strategy in the PMBOK Guide, 5th edition, in Chapter 1, section 1.5.

---

As you already know, project management is all about delivering a product, service, or result. After this product, service, or result has been delivered as part of the entire project work or simply as part of a project phase, it normally gets handed over to operational management. Operational management differs from project management in that it is a permanent part of any organization and is focused on the ongoing activities of the business, whereas project management is focused on the temporary activities of project delivery. Operational management also provides the overall strategy for the organization, which is used to help select the right projects.

Obviously, each area intersects at the point where the deliverable is handed over. At this point, the normal operations of the organization may need to change or adapt to accommodate the deliverable. This is one role of operational managers.

---

▓ **Exam Tip**    For the exam, you need to know the difference between operational work and project work, and that operational management often takes responsibility for the deliverable for the project when it has been completed.

---

| REAL WORLD |
| :---: |

An important tip for any project manager is to include the end users responsible for use and maintenance of any deliverable in the list of stakeholders to be consulted. They often have real-world experience in the use and ongoing maintenance of the deliverable that perhaps the people who design the deliverable don't.

The *business value* is the sum of all tangible and intangible values in the organization. It can include all capital assets of an organization as well as intangible elements such as brand recognition. Organizations strive to increase their business value, and they can use project management to help them do this. The successful creation of business value is enhanced by having a clear strategy and using the strategy to select projects that deliver appropriate business value. In this way, project management can contribute to the business value of an organization.

More specifically, portfolio management selects the projects that align with organizational strategy, program management manages interconnected projects, and project management delivers unique products, service, and results, all of which contribute to greater business value. The creation of business value is the final link in the process whereby project management can be seen as a key strategic enabler for a business.

Project management and organizational strategy are interrelated insofar as organizations achieve strategic goals by delivering successful projects. Although a project manager may not be involved in checking strategic alignment of all projects prior to approval, they should ensure that any project they are given to manage can be mapped back to a strategic goal of the organization. Projects that are not aligned with organizational strategy may suffer from lack of political support, and the organization may not have the core competencies required to complete the project.

## REAL WORLD

It is important that project managers have a sound understanding of operational management objectives so they understand why their projects are important and how they fit into the overall organization strategy and add business value. In my own career, I have found that a business education has helped my project management, and, conversely, my project management experience has helped my operational management efforts.

### Quick Check

1.  Describe the two main points at which the worlds of operational management and project management intersect.

2.  What are the key elements that make up business value?

3.  How can project management contribute to the creation of business value?

4.  How does portfolio management assist in the creation of business value?

### Quick Check Answers

1.  The first point of intersection is that operational management provides the overall organizational strategy that is used to select the right projects. The second main point where the two worlds meet is when operational management takes ownership of any project deliverable.

2.  Business value is made up of both the tangible and intangible elements of a business.

3.  Project management delivers products, services, or results that add either tangible or intangible business value.

4.  Portfolio management focuses on ensuring that any projects selected are aligned with the organizational strategy and that the strategy delivers increased business value.

# Organizational Influences on Project Management

▦ **More Info**   Organizational Influences

You can read more about the organizational influences on project management in the PMBOK Guide, 5th edition, in Chapter 2, section 2.1.

Projects are not completed in a vacuum, devoid of influence from an organization's culture, style, or structure. It is important for a project manager to recognize that each of these elements can positively or negatively influence the outcome of a project. Different organizations have different cultures. These cultures can be observed by noting such things as the values, beliefs, and expectations held by senior management; any relevant policies and procedures that the organization has; the motivation and reward systems; its tolerance toward risk; its attitudes toward hierarchy and power and authority relationships; and such things as the expected work and work hours. The organizational culture is usually established by the founders of the organization, developed by the current employees, and perpetuated through ongoing recruitment policies.

| REAL WORLD |
|---|

Often in the real world you will see organizations that do the same work technically but have completely different organizational cultures. I know of several people who have left one organization to go to a competitor, only to return in a few months because they didn't like the particular organizational culture.

In addition to the internal organizational culture founded by recruitment policies and current employees, an organization's culture can also be influenced by the broader cultural environment in which it operates. This includes factors such as employment market conditions, level of competition, and external political influences. It is up to project managers to make sure they assess and understand how these cultural factors may impact a project. This creates challenges for the project manager, who must be aware of issues around multiculturalism, particularly with the increase of globalization and the use of project team members from different countries.

■ **Exam Tip**  Both the organization's culture and its structure are enterprise environmental factors, because they sit outside the direct realm of the project and can assist or constrain the project.

So far, this chapter has looked at the impact of organizational culture on projects. Other important aspects of organizational influence on projects are organizational process assets and enterprise environmental factors.

*Organizational process assets,* as the name suggests, are any existing plans, procedures, policies, templates, and knowledge bases that the organization owns that can be used to assist the project. Organizational process assets appear as inputs into most of the 47 planning processes in the PMBOK Guide. Specific examples of organizational process assets include the project management methodology, any blank templates, any change-control processes and procedures, any financial control reporting requirements, any defined communication methods, any standardized approach to risk management the organization has, and any project closure guidelines, requirements, or checklists.

*Enterprise environmental factors* are always external to the project but not necessarily external to the organization; they are just not under the control of the project team. Enterprise environmental factors feature as inputs into most of the 47 planning processes in the PMBOK Guide. Specific examples of enterprise environmental factors include the organizational culture and structure, any relevant government or industry standards that can affect the project, any personnel administration requirements, any external marketplace conditions, the stakeholder risk tolerances, the external political climate, and any project management information systems, including any software purchased or licensed by the organization. Many people assume that project management software is an organizational process asset; however, it is generally considered to be an enterprise environmental factor because it is usually licensed rather than owned.

## REAL WORLD

The most common form of organizational process asset that most project managers encounter is the organization's project management methodology. A *project management methodology* itself can mean many things. It can be as simple as a range of blank templates available to the project manager; or, at the other end of the spectrum, it can be a fully defined set of processes, procedures, templates, and databases that must be used for all projects.

■ **Exam Tip**   A general rule of thumb for remembering the difference between organizational process assets and enterprise environmental factors is that, generally speaking, organizational process assets can be used to assist a project, whereas enterprise environmental factors often constrain a project. Additionally, as the name suggests, with organizational process assets, the organization must own the assets.

**Quick Check**

1.   What are some of the main defining characteristics of an organization's culture?

2.   Why should a project manager be aware of the organizational culture?

3.   How is an organizations culture established and perpetuated?

**Quick Check Answers**

1.   The main defining characteristics of an organizational culture can be observed in the organization's visions and values, beliefs, policies, procedures, reward systems, tolerance for risk, work ethic, and view of authority relationships.

2.   A project manager needs to be aware of the overall organizational culture and specific elements within it because these will affect the projects they are working on. It is best to take advantage of those parts of the organizational culture that contribute to project success and mitigate those parts of the organizational culture that may increase the chances of project failure.

3.   The culture of an organization generally reflects the values of its founding members and is then perpetuated and reproduced by both senior managers and leaders and the organization's recruitment policies.

# The Project Life Cycle

■ **More Info**   Project Life Cycle

You can read more about the project life cycle in the PMBOK Guide, 5th edition, in Chapter 2, section 2.4.

The project *life cycle* is central to the PMBOK Guide. It forms the basis for the five PMBOK Guide process groups. The project life cycle provides a framework and also describes the generally sequential activities undertaken in any project, beginning with the process of starting or initiating the project, organizing and preparing to do the work of the project, then carrying out the defined project work, and finally recognizing the closeout of a project.

There are three ways to describe typical project life cycles. The first is the *predictive* life cycle, where a lot of planning work can be done up front and then the work is carried out according to this plan with relatively little change. We often see these types of project life cycles in the construction industry.

The *iterative* or *incremental* project life cycle features planning and executing work being done concurrently (at the same time) to deal with projects where there is a lot of change. We see iterative or incremental project life cycles in many types of information technology projects.

The *adaptive* project life cycle is used when there is a great deal of uncertainty; it recognizes that very little planning work can be done up front. Highly complex information technology projects are good examples of adaptive life cycles.

The concept of the project life cycle moving from a project's beginnings to its closure can be applied to an entire project or to the different *phases* in the project. Project phases are best used when there is a clear and defining milestone between activities. For example, a project may have a design phase that requires signoff on the design (which would be the milestone) before the project is allowed to proceed to the implementation phase. Project phases can be performed in a linear, sequential fashion, with successive phases having to wait until a predecessor phase is complete before proceeding. Alternatively, phases can overlap, with the successive phase able to start prior to the completion of the predecessor phase.

---

░ **Exam Tip**    Be prepared to see terms such as *milestone*, *stage gate*, *phase gate*, *kill point*, and *stop/go point* in questions relating to phases of a project.

---

A project management *methodology* takes an approach based on the project life cycle and perhaps its phases, and describes the processes that will be followed and the tools and templates to be used. Most project management methodologies are built on the concept of the project life cycle and have different procedures that reflect different parts of that life cycle.

## REAL WORLD

There are many different types of project management methodologies. They range from the highly iterative agile methodologies used in information technology projects to the more predictive methodologies also known as *waterfall* methodologies, where there is a clear linear progression from startup through closure of a project. In developing an appropriate project management methodology for an organization, consideration must be given to the type of projects, the size of projects, the organizational culture, the timeframe for project delivery, and the maturity of the organization. The development of a project management methodology is not a one-size-fits-all proposition. In fact, a good methodology will always be flexible enough to accommodate different projects.

The concept of the project life cycle incorporating the initiation, planning, execution, and closing phases of the project is based on the Shewhart and Deming *Plan-Do-Check-Act (PDCA) cycle*. This cycle starts with making a plan, then doing what you planned, then checking that what you are doing is what you planned, then acting if you find any variance between what you are doing and what you planned to do, and then going back and planning again. Figure 1-3 shows this PDCA cycle.

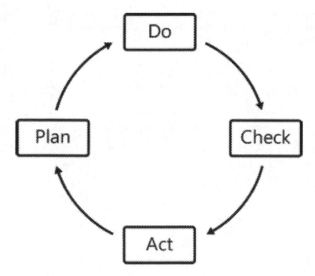

**Figure 1-3.** *The Shewhart and Deming Plan-Do-Check-Act cycle showing the iterative nature of project management*

This cycle forms the basis of the initiating, planning (Plan), executing (Do), monitoring and controlling (Check and Act), and closing process groups of the PMBOK Guide. Figure 1-4 shows the PMBOK Guide process groups.

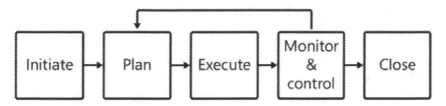

*Figure 1-4.* *The PMBOK Guide process groups shown as an iterative cycle of activity*

---

▒ **Exam Tip**   Take care to read any questions about life cycles to determine whether they are referring to the project life cycle or the product life cycle. The project life cycle refers to the project from initiation to closing. The product life cycle refers to the design, manufacturing, use, and obsolescence of the product. The product life cycle can be many years longer than the project life cycle.

---

The five PMBOK Guide process groups describe work to be done in each of the ten specific knowledge areas. Table 1-1 shows how the five process groups and the ten knowledge areas from the PMBOK Guide overlap.

*Table 1-1.* *The PMBOK Guide Process Groups and Knowledge Areas*

| | Initiating Processes | Planning Processes | Executing Processes | Monitoring and Controlling Processes | Closing Processes |
|---|---|---|---|---|---|
| Project Integration Management | • Develop Project Charter | • Develop Project Management Plan | • Direct and Manage Project Work | • Monitor and Control Project Work<br>• Perform Integrated Change Control | • Close Project or Phase |
| Project Scope Management | | • Plan Scope Management<br>• Collect Requirements<br>• Define Scope<br>• Create WBS | | • Validate Scope<br>• Control Scope | |
| Project Time Management | | • Plan Schedule Management<br>• Define Activities<br>• Sequence Activities<br>• Estimate Activity Resources<br>• Estimate Activity Durations<br>• Develop Schedule | | • Control Schedule | |
| Project Cost Management | | • Plan Cost Management<br>• Estimate Costs<br>• Determine Budget | | • Control Costs | |
| Project Quality Management | | • Plan Quality Management | • Perform Quality Assurance | • Control Quality | |

*(continued)*

*Table 1-1. (continued)*

| | Initiating Processes | Planning Processes | Executing Processes | Monitoring and Controlling Processes | Closing Processes |
|---|---|---|---|---|---|
| Project Human Resource Management | | • Plan Human Resource Management | • Acquire Project Team<br>• Develop Project Team<br>• Manage Project Team | | |
| Project Communications Management | | • Plan Communications Management | • Manage Communications | • Control Communications | |
| Project Risk Management | | • Plan Risk Management<br>• Identify Risks<br>• Perform Qualitative Risk Analysis<br>• Perform Quantitative Risk Analysis<br>• Plan Risk Responses | | • Control Risks | |
| Project Procurement Management | | • Plan Procurement Management | • Conduct Procurement | • Control Procurements | • Close Procurements |
| Project Stakeholder Management | • Identify Stakeholders | • Plan Stakeholder Management | • Manage Stakeholder Engagement | • Control Stakeholder Engagement | |

▓ **Exam Tip** Try memorizing this table to help you remember the sequence of processes on the exam. An easy way to remember the knowledge areas is to use a mnemonic. My favorite, once you remove the word Project from each one, is: *In Summer The Cruel Queen Hates Cold Runny Porridge Snacks.* Notice that the first letter of each word in the sentence links to the first letter in each of the knowledge areas. Try making up your own mnemonic. If you are a numbers sort of person, try remembering the following number sequence 2 - 24 - 8 - 11 - 2. Those numbers are the number of processes in the Initiating, Planning, Executing, Monitoring and Controlling, and Closing process groups, respectively. Another set of numbers is 6 - 6 - 7 - 4 - 3 - 4 - 3 - 6 - 4 - 4, which are the numbers of processes in each knowledge area from Integration Management through Stakeholder Management.

**Quick Check**

1.  What sort of projects benefit from a phased approach?

2.  What are the four parts of the Shewhart and Deming cycle?

3.  What are the five PMBOK Guide process groups?

**Quick Check Answers**

1.  Projects that have well-defined milestones are suitable for a phased approach.

2.  The four parts are Plan, Do, Check, and Act.

3.  The five PMBOK Guide process groups are Initiating, Planning, Executing, Monitoring and Controlling, and Closing a project.

# Chapter Summary

- This chapter introduced you to many foundational concepts of the PMBOK Guide. It began by looking at the purpose and contents of the PMBOK Guide and then went on to define a project and the unique characteristics that differentiate projects from ongoing or repetitive work. It is important that you understand how project work is different from ongoing or operational work.

- The chapter then looked at the differences between and the relationships among project management, program management, and portfolio management. The link to portfolio management also includes consideration of the link between projects and strategic planning and how project management can be a strategic enabler for an organization. Ultimately, the strategic decisions made and the way in which project management can support them will deliver increased business value.

- The role of the project management office (PMO) in any organization is an important one and reflects the level of organizational project management maturity that the organization has attained. The primary function of a PMO and whether it is supportive, controlling, or directive is a direct reflection of the level of maturity of the organization.

- The role of organizational process assets and enterprise environmental factors in the success or failure of project management is important. Additionally, organizational process assets and enterprise environmental factors feature as inputs in many of the 47 processes of the PMBOK Guide.

- The concept of the project life cycle, which begins with the start of a project and moves through the organization, preparation, execution of the planned project work, and finally the closing of the project, is central to many of the processes and knowledge areas in the PMBOK Guide. The concept of the project life cycle can also be applied to separate project phases.

# Exercises

1. Consider the following 12 scenarios. For each scenario, decide whether it is a project, a program, a portfolio, or ongoing work.

   A. The implementation of a new piece of software to run an organization's payroll

   B. The construction of a new house

   C. The development of a new housing subdivision

   D. Filming the first movie of a movie trilogy

   E. Increasing sales from the previous year

   F. The design phase of a new piece of software

   G. The range of projects an organization is undertaking to increase market share

   H. The installation of new servers as part of a major upgrade to an organization's software and hardware systems

   I. A new marketing campaign designed to bring in more business

   J. The development of a new product that will increase operational profit

    K.  Several different pieces of software being developed that use the same developers

    L.  All the new house projects being undertaken by a construction company

2.  Practice filling out the following blank table with process groups, knowledge areas, and processes from the PMBOK Guide.

**The PMBOK Guide Process Groups**

| | | | | | |
|---|---|---|---|---|---|
| | | | | | |
| | | | | | |
| | | | | | |
| | | | | | |
| | | | | | |
| | | | | | |
| | | | | | |
| | | | | | |
| | | | | | |

*The PMBOK Guide Knowledge Areas*

# Review Questions

Test your knowledge of the information in Chapter 1 by answering these questions. The answers to these questions, and the explanation of why each answer choice is correct or incorrect, are located in the "Answers" section at the end of this chapter.

1.  What is the primary role of the portfolio manager?

    A.  To deliver the unique product, service, or result of the project

    B.  To provide project governance and sponsorship

    C.  To assess all potential projects against known organizational strategic goals

    D.  To directly manage people assigned to several different projects

2. What is the primary purpose of the PMBOK Guide?

    A. To provide a flexible methodology for all projects, no matter how large or small

    B. To identify a project management framework based on what is generally recognized as good practice

    C. To define a prescriptive approach to managing projects

    D. To present all the known project management information in a concise manner

3. What is the best description of rolling wave planning?

    A. Project management planning activities that become more detailed as you move through the project

    B. Only planning the first phase of a project

    C. Planning the entire project before starting execution

    D. Only planning the next phase in a project

4. What is the relationship between successful projects and an organization's strategic goals?

    A. There is no relationship between the two, because they are separate and distinct parts of an organization.

    B. The successful delivery of projects can be a strategic enabler and deliver strategic goals.

    C. The project selection methodology will determine what an organization's strategic goals are.

    D. Projects deliver programs, which in turn deliver portfolios, which in turn deliver strategy.

5. What is the best role for a project management office in an organization with a low level of project management maturity?

    A. Directive

    B. Controlling

    C. Supportive

    D. Enabling

6.  What is the name for a group of related projects managed in a coordinated way to obtain a synergy not found by managing them individually?

    A.  Multi projects

    B.  Portfolio

    C.  Program

    D.  Strategy

7.  The PMBOK Guide process groups are based on which life cycle model?

    A.  The Check-Plan-Do-Act cycle

    B.  The Plan-Do-Check-Act cycle

    C.  The Plan-Check-Act-Do cycle

    D.  The Do-Check-Act-Plan cycle

8.  How many processes are there in the Risk Management knowledge area?

    A.  Three

    B.  Four

    C.  Five

    D.  Six

9.  How many processes are there in the Monitoring and Controlling process group?

    A.  9

    B.  10

    C.  11

    D.  12

10. Which knowledge area does not have a Monitoring and Controlling process?

    A.  Cost Management

    B.  Initiating

    C.  Human Resource Management

    D.  Closing

# Answers

This section contains the answers to the questions for the "Exercises" and "Review Questions" in this chapter.

## Exercises

1. Consider the following scenarios. For each scenario, decide whether it is a project, a program, a portfolio, or ongoing work.

    A. The implementation of a new piece of software to run an organization's payroll
    This is an example of a project.

    B. The construction of a new house
    This is an example of a project.

    C. The development of a new housing subdivision
    This would generally be seen as either a very large project or a program. This demonstrates that there is a grey area between projects, programs, and portfolios.

    D. Filming the first movie of a movie trilogy
    The first movie will be seen as a project; the entire trilogy would be seen as a program.

    E. Increasing sales from the previous year
    This is an example of ongoing work.

    F. The design phase of a new piece of software
    Because this is a phase, it would best be viewed as part of a project.

    G. The range of projects an organization is undertaking to increase market share
    This is an example of a program with a common goal of increasing market share.

    H. The installation of new servers as part of a major upgrade to an organization's software and hardware systems
    This is an example of a project that is part of a broader program.

    I. A new marketing campaign designed to bring in more business
    Marketing is generally considered to be an ongoing activity rather than a project.

J.  The development of a new product that will increase operational profit
    This is an example of a project that will be handed over to the operations side of the organization.

K.  Several different pieces of software being developed that use the same developers
    Merely using the same developers doesn't mean that these projects are part of a program. Instead, they should be considered individual projects that are part of a portfolio.

L.  All the new house projects being undertaken by a construction company
    This is an example of a portfolio of projects.

2.  Practice filling out the following blank table with process groups, knowledge areas, and processes.

**The PMBOK Guide Process Groups**

| | Initiating processes | Planning processes | Executing processes | Monitoring and Controlling processes | Closing processes |
|---|---|---|---|---|---|
| **The PMBOK Guide Knowledge Areas** | | | | | |
| **Integration management** | • Develop Project Charter | • Develop Project Management Plan | • Direct and Manage Project Work | • Monitor and Control Project Work<br>• Perform Integrated Change Control | • Close Project or Phase |
| **Scope management** | | • Plan Scope Management<br>• Collect Requirements<br>• Define Scope<br>• Create WBS | | • Validate Scope<br>• Control Scope | |
| **Time management** | | • Plan Schedule Management<br>• Define Activities<br>• Sequence Activities<br>• Estimate Activity Resources<br>• Estimate Activity Durations<br>• Develop Schedule | | • Control Schedule | |
| **Cost management** | | • Plan Cost Management<br>• Estimate Costs<br>• Determine Budget | | • Control Costs | |

| Knowledge Area | Initiating | Planning | Executing | Monitoring & Controlling | Closing |
|---|---|---|---|---|---|
| **Quality management** | | • Plan Quality Management | • Perform Quality Assurance | • Control Quality | |
| **Human Resource management** | | • Plan Human Resource Management | • Acquire Project Team<br>• Develop Project Team<br>• Manage Project Team | | |
| **Communications management** | | • Plan Communications Management | • Manage Communications | • Control Communications | |
| **Risk management** | | • Plan Risk Management<br>• Identify Risks<br>• Perform Qualitative Risk Analysis<br>• Perform Quantitative Risk Analysis<br>• Plan Risk Responses | | • Control Risks | |
| **Procurement management** | | • Plan Procurement Management | • Conduct Procurement | • Control Procurements | • Close Procurements |
| **Stakeholder management** | • Identify Stakeholders | • Plan Stakeholder Management | • Manage Stakeholder Engagement | • Control Stakeholder Engagement | |

# Review Questions

1.  **Correct answer: C**

    A.  **Incorrect:** The project manager takes responsibility for delivering the product, service, or result of a project.

    B.  **Incorrect**: On occasion a portfolio manager may provide some governance and sponsorship advice, but it is not the portfolio manager's primary role.

    C.  **Correct:** The portfolio manager operates at a strategic level within the organization.

    D.  **Incorrect:** It would be the program manager or even a functional manager who would take responsibility for managing people on several projects, depending on the type of organizational structure in place.

2.  **Correct Answer: B**

    A.  **Incorrect:** The PMBOK Guide does not provide a methodology. You are able to build a methodology from the contents of the PMBOK Guide via the process of tailoring.

    B.  **Correct:** The PMBOK Guide collects and presents what is generally considered to be good practice across a wide range of industries and presents this information as a framework rather than a methodology.

    C.  **Incorrect:** The PMBOK Guide emphasizes in several places that, through the process of tailoring, you should only take from the PMBOK Guide what is appropriate to your project.

    D.  **Incorrect:** The PMBOK Guide does not claim to present all known project management information, only that which is generally considered good practice across a wide range of industries.

3.  **Correct Answer: A**

    A.  **Correct:** Rolling-wave planning acknowledges that you will iteratively plan the project as you move along the project life cycle.

    B.  **Incorrect:** Only planning the first phase of a project is typical for phased projects, because there may be an important milestone between phases that prevents further planning.

C. **Incorrect**: Planning the entire project before starting is a very rare occurrence and probably only suitable for small, easily defined projects.

D. **Incorrect:** Iteratively planning a phase of a project is not an example of rolling-wave planning.

4. **Correct Answer: B**

A. **Incorrect:** There is a strong relationship between successful projects and an organization achieving its strategic goals.

B. **Correct:** By selecting projects that deliver strategic goals and then successfully delivering these projects, an organization can achieve its strategic goals.

C. **Incorrect**: It is the organization's strategy that dictates which projects get selected.

D. **Incorrect:** There is not always a direct linear connection between projects, programs, portfolios, and strategy.

5. **Correct answer: C**

A. **Incorrect:** Directive project management offices are generally best in an organization with a high level of project management maturity.

B. **Incorrect:** Controlling project management offices are generally a sign of an organization improving its organizational project management maturity.

C. **Correct:** Supportive project management offices are generally a sign of a low level of project management maturity, because they do not support a lot of complexity.

D. **Incorrect:** This is a made-up term and is not from the PMBOK Guide.

6. **Correct Answer: C**

A. **Incorrect:** Multi projects is a made-up term that does not describe a coordinated approach to interrelated projects.

B. **Incorrect:** Portfolios are groups of projects related only by the fact that they are being performed by a single organization.

C. **Correct:** A program is a group of projects that are related in some way and that are managed to achieve benefits not gained by managing them independently.

D. **Incorrect:** Strategy is the organization's future direction and how it is going to achieve this.

7. **Correct Answer: B**

   A. **Incorrect:** The correct order requires planning to come first and checking to come after doing.

   B. **Correct:** The Plan-Do-Check-Act cycle by Shewhart and Deming describes an iterative approach to management.

   C. **Incorrect:** The correct order requires checking to come after doing and before acting.

   D. **Incorrect:** The correct order requires planning to come first.

8. **Correct Answer: D**

   A. **Incorrect:** There are six processes, not three, in the Risk Management knowledge area.

   B. **Incorrect:** There are six processes, not four, in the Risk Management knowledge area.

   C. **Incorrect:** There are six processes, not five, in the Risk Management knowledge area.

   D. **Correct:** The six processes in the Risk Management knowledge area are Plan Risk Management, Identify Risks, Perform Qualitative Risk Analysis, Perform Quantitative Risk Analysis, Plan Risk Responses, and Control Risks.

9. **Correct Answer: C**

   A. **Incorrect:** There are 11 processes, not 9, in the Monitoring and Controlling process group.

   B. **Incorrect:** There are 11 processes, not 10, in the Monitoring and Controlling process group.

   C. **Correct:** The 11 processes in the Monitoring and Controlling process group are Monitor and Control Project Work, Perform Integrated Change Control, Validate Scope, Control Scope, Control Schedule, Control Costs, Control Quality, Control Communications, Control Risks, Control Procurements, and Control Stakeholder Engagement.

   D. **Incorrect:** There are 11 processes, not 12, in the Monitoring and Controlling process group.

10. **Correct Answer: C**

   A. **Incorrect:** The Cost Management knowledge area has the Control Costs process, which is part of the Monitoring and Controlling process group.

   B. **Incorrect:** The Initiating process group is not a knowledge area.

   C. **Correct:** The Human Resource Management knowledge area does not have a Monitoring and Controlling process, because it is usually the functional manager who monitors and controls project staff.

   D. **Incorrect:** The Closing process group is not a knowledge area.

# CHAPTER 2

■ ■ ■

# Integration Management

This chapter focuses on project integration management. Project Integration Management recognizes that no part of the profession of project management acts in isolation, and in fact there is a high degree of interdependency between different parts of the profession. As such, a lot of the information discussed in this chapter reaches across many other knowledge areas in the profession. In addition to recognizing the interdependency of all other knowledge areas, project integration management also specifically addresses those activities, such as change control processes, which are carried out over more than one knowledge area.

**The PMBOK® Guide Processes**
**Project Integration Management Knowledge Area**

The six processes in the Project Integration Management knowledge area are as follows:

- Develop Project Charter (Initiating process)

- Develop Project Management Plan (Planning process)

- Direct and Manage Project Work (Executing process)

- Monitor and Control Project Work (Monitoring and Controlling process)

- Perform Integrated Change Control (Monitoring and Controlling process)

- Close Project or Phase (Closing process)

# What Is Project Integration Management?

The other nine knowledge areas in the PMBOK Guide focus on a specific knowledge area and have key inputs from, and provide outputs for, other knowledge areas. Project Integration Management is the only knowledge area that actually works across all the other knowledge areas. It has been described as the forest whereas the other knowledge areas are the trees. It is very much a coordination process that recognizes that none of the PMBOK Guide knowledge areas are isolated and discrete. Project Integration Management recognizes that the knowledge areas are all interdependent and rely on

© Sean Whitaker 2016
S. Whitaker, *Pass the PMP® Exam*, DOI 10.1007/978-1-4842-2074-0_2

each other to a greater or lesser extent. They are also able to affect each other; as such, when defining, planning, executing, and controlling the project, a project manager must recognize this and take an integrated point of view. This is true of activity between knowledge areas and also between processes in the same knowledge area. They can also be highly iterative and are not necessarily a direct linear progression from one process to another.

For example, when preparing a cost estimate, you need to have a defined project scope and also be aware of resources available, risks, and any other factors from the other knowledge areas that may affect the cost estimate. If you consider each knowledge area as a separate and discrete activity, then developing cost estimates in isolation would result in highly inaccurate estimates. Project Integration Management reminds us that all knowledge areas and processes are connected.

The Project Integration Management knowledge area produces the project charter (Develop Project Charter), which is a foundational document for the project and most of the other processes. It also delivers the project management plan in its many iterations (Develop Project Management Plan), takes a coordinated and high-level view of all the work being done on the project to achieve the plans (Direct and Manage Project Work), checks the project progress (Monitor and Control Project Work), and assesses, influences, and controls changes as they occur (Perform Integrated Change Control). In addition to providing the foundational documents that initiate the project, this knowledge area also manages the closure of the project or a phase in a project (Close Project or Phase).

Additionally, the Project Integration Management knowledge area reinforces the fact that there are many successful ways to manage a project. Projects vary considerably in terms of depth, complexity, size, industry, and deliverables. As such, the level of interaction between selected processes is also different. The process called *tailoring* involves selecting those processes that are appropriate to a project and ensuring throughout the life of the project that constant checking is done to ensure that the selected processes and their application are still appropriate. Having broad oversight of the project via the Project Integration Management knowledge area helps in selecting the right processes and applying them appropriately.

## REAL WORLD

I am a big advocate of tailoring tools, techniques, and processes to appropriately fit your organization and your project. All sorts of potential problems can arise from applying too many, or too few, project management practices to a project. Take the time at the beginning of the project to choose those processes, tools, and techniques that will actually add value to your project, and throughout the life of the project be prepared to reexamine your decisions to ensure that they are still correct. For example, during one small IT project I worked on, our project management methodology was tailored to be flexible and very simple because the project was simple and took place over a short time frame. A larger IT project I worked on had a very rigid methodology with many processes, reflecting the complexity of the project.

▓ **Exam Tip**   A high proportion of questions on the PMP exam expect you to know how one process or knowledge area interacts with, or is dependent on, other processes or knowledge areas. Do not be surprised if you have to read a question several times to determine exactly how many, and which, processes it is referring to. You should also get used to looking not just at the entire process, but also at the way in which inputs become outputs with the application of selected tools and techniques.

# Develop Project Charter

▓ **More Info**   Develop Project Charter

You can read more about the Develop Project Charter process in the PMBOK Guide, 5th edition, in Chapter 4, section 4.1. Table 2-1 identifies the process inputs, tools and techniques, and outputs.

*Table 2-1.* *Develop Project Charter Process*

| Inputs ⇨ | Tools and Techniques ⇨ | Outputs |
| --- | --- | --- |
| • Project statement of work<br>• Business case<br>• Agreements<br>• Enterprise environmental factors<br>• Organizational process assets | • Expert judgment<br>• Facilitation techniques | • Project charter |

The Develop Project Charter process is an initiating process with a single output—not surprisingly, given the name of the process, it is the project charter. The Develop Project Charter process is one of only two initiating processes in the PMBOK Guide.

*Domain Task Alignment*

The Develop Project Charter process covers the following eight initiating domain tasks:

- Task 1: Perform project assessment based on available information, lessons learned from previous projects, and meetings with relevant stakeholders, in order to support the evaluation of the feasibility of new products or services in the given assumptions and/or constraints.

- Task 2: Identify key deliverables based on the business requirements, in order to manage customer expectations and direct the achievement of project goals.

- Task 4: Identify high-level risks, assumptions, and constraints based on the current environment, organizational factors, historical data, and expert judgment, in order to propose an implementation strategy.

- Task 5: Participate in the development of the project charter by compiling and analyzing gathered information, in order to ensure that project stakeholders are in agreement on its elements.

- Task 6: Obtain project charter approval from the sponsor, in order to formalize the authority assigned to the project manager and gain commitment and acceptance for the project.

- Task 7: Conduct benefit analysis with stakeholders (including sponsor, customer, and subject matter experts), in order to validate project alignment with organizational strategy and expected business value.

- Task 8: Inform stakeholders of the approved project charter, in order to ensure common understanding of the key deliverables, milestones, and their roles and responsibilities.

It is the first process to be completed and the one that kicks off a project. Unlike most of the other processes in the PMBOK Guide, the Develop Project Charter process features inputs that are not outputs from other processes. In this case, the inputs come from either the project sponsor (for example, any contracts or agreements, a business case, or the known project statement of work) or the organization or the environment in which the project must work and is constrained by (enterprise environmental factors and organizational process assets). The project sponsor is critical to this process, because the sponsor takes responsibility not only for providing some necessary inputs into this process but also for initiating and signing off on the development of the project charter.

The project manager may not always be directly responsible for preparation of the project charter. In a perfect world, they would be, but they are often handed a completed project charter and expected to then complete detailed planning.

---

▒ **Exam Tip**    The Develop Project Charter process is one of two initiating processes in the PMBOK Guide. The other is the Identify Stakeholders process from Project Stakeholder Identification Management. Because the project charter is an input into the Identify Stakeholders process, it must be done first.

---

Broadly speaking, many of the inputs used in this process are part of a project-selection process that assesses any potential project against the organizational strategic goals and also against financial and non-financial criteria to help the organization make decisions about which projects it will undertake and which it won't. Understanding this process will assist your understanding of the Develop Project Charter process. Only projects that are of a compliance nature, or emergency works, should be able to bypass this project-selection process, which is illustrated in Figure 2-1. Examples of compliance projects are those that are necessitated when legal reporting requirements are changed and your organization must comply with them, even though there is no business value in doing so. An example of emergency work could be the work you must do after a natural disaster strikes, to get your organization up and running again. There is not time to go through a formal process to justify these types of projects.

***Figure 2-1.*** *Project-selection process*

Figure 2-1 shows that after an organization has identified all the potential projects it could undertake, it must put each project through a series of filters and criteria to enable it to choose the ones it will undertake. From this approved portfolio of projects, it can then prioritize them and begin to develop a project charter. The first step in this selection process is for an organization to only choose those projects that align with and deliver its strategic goals. This is because they will help an organization stay in business and meets its goals, and also because those strategic goals represent the organization's core competencies.

## REAL WORLD

The profession of project management is seen as a critical strategic enabler for organizations. This is because most organizations seek to deliver their strategic goals, and therefore the success or failure of the projects undertaken is a critical indicator of whether organizations will achieve their strategic goals.

After a project has been confirmed as meeting the strategic goals of an organization, it may go through either financial or non-financial criteria processes, or both, that either deny or further refine and approve projects that will be undertaken as part of the organization's approved portfolio of projects. This is usually done during the preparation of a business case.

The following list describes the most common financial criteria that can be used to determine which projects are suitable:

- **Benefit-Cost Ratio (BCR)**   A ratio that looks at the financially quantifiable benefits expected from the project and weighs them against the cost of achieving those benefits. If the benefits outweigh the costs, then the project can be given the go-ahead.

- **Economic Value Add (EVA)**   The profit earned by the organization after the cost of capital has been subtracted. Many organizations set a target for this and only approve projects that meet or exceed this target.

- **Internal Rate of Return (IRR)**   The rate of return after external factors affecting cash flow (for example, interest or cost of capital, and inflation) have been deducted. The higher the IRR, the better the project.

- **Present Value (PV)**   The value of future cash flows in today's dollars. The formula for calculating PV is

$$PV = \frac{FV}{\left(1 + r\right)^n}$$

  where FV equals the future value of cash flows, r equals the interest rate, and n equals the number of time periods.

- **Net Present Value (NPV)**   The value in today's dollars of future benefits minus the costs to achieve the benefits. The organization's own discount rate is applied to future cash flows to calculate today's value. A positive NPV is good, whereas a negative NPV is bad. NPV is calculated by subtracting the PV of costs from the PV of income and is the sum of all the PV calculations for income generated for a particular time period, subtracted from the initial spend on the project. To calculate NPV, simply add up all the PV calculations for the expected income and then subtract this PV from the initial spend. The formula is

| NPV = Initial Outlay + | Year 1 Income | Year 2 Income | Year 3 Income | Year 4 Income |
|---|---|---|---|---|
| | + | + | + | |
| | $(1+r)$ | $(1+r)^2$ | $(1+r)^3$ | $(1+r)^4$ |

For example, if your project had an initial spend of $100,000 and was supposed to generate income of $30,000 in the first year, $35,000 in the second year, $37,000 in the third year, and $39,000 in the fourth year with a discount or interest rate of 10%, the NPV of the project would be $10,634.52.

- **Opportunity Cost**   The cost of not doing other projects and the profit, or financial surplus, they would bring the organization.

- **Payback Period**   The time taken to pay back the investment in the project. An organization may set a required Payback Period, such five years, within which time the project must pay back the original investment. Payback Period is calculated by dividing the initial investment by the projected annual income.

- **Return on Investment (ROI)**   The cost of a project subtracted from dollar gains on a project, divided by the cost of the project, expressed as a percentage. An organization sets criteria specifying that a ROI must first be positive, and the higher the ROI the better. Often organizations also specify that the ROI must be greater than bank interest rates to reflect the risk in a project. Otherwise, from a commercial point of view, the organization is better off putting its money in a bank.

- **Return on Invested Capital (ROIC)**   Used to describe in percentage terms how well an organization is using its money, or capital, on its projects. Positive is good, and the higher the better when it comes to selecting projects.

- **Future Value (FV)**   Used to calculate the future value of an asset with a known interest rate to measure accumulation of value over time.

---

▓ **Exam Tip**   If you find *linear programming* or *non-linear programming* referred to in an exam question, the question is referring to a constrained optimization method for project selection. This is a complex mathematical process of maximizing the cost function of any calculation. The other category you will find is the benefit-measurement model, in which an organization seeks to compare benefits and features of a particular proposal and make the selection on that basis.

---

# Inputs

The Develop Project Charter process uses some or all of the following inputs as part of the development of the project charter for the project.

# Project Statement of Work

The project *statement of work* (SOW) is a high-level narrative description of the work to be done on a project. It reflects what is known about the project work at the early stage of initiating a project. The project SOW describes the known scope of work, the business needs, and the product or service to be delivered. The SOW may also refer to the ways in which the project aligns with and delivers the organization's strategic goals. It may also contain information about known milestones and project constraints, as well as any preliminary budget and time estimates. In the absence of this information during this initiating process, the SOW may describe the work to be done to develop these estimates.

If you are using a SOW, then it leaves room for further definition of the project scope but gives enough information to authorize the project and do a preliminary assessment of time, cost, and other relevant factors. If a project is based on a signed contract or agreement, then the SOW is replaced by the project scope contained in the contract, which tends to be much more detailed in its description of the work to be done.

---

▓ **Exam Tip**   The SOW is a primary input into the Develop Project Charter process but not a mandatory one. If a business case has been developed, or a fully defined contract or agreement is available, then there is no need for a SOW.

---

# Business Case

A business case can be used as an input into the project charter or even as a project charter itself. Typically, the business case examines the financial and non-financial criteria that are used to assess whether the organization will commit to the project. These criteria are best used against a predefined expectation of what constitutes an acceptable project. For example, an organization might require a project to deliver a certain level of ROI or a certain percentage of increase in market share before approving it. Projects that don't deliver these defined metrics are not considered for approval. These predefined metrics can also be further used to prioritize which projects are done first, with the project scoring better being done first. These financial criteria were discussed in greater detail earlier in the chapter.

---

▓ **Exam Tip**   Assume that all projects must go through a rigorous and defined business case process prior to approval. This process considers strategic alignment and financial and non-financial matters, which are all captured in the business case.

---

The business case also looks at any predefined non-financial criteria that the organization wishes to consider. Examples of non-financial criteria an organization may consider are projects that increase market share, those that make it difficult for competitors to enter the market, projects that reduce dependencies on suppliers, and projects focused on delivering social, environmental, health, or educational benefits.

If the project is being executed in several phases with milestones between each phase, the business case can be revisited at these points to ensure that it is both still valid and delivering the expected outcomes.

A business case usually includes most of the following elements:

- A description of the forecast or actual market demand for the product or service

- A description the organizational need for the project

- If it is for an external client, a description of the customer request

- A description of any technical advances that are presenting the opportunity to undertake the project

- Any legal or compliance requirements that are being addressed and met as a result of the project

- Any ecological or natural environmental impacts

- A description of the social need being fulfilled by the project

Clearly, the business case can be a very comprehensive document. If the project is large and complex, then the business case should reflect this. However, if the project is relatively simple and straightforward, the business case can be less complex.

# Agreements

The project charter can be based on any type of agreement between a performing organization and a requesting organization, or customer. An *agreement* can take the form of a signed contract, which in turn may be the result of a procurement process run by an external organization as part of its own project processes. The agreement may also be in the form of a memorandum of understanding (MOU), letter of agreement, or heads of agreement. An exchange of email messages with an offer and acceptance is also a form of valid agreement. A valid agreement can also be formed via a verbal exchange, in which case you should document the exchange as part of the project charter process.

If an agreement with an external party is used as an input into the Develop Project Charter process, the external party should be able to review and agree to the eventual project charter as it relates to them. This does not mean they need to view the entire project charter, because there may be commercially sensitive information contained within it, but they should have the opportunity to comment on and agree to the content that relates to any agreement between the parties.

---

▓ **Note**   Verbal Agreements

Projects that are undertaken with a simple verbal agreement must document the agreement at some point to ensure that all parties understand and agree to what was talked about and to ensure that everyone's expectations are recorded and communicated. This is best done during the Develop Project Charter process before any planning work is done.

---

# Enterprise Environmental Factors

Enterprise environmental factors are some of the most common inputs used throughout the PMBOK Guide. They can refer to many separate and distinct factors that can affect, and be used as inputs to, projects. In the Develop Project Charter process, the specific enterprise environmental factors that can influence the project charter development are any relevant government or industry standards that the project must comply with, any organizational infrastructure issues or constraints, and any known or forecast market conditions affecting the project selection process.

---

**Exam Tip** Enterprise environmental factors are some of the most widely used inputs throughout the PMBOK Guide. The term covers a lot of different factors that can influence a project. The environment referred to is not the ecological environment: it is the financial and human resource market environment, the legislative and legal environment, and the innovation and competitive environment, and it also includes external cultural factors. Take time to understand the variety of factors that are enterprise environmental factors and be able to differentiate them from organizational process assets. Very broadly, enterprise environmental factors can be considered as constraining the project, whereas organizational process assets can be considered as assisting the project.

---

# Organizational Process Assets

An *organizational process asset* is any concept, process, or structure documented by the organization for use in project management. For the Develop Project Charter process, the relevant organizational process assets include any organizational processes relating to the project selection, business cases, and development of the project charter, including any templates the organization may have. It also includes any existing project management methodology the organization has. Organizational process assets that are useful in the initiation phase and the development of the project charter also include historical information and lessons learned from previous projects.

---

**Exam Tip** The PMBOK Guide places a large emphasis on the importance of gathering and referring to historical information and lessons learned. You should always assume that this is done and available to you as a project manager. You should always assume that you will contribute to the development of an organization's historical information and lessons-learned database as part of the project management activities completed on your project. This is an extremely important part of a closeout process and should be part of your closure checklist. You should look to complete closeout interviews and meetings with all stakeholders, complete post-implementation reviews, and also complete benefits-realization analysis to measure whether the intended benefits were achieved. All of this information becomes valuable lessons learned and historical information for future projects.

---

# Tools and Techniques

The following tools and techniques are available to be used to develop the inputs into this process in order to produce the project charter.

## Expert Judgment

*Expert judgment* is the most often-used tool in the PMBOK Guide. Using expert judgment to help you use and optimize the inputs in the process allows you to consult with and seek guidance from any person or group who you consider can contribute to the process. This expertise may come from within your organization, from individuals, or from the Project Management Office (PMO). You may also choose to seek expert judgment from external consultants, competitors, and trade associations with expertise in the particular area you need guidance on. For example, you may seek guidance from experts in financial analysis as part of the business case.

The client or customer is also a valuable source of expert judgment, because they have clear expectations and experience with the product or service being delivered. Professional organizations, such as the Project Management Institute, may be consulted, as well as industry groups and subject matter experts.

## Facilitation Techniques

The purpose of *facilitation techniques* is to solicit information from team members and other key stakeholders who have a contribution to make in terms of using the process inputs and providing advice or further information to enable you to develop the project charter. Many facilitation techniques can be used; the most relevant for the Develop Project Charter process are as follows:

- **Brainstorming**    This involves holding structured workshops or sessions where participants are encouraged to think broadly about every possible action or consequence, no matter how strange it may seem. A process of elimination is then used to get to those ideas that are most useful.

- **Conflict resolution**    This uses a variety of techniques to ensure that any conflict of opinions between experts does not derail the process. Conflict resolution includes problem-solving techniques that use a wide variety of methods to directly address and permanently resolve any problems that arise.

- **Effective meeting management**    Getting your experts together and getting the best from them requires effective meeting-management techniques that include structured and purposeful meetings with defined outcomes.

# Outputs

After applying the appropriate tools and techniques to the selected inputs, the Develop Project Charter process has the following output.

## Project Charter

The Develop Project Charter process has only a single output—the project charter. The *project charter* is the foundational document for a project and is like the project's birth certificate. It proves the project exists and has financial and political support from the organization and, if applicable, an external client. It should be issued once the project has been through an appropriate project-selection process.

The project charter authorizes the initial spend; defines the scope of work known at that time; lists any known constraints, risks, and milestones; and also identifies and authorizes the project manager and project sponsor. Ideally, the project manager is identified and authorized in the project charter and assists with its development; but if not, the project manager should definitely be identified before any of the project-planning processes begin.

Because the project charter is the foundational document for the project, changing it requires significant consideration and should not be done unless there are serious reasons. For this reason, it can be left broad enough to allow the normal process of change control to take place through the project without having to constantly change the project charter. Any potential changes to the project charter must be referred to the project sponsor.

Not all project charters are created equal, and the size and complexity of the project determines the size and complexity of the project charter. Additionally, if not much is known about the project, the charter may be big enough to authorize an investigation phase that is part of an iterative planning process. If the scope of the project is well known, the project charter may be a one-off—that is, a complete and complex business case.

---

▒ **Note**    Project Charter

The foundational document for a project is the *project charter.* Although in a perfect world it would probably be called a *project charter* by everyone involved in project management, you may call it by other names, such as *project mandate*, *business case*, or *work order.* Remember, though, during the exam you must use the PMBOK Guide terminology.

▒ **Exam Tip**    Always assume that a project has a project charter of some sort and that you will refer to it when seeking answers to why the project exists and what its original goals were.

---

The project charter is then a key input into the following processes, all of which are planning processes:

- Plan Scope Management
- Collect Requirements
- Define Scope
- Plan Schedule Management
- Plan Cost Management
- Plan Risk Management
- Identify Stakeholders

# Develop Project Management Plan

▧ **More Info**   Develop Project Management Plan

You can read more about the Develop Project Management Plan process in the PMBOK Guide, 5th edition, in Chapter 4, section 4.2. Table 2-2 identifies the process inputs, tools and techniques, and outputs.

*Table 2-2.* *Develop Project Management Plan Process*

| Inputs ⇨ | Tools and Techniques ⇨ | Outputs |
|---|---|---|
| • Project charter<br>• Outputs from other processes<br>• Enterprise environmental factors<br>• Organizational process assets | • Expert judgment<br>• Facilitation techniques | • Project management plan |

The Develop Project Management Plan process is a planning process that initiates and encompasses the planning activities of all the other knowledge areas. It is the only planning process for the Project Integration Management knowledge area, and one of 24 planning processes in total.

The Develop Project Management Plan process covers the broad range of work covered in other planning domain tasks but specifically includes the following planning domain tasks:

- Task 9: Develop the change management plan by defining how changes will be addressed and controlled, in order to track and manage change.

- Task 11: Present the project management plan to the relevant stakeholders according to applicable policies and procedures, in order to obtain approval to proceed with project execution.

- Task 12: Conduct a kick-off meeting, communicating the start of the project, key milestones, and other relevant information, in order to inform and engage stakeholders and gain commitment.

The *project management plan* itself is a document made up of all the other plans, and it provides a centralized means of planning your project. It does not necessarily have to be contained in a single document, because different formats, such as word processing, spreadsheets, project management software, and other formats can be used to develop and record the different plans. The Develop Project Management Plan process is a highly iterative process that may start with blank templates that eventually become the project management plan for a project.

The primary purpose of this process is to record and document how your project is going to be executed, monitored and controlled, and closed. As such, it should contain plans for each of these elements in the relevant knowledge areas. When your project is underway, you can use the project management plan that has been developed to ensure that progress is as per the plan and act accordingly if there is a variance.

## REAL WORLD

I have worked for organizations that have a single template for their project management plan: it has sections that need to be filled out and guidance as to how to do so. However, I have also worked for organizations for whom the project management plan was a series of disparate documents held in both hard and electronic document versions; when viewed together, they formed a consolidated plan for managing the project. It is important that a project management plan reflect the complexity, size, and industry of the project. Too small a project management plan for a large, complex project increases the chances of project failure. On the other hand, too large a project management plan for a simple project also increases the chances of project failure.

# Inputs

The development of the project management plan uses some or all of the following four inputs.

# Project Charter

The project charter is an output from the Develop Project Charter process. It can take many forms, depending on the size and complexity of a project. It acts as the starting point that authorizes and guides the development of the project management plan, because it contains the known description of the work to be done and any assumptions, constraints, and milestones.

# Outputs from Other Processes

The Develop Project Management Plan process is an iterative process and uses many of the outputs from other knowledge areas as inputs.

---

▒ **Exam Tip**    Take note of outputs from other planning, executing, monitoring and controlling, and closing processes for project management plan updates that indicate that they will be used as inputs into the Develop Project Management Plan process.

---

These outputs include, but are not limited to, the successive iterations of the following:

- The requirements management plan
- The requirements documentation
- The schedule management plan
- The schedule baseline
- The cost management plan
- The cost baseline
- The quality management plan
- The process improvement plan
- The human resource plan
- The staffing management plan
- The communications management plan
- The risk management plan
- The procurement management plan
- The stakeholder management plan

# Enterprise Environmental Factors

Enterprise environmental factors are both external and internal factors outside the realm of the project that a project manager does not have control over but that can influence the processes in a project. Specific enterprise environmental factors that can be used as inputs to aid the development of the project management plan may include the following:

- Any relevant government standards, such as mandatory compliance standards.

- Any relevant industry standards that the project must comply with.

- Any software being used as part of the project management information systems to develop any aspect of the project management plan. Software is considered an external factor because it is generally licensed from a third party.

- The organizational culture and structure of all organizations involved in the project. Organizational culture in terms of acceptable behaviors, attitudes toward risk, the amount of power and authority the project manager has, and a flat versus tall organizational structure are some of the external factors that can affect how a project management plan is developed.

- Any internal organization policies for the recruitment and release of staff.

# Organizational Process Assets

Organizational process assets are a very common input into many processes. It is also worth remembering that several processes have organizational process asset updates as outputs. The specific organizational process assets that can be used as inputs into the Develop Project Management Plan process include the following:

- Any standard templates or checklists the organization has. For example, it may have a blank template for some or all of the content of a project management plan or a checklist for project closure.

- Any processes or project management methodology the organization has that defines when, how, and by whom the project management plan is put together.

- Any predefined change-control procedures and levels of delegated authority the project manager and team have.

- The organization's standard configuration management system that defines how different versions of documents are recorded, controlled, and updated. This is particularly important to ensure that you are always working on the correct version of any document in what can be a highly iterative process.

- Any historical information from past projects that can be used to assist in the compilation of the current project management plan.

---

▓ **Exam Tip**   The PMBOK Guide places a great deal of importance on the value of historical information, particularly lessons learned. Even if you work for an organization that does not currently collect historical information about projects, you must remember that it is considered one of the most valuable organizational process assets in project management.

---

# Tools and Techniques

The following two tools and techniques are used on the inputs to deliver the project management plan.

## Expert Judgment

Expert judgment is a great tool to use, and it is used several times as a tool to help take inputs and use them correctly and wisely in order to generate the outputs from a particular process. The experts providing the judgment can come from any source that is relevant to the needs at hand and can include you as project manager as well. In this instance, when you are developing the project management plan, expert judgment can first be used to *tailor* the processes that are applicable and useful to the development of your particular project management plan. You can also use expert judgment during successive iterations of the development of the project management plan to determine whether the inputs are still valid and applicable.

Expert judgment can also be used to help evaluate any other aspect of the inputs into this process, particularly the outputs from other processes. Because of the large number of outputs from other processes that can be used as inputs into the Develop Project Management Plan process, you may end up using several experts with skills and experience in different areas.

```
╔══════════════════════════════════════════════════════════╗
║                      REAL WORLD                           ║
╚══════════════════════════════════════════════════════════╝
```

During my career as a project manager, I have made repeated and frequent use of experts with knowledge greater than my own. Not only does it assist with a better output, but it is also a great way to learn. Don't hesitate to gather around you experts who can help you with any aspect of project management. Additionally, don't discount your own experience when it comes to providing an expert opinion.

## Facilitation Techniques

Facilitation techniques are used to gather information from individuals or groups of people in a constructive way that produces positive outcomes for your project. As the name suggests, they are means of facilitating information gathering from people. It is up to you as project manager to initiate, define, and lead many of these facilitation techniques. Depending on whether they are useful to you at this point, you may wish to consider using some or all the following facilitation techniques to help you make sense of, develop, redefine, and use the inputs into this process:

- **Brainstorming** This involves gathering people together in a room and asking them to think about all possible ideas. The ideas can be as wide and as varied as possible with no limitation placed on the brainstorming process. After all possible options, no matter how seemingly irrelevant, have been gathered, you can then go through a process of refining them.

- **Conflict-resolution techniques** These are important because dysfunctional conflict needs to be addressed promptly and dealt with and not swept under the carpet. The other element is using conflict to generate healthy debate, which often results in a more thought-out and considered end result. Problem solving, collaborating, compromise, smoothing, forcing, and withdrawing are all examples of conflict-resolution techniques.

- **Productive and effective meetings** Meetings are also an excellent example of facilitation techniques. The use of and adherence to a clear agenda, rules for participants, and clear minutes and action points will greatly assist in gathering information relevant to the development of the project management plan.

# Outputs

The Develop Project Management Plan process produces the following output.

# Project Management Plan

There is only a single output from the Develop Project Management Plan process, and that is the *project management plan* in all of its many iterations. The project management plan can be many different things to many different people, depending on the project management maturity of the organization, the size and complexity of its projects, and the industry it is working in. The plan can be a single document or a collection of many documents in different formats. A mature organization will have established organizational process assets that help the project manager complete the project management plan.

---

▓ **Exam Tip** The project management plan is not a Gantt chart. It is not uncommon for people to think that the Gantt chart is the project management plan, but it is simply a scheduling and a communications tool.

---

The content and depth of the project management plan reflect what is known about the project at that time, because you can only plan what is known. As such, the development of the project management plan is a great example of progressive elaboration and rolling-wave planning on a lot of projects. The project management plan can contain all or some of the following plans and baselines:

- The change-control process
- The requirements management plan
- The requirements documentation
- The schedule management plan
- The schedule baseline and milestone list
- The cost management plan
- The cost baseline
- The quality management plan
- The process improvement plan
- The human resource plan
- The resource calendar
- The communications management plan
- The risk management plan
- The risk register
- The procurement management plan
- The stakeholder management plan

| REAL WORLD |
| --- |

When putting together a project management plan, I always make sure it is appropriate to the size and complexity of the project I am working on. I also recognize that it is a highly iterative process and you can only plan for those parts of the project you can define. This means parts of the project off in the distance of time may not be able to be planned as well as parts of the project to be completed in the short term. It is important to communicate this well to stakeholders, who may think it is possible to plan a long-term project in its entirety.

Despite being a singular output, the project management plan is used, either in its entirety or in its component parts and subset plans, as an input into many other processes throughout the PMBOK Guide. The project management plan is a key input into the following processes:

- Direct and Manage Project Work
- Monitor and Control Project Work
- Perform Integrated Change Control
- Close Project or Phase
- Plan Scope Management
- Control Scope
- Plan Schedule Management
- Control Schedule
- Plan Cost Management
- Control Costs
- Plan Quality Management
- Plan Human Resource Management
- Plan Communications Management
- Control Communications
- Plan Risk Management
- Control Risks
- Plan Procurement Management
- Control Procurements
- Close Procurements
- Plan Stakeholder Management
- Control Stakeholder Engagement

**Quick Check**

1. Why is the project charter used as an input into the Develop Project Management Plan process?

2. Why do project management plan updates feature so much as outputs from other the PMBOK Guide processes?

3. Why does the development of the project management plan appear as part of the Project Integration Management knowledge area?

**Quick Check Answers**

1. During the first iteration of the development of the project management plan, the project charter is the document that authorizes time, money, and energy being directed towards the development of the project management plan, and it contains the initial information on which to base the planning processes.

2. The development of the project management plan is a highly iterative process and, as such, it receives constant updates from other processes as it is fully developed.

3. The development of a project management plan requires the development of plans and baselines in all the other knowledge areas in the PMBOK Guide.

# Direct and Manage Project Work

▓ **More Info**    Direct and Manage Project Work

You can read more about the Direct and Manage Project Work process in the PMBOK Guide, 5th edition, in Chapter 4, section 4.3. Table 2-3 identifies the process inputs, tools and techniques, and outputs.

*Table 2-3.* *Direct and Manage Project Work Process*

| Inputs ⇨ | Tools and Techniques ⇨ | Outputs |
|---|---|---|
| • Project management plan<br>• Approved change requests<br>• Enterprise environmental factors<br>• Organizational process assets | • Expert judgment<br>• Project management information system<br>• Meetings | • Deliverables<br>• Work performance data<br>• Change requests<br>• Project management plan updates<br>• Project document updates |

The Direct and Manage Project Work process is an executing process. It is one of six processes in the Project Integration Management knowledge area, and one of a total of eight executing processes in the PMBOK Guide.

The Direct and Manage Project Work process covers the following executing domain tasks:

- Task 2: Manage task execution based on the project management plan by leading and developing the project team, in order to achieve project deliverables.

- Task 4: Implement approved changes and corrective actions by following the change management plan, in order to meet project requirements.

- Task 5: Implement approved actions by following the risk management plan, in order to minimize the impact of the risks and take advantage of opportunities on the project.

The main focus of the Direct and Manage Project Work process is doing instead of planning, which means the execution and completion of the work on the project and the product, or deliverable, you have planned to do. This is why you do all that planning, so when it comes time to start doing work you know what to do.

There are three main components of the Direct and Manage Project Work process, each focused on a slightly different area of project execution. The first and probably largest area is the implementation of the project plans you have made that specify both project and product requirements. The second area of focus for this process is the iterative process whereby you must repair any defects discovered in deliverables in the Monitoring and Controlling processes. The third area is the focus on implementation of any approved changes. As you can see, they all involve doing something.

---

▓ **Exam Tip**  This process focuses on all the work that has to be done on the project and product, and the integration and interdependencies between all the executing processes. The other executing processes deal specifically with the execution of the quality, human resources, communications, procurement, and stakeholder management plans.

---

The role of the project manager is extremely important in this process and all the executing processes because, along with the rest of the project team members, the manager is responsible for the execution of the plans. The primary focus of this process is the production of deliverables. The Direct and Manage Project Work process is also where any approved changes are implemented.

# Inputs

The inputs used in this process reflect its focus on doing the work that was planned and also implementing any approved change requests.

# Project Management Plan

The project management plan is the primary input here for obvious reasons. Obviously, you can't execute any project or product work without a proper plan to work to. You can, however, start work without the project management plan being entirely complete due to the iterative nature of the executing process and of the profession of project management generally. You can start work on just those areas you have planned while other areas are still being planned.

---
**REAL WORLD**
---

I remember being new to the profession of project management and thinking it was better just to get on with the job and that planning was a negative outcome on a cost-benefit analysis. It was with the wisdom gained with experience (and mistakes) that I learned that proper planning precedes execution, resulting in a much greater chance of project success.

# Approved Change Requests

The Direct and Manage Project Work process is not just about executing the project and product work detailed in the plans you have prepared. It is also about carrying out the work required as a result of approved changes. As such, *approved change requests* are an important input, because they describe the work to be done. Approved change requests can include a requirement for corrective action, a preventive action, or a defect repair. Approved change requests are an output from the Perform Integrated Change Control process.

# Enterprise Environmental Factors

The specific enterprise environmental factors that can influence or constrain this particular process are any organizational culture or structure that affects the timing, commitment, and support for the execution process. Other factors that also influence or constrain the speed, timing, and execution of the plans prepared include decisions around project personnel and risk tolerances for stakeholders within and outside the performing organization. Access to adequate and appropriate project management information systems also affects this process.

# Organizational Process Assets

By now you will have figured out how often organizational process assets appear as a process input. For this process, the specific organizational process assets that can help are things such as standardized guides and work instructions that the organization has to assist the project manager and the project team in doing the planned work. Other organizational process assets that can assist in the execution of the planned work include historical information from similar projects, and any standardized and established communication requirements.

# Tools and Techniques

The three tools and techniques of this process are all used on the separate inputs to deliver the planned work or the approved changes.

## Expert Judgment

Expert judgment as a tool for the Direct and Manage Project Work process is essential for taking the plans and other inputs and carrying out the implementation and execution of those plans. It is the job of the project manager and project team members to provide the expert judgment necessary to carry out the planning work and approved change requests to ensure that this process delivers its expected outputs.

In addition to the expertise of the project manager and project team members, you can also seek guidance from external experts and other stakeholders with skills and experience you require.

## Project Management Information System

The *project management information system* is an automatic or manual system, such as common project management software or databases, used for storing and disseminating project information. Here it is used to track the work being done and communicate it effectively to the correct stakeholders.

---

▩ **Exam Tip**   Project management information systems can include software used for creating and monitoring schedule information such as Microsoft Project, Primavera, Trello, Atlassian, Wrike, Basecamp, ProjectLibre, or any one of the hundreds of other great examples. They can also include databases used for cost estimating and control, and range from standalone installations to larger enterprise resource planning systems.

---

## Meetings

*Meetings* have many purposes throughout the PMBOK Guide, in this process and also in communications processes. In this instance, meetings are used as a tool by the project manager to discuss and make decisions on matters affecting the execution of the project.

```
┌─────────────────────────────────────────────────────────────┐
│                       REAL WORLD                              │
└─────────────────────────────────────────────────────────────┘
```

I have found that a properly organized meeting can be one of the most productive ways of sharing information, getting decisions made, and also building team spirit. To run one well, you need to spend time preplanning the meeting, set a clear agenda, have a real reason for the meeting, and set the expectation of the outcome from the meeting. You also need to invite only those people who need to be present and establish some ground rules. The absence of these basic points will result in a meeting that could potentially be a waste of time for all involved.

# Outputs

The major output from the Direct and Manage Project Work process is the project deliverables.

## Deliverables

The *deliverables* are often the major focus of any project. They are what the project was set up to do in the first place, and they are the primary output from this process. It can be a single deliverable or one of many deliverables. The product deliverable is the output from this executing process, whereas the other executing processes have outputs focused on project, not product, work.

The deliverables go on to become an input into the Control Quality process prior to becoming verified deliverables if they are approved. Once approved by the project team, verified deliverables then become an input into the Validate Scope process prior to becoming accepted deliverables if they are accepted by the customer.

Examples of deliverables include software modules for an IT project. If you are completing a construction project, the deliverable could be the entire building or significant parts of it. Clearly it is important that you are able to measure when a deliverable is complete, so you know when to complete this process.

## Work Performance Data

Another output from this process is the *work performance data*, which is the documented record of observation and measurements of the deliverables taken during this executing process. The work performance data can include any data that records the percent complete, any technical measurements taken, the number of change requests made and approved, the number of defects found and corrected, and start and finish times, both expected and actual. You can probably tell that some of this data is generated by other executing processes. But due to the integrated nature of the Direct and Manage Project Work process, it gets included here as an output because it may affect and be used as an input by the following monitoring and controlling processes:

- Validate Scope

- Control Scope

- Control Schedule

- Control Costs

- Control Quality

- Control Communications

- Control Risks

- Control Procurements

- Control Stakeholder Engagement

## Change Requests

As a result of doing the planned work, you may discover that there are some changes to part of the project management plan or product requirements. The *change requests* generated as a result of this process go on to become inputs into the Perform Integrated Change Control process.

---

▓ **Exam Tip**    All change requests must go through a documented and agreed-on change-control process and be either approved or declined. Change requests fall into one of the following four categories: corrective action, preventive action, defect repair, and updates.

---

## Project Management Plan Updates

As part of doing the planned work, you may choose to update some or all the component plans that make up the project management plan. *Project management plan updates* are different from change requests. Change requests signify that something new needs to be considered in an integrated manner. Project management plan updates are simply updates to documents and plans for clarification or revised approaches to executing the planned work and do not require a formal change request to be initiated.

## Project Document Updates

In addition to updates to specific plans that form the project management plan, you can also carry out project document updates to provide clarification or to note any new information such as new issues, assumptions made, and decisions made.

**Quick Check**

1. Why is it important to complete project planning prior to beginning the Direct and Manage Project Work process?

2. Why does the Direct and Manage Project Work process appear in the Project Integration Management knowledge area?

3. What sort of work do the project deliverables include?

**Quick Check Answers**

1. The Direct and Manage Project Work process is a doing process, and before you can do any work you must have planned what it is you are going to do.

2. Several other knowledge areas have executing processes that focus on their particular specialty. However, very rarely is there an executing process that does not, actually or potentially, have an impact on other knowledge areas. As such, the Direct and Manage Project Work process focuses on the integrated nature of project management and the interrelationship between processes.

3. The project deliverables include all the project and product work required to be completed by the project management plan.

# Monitor and Control Project Work

▦ **More Info**  Monitor and Control Project Work

You can read more about the Monitor and Control Project Work process in the PMBOK Guide, 5th edition, in Chapter 4, section 4.4. Table 2-4 identifies the process inputs, tools and techniques, and outputs.

*Table 2-4.* *Monitor and Control Project Work Process*

| Inputs ⇨ | Tools and Techniques ⇨ | Outputs |
|---|---|---|
| • Project management plan<br>• Schedule forecasts<br>• Cost forecasts<br>• Validated changes<br>• Work performance information<br>• Enterprise environmental factors<br>• Organizational process assets | • Expert judgment<br>• Analytical techniques<br>• Project management information system<br>• Meetings | • Change requests<br>• Work performance reports<br>• Project management plan updates<br>• Project document updates |

The key area of focus in the Monitor and Control Project Work process is checking that what you are doing matches what you planned to do. Obviously, to do this you must have done some planning and use these plans and baselines to check that the work you are doing matches what you planned to do. Remember that the work you are doing is not just the product work but also all the project work defined in your project management plan.

The Monitor and Control Project Work process is one of two monitoring and controlling processes in the Project Integration knowledge area and one of a total of 11 monitoring and controlling processes overall. Monitoring and controlling work is done throughout the life of the project, from initiation to closure.

The Monitor and Control Project Work process covers the following Monitoring and Controlling domain tasks:

- Task 1: Measure project performance using appropriate tools and techniques, in order to identify and quantify any variances and corrective actions.

- Task 5: Review the issue log, update if necessary, and determine corrective actions by using appropriate tools and techniques, in order to minimize the impact on the project.

- Task 6: Capture, analyze, and manage lessons learned using lessons-learned management techniques, in order to enable continuous improvement.

---

▓ **Exam Tip**    Hopefully by now you have started the process of immediately trying to determine what sort of inputs would be useful for completing a process and what sort of outputs that process will produce. Before reading any further, think about what sort of inputs would be useful for checking that what you are actually doing is what you planned to do.

---

# Inputs

There are seven inputs into the Monitor and Control Project Work process, all specifically designed to assist you in producing the outputs of change requests, work performance reports, project management plan updates, and project document updates.

## Project Management Plan

Once again, the project management plan forms a key input into a process, this time because if you are going to check that what you are doing is what you planned to do, you should have available to you as an input the project management plan and all its subsidiary plans—this is what you will be checking your work against. The project management plan is an output from the Develop Project Management Plan process.

## Schedule Forecasts

*Schedule forecasts* are an output from the Control Schedule process in the Project Time Management knowledge area. They are obviously useful for determining if what you are actually achieving in terms of your project schedule is accurate and matches what you had planned or forecast.

## Cost Forecasts

*Cost forecasts* are an output from the Control Costs process in the Project Cost Management knowledge area. As with the schedule forecasts, they are essential for monitoring and controlling progress on project costs.

## Validated Changes

*Validated changes* are an output of the Control Quality process in the Project Quality Management knowledge area. They involve checking that any approved change requests and associated remedial actions have been undertaken as per the approval given. In this process, they are used as a part of the baseline of work being done, and you will now monitor and control these approved additional pieces of work.

---

░ **Exam Tip**   To fully understand what *validated changes* means, you must understand the difference between the words *validate* and *verify.* The PMBOK Guide has an extensive glossary at the back of the book that describes in detail the words used throughout. *Validation* means the product, service, or system meets the needs and requirements of the customer and other important stakeholders. *Verification* means the product, service, or system complies with documented regulations, specifications, or imposed technical conditions. Think of validation as an external process and verification as an internal process done before validation.

---

# Work Performance Information

*Work performance information* is a very common output of a lot of the other monitoring and controlling processes. It is an output from the following processes:

- Validate Scope
- Control Scope
- Control Schedule
- Control Costs
- Control Quality
- Control Communications
- Control Risks
- Control Procurements
- Control Stakeholder Engagement

It includes all the data collected during these processes, and as an input into this process it is valuable for assessing what is actually happening against what you had planned to happen.

---

░ **Exam Tip**   You may recognize that work performance data becomes work performance information, which in turn becomes work performance reports. Each step is a further refinement of the information.

---

## Enterprise Environmental Factors

The specific types of enterprise environmental factors that can be used in this process include any relevant government or industry standards, stakeholder risk tolerances, and your project management information system being used to provide information into this process and record and disseminate any results from the process.

## Organizational Process Assets

The specific types of organizational process assets that can be used as inputs into this process include any existing processes and templates the organization has, lessons-learned databases, risk-management procedures, documented change-control processes and procedures, and issue and defect management procedures.

# Tools and Techniques

The following tools and techniques are available, if appropriate, to use on the selected inputs.

## Expert Judgment

Once again, expert judgment appears as a key tool to assist in gathering, interpreting, and making sense of the inputs into the process to produce useful and meaningful outputs. In this process, the project manager and members of the project team are the most relevant and easily accessible experts to consult.

## Analytical Techniques

*Analytical techniques* allow you to make sense of the inputs into the processes and the data they contain to forecast potential future scenarios. The PMBOK Guide specifically mentions the following analytical techniques:

- **Regression analysis**   The analysis of a dependent variable against one or more independent variables to determine the nature of the relationship, if any, between the variables and to extrapolate from this a likely future scenario. In this process, it is used to forecast a likely future state of perhaps time or costs based on past performance and the mathematical trend observed. It is often displayed in graph format, as shown in Figure 2-2.

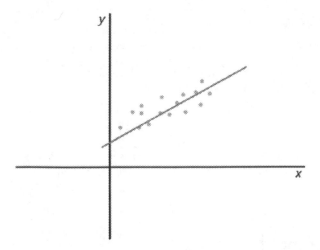

*Figure 2-2. A graph showing an example of linear regression*

- **Grouping methods**   Techniques for taking what you have observed and classifying the data into relevant groups for further study and comparison. A specific type of *grouping method* uses *exploratory study* to compare sets of data and to look for patterns and correlations between the data for causal effects.

- **Multiple-equation models**   Tools that use simultaneous equations to describe a relationship between variables and forecast likely future outcomes.

- **Failure mode and effect analysis *(FMEA)***   A widely used technique to examine the consequence of failure in any part of the system and the use of those observations to ensure that failure does not actually occur or that, if it does, the impact is anticipated and mitigated. In this process, you could use this tool to determine the likely effect of failure in the product and prepare to ensure that it doesn't happen.

- **Reserve analysis**   A tool for determining how much reserve you will need in any of the cost or time management processes or project management plan components.

- **Trend analysis**   A technique for observing data, trying to spot a trend in the data and use this observed trend to forecast a future state. You could use this in this process to spot a constant and regular trend in the product deliverable indicating that if the trend continues, you will end up with a product the client doesn't want.

▓ **Exam Tip**   All of these analytical tools and techniques feature some form of mathematical modeling and use the results to forecast a future state. On the exam, if a mathematical tool or technique is referred to, and it is in a monitoring and controlling process, then it is probably one of these tools.

## Project Management Information System

The project management information system is used here to record new data, retrieve existing data, and distribute any relevant data to stakeholders.

▓ **Exam Tip**   Remember that your project management information system is part of your enterprise environmental factors.

## Meetings

Meetings are a useful tool for the project manager, project team members, and relevant stakeholders to exchange and discuss information. They are best held in a face-to-face environment where participants can see each other, but they can also be held in virtual formats. Meetings that would be useful during this process are kick-off meetings and review meetings.

The *kick-off meeting* is done on site with all relevant stakeholders as a means of communicating that the project has done enough planning work to begin executing. As such, this meeting is generally done immediately prior to beginning project execution.

# Outputs

The following outputs are generated by the Monitor and Control Project Work process.

## Change Requests

The key outputs from the Monitor and Control Project Work process are change requests generated as a result of observing and comparing what is actually occurring against what was planned and also generated by changing requirements. Several different categories of change requests can be made; these include *corrective actions*, *preventive actions*, and *defect repair*.

Change requests become an input into the Perform Integrated Change Control process, where they are assessed and decisions are made as to whether they are approved or declined. They are not acted on until they have been approved.

# Work Performance Reports

*Work performance reports* are generated by your project management information system in physical or electronic form and show how the project is progressing against what was planned, and any changes requested and subsequent actions taken. Typically work performance reports include any regular status updates, project memos, explanatory notes, and any other updates to project team members and stakeholders.

---

## REAL WORLD

I find that not only are reports on work performance information a valuable means of communicating technical information, but they are also a valuable means of establishing and maintaining effective communications with team members and stakeholders. I have always been selective about what information goes to certain people and also what the best format is to ensure that the information I am distributing is understood by the recipients.

---

# Project Management Plan Updates

As a result of monitoring and controlling the actual results against the planned results, you will detect variations, and as a result there will be some changes to your project, probably in several different areas. These need to be captured in updates to the relevant parts of your project management plan.

# Project Document Updates

Just as there will be updates to parts of your project management plan, there will also need to be updates to project documents that deal with forecast, performance, or issues.

### Quick Check

1.  How are the Monitor and Control Project Work process and the Perform Integrated Change Control process linked?

2.  Why is the project management plan an important input into the Monitor and Control Project Work process?

3.  When would you start the Monitor and Control Project Work process?

**Quick Check Answers**

1.  The two processes are linked by change requests. These are a primary output from the Monitor and Control Project Work process and are an input in the Perform Integrated Change Control process, where decisions are made about the change request.

2.  The project management plan provides a description of how the work is expected to be done and can be used to compare with what is actually occurring.

3.  Monitoring and controlling activities are done throughout the life of the project and begin as soon as the project begins initiation and end when the project is closed.

# Perform Integrated Change Control

▓ **More Info**    Perform Integrated Change Control

You can read more about the Perform Integrated Change Control process in the PMBOK Guide, 5th edition, in Chapter 4, section 4.5. Table 2-5 identifies the process inputs, tools and techniques, and outputs.

*Table 2-5.* *Perform Integrated Change Control Process*

| Inputs ⇨ | Tools and Techniques ⇨ | Outputs |
|---|---|---|
| • Project management plan <br> • Work performance reports <br> • Change requests <br> • Enterprise environmental factors <br> • Organizational process assets | • Expert judgment <br> • Meetings <br> • Change control tools | • Approved change requests <br> • Change log <br> • Project management plan updates <br> • Project document updates |

The Perform Integrated Change Control process is one of two monitoring and controlling processes in the Project Integration Management knowledge area, and one of a total of 11 monitoring and control processes. The other 10 monitoring and controlling processes are focused on discovering any variations between what is planned and what is actually occurring, and generating change requests where appropriate. The Perform Integrated Change Control process deals with these change requests.

The Perform Integrated Change Control process covers the following Monitoring and Controlling domain task:

- Task 2: Manage changes to the project by following the change management plan, in order to ensure that project goals remain aligned with business needs.

This is the process where all changes to any part of the project are considered and decisions are made about whether they are approved or rejected. As such, it receives inputs from all the other monitoring and control processes in the form of change requests that have been generated by these other processes. It is completed throughout the life of the project, as are all monitoring and control processes.

Change requests can come from many sources, including any stakeholder on the project. All changes, no matter how small, should be documented. Many change requests are initiated with a simple verbal request, but even these should be documented and recorded in some way. Documentation of change requests can range from simple email verification of verbal requests to completion of a formal change request document, right up to a complete business case for major changes to a project. Failure to document changes will result in scope creep. *Scope creep* occurs when undocumented change control is allowed to happen, involving small changes that are regarded as insignificant. Individually they may not pose a problem, but collectively they increase the chances of project failure.

*Gold plating* is the process of making small undocumented changes to a project that result in a better outcome for the client. Although it sounds good in theory, the key here is that it is still undocumented changes to a project. This is not to say that you should not pursue better outcomes for the project and the client, but that all changes should be documented and assessed according to an agreed-on change-control process.

---

▓ **Exam Tip**    At all times you should be delivering what is documented and only what is documented. This doesn't mean you can't change what is being delivered, but that all changes should be documented.

---

All changes should be recorded in a change log that assigns them a tracking number and records progress and outcomes on the decision-making process.

---

▓ **Exam Tip**    The identification and numbering of the changes in a change log is one example of a configuration management system at work. It is a system whereby you identify all the plans and the version of those plans to ensure that you are always working on the latest plans or parts of a project. *Configuration verification and audit* is the process of checking that the configuration management system is being used correctly and that all changes to it are

---

recorded appropriately. You will find the configuration management system used in several areas throughout the PMBOK Guide, where it is broken down into the following three parts:

- *Configuration identification:* Deciding on the type and format of an appropriate configuration system to use.

- *Configuration status accounting:* Actually using each of the configuration management systems to track and surveil the project.

- *Configuration verification and audit:* Checking that people are using the configuration management system to ensure that documents are being tracked, the correct version of software is being used, processes are being used, and the right parts are being used.

# Inputs

The following inputs can be used in this process.

## Project Management Plan

The project management plan is a key input into this process, because it outlines what is planned to happen on the project. Many change requests are initiated as a result of observing a difference between what was planned and what is actually occurring. The project management plan is an output from the Develop Project Management Plan process.

## Work Performance Reports

If you are going to assess the impact and nature of any changes, it is important that you have the work performance reports to assist you. They provide information about specific areas of the project and also allow the project manager and project team members to consider any impacts of a change in one area on other areas of the project.

The work performance reports are an output of the Monitor and Control Project Work process.

---

▓ **Exam Tip** The difference between work performance reports, work performance information, and work performance data is that the work performance data is the raw information; work performance information is the raw information after it has been analyzed and contextualized, and after it incorporates the integrated nature of project management; and work performance reports are the information presented in a particular way to a particular group of stakeholders.

---

## Change Requests

The change requests are an essential input into this process, because it is focused on receiving a change request, considering it in light of the entire project, and making a decision about whether to approve or reject the change request.

As you have already learned, change requests are outputs of the other ten monitoring and controlling processes.

## Enterprise Environmental Factors

The specific enterprise environmental factor that can affect the Perform Integrated Change Control process is primarily the project management information system, because it records all the changes, the work performance information and reports, and the decisions made about the change requests.

## Organizational Process Assets

The organizational process assets that can be used to assist the Perform Integrated Change Control process are any change-control processes, templates, and procedures the organization has that guide assessment, delegated authority, and decision-making.

---

### REAL WORLD

I am a strong advocate of documenting very clearly the levels of delegated authority that project managers have when it comes to making assessment and decisions about change requests. It is simply not practical for all changes to go to a change-control board that perhaps meets monthly. It is far more sensible to allocate a certain amount of delegated authority to the project manager so the project can keep moving along. This view is reflected in the PMBOK Guide.

---

# Tools and Techniques

The following tools and techniques can be used on the selected and available inputs to generate the outputs.

## Expert Judgment

The specific type of expert judgment you will use as a tool in this process consists of those people with skills and experience to be able to assist in considering change requests and the information that will help decide whether to accept or reject the change requests. These experts can be individuals who are consulted about particular issues, or they can be groups of stakeholders who form the change-control board that meets to consider change requests.

## Meetings

Meetings, in this case *change-control meetings,* are attended by the *change-control board* that is responsible for assessing change requests and making the decisions to approve or reject change requests. Not all changes need to go to the change-control board via change-control meetings, though—only those specified in the documented change-control process, which ideally should be part of your project management methodology, itself part of your organizational process assets.

## Change-Control Tools

*Change-control tools* used in the Perform Integrated Change Control process can be any automated or manual system for organizing, recording, documenting, assessing, storing, and distributing decisions about change requests and the subsequent decisions made. You can tell that your project management information system is one example of the sort of change-control tool that can be used.

# Outputs

The Perform Integrated Change Control process produces some or all the following outputs.

## Approved Change Requests

*Approved change requests* are the primary output from the Perform Integrated Change Control process. They are the result of the selected inputs and the tools and techniques applied. All approved change requests are recorded in the change-request log.

The approved change requests go on to be incorporated into existing baselines and become an input in the following processes:

- Direct and Manage Project Work
- Control Quality
- Control Procurements
- Manage Stakeholder Engagement

## Change Log

The *change log* is the document kept to record the change requests received and their status. It is used as an input in the Manage Stakeholder Engagement process.

# Project Management Plan Updates

Approved change requests are added to existing baselines to become new baselines. Additionally, many approved change requests also affect other subsidiary project management plans. Project management plan updates are used as an input into the Develop Project Management Plan process.

---

▨ **Exam Tip**   According to the PMBOK Guide, a baseline is the original baseline plus any approved changes. This may differ from your current understanding of the baseline being only what you originally started with.

---

# Project Document Updates

Just as approved change requests can change parts of the project management plan, they can also affect other project documents and require them to be updated, particularly those associated with the change-control process.

### Quick Check

1.   Why is the Perform Integrated Change Control process performed after other monitoring and controlling processes?

2.   During what parts of the project life cycle are the activities associated with Perform Integrated Change Control process performed?

3.   What is the role of the change-control board?

### Quick Check Answers

1.   The Perform Integrated Change Control process requires change requests as a key input. These change requests are generated as outputs from other monitoring and controlling processes.

2.   The activities of the Perform Integrated Change Control process are carried out throughout the entire project life cycle, from initiation to closing.

3.   The change-control board is the group of experts who meet to consider change requests. They are defined by the documented change-control processes in place in the organization.

# Close Project or Phase

▓ **More Info**   Close Project or Phase

You can read more about the Close Project or Phase process in the PMBOK Guide, 5th edition, in Chapter 4, section 4.6. Table 2-6 identifies the process inputs, tools and techniques, and outputs.

*Table 2-6.*  *Close Project or Phase Process*

| Inputs ⇨ | Tools and Techniques ⇨ | Outputs |
|---|---|---|
| • Project management plan<br>• Accepted deliverables<br>• Organizational process assets | • Expert judgment<br>• Analytical techniques<br>• Meetings | • Final product, service, or result transition<br>• Organizational process asset updates |

The Close Project or Phase process is one of two closing processes in the PMBOK Guide; the other is Close Procurements in the Project Procurement Management knowledge area.

The Close Project or Phase process covers the following seven closing domain tasks:

- Task 1: Obtain final acceptance of the project deliverables from relevant stakeholders, in order to confirm that project scope and deliverables were achieved.

- Task 2: Transfer the ownership of deliverables to the assigned stakeholders in accordance with the project plan, in order to facilitate project closure.

- Task 3: Obtain financial, legal, and administrative closure using generally accepted practices and policies, in order to communicate formal project closure and ensure transfer of liability.

- Task 4: Prepare and share the final project report according to the communications management plan, in order to document and convey project performance and assist in project evaluation.

- Task 5: Collate lessons learned that were documented throughout the project, and conduct a comprehensive project review, in order to update the organization's knowledge base.

- Task 6: Archive project documents and materials using generally accepted practices, in order to comply with statutory requirements and for potential use in future projects and audits.

- Task 7: Obtain feedback from relevant stakeholders, using appropriate tools and techniques and based on the stakeholder management plan, in order to evaluate their satisfaction.

This process is the only closing process in the Project Integration Management knowledge area and is focused on the activities involved in completing the work required in a project or a phase of a project. Because it is an integrated process, it involves closure over all the processes being used in the project and not just the deliverable. As the name of the process suggests, it is used when closing a project prior to deliverable handover, or when completing a phase of a project prior to awaiting approval to proceed to the next phase.

The role of the project manager during this process is important, because the project manager must take responsibility for closing the project and overseeing the required tasks. The project manager has responsibility for reviewing all the documents created and ensuring that what is being delivered matches what is documented. Having a closeout checklist as part of your organizational process assets is an effective way to document exactly what *closure* means, the tasks that must be done, the signatures that must be obtained, and the final steps to confirm the project is complete. The role of the project sponsor is also important, because that individual officially signs off on project or phase closure.

---

▓ **Exam Tip**　The PMBOK Guide places a high degree of importance on the value of creating lessons learned during the project and finalizing these during the closeout process through informal means, surveys, interviews, workshops, and post-implementation reviews. You should always assume that you will create lessons learned as part of your project, and always assume that lessons learned are available to you from previous projects when you begin a new one.

---

One of the key ways to distinguish this process from the Close Procurements process is that the Close Project or Phase process is focused not only on contractual closure but on all the aspects of administrative closure as well. Being an integrated process, it considers how contractual closure processes as part of the Close Procurements process may impact other areas of the project, and it also goes through the defined and approved closure process the organization has as part of its organizational process assets.

---

▓ **Exam Tip**　All projects must be closed, even if they end in less-than-perfect situations. If a project ends suddenly, then you must have a process in place to follow in this instance. If a question on the PMP exam poses this scenario, you should also assume that whatever the situation, you will enter some form of project-closure process.

---

| REAL WORLD |
|---|

Project closure is one of those processes that we know we should do, but usually by the time we move into the part of the project where the bulk of our effort is on project closure, we are being called away to start a new project. I have learned that there are tangible benefits to staying focused on project closure in the face of these calls to join new projects. It is important to make sure you get formal signoff that the project is complete, collect and store lessons learned, and, if possible, hold a post-implementation review some time later to determine whether the deliverable is actually doing what it was supposed to do.

# Inputs

The Close Project or Phase process uses the following inputs.

## Project Management Plan

The project management plan defines the work to be done, and so, as part of seeking to close a project or phase of a project, you need the project management plan and must be able to prove that all the work planned has been completed. The PMBOK Guide describes the project management plan as the contract between the project manager and the project sponsor, because it is the document that defines what constitutes project completion. The project management plan is an output from the Develop Project Management Plan process.

## Accepted Deliverables

*Accepted deliverables* are an output from the Validate Scope process in the Project Scope Management knowledge area. Because they are validated by your documented processes, they are now ready to be handed over as part of the project closure process.

## Organizational Process Assets

The specific organizational process assets that can be used to assist the Close Project or Phase process are any documented closeout checklists, templates, processes, or requirements. Additionally, you can use any relevant historical information or lessons learned to assist you with this process.

---

▨ **Exam Tip**   You should always do your closure planning during the Develop Project Management Plan process and the other planning processes. Along with all your other plans, you should also have a plan for how to close the project.

---

# Tools and Techniques

The following tools and techniques can be used on the inputs into the Close Project or Phase process.

## Expert Judgment

The type of expert judgment you use during this process includes the project manager, the project team members, the project sponsors, the client, your legal team, and any other stakeholders who can provide advice and opinion on project closure.

## Analytical Techniques

Analytical techniques were used as a tool or technique in the Monitor and Control Project Work process to analyze data and forecast future trends. As a tool in this process, they are used to substantiate any information that can be used to confirm project or product deliverables. Of the possible analytical techniques that could be used, regression analysis and trend analysis are the most applicable and useful.

## Meetings

Meetings between experts and other stakeholders involved in discussing and deciding on aspects of project or phase closure are an important tool in the process. Specific types of meetings that can be held include lessons-learned meetings, closeout meetings, and post-implementation review meetings.

# Outputs

The Close Project or Phase process produces the following outputs.

## Final Product, Service, or Result Transition

This is the whole point of the project—the reason it was initiated in the first place. This is the deliverable the entire project was planned to provide for the customer. In the case of phase closure, it is the milestone that is expected before approval is given to proceed to the next phase. The *final product, service, or result* is handed over to the customer as the final part of contractual closure.

# Organizational Process Asset Updates

The end of a project and the time spent examining what was done well and what was not done so well is a great opportunity to look at updating any relevant organizational process assets as part of your commitment to continuous improvement. The project files, including all the documentation resulting from the completion of project activities, should be used to update any relevant organizational process assets. Gathering historical information and lessons learned, and using this information to update and improve organizational process assets, is also an important step. *Organizational process asset updates* are the final act of administrative closure.

---

▒ **Exam Tip**   Know the difference between contractual and administrative closure, and understand that contractual closure is always completed before administrative closure is completed.

---

### Quick Check

1.   Why is the completion of the lessons-learned documentation during the Close Project or Phase process so important?

2.   What is the difference between closing a project and closing a phase of a project?

3.   What is the role of the project sponsor during the Close Project or Phase process?

### Quick Check Answers

1.   The lessons-learned documents ensure that any part of the project that was done well and any part of the project that was not done well are documented for future project managers to use so they can take advantage of the strengths and avoid repeating the weaknesses in your project.

2.   Closing a project means the completion of all work on a project. Closing a phase of a project is the end of one phase and not necessarily the end of the project. The successful end of a phase means waiting for approval to move to the next phase, usually with the output from the phase that is being closed.

3.   The project sponsor's role in the Close Project or Phase process is to accept the deliverable on behalf of the delivering organization and provide formal signoff for project closure.

# Chapter Summary

- The Project Integration Management knowledge area recognizes and is focused on the way in which project work is not completed in separate discrete chunks. There is the need to take a high-level view across all project activities, and activities in one knowledge area may influence activities in another knowledge area.

- The project charter is the foundational document for the project, and all projects must have a project charter.

- The project management plan contains all the elements of integrated project planning and also all the other outputs from the other planning processes.

- The project management plan is an output from the Develop Project Management Plan process and an essential input into the Direct and Manage Project Work, Monitor and Control Project Work, Perform Integrated Change Control, and Close Project or Phase processes.

- The Direct and Manage Project Work process is focused on completing the work described in the project management plan. The project deliverables are the primary output from this process.

- The Monitor and Control Project Work process is focused on checking that what is being completed as part of the Direct and Mange Project Work process is what was planned. Any changes are issued as outputs from the process as change requests for the Perform Integrated Change Control process to deal with. Change requests can be outputs from any of the other monitoring and controlling processes in the PMBOK Guide, with the exception of the Perform Integrated Change Control process, for which they are an input.

- The Perform Integrated Change Control process is focused on receiving and considering all change requests and processing them as per the approved and documented change-control process. Change requests can be approved or rejected.

- The Close Project or Phase process is focused on completing all the activities associated with administrative and contractual closure. It provides the deliverable and closure for a project, or the milestone for a project being delivered in phases.

# Exercises

The answers for these exercises are located in the "Answers" section at the end of this chapter.

1.  Calculate the following financial selection criteria for projects:

    A.  Calculate Present Value, where the Future Value is $300,000, the interest rate is 10%, and the time period is 3 years.

    Calculate Net Present Value where the Present Value of Income is $250,000 and the Present Value of Costs is $180,000.

    Calculate the Payback Period for a project with an initial cost of $450,000 and annual income of $110,000.

2.  All of the following are either inputs, outputs, or both into processes in the Project Integration Management knowledge area. As such, it is possible to place them in the order in which they are generally completed so that one is completed prior to it being used as an input in a subsequent process. Place the following in order from first to last in relation to where they appear in the overall flow of inputs and outputs between the processes in the Project Integration Management knowledge area:

    A.  Change requests

    B.  Agreements

    C.  Schedule forecasts

    D.  Project management plan

    E.  Final product, service, or result

    F.  Accepted deliverables

    G.  Business case

    H.  Deliverables

    I.  Project charter

    J.  Validated changes

    K.  Project statement of work

    L.  Cost forecast

    M.  Approved change requests

# Review Questions

Test your knowledge of the information in Chapter 2 by answering these questions. The answers to these questions and the explanations of why each answer choice is correct or incorrect are located in the "Answers" section at the end of this chapter.

1.  Which of the following answers best describes a key benefit of the Develop Project Charter process?

    A.  Assess and manage all change requests.

    B.  Define the project start, and create a formal record of the project.

    C.  Iteratively prepare plans for execution throughout a project.

    D.  Ensure that all projects are closed.

2.  The high-level narrative description of the work to be done on the project is known as which of the following?

    A.  Strategic plan

    B.  Product scope description

    C.  Statement of work

    D.  Business case

3.  Which of the following answers best describes the main purpose of the project management plan?

    A.  To initiate and approve the project

    B.  To define both project and product scope

    C.  To describe how the project will be executed, monitored, and controlled

    D.  To assess which projects should be done

4.  Which project change requests must go through the approved change-control process?

    A.  Only those that have an impact on project scope

    B.  Any change request that affects scope, time, cost, or quality

    C.  Only those change requests that the project manager decides should go through the process

    D.  All change requests must go through the change-control process.

5. What is the name of the group of people responsible for reviewing, evaluating, and deciding on changes to the project?

   A. Change-control board

   B. Project steering group

   C. Project team

   D. Stakeholders

6. Which of the following is not an organizational process asset that would be updated as a result of completing project closure?

   A. Historical information

   B. Project files

   C. Project charter

   D. Project closure checklist

7. Consulting stakeholders and project team members, and using your own knowledge, are all examples of what sort of tool or technique used in the Project Integration Management knowledge area?

   A. Stakeholder engagement

   B. Meetings

   C. Expert judgment

   D. Analytical techniques

8. What is the correct order of project activities?

   A. Develop project management plan, execute project, develop project charter, conduct project selection

   B. Conduct project selection, develop project charter, execute project, develop project management plan

   C. Conduct project selection, develop project charter, develop project management plan, execute project

   D. Develop project charter, develop project management plan, execute project, conduct project selection

9.  Which process in the Project Integration Management knowledge area deals with making decisions on change requests?

    A.   Monitor and Control Project Work

    B.   Develop Project Charter

    C.   Direct and Manage Project Work

    D.   Perform Integrated Change Control

10. What are the existing change-control processes, policies, and templates referred to as?

    A.   Organizational process assets

    B.   Enterprise environmental factors

    C.   Project documents

    D.   Project management plan

11. The final product, service, or result is an output of the Close Project or Phase process. Where does it go after this process?

    A.   The Monitor and Control Project Work process

    B.   The customer

    C.   The Perform Integrated Change Control process

    D.   The Direct and Manage Project Work process

12. The document that authorizes the project is called what?

    A.   Project management plan

    B.   Project document

    C.   Organizational process asset

    D.   Project charter

# Answers

This section contains the answers to the questions for the "Exercises" and "Review Questions" in this chapter.

## Exercises

1.  Calculate the following financial selection criteria for projects:

    A.  Calculate Present Value where the Future Value is $300,000, the interest rate is 10%, and the time period is 3 years.

    $$PV = \frac{FV}{(1 + r)^n}$$

    where *FV* equals the future value of cash flows, *r* equals the interest rate, and *n* equals the number of time periods.

    Therefore, the calculation is

    $$PV = \frac{\$300,000}{(1 + 0.1)^3}$$

    $$PV = \$225,394$$

    Calculate Net Present Value where the Present Value of Income is $250,000 and the Present Value of Costs is $180,000.

    NPV is calculated by subtracting the Present Value of Costs from the Present Value of Income:

    = *$250,000 – $180,000 = $70,000*

    Calculate the Payback Period for a project with an initial cost of $450,000 and annual income of $110,000.

    Payback Period is calculated by dividing the initial investment by the projected annual income:

    = *$450,000/ $110,000 = 4.09 years*

2. The following order presents the inputs before they are required in a process, and subsequent outputs are presented before they are first used as an input.

A. Project statement of work (input into Develop Project Charter)

B. Business case (input into Develop Project Charter)

C. Agreements (input into Develop Project Charter)

D. Project charter (output from Develop Project Charter; input into Develop Project Management Plan)

E. Project management plan (output from Develop Project Management Plan; input into all subsequent processes)

F. Deliverables (output from Direct and Manage Project Work)

G. Change requests (output from Direct and Manage Project Work and Monitor and Control Project work; input into Perform Integrated Change Control)

H. Validated changes (input into Monitor and Control Project Work)

I. Schedule forecasts (input into Monitor and Control Project Work)

J. Cost forecasts (input into Monitor and Control Project Work)

K. Approved change requests (output from Perform Integrated Change Control)

L. Accepted deliverables (input into Close Project or Phase)

M. Final product, service, or result (output from Close Project or Phase)

# Review Questions

1. **Correct Answer: B**

A. **Incorrect:** The Perform Integrated Change Control process assesses and manages change requests.

B. **Correct**: The Develop Project Charter process does result in outputs that define the start of the project and does create a formal record of the project with the project charter.

C. **Incorrect:** The Develop Project Management Plan process iteratively prepares the different plans to guide project execution.

D. **Incorrect:** The Close Project or Phase process ensures that all projects are formally closed.

2. **Correct Answer: C**

A. **Incorrect:** The strategic plan is developed by the organization and is used to help it select the correct projects.

B. **Incorrect**: The product scope description is a well-defined description of the deliverable.

C. **Correct:** The statement of work is a high-level narrative description of the work to be done on the project and is used as an input into the Develop Project Charter process.

D. **Incorrect:** The business case prepares a justification for undertaking the project.

3. **Correct Answer: C**

A. **Incorrect:** The project charter initiates and approves the project.

B. **Incorrect**: The scope statement defines both project and product scope.

C. **Correct:** The project management plan describes how the rest of the project will be executed, monitored, and controlled.

D. **Incorrect:** The business case can be used to assess which projects should be done.

4. **Correct Answer: D**

A. **Incorrect:** All change requests, not just those that affect project scope, must go through the defined change-control process.

B. **Incorrect**: All change requests, not just those that affect scope, time, quality, and cost, must go through the defined change-control process.

C. **Incorrect:** The project manager does play a proactive part in influencing those factors that may lead to change requests being initiated; but once initiated, the requests must all go through the approved change-control process.

D. **Correct:** All change requests must be considered as per the approved change-control process.

5.    **Correct Answer: A**

A.    **Correct:** The change-control board is responsible for reviewing, evaluating, and deciding on changes to the project.

B.    **Incorrect**: The project steering group is responsible for providing senior-level advice, oversight, and project governance.

C.    **Incorrect:** The project team is responsible for carrying out the project work under the guidance of the project manager.

D.    **Incorrect:** Stakeholders have many roles within the project, and members of the change-control board are certainly stakeholders, but the broadest definition includes everyone who can affect or be affected by the project.

6.    **Correct Answer: C**

A.    **Incorrect:** Historical information is updated as part of project closure.

B.    **Incorrect**: Many types of project files are updated as part of project closure.

C.    **Correct:** The project charter is an initiating document and is not updated as part of project closure, although some historical information may refer to lessons learned about the project charter.

D.    **Incorrect:** The project closure checklist is completed and updated as part of project closure.

7.    **Correct Answer: C**

A.    **Incorrect:** Stakeholder engagement is the activity carried out as the focus of the Project Stakeholder Expectation Management knowledge area.

B.    **Incorrect**: Meetings are used to gather groups of stakeholders together to discuss and make decisions.

C.    **Correct:** The description in the question refers to different categories of experts who may be consulted for their advice and opinion.

D.    **Incorrect:** Analytical techniques are mathematical techniques used to interpret raw data.

8. **Correct Answer: C**

    A.     **Incorrect:** Project selection and development of the project charter must be carried out before the development of the project management plan.

    B.     **Incorrect**: The development of the project management plan must occur before execution of the work.

    C.     **Correct:** Project selection feeds into the project charter, which in turns feeds into the development of the project management plan. The project management plan is used as the basis for project execution.

    D.     **Incorrect:** Conducting project selection must be done first in the process.

9. **Correct Answer: D**

    A.     **Incorrect:** The Monitor and Control Project Work process focuses on monitoring the actual work being done against the planned work. Change requests are an output from this process.

    B.     **Incorrect**: The Develop Project Charter process is focused on project selection methods and the development of the project charter.

    C.     **Incorrect:** The Direct and Manage Project Work process is focused on executing the work contained in the project management plan.

    D.     **Correct:** The Perform Integrated Change Control process uses change requests as an input and, with the appropriate tools and techniques, decides whether to accept or reject the change requests.

10. **Correct Answer: A**

    A.     **Correct:** The existing change-control processes, policies, and templates are all examples of process assets owned by the organization.

    B.     **Incorrect**: Enterprise environmental factors are external to the project, although they may still be in the performing organization. They can often be seen as constraining rather than assisting a project.

    C.     **Incorrect:** Project documents are produced as part of many processes. Some documents are part of the organizational process assets.

    D.     **Incorrect:** The project management plan is the overall combination of subsidiary plans across all the PMBOK Guide knowledge areas.

11. **Correct Answer: B**

    A.    **Incorrect:** The Monitor and Control Project Work process uses forecast information and the project management plan to check actual against planned work.

    B.    **Correct**: The customer receives the deliverables from the project.

    C.    **Incorrect:** The Perform Integrated Change Control process uses change requests and work performance reports as inputs.

    D.    **Incorrect:** The Direct and Manage Project Work process uses the project management plan and approved change requests as inputs.

12. **Correct Answer: D**

    A.    **Incorrect:** The project management plan combines all subsidiary plans from other planning processes. The project charter feeds the development of the project management plan.

    B.    **Incorrect:** *Project document* is a generic term for any document used to plan, record, and store information about the project. The project charter is one example of a project document.

    C.    **Incorrect:** The process to produce the project charter and the blank template can produce organizational process assets but are not examples of organizational process assets themselves.

    D.    **Correct:** The project charter is the foundation document for any project; it authorizes resources to be used on the project.

# CHAPTER 3

■ ■ ■

# Scope Management

This chapter looks at the processes focused on how to plan, define, manage, and control changes to the project requirements, scope, and work breakdown structure (WBS).

The Project Scope Management knowledge area includes six processes. Four of the six processes are planning processes; the other two are monitoring and controlling processes. Properly defining the project scope statement is critical in order to complete other planning activities such as planning the project cost, project time, quality, communications, human resources, and procurement. Without properly defined requirements, scope, and WBS, you simply cannot complete these other activities well.

**The PMBOK® Guide Processes**
**Project Scope Management Knowledge Area**
The six processes in the Project Scope Management knowledge area are as follows:

- Plan Scope Management (planning process)

- Collect Requirements (planning process)

- Define Scope (planning process)

- Create WBS (planning process)

- Validate Scope (monitoring and controlling process)

- Control Scope (monitoring and controlling process)

Defining and documenting the project scope is about documenting all the work to be completed and the work not to be completed, as part of the project and the product. It is important to note that the product scope is a subset of the project scope. Figure 3-1 shows the product scope as a subset of the project scope.

© Sean Whitaker 2016
S. Whitaker, *Pass the PMP® Exam*, DOI 10.1007/978-1-4842-2074-0_3

*Figure 3-1.* *Product scope as a subset of project scope*

---

▒ **Exam Tip**    Many people are used to focusing on defining the product scope as part of their scope management work. It is important to realize that there is more to the scope of the project than just the scope of delivering the product and its technical requirements. The project scope includes all the planning work, executing work, monitoring and control work, and closing work that has to be done in addition to the delivery of the product.

---

# What Is Project Scope Management?

Project scope management is focused on defining and managing the scope of work to be completed as part of the project. It is a highly iterative process that begins with the initiation of the project and the statement of work contained in the project charter. The project charter is then used as an input into gathering the requirements, which results in requirements documentation; it may also result in a preliminary scope statement. After you have performed these next iterations of defining the scope statement, you arrive at a project scope statement, which in itself may only define and detail the work to be done in the short term and may leave some of the work to be done in the longer term relatively undefined.

| REAL WORLD |
| --- |

Most people focus on the three pillars of project management: the scope, the time, and the cost of the project. This is for good reason, because these three foundational elements are most often used as the primary metrics of success in a project, and they also feed into the other areas of the profession of project management. Therefore, you should pay extra attention to the time and effort committed to defining the scope of a project: of the three pillars, it is the most crucial because it allows you to complete cost and time estimates.

Distinct terms are used to describe successive iterations of the work to be done on a project. Figure 3-2 shows a hierarchical view of the different terms used to describe successive and progressively more detailed iterations of the scope.

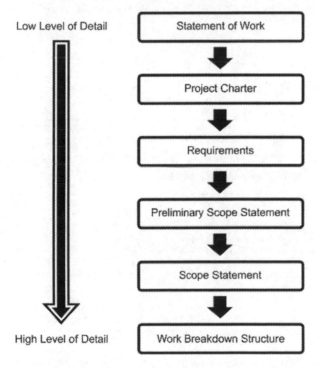

**Figure 3-2.** *Descriptions of project work reflecting the level of detail contained in the description*

```
┌────────────────────────────────────────────────────────────┐
│                        REAL WORLD                            │
└────────────────────────────────────────────────────────────┘
```

When working on a project, I have found that most people want to spend a lot of time and energy defining the product without giving much thought to planning and defining all the other work that must be done on a project Not only does the lack of wider project work information create problems with your project as you proceed, but it also creates a false impression that all of your work as a project manager is focused on delivery of the product.

▓ **Exam Tip**　Make sure when reading a question on the exam that you are careful to look out for the words *project* and *product*" This is particularly important in questions relating to the project scope or the product scope. It is also important in the Project Quality Management knowledge area, where there are separate quality processes for the project and the product.

# Plan Scope Management

▓ **More Info**　Plan Scope Management You can read more about the Plan Scope Management process in the PMBOK Guide, 5th edition, in Chapter 5, section 5.1. Table 3-1 identifies the process inputs, tools and techniques, and outputs.

**Table 3-1.**  *Plan Scope Management Process*

| Inputs ⇨ | Tools and Techniques ⇨ | Outputs |
|---|---|---|
| • Project management plan<br>• Project charter<br>• Enterprise environmental factors<br>• Organizational process assets | • Expert judgment<br>• Meetings | • Scope management plan<br>• Requirements management plan |

The Plan Scope Management process is a planning process with two major outputs: the scope management plan and the requirements management plan.

The Plan Scope Management process addresses the following planning domain task:

- Task 2: Develop a scope management plan, based on the approved project scope and using scope management techniques, in order to define, maintain, and manage the scope of the project.

The Plan Scope Management process, like most of the other planning processes, sets out and defines your particular approach for further definition of the project and product scope, and the way in which you are going to validate scope and control any changes to the scope. All of these elements are captured in the scope management plan.

---

▓ **Exam Tip**    You may begin to notice that the key output from the initial planning processes in any knowledge area is some form of plan. For example, a key output from the Plan Scope Management process is the scope management plan.

---

# Inputs

The Plan Scope Management process uses some or all of the following inputs as part of the development of the scope management plan for the project.

## Project Management Plan

The project management plan, at whatever stage of its development, is used as an input here into planning your approach to managing your scope. Keep in mind that early on in the project, the project management plan and its subsidiary plans will be relatively ill defined. As the project progresses and more details are known about the project and the subsidiary elements of the project, the project management plan itself will become more fleshed out. This clearly demonstrates the highly iterative nature of planning how you will manage your project and product scope. The project management plan is the key output from the Develop Project Management Plan process.

---

▓ **Exam Tip**    Keep in mind that the project management plan is the collection of all the other subsidiary plans and baselines.

---

## Project Charter

The project charter is used here as an input into the Plan Scope Management process because it contains the description of the project scope that is known at that point. If the project charter contains a statement of work, this will need to be further developed and defined into a full scope statement. If the project charter is built on the results of a negotiated contract, it may include a fully defined scope of work. The project charter is the sole output from the Develop Project Charter process.

## Enterprise Environmental Factors

The types of enterprise environmental factors that can play a role in how you manage scope can include things such as the culture of the organization and its attention to detail, risk, and quality; and any external marketplace conditions that the project is being initiated to take advantage of.

---

▨ **Exam Tip**  Enterprise environmental factors are one of the most widely used inputs throughout the PMBOK Guide. The term covers a lot of different factors that can influence a project. Take time to understand the variety of factors that are enterprise environmental factors and be able to differentiate them from organizational process assets.

---

## Organizational Process Assets

Once again, organizational process assets play an important role as an input into a planning process. The types of organizational process assets that are most useful in this section are any blank templates, defined policies and procedures, any historical information, lessons learned, and any project management methodology already in place.

# Tools and Techniques

The following tools and techniques are available to be used to develop the inputs into this process in order to produce the scope management plan.

## Expert Judgment

Expert judgment is one of the key tools used throughout the entire PMBOK guide. In relation to the Plan Scope Management process, the experts you will call on include your own expert judgment, the expert judgment of team members, and any other experts you want to consult to help you define your particular approach to scope management.

## Meetings

Meetings in which you gather project team members and relevant stakeholders together are an important tool and technique in defining your approach to scope management. Attendees at such meetings should include anyone with responsibility for any part of the scope management process.

---

▓ **Exam Tip**   The way in which your run your meetings determines how effective they are. Meetings are both an important way to gather technical information and an important means of distributing information and building a high-performing team. These latter attributes of a meeting are more fully discussed in the Project Communications Management knowledge area and the Project Human Resource Management knowledge area.

---

# Outputs

After applying the appropriate tools and techniques to the selected inputs, the Plan Scope Management process has the following outputs.

## Scope Management Plan

The *scope management plan* is one of the more important subsidiary plans contained in the project management plan. It outlines your particular process for iteratively defining the detail of the project and product scope, the process of decomposition for the creation of your work breakdown structure (a process that uses the scope statement that has been developed to execute project work), and the process by which any requested changes are considered and either approved or declined. In addition to these elements, it also sets out the process of validating the project scope and deliverables, and how signoff for closure will be obtained. Again, the detail in the scope management plan reflects the detail of the project scope. A highly defined scope results in a well-defined scope management plan, and a loosely defined scope results in a more flexible scope management plan, allowing for further iterations.

The scope management plan is used as an input into the following processes:

　　　　5.2 Collect Requirements

　　　　5.3 Define Scope

　　　　5.4 Create WBS

　　　　5.5 Validate Scope

---

## REAL WORLD

As a general rule of thumb, I like to make sure about one-third of the content of the scope statement refers to what is not included in both the project and product scope of work. If you don't specifically list the exclusions, stakeholders will make assumptions about what is, and what isn't, included in the scope of work, and it is these assumptions that lead to disagreements.

---

## Requirements Management Plan

The *requirements management plan* is a specific plan that addresses how the product requirements are documented, defined, tracked, and reported against. It is also in the requirements management plan that detail of the configuration management activities are defined. The requirements management plan also contains methods for prioritizing the requirements, and any defined metrics to define the product. The requirements management plan is used as an input into the Collect Requirements process.

**Quick Check**

1.  What is the main focus of the Plan Scope Management process?

2.  What is the difference between the project scope and the product scope?

3.  What are the key differences between the scope management plan and the requirements management plan?

**Quick Check Answers**

1.  The main focus of the Plan Scope Management process is to develop a scope management plan that will guide your activities in defining the project requirements, scope, and work breakdown structure.

2.  The project scope includes a definition of all the work required in the project, whereas the product scope focuses on defining the technical requirements of the expected deliverable.

3.  The scope management plan can be seen as the broader of the two management plans because it focuses on the entire project and product scope and how it will be defined, documented, and controlled. The requirements management plan focuses solely on further iterations and definition of the requirements of the project deliverable.

# Collect Requirements

---

▨ **More Info**  Collect Requirements You can read more about the Collect Requirements process in the PMBOK Guide, 5th edition, in Chapter 5, section 5.2. Table 3-2 identifies the process inputs, tools and techniques, and outputs.

---

*Table 3-2.* *Collect Requirements Process*

| Inputs ⇨ | Tools and Techniques ⇨ | Outputs |
|---|---|---|
| • Scope management plan<br>• Requirements management plan<br>• Stakeholder management plan<br>• Project charter<br>• Stakeholder register | • Interviews<br>• Focus groups<br>• Facilitated workshops<br>• Group creativity techniques<br>• Group decision-making techniques<br>• Questionnaires and surveys<br>• Observations<br>• Prototypes<br>• Benchmarking<br>• Context diagrams<br>• Document analysis | • Requirements documentation<br>• Requirements traceability matrix |

The Collect Requirements process addresses the following planning domain task:

- Task 1: Review and assess detailed project requirements, constraints, and assumptions with stakeholders based on the project charter and lessons learned, and by using requirements-gathering techniques, in order to establish detailed project deliverables.

*Requirements* can best be defined as a definition of the stakeholders' needs to meet the project's objectives. They can include technical requirements or known constraints. Therefore, the process of collecting requirements involves stakeholders and documentation of what they believe the project objectives are. It is important to note that the project requirements can be much more than the product requirements.

▓ **Exam Tip**   On the exam, you should assume that unless otherwise explicitly stated, you must go through a requirements-gathering process prior to completing the scope statement.

```
╔══════════════════════════════════════════════════════════╗
║                      REAL WORLD                            ║
╚══════════════════════════════════════════════════════════╝
```

I have often found that broader project requirements can be captured and documented as key performance indicators for determining the success or otherwise of the project, beyond the strict technical requirements of the product. For example, you could have customer satisfaction, health and safety compliance, environmental management requirements, or any other factors set as key performance indicators of project success, and these factors would be gathered in the requirements documentation.

# Inputs

The following inputs are used in the Collect Requirements process.

## Scope Management Plan

Obviously, in order to collect and define the project requirements, it is important that you act according to your scope management plan, because the requirements are a subset of the project scope. The scope management plan is a key output from the Plan Scope Management process.

## Requirements Management Plan

The requirements management plan is an important input into this process because it guides you as you seek to further define and document the requirements of the project and product. The requirements management plan is an output from the Plan Scope Management process.

## Stakeholder Management Plan

The *stakeholder management plan* is an important input into this process because you will be approaching stakeholders and asking what the requirements are for the project and the product. Thus, the stakeholder management plan and the information it contains about how you identify and manage stakeholder expectations is a critical part of and input into this process. The stakeholder management plan is a key output from the Plan Stakeholder Management process.

## Project Charter

The project charter authorizes the project and contains any high-level information about the product and project deliverable that can be used to assist the process of collecting more detailed requirements. The project charter is the sole output from the Develop Project Charter process.

## Stakeholder Register

The *stakeholder register* identifies the known stakeholders, their power and interest in the project, an assessment of their expectations, and an analysis of their communication needs. You can use this information to effectively interact with the stakeholders to ensure that you have gathered all the project and product requirements. The stakeholder register is an output from the Identify Stakeholders process.

# Tools and Techniques

The following tools and techniques can be used to produce the outputs from the Collect Requirements process.

## Interviews

When dealing with stakeholders, one of the most effective ways of soliciting information from them is by using *interviews*. Interviews can be formal or informal, and they can be conducted in person or via email or surveys.

## Focus Groups

*Focus groups* are a very effective means of bringing together relevant stakeholders and subject matter experts and gathering information from them in a structured way.

## Facilitated Workshops

*Facilitated workshops* provide a forum to solicit information from various stakeholders in a controlled manner. They are focused and interactive by their nature and are often facilitated by an independent party. Examples of specific types of facilitated workshops include the joint application design/development sessions (JAD) and the quality function deployment (QFD) facilitated workshops used in new product development.

## Group Creativity Techniques

Several types of *group creativity techniques* can be used as tools in this process to further define and document project and product requirements. Brainstorming is a particularly popular one, in which you bring together relevant stakeholders with the experience and skills needed and run a free-flowing session where all ideas are considered good ideas and are further refined by the group.

The nominal group technique is a group creativity technique that uses a variety of voting methods by which group members rank the most useful ideas for further brainstorming. Examples include the fist-of-fives, where group members display their support for an idea by raising a number of fingers on their hands; weighted voting systems, where each member is given a certain number of votes to allocate between different ideas; and a simple, straightforward voting system to rank different ideas in terms of validity and prioritization.

## Group Decision-Making Techniques

The goal of *group decision-making techniques* is to generate either a consensus among group members or a decision to abide by majority opinion. Obviously, there will be dissenting and differing views on which ideas should have greatest priority. An important part of running any group decision-making process is to establish early on how decisions will be made so that all participants are aware of the process for decision-making. You can agree on any one of the following group decision-making techniques to aid your decision-making process:

- Unanimity or consensus is where everybody agrees on a single course of action.

- The Delphi technique, which gathers information anonymously from experts to avoid peer pressure, can be used if you want to allow experts to provide anonymous feedback.

- You can decide to use a simple majority for any decisions made. If a majority (more than 50% of the members of the group) cannot be obtained, you may decide to use plurality, in which the largest bloc in a group decides.

- A final method of obtaining a group decision in the face of dissenting opinions is to agree to allow one individual in the group to make the decision for the group. This is commonly referred to as a dictatorship group decision-making technique.

## Questionnaires and Surveys

A key element of the Collect Requirements process is the gathering of information that can then be used to further define the requirements for the project and the product. *Questionnaires and surveys* present a very effective means of gathering this information from identified stakeholders. Depending on the development of the questionnaires and surveys, the information gathered may be able to have some statistical analysis applied to it to aid in your requirements-gathering process.

## Observations

*Observations* are a very accurate way of determining how a potential project or product scope will be implemented or used in real life. If the project scope includes certain processes, observing who will use these processes, how they will be used, and any other aspects in the real world will help define the process. If part of the project scope includes any product, observing the users of the product in the real world will also help define the product further.

## Prototypes

*Prototypes* are a great way to get fast feedback on any element of the product by producing drafts and seeking feedback from stakeholders as to whether this is what they wanted. The practice of prototyping is quickly gaining support with the rise of technology that allows rapid prototyping. In addition to physical prototypes, storyboarding can be used to show the sequence of processes or product development to solicit feedback from stakeholders, particularly in the production of web pages or user interfaces.

# Benchmarking

*Benchmarking* is a tool used in several processes. It involves comparing what you planned to do against other projects or organizations to determining whether you are better or worse than them. You can gather this important information from competitors, trade and industry associations, and the Project Management Institute.

# Context Diagrams

A *context diagram* is a simple tool showing visually how a business system and users interact. Figure 3-3 shows an example of a context diagram.

**Figure 3-3.** *A context diagram showing the relationship between supplier, ordering software, accounts department, and warehouse*

# Document Analysis

As part of refining the requirements, you may want to carry out a document analysis and examine any relevant documents such as business plans, data models, software documentation, and issues logs to help you summarize the requirements.

# Outputs

The following outputs are generated from the Collect Requirements process.

# Requirements Documentation

The *requirements documentation* is highly iterative; you may be able to fully define certain requirements and not yet define other requirements. When requirements are fully defined and documented, they include a description of how the requirement meets the identified business need, objectives, or stakeholder requirements. They also include a traceability matrix identifying which stakeholders requested each requirement, defining acceptance criteria, and providing a link back to the business objective that the requirement is intended to meet.

---

▓ **Exam Tip**   You can view the requirements documentation as a subsidiary of the scope statement. Rather than referring to the entire project and product scope, the requirements documentation focuses on individual requirements of parts of the project.

---

The requirements documentation as an output goes on to be used as an input into the following processes:

>   5.3 Define Scope

>   5.4 Create WBS

>   5.5 Validate Scope

>   5.6 Control Scope

>   8.1 Plan Quality Management

>   12.1 Plan Procurement Management

## Requirements Traceability Matrix

The *requirements traceability matrix* is a valuable tool for ensuring that the documented requirements are mapped directly back to business objectives. A requirements traceability matrix is a table that links the origins of individual product requirements to the expected deliverable that meets those requirements so that you can track requirements throughout the project life cycle. This is particularly important if you want to either change a requirement and assess the impact it will have on deliverables or check that a deliverable still meets the original requirement.

The requirements traceability matrix is used as an input into the following two processes:

>   5.5 Validate Scope

>   5.6 Control Scope

### Quick Check

1.   What is the main focus of the Collect Requirements process?

2.   How is the requirements documentation different from the project scope statement?

3.   Why is consultation with stakeholders critical to successfully documenting project requirements?

### Quick Check Answers

1.   The main focus of the Collect Requirements process is to use a variety of means to gather from stakeholders their technical requirements, which are then used to define the scope of work.

2. The requirements documentation is a subset of the total project scope statement and relates specifically to how requirements of the project and product align with and deliver project objectives. The project scope statement describes and defines the total work to be done in delivering the project and product.

3. Consultation with stakeholders is critical to successfully documenting and defining project requirements, because the wishes of stakeholders are driving the project, and by consulting them you can ensure that you meet their expectations by delivering the requirements.

# Define Scope

▓ **More Info**   Define Scope You can read more about the Define Scope process in the PMBOK Guide, 5th edition, in Chapter 5, section 5.3. Table 3-3 identifies the process inputs, tools and techniques, and outputs.

*Table 3-3.* *Define Scope Process*

| Inputs ⇨ | Tools and Techniques ⇨ | Outputs |
|---|---|---|
| • Scope management plan<br>• Project charter<br>• Requirements documentation<br>• Organizational process assets | • Expert judgment<br>• Product analysis<br>• Alternatives generation<br>• Facilitated workshops | • Project scope statement<br>• Project document updates |

The Define Scope process is one of four planning processes in the Project Scope Management knowledge area. The Define Scope process covers the following planning domain task:

• Task 2: Develop a scope management plan, based on the approved project scope and using scope management techniques, in order to define, maintain, and manage the scope of the project.

```
┌─────────────────────────────────────────────────────────────┐
│                       REAL WORLD                              │
└─────────────────────────────────────────────────────────────┘
```

It is very rare that you will ever begin a project with a complete and detailed description of the scope. Often this occurs only as a result of lengthy contractual negotiations. In almost every other situation, you will begin a project with enough of the scope defined to allow you to start, and then you will undertake successive iterations of definition and documentation as you go. You may also decide to commit time and energy to defining the scope for the immediate timeframe, and leave definition of the remainder of the scope until you get closer to the time of delivery.

# Inputs

The following inputs can be used in the Define Scope process.

## Scope Management Plan

Obviously, in order to define the scope, you are going to have to work according to your scope management plan, which sets out the process you will use to iteratively define and document the scope of both your project and the product. The project scope management plan is the key output from the Plan Scope Management process.

## Project Charter

The project charter can be used as a key input into the Define Scope process because it contains the project approvals and any known description of the project and product scope. The project charter is the sole output from the Develop Project Charter process.

## Requirements Documentation

The requirements documentation is an output from the Collect Requirements process and contains the defined and documented project and product requirements. These requirements form an important part of both the project and product scope.

## Organizational Process Assets

Organizational process assets that can be used to define the scope include any project management methodology, policies, and blank templates that the organization has. There is also a high probability that the organization has completed a project with a similar scope in the past, and thus any lessons learned or historical information from previous projects or phases are important organizational process assets that can be used when defining the scope. These resources can also include important internal stakeholders such as the project sponsor.

# Tools and Techniques

The following tools and techniques can be used on the inputs to generate the process outputs.

## Expert Judgment

Again we can see expert judgment as an effective tool; expert experience and skill can help you refine process inputs and develop them into the expected outputs. In this instance, you as project manager are one of the more important experts, as are your project team members, who are responsible for completing the project work, and any other stakeholders with relevant experience and skill in defining the scope.

## Product Analysis

*Product analysis* is best used when a project is delivering a product, instead of a service or result, as its major deliverable. Breaking down the product into its component parts and ensuring that each part meets the requirements and technical specifications assists with documenting the product scope. Product analysis can also include value-engineering processes in which you try to use innovation to deliver the product as efficiently as possible.

## Alternatives Generation

The process of *alternatives generation* considers all the potential ways in which the project and product work can be performed in order to determine whether you are using the most efficient way of delivering the project and product scope.

## Facilitated Workshops

*Facilitated workshops* involve bringing experts together in a workshop setting and having an independent facilitator guide the group to produce successive iterations of the project and product scope. The role of the independent facilitator is to stay neutral, set and enforce rules about how participants contribute, keep the workshop focused and on track, and make sure expectations are clearly understood.

# Outputs

The following outputs are produced by the Define Scope process.

## Project Scope Statement

The major output from the Define Scope process is the *project scope statement*, which describes in increasing detail the deliverables, assumptions, and constraints of the project. The project scope statement defines all the work to be done on the project, and *only* the work to be done on the project. It includes a detailed description of the exclusions and the work that will not be done as part of the project. The project scope statement also includes a full description of the work to be done to deliver the scope of the product.

---

▓ **Note**    Scope creep and gold plating One of the primary reasons to conduct scope management planning exercises and produce a clear definition of the scope statement with a documented change-control process is to ensure that your project is not subject to scope creep. *Scope creep* happens because of undocumented scope change. At all times, you must deliver only what is documented for your project and product scope. This does not mean that change will not occur on your project; in fact, quite the opposite—you can expect change at all points in your project. What it means is that you consider all changes, no matter how small or large, and if the change is accepted, you document this and incorporate it into your scope statement, thereby stopping scope creep. The other element to watch for with undocumented scope is gold plating. *Gold plating* occurs when you see the opportunity to deliver greater quality for less cost and in less time to the client and decide to proceed with this without documenting it. There is nothing wrong with delivering greater quality and exceeding expectations, but once again, at all times you must only be producing what is documented.

---

The project scope statement as an output goes on to be used as an input into the following processes:

>5.4 Create WBS
>
>6.3 Sequence Activities
>
>6.5 Estimate Activity Durations
>
>6.6 Develop Schedule

# Project Document Updates

The process of defining the scope will probably result in the requirement to update other project documents such as the stakeholder register, to identify any changes to stakeholder expectations; the requirements documentation, to account for any iterative development of the scope that affects requirements; and, dissociated from the requirements documentation, the requirements traceability matrix.

**Quick Check**

1. How do the Collect Requirements and Define Scope processes interact with each other?

2. Why is it important to define exclusions in the project scope statement?

3. How is the information about the project and product scope statement contained in the project charter different from the information contained in the project scope statement?

**Quick Check Answers**

1. The Collect Requirements process takes the statement of work and project charter and seeks to gather requirements from stakeholders that are then used as an input into the Define Scope process to help define the scope statement.

2. It is important to define the known project and product exclusions as part of the project scope statement in order to avoid ambiguity and assumptions about what is, and what is not, included in the work to be done.

3. The project charter contains a description of the project and product work to be done that is known at the time of initiating the project. As such, it may be at a much higher level than the information contained in the project scope statement. Additionally, the project charter contains other information such as the project's purpose, justification, and any required approvals.

# Create WBS

░ **More Info**   Create WBS You can read more about the Create WBS process in the PMBOK Guide, 5th edition, in Chapter 5, section 5.4. Table 3-4 identifies the process inputs, tools and techniques, and outputs.

***Table 3-4.*** *Create WBS Process*

| Inputs ⇨ | Tools and Techniques ⇨ | Outputs |
|---|---|---|
| • Scope management plan<br>• Project scope statement<br>• Requirements documentation<br>• Enterprise environmental factors<br>• Organizational process assets | • Decomposition<br>• Expert judgment | • Scope baseline<br>• Project document<br>  updates |

The Create WBS process is the last of the planning processes in the Project Scope Management knowledge area and relies on the Collect Requirements and Define Scope processes to be complete. The Create WBS process covers the following planning domain task:

- Task 2: Develop a scope management plan, based on the approved project scope and using scope management techniques, in order to define, maintain, and manage the scope of the project.

---

▒ **Exam Tip**    On the exam, unless it is otherwise stated, you should assume that the processes of collecting requirements and defining the scope have occurred before beginning the process of creating the WBS.

---

# Inputs

The following inputs can be used to generate the outputs of the Create WBS process.

## Scope Management Plan

The scope management plan is a key input because in this plan you have detailed how you will approach the process of decomposing the project scope statement and creating the work breakdown structure (WBS). The scope management plan is a key output from the Plan Scope Management process.

## Project Scope Statement

The WBS is a breakdown of the entire project scope statement into its component parts; therefore, the project scope statement is a key input into the Create WBS process. The project scope statement is the key output from the Defined Scope process.

# Requirements Documentation

The requirements documentation is a key output from the Collect Requirements process. In addition to the project scope statement, having access to the requirements documentation and the requirements traceability matrix enables you to ensure that your process of decomposition to create the WBS captures all of the project and product scope and the associated requirements.

# Enterprise Environmental Factors

There are some industry-wide enterprise environmental factors that can be useful as an input into the Create WBS process. For example, the ISO/IEC 15288 standard on systems engineering-system life cycle processes could be used for engineering projects.

# Organizational Process Assets

The most useful organizational process assets to be used as an input into the Create WBS process include any project management methodology, policies, or blank templates for the creation of a WBS, and any historical information or lessons learned from previous projects.

# Tools and Techniques

Two techniques are used in the Create WBS process.

# Decomposition

The process of *decomposition* involves taking a high-level description of the work to be done for the project and product, and successively breaking it down into deliverables, sub-deliverables, and finally *work packages*. The work package is the lowest level to which you should break down the WBS. A work package is defined as a package of work that can reliably be estimated for time and cost. This means you can easily allocate the work to one person and that it doesn't make sense to decompose it any further, because at that level you can develop an accurate estimate of the time it will take and the amount of money it will cost to complete the work package. Below the level of work packages are individual activities, which are used in the Project Time Management knowledge area to assist in building a project schedule.

The WBS is a graphical representation of the total project scope; therefore, work that is not included in the WBS is not part of the project. If the project scope is being developed iteratively, this is represented in the development of the WBS, and it too develops iteratively.

---

**REAL WORLD**

---

I always use my project team members who are responsible for completing the work to help complete the WBS. Not only does this give me the right technical input from the people responsible for completing the work, but it also creates commitment to the process of completing the work, because people feel they have made a significant and personal contribution.

---

▓ **Note**    Decomposition is used in any of the breakdown structures used in project management. It simply describes a process of breaking down a larger concept into its component parts. It is used to create the WBS, the organizational breakdown structure (OBS), the risk breakdown structure (RBS), and another RBS, the resource breakdown structure (RBS).

---

## Expert Judgment

Expert judgment is a key tool in the Create WBS process because the creation of the WBS is best done by those experts with knowledge about the work to be done and how it can best be decomposed into its component parts.

# Outputs

The following outputs are generated by the Create WBS process.

## Scope Baseline

The *scope baseline* is used to measure what is actually being produced against what is expected to be produced in relation to the project and product scope. It is made up of three key, distinct elements: the project scope statement, the WBS, and the WBS dictionary.

---

▓ **Exam Tip**    The scope baseline is what you use to measure progress against in the project. Any baselines in project management can only be changed through the formal change-control process. After an approved change is integrated into a baseline, the baseline itself is changed; thus the easiest way to think of a baseline is that it is what you originally started with plus any approved changes.

---

The WBS is often called the *backbone* of a project. This is because it acts as an input into many other planning processes. Without a complete and accurate WBS, your efforts in cost estimating, budget estimating, activity definition, risk identification, scope validation, and all the subsequent processes they provide inputs into would be extremely difficult. Creation of the WBS is done by decomposing the top-level descriptions of project work into their component parts. The highest level is broken down into deliverables, then into sub-deliverables, and then into individual work packages. A work package is an amount of work that can reliably be estimated for time and cost and can generally be performed by one person. Below work packages are activities, which are used in developing a project schedule, as described in the next chapter.

Figure 3-4 shows a WBS for a new house project, with the breakdown of different work streams to work package level. Note that all nodes in the WBS have a unique identifying number that allows you to track work being done and also to allocate costs to specific work packages for better cost reporting. The numbering system should clearly identify each node and relate to the node above so you can easily see related nodes and the way they are decomposed. This numbering system is an example of a configuration management system.

*Figure 3-4. A work breakdown structure (WBS) showing the total project, deliverables, sub-deliverables, and work packages*

---

░ **Note**    WBS dictionary When you are representing a WBS graphically, each node in the WBS can contain only summary information, such as the configuration management details; the name of the deliverable, sub-deliverable, or work package; and summary information about the time, cost, and resources allocated to each node. The WBS dictionary is a text-based document that provides additional information about the summary information contained in each WBS node.

---

The WBS becomes an input into the following processes:

> 5.5 Validate Scope
>
> 6.2 Define Activities
>
> 7.2 Estimate Costs
>
> 7.3 Determine Budget
>
> 11.2 Identify Risks
>
> 11.3 Perform Qualitative Risk Analysis

---

▩ **Exam Tip** Many exam questions pose a scenario where something is missing and ask what you should do. In most instances, it is acceptable to continue with the project and develop something in the interim to help tide you over. The only exception to this is if it is the WBS that is missing. If is you are working on a project and do not have the WBS, you must stop and create the WBS, because without it you cannot complete the planning processes of your project.

---

## Project Document updates

As a result of creating the WBS, information may be gathered that requires other project documents to be updated, such as the project scope statement and the requirements documentation.

### Quick Check

1. To what level of detail do you decompose the project scope when creating the WBS?
2. How would you define the key elements of a work package?
3. What elements make up the scope baseline?

### Quick Check Answers

1. The project scope statement is decomposed to major deliverables, to sub-deliverables, down to the work package level.
2. A work package can best be defined as an amount of work that can reliably be estimated for time and cost. Going any further in the decomposition process delivers little benefit for the time taken to do the work.
3. The three key elements of the scope baseline are the project scope statement, the WBS, and the WBS dictionary.

# Validate Scope

▨ **More Info**   Validate Scope You can read more about the Validate Scope process in the PMBOK Guide, 5th edition, in Chapter 5, section 5.5. Table 3-5 identifies the process inputs, tools and techniques, and outputs.

***Table 3-5.*** *Validate Scope Process*

| Inputs ⇨ | Tools and Techniques ⇨ | Outputs |
|---|---|---|
| • Project management plan <br> • Requirements documentation <br> • Requirements traceability matrix <br> • Verified deliverables <br> • Work performance data | • Inspection <br> • Group decision-making techniques | • Accepted deliverables <br> • Change requests <br> • Work performance information <br> • Project document updates |

The Validate Scope process is a monitoring and control process, one of two monitoring and control processes in the Project Scope Management knowledge area.

The Validate Scope process covers the following domain monitoring and controlling task:

- Task 1: Measure project performance using appropriate tools and techniques, in order to identify and quantify any variances and corrective actions.

▨ **Note**   Validation compared to verification The process of validation is important to understand, as is the difference between it and the process of verification. Verification is about confirmation that the product, service, or result produced complies with agreed specifications or requirements. It is primarily an internal process that the delivering organization performs prior to submitting the product, service, or result for validation, which involves the customer as well. Validation also involves a check that the product, service, or result meets stakeholder requirements. Verification occurs before validation.

# Inputs

The Validate Scope process uses some or all of the following inputs.

# Project Management Plan

The project management plan guides how you execute and monitor your project, and, as such, it contains plans and baselines useful for validating the project scope. The particular parts of the project management plan that are most useful as inputs into the Validate Scope process are the scope management plan and the scope baseline. The scope management plan is used as an input because it details how you plan to manage your scope in its entirety, including validation. The scope baseline, which includes the scope statement, the WBS, and the WBS dictionary, is absolutely necessary in validating the scope because it represents the baseline against which you are comparing the actual work performed. The project management plan is an output from the Develop Project Management Plan process; the scope management plan is a key output from the Plan Scope Management process; and the scope baseline is the key output from the Create WBS process.

# Requirements Documentation

The requirements documentation lists the project objectives and the requirements that will deliver those objectives, and as such it is an essential input into validating the scope. Requirements documentation is the key output from the Collect Requirements process.

# Requirements Traceability Matrix

The requirements traceability matrix provides an additional measure of rigor when validating the scope, because you are able to link specific requirements back to identified business objectives. The requirements traceability matrix is an output from the Collect Requirements process.

# Verified Deliverables

The *verified deliverables* are deliverables that have already been completed and checked for correctness against the required specifications through the control quality process and, as such, now need to be validated in order to become accepted deliverables and used in the Close Project or Phase process. Verified deliverables are a key output from the Control Quality process.

---

▓ **Note**    Deliverables Project deliverables must go through the process of first being verified and then being accepted. Verification is an internal process that ensures correctness against predetermined quality standards, whereas validation is an external acceptance process completed by the project sponsor or customer.

---

## Work Performance Data

The work performance data indicates whether there is compliance with the documented requirements. Work performance data is an output from the Direct and Manage Project Work process.

# Tools and Techniques

The following two tools and techniques can be used to deliver the process outputs.

## Inspection

*Inspection* as a technique literally means inspecting the deliverables to ascertain whether they meet the documented requirements and acceptance criteria.

## Group Decision-Making Techniques

Group decision-making techniques are any techniques used to allow a group of people to reach a decision. It is best if the decision-making technique is outlined to the group prior to the decision-making process being undertaken, to be sure that all group members understand how the decision will be made.

# Outputs

The Validate Scope process has the following outputs.

## Accepted Deliverables

Accepted deliverables meet the acceptance criteria and are signed off and accepted by either the customer or the project sponsor. Accepted deliverables are used as the key input into the Close Project or Phase process.

---

▓ **Exam Tip** A key role of the project sponsor is to act as the person internal to the performing organization who formally accepts the product. The customer is usually a person external to the organization who accepts the product.

---

## Change Requests

If a deliverable is not accepted due to some areas of noncompliance or noncorrectness, a change request for defect repair may be generated. Change requests are a key input into the Perform Integrated Change Control process.

# Work Performance Information

Work performance information takes the work performance data and presents it in such a way that project progress can easily be determined and identified. This information is communicated to stakeholders as appropriate. Work performance information is used as an input into the Monitor and Control Project Work process.

---

▓ **Note**    Work performance Work performance data is the raw data gathered in any process. Work performance information is the data after it has been interpreted into something meaningful. Work performance data becomes work performance information, which in turn is used in work performance reports.

---

# Project Document Updates

The types of project documents that may be updated include requirements documentation, the scope statement, and quality control documents.

### Quick Check

1. What is the main focus of the Validate Scope process?

2. What is the difference between validation and verification?

3. Who formally accepts the project deliverables?

### Quick Check Answers

1. The main focus of the Validate Scope process is to formally accept the completed project deliverables.

2. Verification is an internal process completed by the performing organization measuring the product, service, or result against defined requirements and specifications. It is completed prior to validation. Validation involves taking the verified product, service, or result and, in conjunction with key stakeholders, confirming that it meets stakeholder requirements.

3. The project sponsor formally accepts the project deliverables on behalf of the performing organization. The customer formally accepts the project deliverables on behalf of the external organization requesting the work to be done.

# Control Scope

▒ **More Info**  Control Scope You can read more about the Control Scope process in the PMBOK Guide, 5th edition, in Chapter 5, section 5.6. Table 3-6 identifies the process inputs, tools and techniques, and outputs.

*Table 3-6.*  *Control Scope Process*

| Inputs ⇨ | Tools and Techniques ⇨ | Outputs |
| --- | --- | --- |
| • Project management plan <br> • Requirements documentation <br> • Requirements traceability matrix <br> • Work performance data <br> • Organizational process assets | • Variance analysis | • Work performance information <br> • Change requests <br> • Project management plan updates <br> • Project document updates <br> • Organizational process assets updates |

The Control Scope process is a monitoring and control process, one of two monitoring and control processes in the Project Scope Management knowledge area.

The Control Scope process covers the following monitoring and controlling domain task:

- Task 1: Measure project performance using appropriate tools and techniques, in order to identify and quantify any variances and corrective actions.

# Inputs

The following inputs can be used in the Control Scope process.

## Project Management Plan

The project management plan, or, more correctly, some of the subsidiary plans of the project management plan, are used as inputs to enable you to control the scope. By using a description of what you planned to do and comparing that to what you are actually doing, you can spot any variances. The project management plan is a key output from the Develop Project Management Plan process.

---

▓ **Exam Tip**   Whenever you see the project management plan listed as an input into a process, it indicates that more than one subsidiary plan is used in this process. In this instance, elements of the scope management plan, change management plan, configuration management plan, and requirements management plan are used as inputs to control the scope.

---

## Requirements Documentation

The clearly defined requirements documentation for the project and product can be used to detect any deviation in the scope during the Control Scope process. The requirements documentation is a key output from the Collect Requirements process.

## Requirements Traceability Matrix

Using the requirements traceability matrix as an input helps bring an additional level of rigor into the Control Scope process by enabling you to map requirements back to project objectives. The requirements traceability matrix is a key output from the Collect Requirements process.

## Work Performance Data

Work performance data in this instance refers to information about change requests received or the number and type of deliverables completed. Work performance data is the key output from the Direct and Manage Project Work process.

## Organizational Process Assets

Key organizational process assets that can be useful as inputs into the Control Scope process include any change control–related or scope control–related guidelines, policies, or templates, and any documented monitoring and reporting methods.

# Tools and Techniques

There is a single technique used in the Control Scope process.

## Variance Analysis

Any *variance analysis* is simply an examination of what is actually occurring against what was planned to occur, looking for any variances, positive or negative, and acting on them accordingly. If you discover any variance, you can decide to undertake corrective or preventive actions or initiate changes.

---

▓ **Exam Tip**   Variance analysis is a key tool in all the monitoring and controlling processes. Wherever you see variance analysis as a tool in a process, you should also look for some sort of baseline that is being checked for variance.

---

# Outputs

The following outputs are produced by the Control Scope process.

## Work Performance Information

*Work performance information* as an output from this process includes information relating to the type and category of change requests received and how they may potentially affect other areas of the project. Work performance information goes on to be used as an input in the Monitor and Control Project Work process.

## Change Requests

Change requests are a result of variances detected. All change requests must be processed according to the predefined change management process. Change requests go on to be used in the Perform Integrated Change Control process.

## Project Management Plan Updates

Elements of the project management plan that may be updated as a result of the work done during the Control Scope process include the project scope statement, WBS, and WBS dictionary.

## Project Document Updates

As a result of performing the Control Scope process, you may choose to update the requirements documentation to reflect new or changed information.

## Organizational Process Assets Updates

Organizational process assets that may be updated as a result of the Control Scope process include any elements of the project scope management plan, change management plan, or lessons learned that have been gathered.

### Quick Check

1. What is the main focus of the Control Scope process?

2. Why is variance analysis important to the Control Scope process?

3. What is the relationship between work performance data and work performance information?

### Quick Check Answers

1. The main focus of the Control Scope process is to check the progress of the project against planned baselines, looking for variances and acting on any that are discovered.

2. Variance analysis is the process of checking what you planned to do against what you are actually doing. If you discover a variance between the two, then you must act.

3. Work performance data is the raw data collected while observing work being performed; it is turned into work performance information by applying metrics, formulas, and other ways of interpreting the data in order for it to make sense and be usable for measuring project progress.

# Chapter Summary

- The Project Scope Management knowledge area is focused on the processes of planning, defining, documenting, and managing change to the project requirements, scope, and work breakdown structure (WBS).

- Like other knowledge areas, the Project Scope Management knowledge area begins with a process of planning how you will manage the project scope. The key output from this is the scope management plan, which becomes a subsidiary plan of the project management plan.

- The first step in a linear process of defining the full project scope is to collect project requirements from stakeholders and develop both the requirements documentation and requirements traceability matrix.

- The process of defining the project scope is highly iterative and may be subject to rolling-wave planning throughout the life of the project. After it is defined, the project scope is captured in the project scope statement. The scope of the product is a subset of the total project scope.

- The WBS is a graphical representation of the project scope statement; thus any work not included in the WBS is not included as part of the project. The WBS forms one of three key elements of the scope baseline. The scope baseline is made up of the project scope statement, the WBS, and the WBS dictionary.

- The WBS, after it is completed, serves as a valuable input into several other processes, including Project Cost Management, Project Time Management, and Project Risk Management.

- The process of validating the project scope involves internal and external stakeholders checking that the deliverables conform to stakeholder requirements and expectations. It is performed after scope verification.

- All changes to the project scope or requirements must go through the documented change control process. Any approved changes are incorporated into the scope baseline.

# Exercises

The answers for these exercises are located in the "Answers" section at the end of this chapter.

1.  Create a WBS.

    You are working on a project, Project BlueTalk, to develop a new piece of software. As part of the development of the scope, you have identified that the four major deliverables are the software design, the testing of the software, the user training of the software, and the implementation of the software. At this early stage in the project, you are only able to further define the software design process and have broken that down into the sub-deliverables for module 1 and module 2. Using your project team members responsible for the software design, you have broken module 1 down into three work packages: database, user interface, and backup.

    Use this information to complete a WBS for the project.

2. Map each of the following terms on the left to the definition that best fits it on the right:

| | |
|---|---|
| a) Project charter | i. An early iteration of the project scope statement |
| b) Statement of work | ii. A description of all the work to be done on a project |
| c) Requirements | iii. A description of the product, service, or result to be delivered as part of the project work |
| d) Preliminary scope statement | iv. A narrative description of the work to be completed; used as an input into the project charter |
| e) Project scope statement | v. The documented list of expectations and specifications from project stakeholders |
| f) Product scope | vi. The foundational document for a project, which contains a high-level description of the work to be completed |

# Review Questions

Test your knowledge of the information in Chapter 3 by answering these questions. The answers to these questions, and the explanation of why each answer choice is correct or incorrect, are located in the "Answers" section at the end of this chapter.

1. What is the correct order of activities in the Project Scope Management knowledge area?

    A. Define Scope, Collect Requirements, Plan Scope Management, Create WBS

    B. Plan Scope Management, Define Scope, Collect Requirements, Create WBS

    C. Plan Scope Management, Collect Requirements, Define Scope, Create WBS

    D. Collect Requirements, Define Scope, Create WBS, Plan Scope Management

2. What are the elements of the scope baseline?

    A. The project scope management plan and requirements documentation

    B. The project scope management plan and project scope statement

    C.    The scope statement, the WBS, and the WBS dictionary

    D.    The project scope statement, the product scope statement, and the WBS

3.    What is the correct term for the component of the project management plan that describes how project requirements will be analyzed, documented, and managed?

    A.    The requirements management plan

    B.    The scope management plan

    C.    The project scope statement

    D.    The scope baseline

4.    Brainstorming is an example of what sort of process tool or technique?

    A.    Group decision-making techniques

    B.    Observations

    C.    Facilitated workshops

    D.    Group creativity techniques

5.    What is the main purpose of the requirements traceability matrix?

    A.    To hold people accountable for work delivery

    B.    To let stakeholders know when the project will be delivered

    C.    To map individual requirements back to specific business needs and objectives

    D.    To describe the work to be completed in the project

6.    Which of the following best describes the relationship between the scope of the project and the scope of the product?

    A.    The scope of the project includes all the planning work to be done, whereas the scope of the product documents the technical requirements of the deliverable.

    B.    The product scope is a subset of the project scope.

    C.    The project scope is delivered as part of the delivery of the product scope.

    D.    There is no difference between the two terms.

7. What is the lowest level of WBS decomposition?

    A.  The deliverable

    B.  Project activities

    C.  The work package

    D.  The scope statement

8. What is the name of the document that provides additional information about each node of the WBS?

    A.  The scope management plan

    B.  The WBS dictionary

    C.  The project scope statement

    D.  The requirements documentation

9. What is the key purpose of the Validate Scope process?

    A.  It is an internal process to determine whether the product meets strict technical requirements.

    B.  It is the process of checking whether the deliverable conforms to requirements.

    C.  It is the process of managing changes to the project scope statement.

    D.  It is a process that involves internal and external stakeholders checking that the deliverable meets project requirements and stakeholder expectations.

10. Change requests that are generated as part of the Control Scope process are used as inputs into which process?

    A.  The Validate Scope process

    B.  The Perform Integrated Change Control process

    C.  The Control Quality process

    D.  The Plan Scope Management process

# Answers

This section contains the answers for the Exercises and Review Questions in this chapter.

## Exercises

1. Create a WBS.

   Your completed WBS should look like the diagram shown in Figure 3-5. Did you remember to include the unique number identifiers in each node?

*Figure 3-5.* A completed work breakdown structure for Project BlueTalk

2. Map each of the following terms on the left to the definition that best fits it on the right:

| | |
|---|---|
| a) Project charter | vi. The foundational document for a project, which contains a high-level description of the work to be completed |
| b) Statement of work | iv. A narrative description of the work to be completed; used as an input into the project charter |
| c) Requirements | v. The documented list of expectations and specifications from project stakeholders |
| d) Preliminary scope statement | i. An early iteration of the project scope statement |
| e) Project scope statement | ii. A description of all the work to be done on a project |
| f) Product scope | iii. A description of the product, service, or result to be delivered as part of the project work |

# Review Questions

1.  **Correct Answer: C**

    A.  **Incorrect:** Plan Scope Management is the first process to be completed so that you have a guide to completing the others.

    B.  **Incorrect:** Define Scope comes after Collect Requirements.

    C.  **Correct:** The sequence of Plan Scope Management, Collect Requirements, Define Scope, Create WBS describes the iterative development of Project Scope Management processes.

    D.  **Incorrect:** Plan Scope Management is the first process to be completed so that you have a guide to completing the others.

2.  **Correct Answer: C**

    A.  **Incorrect:** The project scope management plan and requirements documentation are not part of the scope baseline.

    B.  **Incorrect:** The project scope management plan is not part of the scope baseline.

    C.  **Correct:** The scope statement, the WBS, and the WBS dictionary are the three elements of the scope baseline.

    D.  **Incorrect:** The project scope statement and the product scope statement are a part of but not all of the scope baseline.

3.  **Correct Answer: A**

    A.  **Correct:** The requirements management plan describes how project requirements will be analyzed, documented, and managed.

    B.  **Incorrect:** The scope management plan describes how the project scope will be defined, documented, and managed.

    C.  **Incorrect:** The project scope statement describes the scope of work to be done as part of the project.

    D.  **Incorrect:** The scope baseline is made up of the scope statement, WBS, and WBS dictionary.

4.  **Correct Answer: D**

    A.  **Incorrect:** Group decision-making techniques are techniques to assist groups of people in making decisions in the face of differing, and often dissenting, opinions.

    B.  **Incorrect:** Observations do not require brainstorming.

    C.  **Incorrect:** Facilitated workshops describe focused workshops.

    D.  **Correct:** Brainstorming is an example of a group creativity technique.

5.  **Correct Answer: C**

    A.  **Incorrect:** The requirements traceability matrix does not hold people accountable for work delivery.

    B.  **Incorrect:** Letting stakeholders know when the project will be delivered would be part of your time management plan and communications management plan.

    C.  **Correct:** The main purpose of the requirements traceability matrix is to map individual requirements back to specific business needs and objectives.

    D.  **Incorrect:** The project scope statement is used to describe the work to be completed in the project.

6.  **Correct Answer: B**

    A.  **Incorrect:** The project scope includes all the work and only the work to be done, including a description of the product.

    B.  **Correct:** The product scope is a subset of the project scope that focuses specifically on the product or deliverable of the project.

    C.  **Incorrect:** The project scope is not delivered as part of the delivery of the product scope; it is the other way around.

    D.  **Incorrect:** There is a difference between the two terms, because they describe different things.

7. **Correct Answer: C**

   A.  **Incorrect:** The deliverable is a high-level description of the work to be done.

   B.  **Incorrect:** Project activities are work packages that are further defined and used in developing a project schedule.

   C.  **Correct:** The work package is the lowest level of WBS decomposition.

   D.  **Incorrect:** The scope statement describes all the work to be done on the project.

8. **Correct Answer: B**

   A.  **Incorrect:** The scope management plan describes how the project scope will be defined, documented, and managed.

   B.  **Correct:** The WBS dictionary provides additional information to expand on the summary information contained in each node of the WBS.

   C.  **Incorrect:** The project scope statement describes all the work to be done on the project.

   D.  **Incorrect:** The requirements documentation describes individual requirements for the project.

9. **Correct Answer: D**

   A.  **Incorrect:** The Validate Scope process is not simply an internal process.

   B.  **Incorrect:** The process of checking whether the deliverable conforms to requirements is a Control Quality process.

   C.  **Incorrect:** The Change Management process describes the process of managing changes to the project scope statement.

   D.  **Correct:** The Validate Scope process is a process that involves internal and external stakeholders checking that the deliverable meets project requirements and stakeholder expectations.

10. **Correct Answer: B**

A. **Incorrect:** Change requests are an output from the Validate Scope process.

B. **Correct:** Change requests are used as an input into the Perform Integrated Change Control process.

C. Incorrect: Approved change requests, which are change request that have been through the Perform Integrated Change Control process, are used as an input into the Control Quality process.

D. **Incorrect:** Change requests are not an input into the Plan Scope Management process.

# CHAPTER 4

■ ■ ■

# Time Management

This chapter focuses on the topic of project time management. Project Time Management, like the other knowledge areas, begins with a process of planning that produces a schedule management plan. Then there is an iterative, or repeating, process that produces and updates the project schedule. Then, as with all other knowledge areas with the exception of the Human Resource Management knowledge area, there is a controlling process that seeks to measure planned versus actual progress in relation to time and deal with any changes or corrective or preventive actions.

You may need to pay particular attention in this chapter to those activities that lead up to the construction of the network diagram, because there is quite a bit of technical information you need to learn.

**The PMBOK® Guide Processes**
**Project Time Management Knowledge Area**
The seven processes in the Project Time Management knowledge area are as follows:

- Plan Schedule Management (planning process)

- Define Activities (planning process)

- Sequence Activities (planning process)

- Estimate Activity Resources (planning process)

- Estimate Activity Durations (planning process)

- Develop Schedule (planning process)

- Control Schedule (monitoring and controlling process)

## What Is Project Time Management?

Project time management is focused on the processes of developing a schedule management plan, estimating durations for activities and the overall project, preparing your project schedule, ensuring that the project progresses as planned and that milestones are reached on the communicated schedule, and influencing and assessing any changes to the project schedule.

░ **Exam Tip**    Some industries use the term *schedule* in reference to a schedule of materials to be used in the execution of the project. For the exam, you should note that the word *schedule* is used exclusively to mean project time estimates.

Apart from the Control Schedule process, the processes contained in this knowledge area present what appears to be a wonderfully logical and sequential flow of information, from defining activities through to development of the project schedule. Figure 4-1 shows the general flow through this linear process.

**Figure 4-1.**  *The sequential flow of the Project Schedule Development Process*

---

## REAL WORLD

Even though the project time management processes are often presented as separate, discrete processes, I have always found that the process of developing a project schedule is in fact done as one process, usually all at the same time.

---

░ **Exam Tip**    Remember that the output of the time management processes is the project schedule, which refers to all elements of time management on a project and not just the ubiquitous Gantt chart. Also remember that a project management plan is more than just a Gantt chart.

# Plan Schedule Management

░ **More Info**    Plan Schedule Management You can read more about the Plan Schedule Management process in the PMBOK Guide, 5th edition, in Chapter 6, section 6.1. Table 4-1 identifies the process inputs, tools and techniques, and outputs.

***Table 4-1.*** *Plan Schedule Management Process*

| Inputs ⇨ | Tools and Techniques ⇨ | Outputs |
|---|---|---|
| • Project management plan<br>• Project charter<br>• Enterprise environmental factors<br>• Organizational process assets | • Expert judgment<br>• Analytical techniques<br>• Meetings | • Schedule<br>management plan |

The Plan Schedule Management process is a planning process with a single output—not surprisingly, given the name of the process, it is the schedule management plan. Like all other planning documents, the schedule management plan will guide your efforts in defining and controlling the project schedule. It will form a subsidiary plan to the overall project management plan.

The Plan Schedule Management process covers the following planning domain task:

- Task 4: Develop the project schedule based on the approved project deliverables and milestones, scope, and resource management plans, in order to manage timely completion of the project.

# Inputs

The Plan Schedule Management process uses some or all of the following inputs as part of the development of the schedule management plan for the project.

## Project Management Plan

Any reference to the project management plan includes a reference to all subsidiary management plans that it contains. Obviously, any aspect of work on the project will incur some time; therefore, the project management plan, with its information about other areas, provides a useful input into planning your particular approach to schedule management. Any and all information relating to the project scope, project cost, project risk, project communications, project procurement, and stakeholder expectation management will be useful in assisting you develop your schedule management plan.

## Project Charter

The project charter, which is the foundational document of the project, providing and confirming financial and political support for the project, contains useful information about the known statement of work, any initial known constraints and assumptions, and an assessment of the known risks. This preliminary information contained in the project charter is particularly useful when you first begin defining your project schedule.

## Enterprise Environmental Factors

Enterprise environmental factors are any factors external to the project that can influence the outcome; they can usually be viewed as some sort of constraint on the project. Particular enterprise environmental factors that may assist with development of your schedule management plan include the wider organizational culture and structure and the inherent skills available throughout the organization. Additional enterprise environmental factors that are useful in developing a project schedule include any external published commercial information that can be used to estimate time on a project, and any company work-authorization systems.

## Organizational Process Assets

Organizational process assets that may play an important part as inputs into the development of your schedule management plan include historical information, blank templates, and project management methodology guidelines.

---

■ **Exam Tip**    Historical information and lessons learned are considered to be two of the most important organizational process assets that any project manager can rely on in the development of any part of the project management plan. On the exam, you will find an emphasis on historical information and lessons learned as important inputs into many processes.

---

# Tools and Techniques

The following tools and techniques are available to be used to develop the inputs into this process in order to produce the schedule management plan.

## Expert Judgment

Again, expert judgment is used as a tool. Expert judgment is the advice and opinion of any person or group who holds specific knowledge about a particular area. You as project manager are considered to be an expert, your project team members are experts, and any other person with specialist knowledge you choose to consult is also an expert.

---

■ **Exam Tip**    Deciding to use expert judgment is one thing; how you get the information from selected experts is another matter and is the subject of other information-gathering tools and techniques, such as meetings, the Delphi technique, interviews, questionnaires, and surveys.

---

## Analytical Techniques

As part of the development of the schedule management plan, you have to make decisions about which processes, tools, and techniques are best used in your particular project. This process of analyzing the potential options available to you is referred to as using *analytical techniques*.

## Meetings

Meetings are a useful tool to bring together everyone with experience in developing the schedule management plan. When run properly, they are an effective and efficient means of getting work done. The most useful people to invite to these particular meetings are members of the project team and people with experience in developing schedules.

# Outputs

After applying the appropriate tools and techniques to the selected inputs, the Plan Schedule Management process has the following output.

## Schedule Management Plan

The Plan Schedule Management process has only a single output: the *schedule management plan*. The schedule management plan is a subsidiary plan of the project management plan. The purpose of the schedule management plan is to guide the project manager and the project team; the plan also guides further activities, such as defining and developing the project schedule, checking for variance between what has been planned and what is actually happening, and managing any changes to the project schedule. As such, it is an important plan to have in place in order to provide oversight, standardization, and best practices to ensure that the project schedule, itself an essential part of any successful project, is well developed, monitored, and controlled.

---

▨ **Exam Tip**   Always assume that any aspect of your project management activities has some form of plan guiding it. The absence of a plan will result in inefficient and ineffective efforts that can increase the chances of project failure.

---

The schedule management plan is then a key input into the following processes, all of which are planning processes:

> 6.2 Define Activities
>
> 6.3 Sequence Activities
>
> 6.4 Estimate Activity Resources
>
> 6.5 Estimate Activity Durations
>
> 6.6 Develop Schedule

**Quick Check**

1.  What is the main purpose of the schedule management plan?

2.  Why is the project charter an important input into the Plan Schedule Management process?

3.  What role does the schedule management plan have in the overall project management plan?

**Quick Check Answers**

1.  The main purpose of the schedule management plan is to provide a documented guide as to how your project schedule will be defined, documented, and used to check the actual versus planned schedule, and to outline how any potential changes will be managed and assessed.

2.  At the beginning of the development of your project schedule, the project charter provides a wealth of preliminary information about the statement of work, constraints, assumptions, risks, and other information that will ultimately affect the project schedule.

3.  The schedule management plan is a subsidiary plan of the overall project management plan that focuses on the particular area of project time management.

# Define Activities

▓ **More Info**   Define Activities You can read more about the Define Activities process in the PMBOK Guide, 5th edition, in Chapter 6, section 6.2. Table 4-2 identifies the process inputs, tools and techniques, and outputs.

*Table 4-2.* *Define Activities Process*

| Inputs ⇨ | Tools and Techniques ⇨ | Outputs |
| --- | --- | --- |
| • Schedule management plan | • Decomposition | • Activity list |
| • Scope baseline | • Rolling-wave planning | • Activity attributes |
| • Enterprise environmental factors | • Expert judgment | • Milestone list |
| • Organizational process assets | | |

The Define Activities process is a planning process that takes the already-defined work packages from the Create WBS process and breaks them down further into individual activities.

The Define Activities process covers the following planning domain task:

- Task 4: Develop the project schedule based on the approved project deliverables and milestones, scope, and resource management plans, in order to manage timely completion of the project.

The difference between an activity and a work package is that an *activity* is the smallest component of work to be performed during the course of a project. A *work package* is a convenient level of work to stop at when completing the work breakdown structure (WBS), because at that point the work can reliably be estimated for time and cost. Breaking work packages down into activities for the purposes of the WBS has a decreasing benefit given the time and effort taken to do this. However, for the purpose of putting together an accurate project schedule, you must break work packages down even further to the level of activities.

---

## REAL WORLD

When completing any decomposition of the project scope statement, it sometimes seems arbitrary to stop the decomposition process at the level of work packages and then come back later to break them down further into activities. Therefore, during the process of decomposition of the scope, whether to show it graphically in a WBS or to obtain a list of work packages and activities to put into the project schedule, I generally do both processes at the same time.

---

# Inputs

The Define Activities process uses some or all of the following four inputs.

## Schedule Management Plan

The schedule management plan is obviously a key input into the Define Activities process because the schedule management plan contains information about how you will break down activities and the level of detail expected from the activities listed. The schedule management plan is an output from the Plan Schedule Management process.

## Scope Baseline

The scope baseline is used to ensure that the project manager captures all the activities contained in the project scope. When breaking down the project scope into its component parts, you can use the scope baseline and all the information it contains to ensure that you have captured all the activities required to complete the project. The scope baseline is an output of the Create WBS process.

---

■ **Exam Tip**    Remember that the scope baseline includes the following three elements: the project scope statement, the WBS, and the WBS dictionary.

---

## Enterprise Environmental Factors

The specific types of enterprise environmental factors that are useful as inputs into the Define Activities process are any aspects of the project management information system, any relevant parts of the organizational culture and structure, and any published information from commercial databases.

## Organizational Process Assets

The specific types of organizational process assets that are useful as inputs into the Define Activities process are any existing project management methodologies, processes, and templates that can assist with the development of the project schedule. Additionally, any configuration management system that defines how different versions of the project schedule are recorded, controlled, and updated can be used as an input. This is particularly important to ensure that you are always working on the correct version of any document in what can be a highly iterative process. Of course, any historical information from past projects that can be used to assist in the compilation of the current project management plan is also useful.

# Tools and Techniques

The following three tools and techniques are used on the inputs to deliver the process outputs.

## Decomposition

You have read about the process of decomposition used in the Create WBS process to take the scope of the project and decompose it down to the work package level. As a tool and technique in the Define Activities process, it is used to further decompose the already-defined work packages to activity level.

# Rolling-Wave Planning

Rolling-wave planning is a key iterative element of the project manager's planning process. It is a form of progressive elaboration in which you can plan in detail work that is in the immediate future, and plan in less detail work that is further off.

A good example of rolling-wave planning is when you have a project that is to go on for two and a half years. You will spend most of your planning activity on the work coming up in the next three months. Work to be done from three months to nine months out will have a lesser level of detail attached to it during planning, but still enough to give you confidence about project time and cost. Work that is to be done beyond the nine-month period may have a very low level of detail attached to its time and cost elements.

# Expert Judgment

You may decide to call on the expert judgment of people with skills and experience in this type of project and in the preparation of project schedules, in order to more accurately define your project activities.

# Outputs

The Define Activities process produces some or all of the following outputs.

## Activity List

The *activity list* is a comprehensive list that includes all currently known activities. In addition to listing the title and brief description of the activity, the activity list can provide additional information such as a unique identification number, which is an example of the configuration management system at work, and any other relevant ancillary information.

It is important to note that if you are undertaking any form of progressive elaboration or rolling-wave planning, you may only have identified and defined the activities for the next immediate time period; definition and documentation of activities beyond this may yet need to be done.

The activity list is used as an input into the following processes:

6.3 Sequence Activities

6.4 Estimate Activity Resources

6.5 Estimate Activity Durations

6.6 Develop Schedule

## Activity Attributes

The *activity attributes* are to the activity list what the WBS dictionary is to the WBS. The activity list contains summary information about each activity, whereas the activity attributes document provides more detailed information about each of the activities. This detailed information can include any requirements, known constraints and assumptions, required milestones, and any other information that helps any person wanting to know more about the activity to understand it fully.

The activity attributes document is used as an input into the following processes:

6.3 Sequence Activities

6.4 Estimate Activity Resources

6.5 Estimate Activity Durations

6.6 Develop Schedule

## Milestone List

As part of the development of the project schedule, and after the project activities have been defined, the project manager, in consultation with relevant stakeholders, may be able to produce a list of known milestones that should be achieved on the project. The *milestone list* contains these documented milestones.

---

▦ **Exam Tip**    Remember that a milestone has no duration and indicates a particular moment in time, usually when some specific work package or phase of a project has been completed. A milestone is often used as a point in the project where an assessment of work to date is done and decisions made about whether the project will continue.

---

```
REAL WORLD
```

I often use the milestone list and a description of which milestones have been achieved and which ones have not yet been achieved as a high-level way of communicating project progress quickly to senior stakeholders on the project.

**Quick Check**

1.    What is the difference between an activity and a work package?

2.    How is rolling-wave planning used?

3.    What is the primary purpose of the activity attributes document?

**Quick Check Answers**

1. A work package is the lowest level of decomposition in the work breakdown structure (WBS). It represents a parcel of work that can reliably be estimated for time and cost. On the other hand, an activity is a decomposed work package, broken down into the actual tasks that need to be done on a project.

2. Rolling-wave planning is an important tool to use on long-term projects. With rolling-wave planning, planning and detail is done for the immediate time period, and time periods that are further out are planned in less detail.

3. The primary purpose of the activity attributes document is to provide further and more detailed information about each of the activities in the activity list.

# Sequence Activities

▓ **More Info**   Sequence Activities You can read more about the Sequence Activities process in the PMBOK Guide, 5th edition, in Chapter 6, section 6.3. Table 4-3 identifies the process inputs, tools and techniques, and outputs.

***Table 4-3.*** *Sequence Activities Process*

| Inputs ⇨ | Tools and Techniques ⇨ | Outputs |
|---|---|---|
| • Schedule management plan<br>• Activity list<br>• Activity attributes<br>• Milestone list<br>• Project scope statement<br>• Enterprise environmental factors<br>• Organizational process assets | • Precedence diagramming method (PDM)<br>• Dependency determination<br>• Applying leads and lags | • Project schedule network diagrams<br>• Project document updates |

The Sequence Activities process is a planning process that takes the list of activities that have already been defined and starts to put them in the order in which they will be completed.

The Sequence Activities process covers the following planning domain task:

• Task 4: Develop the project schedule based on the approved project deliverables and milestones, scope, and resource management plans, in order to manage timely completion of the project.

# Inputs

The inputs used in this process allow for sequencing of the already-defined project activities.

## Schedule Management Plan

The schedule management plan is used as a key input into the Sequence Activities process because it outlines and defines how and when you will sequence the activities. The schedule management plan is an output from the Plan Schedule Management process.

## Activity List

The activity list is a very important input into the Sequence Activities process, because you need the list of activities to put them in order. The activity list is an output from the Define Activities process.

## Activity Attributes

The activity attributes document provides additional information about each of the activities that may be useful when it comes to deciding whether they are predecessors or successors for any other activity. The activity attributes document is an output from the Define Activities process.

## Milestone List

The milestone list is an important input because it has a description of the known project milestones, and with this you can determine which activities must be completed before the milestone and which must be completed after the milestone. The milestone list is an output from the Define Activities process.

## Project Scope Statement

The project scope statement is used as an input into the Sequence Activities process because it allows you to understand the complete scope of work to be delivered in the project. Thus you can get a clear idea of which activities must be performed before other activities.

## Enterprise Environmental Factors

The specific types of enterprise environmental factors that are of use during the Sequence Activities process are scheduling tools, government or industry standards, and any other external factors affecting the order in which work is to be completed on your project.

## Organizational Process Assets

The specific organizational process assets that can assist you in sequencing the activities include any existing processes, templates, historical information, or lessons learned documentation that the organization owns.

# Tools and Techniques

The three tools and techniques of this process are all used on the separate inputs to deliver the process outputs.

## Precedence Diagramming Method (PDM)

The *precedence diagramming method* (PDM) is a graphical representation of activities in a project, represented on nodes, with the relationships between them indicated by arrows. This is more commonly called the *activity-on-node* (AON) diagram. It establishes a *predecessor* and *successor* relationship between activities. An activity can be a predecessor of other activities, meaning it must be done before them. The same activity can also be a successor activity to one or more activities, meaning it must be done after them.

As mentioned already, a predecessor activity is one that comes before another activity, and a successor activity is one that comes after another activity. A predecessor activity may have many successor activities, in which case it is known as a *burst* activity. A successor activity may have one or more predecessor activities. If the successor activity has more than one predecessor activity, it is known as a *merge* activity. Figure 4-2 shows an example of Activity A as the predecessor activity, with Activities B and C as the successor activities. Activity A is also a burst activity.

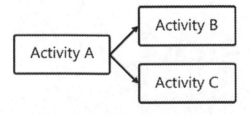

*Figure 4-2.* *Predecessor and successors*

Four types of relationships exist between predecessor and successor activities:

- *Finish-to-start (FS):* The successor activity cannot start until the predecessor activity has finished. For example, you cannot erect the walls of a house until the foundation has been completed. Figure 4-3 depicts how this would be represented diagrammatically.

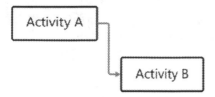

***Figure 4-3.*** *Finish-to-start relationship*

- *Finish-to-finish (FF):* The successor activity cannot finish until the predecessor activity has finished. For example, you cannot finish writing the user manual for a piece of software until the testing is finished. Figure 4-4 depicts how this would be represented diagrammatically.

***Figure 4-4.*** *Finish-to-finish relationship*

- *Start-to-start (SS):* The successor activity cannot start until the predecessor activity starts. For example, you cannot begin testing a new piece of software until you have started writing the code. Figure 4-5 depicts how this can be represented diagrammatically.

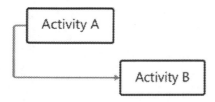

***Figure 4-5.*** *Start-to-start relationship*

- *Start-to-finish (SF):* The successor cannot finish until predecessor starts. For example, you may have an activity that is to send the invoice for a product, but the invoice cannot be sent (finished) until delivery of the product has started. This type of relationship is almost never used, because it seems to indicate that the successor should be the predecessor and vice versa. Figure 4-6 depicts how this would be represented diagrammatically.

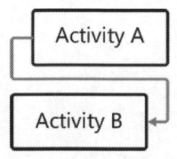

***Figure 4-6.*** *Start-to-finish relationship*

---

## REAL WORLD

In most project management scheduling software, the default relationship for activities is finish-to-start. Check it out: if you enter *FS* after a predecessor, the *FS* disappears. However, if you enter *FF*, *SS*, or *SF*, it remains.

---

## Dependency Determination

In addition to the types of relationships that exist between predecessor and successor activities, there are also four types of dependencies that determine the nature of the relationship between the two activities.

- *Mandatory dependencies:* The successor activity must always occur after the predecessor activity. For example, you must develop the code for a piece of software before you begin testing it.

- *Discretionary dependencies:* The successor activity should occur after the predecessor activity, although the two activities can be performed in another sequence if necessary.

---

■ **Exam Tip**   Be aware that discretionary dependencies have some flexibility built into them in terms of how they are scheduled. Generally, they should be performed in sequence, with successor activities after their predecessor activities, but they can be performed in parallel if necessary. There can be an increased risk associated with performing discretionary dependencies in parallel rather than in sequence, and this additional risk would need to be considered when putting together the project schedule.

---

- *External dependencies:* The activity is dependent on an activity being completed outside of the project. For example, you cannot start construction on the house until you have received building consent.

- *Internal dependencies:* The activity relies on another activity that is external to the project but internal to the broader organization. For example, the recruitment of people on your project may be done by the human resources department, and you have to wait until they complete the work.

## Applying Leads and Lags

As you start to put together your project network diagram by beginning with the sequencing of the activities, you can also choose to apply *leads* and *lags*. A *lead* is the amount of time a successor activity can start before its predecessor activity finishes. For example, generally speaking, you do not start building the walls of a house until construction of the foundation has been completed. However, you can get a lead on the construction of the walls by having them built off site.

The opposite of a lead is a lag. A *lag* is the amount of time a successor activity must wait after its predecessor activity has finished before it can start. For example, in the case of pouring concrete for a house foundation, you must wait several days while the concrete cures before you can start building on it. Because the concrete curing period has neither resources nor costs assigned to it, it cannot be included as an activity in your network diagram. Instead, you indicate that the successor activities must wait via a lag before they can begin.

---
### REAL WORLD
---

If you want to indicate a lead between a successor and its predecessor by using Microsoft Project, Primavera, or ProjectLibre, this can be done by using the relationship acronym, such as finish-to-start (FS), and a minus sign followed by the number of time periods the activity can start before the completion of its predecessor. For example, *FS − 4* means the successor activity has a finish-to-start relationship with its predecessor activity and can start four days before the predecessor activity ends. If you want to indicate a lag, you can do this by using a plus sign after the relationship acronym. For example, if you want to indicate a lag of three days, you simply write the task ID number of the predecessor and then, for a finish-to-start relationship, *FS + 3.*

# Outputs

The major outputs from the Sequence Activities process are the following.

## Project Schedule Network Diagrams

The *project schedule network diagram* represents all the activities in the project and the relationships between them all. The process of completing the sequencing of activities is the first step in the completion of the project schedule network diagram. This first pass, which indicates the relationships between the activities, will be further fleshed out with more information in the coming processes as you use the resource estimates to define the durations of each of the activities. Then you will be able to calculate the total project duration, the amount of slack or float in the project, and the critical path or paths.

Figure 4-7 shows what an activity-on-node (AON) network diagram might look like at the end of the sequencing process. Information about each activity is represented in the nodes on the diagram, and the arrows indicate the relationships between the activities. In this case, they are all finish-to-start (FS) relationships. The AON diagram is the most popular graphical way of representing a network, but there is another less intuitive way called the activity-on-arrow (AOA) diagram.

*Figure 4-7.* *Activity-on-node network diagram*

| REAL WORLD |
| --- |

It is highly unlikely that you will need to know how to construct a network diagram manually in the real world. I have found that the main benefit of knowing how to put together a network diagram, calculate the project duration, calculate any slack in the network diagram, and determine a critical path is for understanding and appreciating how project management software works. Perhaps the only time you will need to know how to do this manually is for a small part of your project schedule at short notice when software isn't available.

■ **Exam Tip**　The other way to graphically represent a network diagram is called the arrow diagramming method or the activity-on-arrow (AOA) diagram. The AOA diagram is not used very much in the project management world, because it seems to run counter to the logical representations of activities and the relationships between them. Because the activities themselves are represented by arrows, it becomes a problem to also use arrows to show relationships between activities; so where there are multiple predecessors to an activity, a dummy activity is used, represented by a dotted line. Figure 4-8 shows an example of an AOA diagram with a dummy activity showing a relationship between Activities B and G. On the exam, if you find a reference to a dummy activity, you know it is referring to AOA diagrams.

*Figure 4-8.*　*Activity-on-arrow (AOA) diagram*

## Project Document Updates

The types of project documents that may be updated as a result of the Sequence Activities process are the activity list, activity attributes, and any other relevant documents.

> **Quick Check**
>
> 1.　What is the most commonly used type of relationship between predecessor and successor activities?
>
> 2.　What is the difference between a lead and a lag?
>
> 3.　What is the difference between an activity-on-node diagram and an activity-on-arrow diagram?

**Quick Check Answers**

1. The most commonly used type of relationship between predecessor and successor activities is a finish-to-start relationship.

2. A lead is the amount of time a successor activity can start before its predecessor finishes, whereas a lag is the amount of time a successor activity must wait after its predecessor activity finishes.

3. An activity-on-node diagram represents the project activities on nodes, with the arrows between the nodes representing the types of relationships. An activity-on-arrow diagram shows the activities of the project occurring on the arrows themselves, with nodes representing where multiple activities join.

# Estimate Activity Resources

▓ **More Info**   Estimate Activity Resources You can read more about the Estimate Activity Resources process in the PMBOK Guide, 5th edition, in Chapter 6, section 6.4. Table 4-4 identifies the process inputs, tools and techniques, and outputs.

*Table 4-4.*  *Estimate Activity Resources Process*

| Inputs ⇨ | Tools and Techniques ⇨ | Outputs |
|---|---|---|
| • Schedule management plan<br>• Activity list<br>• Activity attributes<br>• Resource calendars<br>• Risk register<br>• Activity cost estimates<br>• Enterprise environmental factors<br>• Organizational process assets | • Expert judgment<br>• Alternative analysis<br>• Published estimating data<br>• Bottom-up estimating<br>• Project management software | • Activity resource requirements<br>• Resource breakdown structure<br>• Project document updates |

The key area of focus in the Estimate Activity Resources process is to consider the defined activities and carry out the process of estimating what resources will be required to complete the work.

The Estimate Activity Resources process covers the following planning domain task:

• Task 4: Develop the project schedule based on the approved project deliverables and milestones, scope, and resource management plans, in order to manage timely completion of the project.

---

▓ **Note**    Defining resources A resource can be defined as any person, team, machinery, equipment, material, or funds used to do work on the project.

---

# Inputs

There are eight inputs into the Estimate Activity Resources process, all specifically designed to assist you in producing the outputs.

## Schedule Management Plan

Again, the schedule management plan appears as a primary input into a process devoted to producing the project network diagram. This is because the schedule management plan is the document that describes and defines your approach to producing a project schedule. The schedule management plan is an output from the Plan Schedule Management process.

## Activity List

The activity list provides information about all the activities you have defined. You use this information to estimate individual resources assigned to each activity. The activity list is an output from the Define Activities process.

## Activity Attributes

The activity attributes document provides additional information about each activity on your activity list. This information can refer to which resources are available. The activity attributes document is an output from the Define Activities process.

## Resource Calendars

*Resource calendars* are a key input into this process because they define constraints on when resources are available to work. They define such things as normal working times, holidays, and any other constraints on when resources may be available. Resource calendars are an output from the Acquire Project Team process in the Human Resource Management knowledge area.

## Risk Register

The *risk register* is used to assist with estimating activity resources because it documents any known risks that might affect resources you plan to use on the project. The risk register is an output from the Identify Risks process in the Risk Management knowledge area.

## Activity Cost Estimates

You can use *activity cost estimates* to determine the cost of the resources you may be considering for each activity. Activity cost estimates are an output from the Estimate Costs process in the Cost Management knowledge area.

## Enterprise Environmental Factors

The specific types of enterprise environmental factors that can be used in this process include any constraints imposed on resource availability for the project, such as government regulations on mandatory types of resources that must be used, or perhaps regulations of health and safety that affect the number of people who must be present in a workplace.

## Organizational Process Assets

The specific types of organizational process assets that can be used as inputs into this process include any existing processes and templates, any relevant human resource policies, and any relevant policies in relation to procurement of supplies and equipment that the organization has. Additionally, a key organizational process asset is always historical information from previous projects.

# Tools and Techniques

The following tools and techniques are available, if appropriate, to use on the selected inputs.

## Expert Judgment

Expert judgment is a key tool, because you will use the judgment of experts to help produce the activity resource estimates. The types of experts you should consult are those people with prior and specialized knowledge in resource planning on a project similar to your own.

## Alternative Analysis

The process of *alternative analysis* considers all the permutations of delivering an activity by using different combinations of resources, quantities of resources, and types of resources, and whether you will rent or buy the resources you require.

## Published Estimating Data

*Published estimating data* is a convenient means of getting reliable data from commercial sources. This published estimating data can give you information about what resources are available, the cost of these resources, and the work rate of the resources.

---

▓ **Exam Tip**   You will use published estimating data as a tool for cost-estimating processes as well.

---

## Bottom-Up Estimating

*Bottom-up estimating* is an estimating process that begins at a low level of the WBS, such as at individual work packages or even at the activity level, and works upward by aggregating, or adding up, resource estimates in each level of the WBS to arrive at a high-level estimate. Bottom-up estimating is generally considered to be more accurate than top-down estimating, but it involves more time and effort to complete.

## Project Management Software

Most projects plan to use many different types of resources, and it is neither effective nor efficient to do this process manually. This is where using *project management software* provides a definite advantage, because it can process information more quickly.

# Outputs

The following outputs are generated by the Estimate Activity Resources process.

## Activity Resource Requirements

The *activity resource requirements* list is the documented list of the resources you will require to complete every activity on your activity list. The activity resource requirements list goes on to be used as an input into the Plan Human Resource Management process and the Plan Procurement Management process.

## Resource Breakdown Structure

The *resource breakdown structure*, like other breakdown structures, is used to decompose the categories of resources required and the specific resources required for the project. The resource breakdown structure then goes on to be used as an input into the Estimate Activity Durations process and the Develop Schedule process. Figure 4-9 shows an example of a resource breakdown structure.

*Figure 4-9.* *Resource breakdown structure*

---

░ **Exam Tip** The resource breakdown structure is one of four breakdown structures you should know for the exam. The other three are the organizational breakdown structure, the risk breakdown structure, and of course, perhaps the most important, the work breakdown structure (WBS).

---

## Project Document Updates

Types of project documents that may be updated as a result of the Estimate Activity Resources process are the activity list, activity attributes, resource calendars, and project schedule management plan.

**Quick Check**

1. What is the definition of a project resource?

2. What is the benefit of using published estimating data?

3. What is the advantage of using bottom-up estimating techniques?

4. Why is it important to use resource calendars as an input into the Estimate Activity Resources process?

**Quick Check Answers**

1. A project resource is any person, material, funding, or piece of equipment that is being used to complete activities, and subsequently work, on a project.

2. The benefit of using published estimating data is that it is reliable and is generally prepared by using relevant commercially available data.

3. Bottom-up estimating techniques are generally more accurate than top-down techniques because they aggregate estimates at a low level in the WBS and roll them up.

4.  Resource calendars provide information about resource availability; as such, they are an essential input into the Estimate Activity Resources process because they let you know when resources are available and when resources are not available to work on a project.

# Estimate Activity Durations

▦ **More Info**    Estimate Activity Durations You can read more about the Estimate Activity Durations process in the PMBOK Guide, 5th edition, in Chapter 6, section 6.5. Table 4-5 identifies the process inputs, tools and techniques, and outputs.

*Table 4-5.*  *Estimate Activity Durations Process*

| Inputs ⇨ | Tools and Techniques ⇨ | Outputs |
|---|---|---|
| • Schedule management plan<br>• Activity list<br>• Activity attributes<br>• Activity resource requirements<br>• Resource calendars<br>• Project scope statement<br>• Risk register<br>• Resource breakdown structure<br>• Enterprise environmental factors<br>• Organizational process assets | • Expert judgment<br>• Analogous estimating<br>• Parametric estimating<br>• Three-point estimating<br>• Group decision-making techniques<br>• Reserve analysis | • Activity duration estimates<br>• Project document updates |

The Estimate Activity Durations process is focused on taking the previous data you have produced in defining the activities, sequencing the activities, and estimating the resources required for each activity, and then estimating the duration of each activity so that you can roll up these individual estimates into a total estimate for the project duration.

The Estimate Activity Durations process covers the following planning domain task:

•   Task 4: Develop the project schedule based on the approved project deliverables and milestones, scope, and resource management plans, in order to manage timely completion of the project.

> ▓ **Exam Tip**   The Estimate Activity Resources process comes before the Estimate Activity Durations process because generally you need to know what resources are available in order to be able to estimate how long activity will take. The more resources you have, the faster an activity will be completed.

# Inputs

The following inputs can be used in the Estimate Activity Durations process to generate the outputs.

## Schedule Management Plan

The schedule management plan is again a key input into this process because it outlines the way in which you will complete your estimate of activity durations. The schedule management plan is an output from the Plan Schedule Management process.

## Activity List

The activity list provides information about all the activities on a project and is an essential input, because you are now going to be estimating the duration of each of these activities. The activity list is an output from the Define Activities process.

## Activity Attributes

Although the activity list provides you with a list of all the activities and some summary information about each of them, the activity attributes document provides more detailed information about each of the activities, including the resources allocated to them, any known constraints or assumptions, and any risks. Activity attributes are an output from the Define Activities process.

## Activity Resource Requirements

The activity resource requirements match each activity in your activity list with allocated resources that have been estimated to complete the activity. The activity resource requirements are an output from the Estimate Activity Resources process.

## Resource Calendars

Resource calendars provide you with information about constraints on resource availability. They specify when resources are available and when they are not available. If they are referring to people, they may outline holidays and known non-working times so that you can build these into your duration estimates. Resource calendars are also useful for indicating when resources are allocated to other projects and are thus not available to work on your project. Resource calendars are an output from the Acquire Project Team process.

## Project Scope Statement

The use of the project scope statement as an input into the Estimate Activity Durations process provides a great level of oversight to ensure that you have captured the entire project scope. Furthermore, the project scope statement contains additional information that you may need to be aware of when estimating activity durations, such as any pre-identified skilled resources and any known contract terms and requirements affecting duration estimates. The project scope statement is an output from the Define Scope process in the Scope Management knowledge area.

## Risk Register

The project risk register includes an analysis of the risks associated with resource use on the project, and, as such, contains important information about uncertainty in your activity duration estimates. The risk register is an output from the Identify Risks process in the Risk Management knowledge area.

## Resource Breakdown Structure

The resource breakdown structure provides you with a comprehensive decomposition of the types of resources you will require on the project, and with this information you can estimate durations better. The resource breakdown structure is an output from the Estimate Activity Resources process.

## Enterprise Environmental Factors

The specific types of enterprise environmental factors that may be used as inputs into this process are any estimating databases the organization has accumulated or that are available from external sources, and any known productivity metrics useful in determining the durations of particular activities when completed by specific resources.

## Organizational Process Assets

The organizational process assets that can be used to assist in the Estimate Activity Durations process are any historical information you have from previous projects, any lessons learned from previous projects specifically in relation to estimating, activity durations, and any organizational methodology and processes that can assist you in this process.

# Tools and Techniques

The following tools and techniques can be used on the selected inputs to generate the outputs.

## Expert Judgment

The specific type of expert judgment you will use as a tool in this process will be from anyone with specific knowledge about how long activities should take. This expert judgment can come from team members, others in the organization, or external people with specific experience.

## Analogous Estimating

*Analogous estimating* is an estimating technique in which you take a similar activity and extrapolate from that a current estimate based on the relationship between the other activity and this activity. For example, you may know that a similar activity took three days to complete, and the one you are currently estimating is twice as big; therefore, you would estimate a total duration of six days by using an analogous estimating technique.

---

▓ **Note**    Accuracy of estimates Any estimating technique is simply an attempt to forecast what the future may hold. The better the information that goes into the estimating process is, the better the estimate will be. For example, let's say that you are trying to forecast the weather for tomorrow, for one week from now, for one month from now, and for one year from now. In order to estimate the weather for tomorrow, you have available to you a lot of data, including quantitative data on what today's weather pattern is doing and what historical information and computer simulations tell you this weather pattern will do tomorrow. As a result of this detailed information going into the estimating process, you can be reasonably sure that your estimate about tomorrow's weather will be fairly accurate. As you move out in time with your weather forecasts, the data available to you and the computer simulations and historical information will provide less valuable input, and thus your weather forecast for a year away will basically just be a guess based on the seasonal expectations.

---

## Parametric Estimating

*Parametric estimating* uses known quantities and known units of measurement and multiplies them together to arrive at an estimate. For example, you may know that each person can write 300 lines of code per day and that there are 3,000 lines of code to be written; therefore, your duration estimate using parametric estimating is 10 days.

# Three-Point Estimating

*Three-point estimating* is part of the *Program Evaluation and Review Technique* (PERT), a technique that uses a weighted-average scenario to arrive at an estimate where there are most likely, optimistic, and pessimistic durations for an activity. If you were to take a simple average of three numbers, you would add the three numbers together and then divide by 3. The three-point estimating technique gives a higher weighting to the most likely estimate (tM) and assigns it a weight of 4, while assigning a weight of 1 to each of the optimistic (tO) and pessimistic (tP) duration estimates. With six numbers now instead of three, you divide by 6 to get the weighted average. Therefore, the formula for calculating a three-point estimate using this technique is

$$\frac{tO + (tM \times 4) + tP}{6}$$

---

▨ **Exam Tip**   The same formula is used to estimate project costs. In this section, the letter *t* is used to denote the variable being used to estimate time. When you are using this formula to estimate costs, the letter *c* is used instead. You may find it easier just to remember the formula without the *t* or *c*. Expert judgment, analogous estimating, parametric estimating, and three-point estimating are also used in the Estimate Costs process.

---

For example, if you have an optimistic estimate of 4 days, a most likely estimate of 7 days, and a pessimistic estimate of 12 days and put these estimates into the three-point estimating formula, your three-point estimate for this activity is 7.33 days:

$$\frac{4 + (7 \times 4) + 12}{6}$$
$$= \frac{4 + 28 + 12}{6}$$
$$= \frac{44}{6}$$
$$= 7.33$$

In addition to calculating the expected duration, you can also calculate the *standard deviation* and variance. The standard deviation is a calculation of how far away from the average duration, or the expected duration using the three-point estimating formula, your data is spread. A smaller standard deviation means the data is tightly grouped, whereas a larger standard deviation means the data is more widely spread.

The standard deviation calculation we use in the three-point estimating technique is essentially a heuristic, or rule-of-thumb, way of calculating standard deviation rather than the full formula used by statisticians. The formula subtracts the optimistic from the pessimistic and divides the result by 6:

$$\frac{tP - tO}{6}$$

So, using the previous example, the standard deviation is 8 divided by 6, which equals 1.33 days.

A benefit of calculating the standard deviation is that you can then estimate the confidence interval for a range of estimates. The *confidence interval* states the amount of the data that you expect to fall between the number of standard deviations above and below the mean. A standard deviation of one either side of the mean represents a confidence interval of 68%, a standard deviation of two either side of the mean gives a confidence interval of 95%, and a standard deviation of three either side of the mean gives a confidence interval of 99.7%.

---

▨ **Exam Tip**    Six standard deviation either side of the mean contains 99.999% of the population. More commonly known as *Six Sigma*, it is used as a quality management tool in the Project Quality Management knowledge area.

---

Figure 4-10 shows a normal distribution and the range of a population you would expect to find with either one, two, or three standard deviations (SD) either side of the mean.

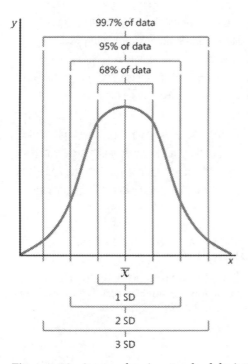

*Figure 4-10.* A curve showing standard deviations

For example, in the previous scenario, you could say that you have a 95% degree of certainty that the estimate for the activity duration is between 7± 2.66 days. This is calculated by realizing that 95% certainty reflects two standard deviations either side of the mean. The standard deviation, as already calculated, equals 1.33 days; therefore, two standard deviations equals 2.66 days.

---

▓ **Exam Tip**   On the exam, you may be asked a question about a range of estimates of which you are either 68%, 95%, or 99.7% certain, which means the question is asking you to calculate one, two, or three standard deviations either side of the mean or average.

---

There is one more formula you need to be aware of: calculating the *variance*. The variance is calculated by multiplying the standard deviation by itself:

$$\left( \frac{tP - tO}{6} \right)^2$$

Using the previous example, the variance is the standard deviation squared, which equals 1.33 × 1.33, which equals 1.77.

---

▓ **Note**   Origins of three-point estimating The origins of the three-point estimating technique are reportedly from the U.S. Navy Polaris submarine program in the 1950s. The technique was developed to help improve the delivery of large, complex projects. It is a subset of the Program Evaluation and Review Technique (PERT), which was one of the first analytical techniques to sequence activities and show the relationship between them.

▓ **Exam Tip**   On the exam, you will probably have to do some calculations using formulas. You should always round your answer to two decimal places. However, you may arrive at an answer that is a fractionally different from one of those presented. If this is the case, it is probably a safe bet, if you have used the right equation, that the answer closest to yours is correct.

---

# Group Decision-Making Techniques

There are many ways to gather information from groups of people, each with its own benefits and drawbacks. The most common group decision-making techniques used are *brainstorming, nominal group techniques,* and the *Delphi technique.*

*Brainstorming* is an excellent way of getting a group of people to think about many possible options. If you are facilitating a brainstorming session, you should encourage all ideas. The *nominal group technique* takes all the ideas and has the group vote on which ideas are worthy of further investigation.

The *Delphi technique* is a technique for soliciting information from experts on an anonymous basis. The reason is that often, bringing experts together into a room to provide expert opinion and advice results in the loudest being heard, or peer pressure influencing the opinions of those present. The Delphi technique aims to get around these potential problems and allow experts to contribute freely by asking each expert anonymously, via a structured questionnaire, for their opinion. After the first round of opinions has been gathered, the summarized results are often circulated again to all experts taking part in the process. They can then review the results and, if they want, change their original opinion.

---

### REAL WORLD

The Delphi technique is a very effective way of getting accurate information from experts; however, it is also time consuming and can cost a significant amount of money to do successfully. I have been part of a Delphi technique that was used to determine the level of risk on IT projects; I never knew how many other experts were being consulted, but the entire process took about three weeks to complete.

---

▓ **Note** Origins of the Delphi technique The Delphi technique is named after the oracle of Delphi, who was a priestess at the Temple of Apollo in ancient Greece. She went into a trance and provided advice about what the future might hold.

---

## Reserve Analysis

A *reserve analysis* is the process of determining a justifiable reserve, or buffer, to be added to activities based on quantitative analysis carried out as part of developing the risk register. This process develops a *contingency reserve*, which is used for known unknowns, or identified uncertainty, in your project. It is a justifiable means of adding in extra time or cost. For example, if, during your quantitative risk assessment, you discovered that there was a 25% chance of a time delay of 10 days to a particular activity, you would add a contingency reserve of 2.5 days to your estimates. If the risk did not manifest, you would not need this contingency reserve.

The other sort of reserve that may be available to a project is a *management reserve*, which is a figure determined at the start of the project and that management and the project sponsor control for unknown unknowns, or unforeseen risks. A project can apply to use the management reserve. Use of the management reserve results in a change to the schedule baseline, because it is not factored into your duration estimates. *Padding* of estimates means making unjustifiable additions to cost or time estimates and is considered unethical.

---

**REAL WORLD**

---

It can be extremely difficult to convince the project sponsor and members of the project steering group to approve a contingency reserve for either time or cost, because they need to be persuaded that your methodology for determining it is sound and based on quantitative data. I have always argued for the provision of a contingency reserve on the basis of "no surprises," and this has generally been successful. When the identified activity has been completed, if there was no need to use the contingency reserve, this is reported, and the overall contingency reserve is decreased.

---

# Outputs

The Estimate Activity Durations process produces some or all of the following outputs.

## Activity Duration Estimates

The main output from the Estimate Activity Durations process is the *activity duration estimates*, which define and record the individual assessments for the time required to complete each activity on the activity list. The individual activity duration estimates include an expected duration for each activity and, if calculated, the range of uncertainty in each activity, which can be aggregated to provide an expected duration with the total range of uncertainty for the entire project. For example, you could report that the total project duration is expected to be 89 days with a 10% probability that it will take 95 days based on the reserve analysis. The activity duration estimates go on to be used as an input into the Develop Schedule process.

## Project Document Updates

The specific types of project documents that may be updated as a result of completing the Estimate Activity Durations process are the activity list, the activity attributes, and any other documents relating to expected durations of activities that the organization has.

**Quick Check**

1. Using the three-point estimating technique, what is the expected duration of an activity with an optimistic duration of 8 days, a most likely estimate of 10 days, and a pessimistic estimate of 16 days?

2. What is the main benefit of using the Delphi technique as and estimating tool?

3. What is the main difference between analogous and parametric estimating techniques?

4.  What percentage of a data population would you expect to find within two standard deviations either side of a mean?

5.  What are the two types of justifiable reserve that may be used on a project?

**Quick Check Answers**

1.  If you apply the three-point estimating formula to this scenario, you will arrive at a three-point estimate of 10.66 days.

2.  The main benefit of using the Delphi technique is to allow experts to contribute their opinions anonymously and without peer pressure.

3.  Analogous estimating uses similar scenarios to extrapolate a current estimate, whereas parametric estimating uses a known quantity and multiplies it by a known metric.

4.  You would expect to find approximately 95% of a population within two standard deviations either side of a mean.

5.  Both the contingency reserve, for "known unknowns," and the management reserve, for "unknown unknowns," are developed by using quantitative data and historical information and, therefore, provide justifiable reserves.

# Develop Schedule

▒ **More Info**   Develop Schedule You can read more about the Develop Schedule process in the PMBOK Guide, 5th edition, in Chapter 6, section 6.6. Table 4-6 identifies the process inputs, tools and techniques, and outputs.

*Table 4-6.* *Develop Schedule Process*

| Inputs ⇨ | Tools and Techniques ⇨ | Outputs |
|---|---|---|
| • Schedule management plan<br>• Activity list<br>• Activity attributes<br>• Project schedule network diagrams<br>• Activity resource requirements<br>• Resource calendars<br>• Activity duration estimates<br>• Project scope statement<br>• Risk register<br>• Project staff assignments<br>• Resource breakdown structure<br>• Enterprise environmental factors<br>• Organizational process assets | • Schedule network analysis<br>• Critical path method<br>• Critical chain method<br>• Resource optimization techniques<br>• Modeling techniques<br>• Leads and lags<br>• Schedule compression<br>• Scheduling tool | • Schedule baseline<br>• Project schedule<br>• Schedule data<br>• Project calendars<br>• Project management plan updates<br>• Project document updates |

The Develop Schedule process takes all the information you have gathered in the previous processes—Define Activities, Sequence Activities, Estimate Activity Resources, and Estimate Activity Durations—and combines them into the project network diagram, which graphically represents the project schedule.

The Develop Schedule process covers the following planning domain task:

- Task 4: Develop the project schedule based on the approved project deliverables and milestones, scope, and resource management plans, in order to manage timely completion of the project.

## REAL WORLD

On most projects I've been involved in, the Develop Schedule process has been our primary focus. The preceding processes have all been completed at the same time, rather than as discrete, separate processes.

# Inputs

The Develop Schedule process uses the following inputs.

## Schedule Management Plan

The schedule management plan is an essential input into the Develop Schedule process because it outlines the way in which you will develop the project schedule. The schedule management plan is an output from the Plan Schedule Management process.

## Activity List

The activity list provides you with a list of all the activities you have defined for the project that need to be completed. Each activity needs to be represented on the completed project schedule, and thus the activity list is a key input into this process. The activity list is an output from the Define Activities process.

## Activity Attributes

The activity attributes give you more detailed information about the activities on the activity list, which only provides summary information about each activity. The activity attributes are an output from the Define Activities process.

## Project Schedule Network Diagrams

The project schedule network diagrams present each of the activities and the relationship each has with predecessors and successors. The full development of the project schedule takes this preliminary information and adds additional detail to it, such as the estimate of activity resources and the individual estimate of activity durations, to produce the final project schedule. The project schedule network diagrams are an output from the Sequence Activities process.

## Activity Resource Requirements

The activity resource requirements are used to allocate resources to each of the activities identified in the project. Activity resource requirements are an output from the Estimate Activity Resources process.

## Resource Calendars

The resource calendars provide information about any known constraints on the use of resources on your project that may affect your scheduling. The resource calendars are an output from the Acquire Project Team process in the Human Resource Management knowledge area.

## Activity Duration Estimates

The activity duration estimates are absolutely essential if you want to complete a project schedule. You use these individual estimates and aggregate them to determine your total project duration. Activity duration estimates are an output from the Estimate Activity Durations process.

## Project Scope Statement

The project scope statement gives you information about the project and product scope of work to be completed, and it also provides information about known constraints and assumptions and any known contractual obligations that will affect your project schedule. The project scope statement is an output from the Develop Project Scope process in the Scope Management knowledge area.

## Risk Register

The risk register contains information about known schedule risks and known resource risks of the project. As part of the analysis of these risks, there may be the development of contingencies relating to time that must be taken into account in developing a project schedule. The risk register is an output from the Identify Risks process in the Risk Management knowledge area.

## Project Staff Assignments

The *project staff assignments* specify which organizational employees are to be allocated to each activity and provide an analysis of experience and skills that each particular person brings. The project staff assignments are an output from the Acquire Project Team process in the Human Resource Management knowledge area.

## Resource Breakdown Structure

The resource breakdown structure is used as an input because it provides the details of the categories of individual skills that resources must be able to bring to the project to complete the assigned activities. The resource breakdown structure is an output from the Estimate Activity Resources process.

## Enterprise Environmental Factors

The specific enterprise environmental factors that may be used as inputs, if appropriate, are any external standards, regulations, contractual obligations, or licensed scheduling tools that you will use to develop the project schedule.

## Organizational Process Assets

The specific organizational process assets that may be useful in developing your project schedule include any existing project management methodology, blank templates, tools, and other techniques owned by the organization for the preparation of a project schedule.

# Tools and Techniques

The following tools and techniques can be used on the inputs into the Develop Schedule process.

## Schedule Network Analysis

*Schedule network analysis* is a primary tool used to bring together all the previous information you have gathered when you defined the activities, sequenced the activities, estimated the activity resources, and estimated the activity durations. You use all of this information to put together your full schedule network diagram; when it is completed, you can use the critical path method, critical chain method, what-if analysis, or resource leveling to determine the total project duration and the amount of *total float or slack* between specific activities and in the overall project.

---

### REAL WORLD

There are many ways of drawing the information contained in each node of an activity-on-node (AON) network diagram, and there are at least two ways of representing the numbering systems used to calculate durations between activities.

---

## Critical Path Method

The *critical path* method focuses on identifying all the paths through a project and, with the aid of a network diagram, determining which of these paths presents the shortest duration and also the least amount of scheduling flexibility as indicated by the length of slack or float. The path with the shortest duration and the least slack or float through the project represents the path of most risk to the project—hence the name *critical path*. There can be many paths through a project, as Figure 4-11 shows.

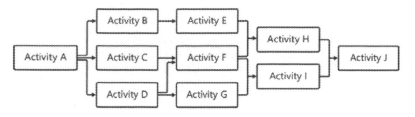

***Figure 4-11.*** *Network paths*

This network diagram contains the following paths:

- A-B-E-H-J

- A-C-F-H-J

- A-C-F-I-J

- A-D-F-H-J

- A-D-F-I-J

- A-D-G-I-J

However, you cannot determine which path or paths are the critical paths until you complete a full schedule network analysis.

---

▓ **Note**    Slack and float There are not many instances in the PMBOK guide for which a single word has two meanings. The case of *slack* and *float* is one of the only times when two words are used to mean the same thing. There are two types of slack or float: *free slack* or *free float*, and *total slack* or *total float*. Free slack, or free float, indicates the amount of time an activity can be delayed before that affects the next activity on the path. Total slack, or total float, indicates the amount of time an activity can be delayed before it affects the total project duration. If an activity has zero total float, it means if it is delayed, it will automatically increase the duration of the project. The critical path or paths through a project are those on which there is no slack or float.

---

In order to complete a full schedule network diagram, you must understand how to complete an activity-on-node (AON) diagram. This section takes you through the process of completing a schedule network diagram, completing a *forward pass* to determine the project duration, and completing a *backward pass* to determine the critical path or paths.

To calculate the critical path on an AON diagram, this example uses the node to represent the information about the activity. The information contained in the node is the task ID, the duration of the activity, the *early start (ES)*, the *early finish (EF)*, the *late start (LS)*, the *late finish (LF)*, and the amount of total float in the activity. Figure 4-12 represents a typical node; however, be aware that in the real world and on the exam, many different forms of nodes may be used, with information displayed in different locations. They all display the same information, just in different ways.

| Early Start (ES) | Duration | Early Finish (EF) |
|---|---|---|
| Activity Name | | |
| Late Start (LS) | Total Float | Late Finish (LF) |

*Figure 4-12.* *The activity node*

Now, if you take the information contained in Table 4-7 and map it out over an entire network diagram, you can calculate the project duration and the critical path or paths.

*Table 4-7.* *Activity Information*

| Activity ID | Duration (Days) | Predecessor |
|---|---|---|
| A | 3 | - |
| B | 5 | A |
| C | 4 | A |
| D | 2 | B, C |
| E | 6 | C |
| F | 5 | D, E |
| G | 4 | E |
| H | 7 | F, G |

The first step in the process is to construct a network diagram showing the relationships between the activities. In this instance, assume that all activities have a finish-to-start relationship and there are no leads and lags. Figure 4-13 shows the network diagram:

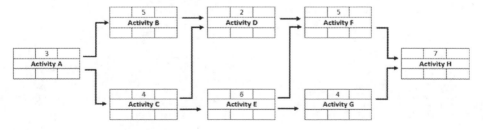

*Figure 4-13.* *Network diagram example*

By examining this network diagram, you can now write out the paths through the diagram as follows:

- A-B-D-F-H

- A-C-D-F-H

- A-C-E-F-H

- A-C-E-G-H

The next step in the process is to complete a *forward pass*. The forward pass is completed by working from left to right and calculating the early start and the early finish for each task. The earliest a task can start is immediately after the latest early finish of all its predecessor activities. For example, if Activity A has an early finish of day 3 (which means it finishes at the end of day 3), then Activity B has an early start of day 4 (which means it starts at the beginning of day 4). If an activity has more than one predecessor, the earliest it can start is immediately after the latest early finish of all its predecessors. Figure 4-14 shows the network diagram with the forward pass completed. You can now determine that the project duration is 25 days.

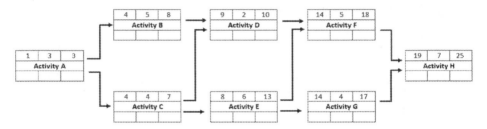

**Figure 4-14.** *Forward pass completed*

The next step in the process is to complete a *backward pass*. This time, you work from right to left, and you calculate the late finish and the late start for each activity. When calculating the late finish for an activity, you must look to its successor activities; the late finish for an activity is immediately prior to the earliest of all successor late start dates. For example, if Activity D is the successor to Activity B, and activity D has a late start of day 12, then Activity B has a late finish of day 11. As you complete the backward pass, you can also calculate the total slack for each task by subtracting the late start from the late finish. Figure 4-15 shows a completed backward pass.

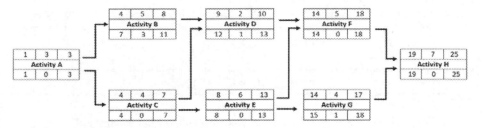

**Figure 4-15.** *Backward pass completed*

To calculate which of the paths through the network diagram is the critical path, you simply look at all the activities that have zero total float, because these represent activities that, if delayed, will affect the total project duration. If you do this, you can determine that the critical path in this network diagram is A-C-E-F-H.

# Critical Chain Method

The *critical chain method* is a means of purposely adding in buffer time to identified activities, usually on the critical path, to account for limited resources and project uncertainties. The amount of buffer is usually worked out by using historical information or quantitative risk analysis. The purpose of adding buffer is to ensure that activities on the critical path that are identified as important feeder activities—that is, those that produce work for successor activities—always have float to ensure that they don't slip and cause the project duration to extend.

---

▓ **Exam Tip**   If a question on the exam asks about the application of buffer time, it is referring to the critical chain method.

---

# Resource Optimization Techniques

Often, the first pass through any estimate of activity resources—equipment, supplies, or people—is what could be referred to as the *optimal use of resources*. However, this may not be the most efficient use of resources, and there may be times when resources are either over-allocated or under-allocated. If resources are over-allocated, you may not be able to use them; and if they are under-allocated, you may be paying for resources to sit around unused. Through the processes of *resource leveling* and *resource smoothing*, you can attempt to make more efficient use of your resources, but this may have an impact on project cost and project duration.

*Resource leveling* involves moving the allocation of resources between time periods to level out periods when a resource will be overused or periods when a resource will be underused. For example, you may have forecast one person to be working 60 hours in a week, while someone else will work 15 hours. Obviously, after you start moving a resource around to get more efficient use, you may end up changing the duration of activities or even the sequence of activities. *Resource smoothing* is a less intensive form of resource leveling because it adjusts resources only within the total float for each activity so as not to extend the total project duration.

---

## REAL WORLD

Typically, resource leveling is best left to sophisticated project management software. If you try to do it manually, you may end up spending too much of your time completing it and not obtaining the optimal results.

---

# Modeling Techniques

*Modeling techniques* typically use computers to present a model of a potential outcome. They are particularly useful when you are developing your project schedule, because you can examine all potential options and easily find problems or opportunities in the project schedule.

A particular type of modeling technique is the *what-if scenario analysis*. What-if scenario analysis is a form of statistical and mathematical analysis that looks at the potential probabilities and likely outcomes of different scenarios occurring. For example, you may be able to use this technique to analyze what would happen to your project schedule if certain events occurred and, from this analysis, choose the scenario that best suits your project-duration goals. Of all the what-if scenario analysis techniques, the most common is *Monte Carlo analysis*. Monte Carlo analysis applies statistical analysis to examining a possible distribution of outcomes and extrapolates from this the likelihood of specific outcomes. Due to its complex use of mathematical modeling, this type of analysis is most often performed by a computer.

---

▓ **Exam Tip**     On the exam, if a question relates to mathematical analysis of different scenarios or the probability of different outcomes, the answer is most likely what-if scenario analysis or Monte Carlo analysis.

▓ **Note**     Origin of Monte Carlo analysis Monte Carlo analysis was used to assist with modeling potential effects of the atomic bomb during the Manhattan Project. It was reportedly so named because the uncle of one of the lead scientists using the method liked to gamble at the casino in Monte Carlo.

---

## Leads and Lags

In completing your entire project schedule with the use of a schedule network diagram, you may choose to use leads and lags as appropriate to represent either the amount of time an activity can start before its predecessor finishes or the amount of time an activity must wait after its predecessor ends before starting, respectively.

## Schedule Compression

Often the first pass through the development of your project schedule results in an optimal timeframe. However, there may be existing schedule constraints, legislation requiring a set date for compliance, market conditions, or stakeholder expectations that mean your original estimate of total project duration is too long. In this case, you need to consider undertaking a variety of *schedule compression* techniques to shorten the duration of the project. The two most common and most often-used techniques are crashing and fast tracking. *Crashing* involves adding extra resources to an activity in order to complete it in a shorter time period, which often involves extra cost. *Fast tracking* allows activities that would normally be done in sequence to be done in parallel for all, or at least a portion, of their duration. Obviously, the type of dependency between the two activities would need to be a discretionary dependency, and you may need to take into account extra risk analysis in relation to starting an activity early.

## Scheduling Tool

A *scheduling tool* can be a piece of project management software dedicated entirely to project scheduling, or it can be a module of a larger piece of project management software, such as Microsoft Project, Primavera, or ProjectLibre, to name just three of the hundreds available.

# Outputs

The Develop Schedule process produces the following outputs.

## Schedule Baseline

The schedule baseline is the final approved version of the project schedule used to track actual progress against planned progress.

---

▧ **Exam Tip**   Four baselines in project management are used to monitor progress after project execution has begun: the scope baseline, the time or schedule baseline, the project budget, and the quality baseline. All project baselines form part of the overall project management plan, because they provide information about what is intended.

---

---

| **REAL WORLD** |
|:---:|

The most often-used form of schedule baseline is the Gantt chart. However, be aware that the Gantt chart is also an exceptional communications tool. On many projects I have worked on, I have used the Gantt chart for both reasons with great success. This is because it presents different levels of information graphically, which means it is easily understood by both technically minded and non-technically minded stakeholders.

---

## Project Schedule

The *project schedule* can be represented in a number of ways. It is most commonly presented graphically by using either a Gantt chart, which is often called a horizontal bar chart, or a horizontal histogram. The project schedule can also be represented by a milestone chart or, less commonly, by the project schedule network diagram. Figure 4-16 shows an example of a Gantt chart.

*Figure 4-16.* *Gantt chart*

---

■ **Note** Origin of the Gantt chart Many people think that Gantt is an acronym for something. I once had a student who was absolutely convinced that it stood for *graphical analysis and numerical tracking tool*. I think the student was just making that up, because it is actually the surname of Henry Gantt, a mechanical engineer credited with using the chart to plot durations on a project.

---

# Schedule Data

The *schedule data* refers to all the data that makes up the project schedule, and it refers to data relating to activity duration estimates, resources, reserves, constraints, and any resource leveling undertaken.

# Project Calendars

The *project calendar* refers to the working time available for the project resources over the life of the project. If the project calendar is for people, then it may refer to the working week; if the project calendar is for machinery, it may refer to a 24-hour, seven-day-a-week schedule.

# Project Management Plan Updates

The parts of the project management plan that may be updated as a result of developing a project schedule are the schedule management plan and the schedule baseline.

# Project Document Updates

The types of project documents that may be updated as a result of completing the Develop Schedule process iteratively are any of the documents that feed into any part of the previous processes, such as activity resource requirements, activity attributes, project calendars, or the risk register.

### Quick Check

1.  Why is identifying the critical path so important?

2.  After completing a forward pass, you will have calculated what?

3.  After completing a backward pass, you will have calculated what?

4.  What method uses time buffers to ensure that feeder activities don't extend the project duration?

5.  What is the key purpose of leveling resources?

6.  What is the main difference between crashing and fast tracking?

**Quick Check Answers**

1.  Activities on the critical path have no total float; if they are delayed, they will extend the overall project duration. Therefore, they represent a high degree of risk on the project.

2.  After completing a forward pass, you will have calculated the project duration.

3.  After completing a backward pass, you will have identified the total float for each activity and can determine the critical path.

4.  The critical chain method uses time buffers inserted into the project schedule to ensure that high-risk activities do not cause the overall project duration to extend.

5.  The key purpose of resource leveling is to maximize the efficient use of resources.

6.  The main difference between crashing and fast tracking is that, generally, crashing costs more because it involves allocating more resources to a particular activity to shorten the duration.

# Control Schedule

▓ **More Info**   Control Schedule You can read more about the Control Schedule process in the PMBOK Guide, 5th edition, in Chapter 6, section 6.7. Table 4-8 identifies the process inputs, tools and techniques, and outputs.

*Table 4-8.*   *Control Schedule Process*

| Inputs ⇨ | Tools and Techniques ⇨ | Outputs |
|---|---|---|
| • Project management plan<br>• Project schedule<br>• Work performance data<br>• Project calendars<br>• Schedule data<br>• Organizational process assets | • Performance reviews<br>• Project management software<br>• Resource optimization techniques<br>• Modeling techniques<br>• Leads and lags<br>• Schedule compression<br>• Scheduling tool | • Work performance information<br>• Schedule forecasts<br>• Change requests<br>• Project management plan updates<br>• Project document updates<br>• Organizational process asset updates |

The Control Schedule process is focused mainly on monitoring any variations between what was planned in terms of individual activity durations and the overall project duration, and what is actually occurring. It is also focused on documenting any requested changes to the project schedule as per the agreed change-control procedure.

The Control Schedule process covers the following monitoring and controlling domain task:

- Task 1: Measure project performance using appropriate tools and techniques, in order to identify and quantify any variances and corrective actions.

# Inputs

The Control Schedule process uses the following inputs.

## Project Management Plan

Obviously, in order to control any process, you need a plan or plans that guide you in determining your particular approach to monitoring and controlling. In this instance, the project management plan contains the plans and documents that are required to control the schedule. Foremost among these are the schedule management plan and the schedule baseline. In addition, your change management plan and other subsidiary plans will be useful in guiding you in this process. The project management plan is an output from the Develop Project Management Plan process.

## Project Schedule

The *project schedule* is an absolutely essential input into the Control Schedule process, because you use this to check for any variance. The project schedule outlines what you had planned to achieve in terms of time progress on the project. Through your efforts of checking this against what is actually happening, you can spot any variances and, as a result, raise any requested changes or corrective or preventive actions. The project schedule is an output from the Develop Schedule process.

## Work Performance Data

*Work performance data* is the information you gather about progress on the activities that have started, what the actual duration is, and the status of any activities considered finished. You use this work performance data as a key input into the Control Schedule process. Work performance data is an output from the Direct and Manage Project Work process.

## Project Calendars

Project calendars, which outline the times that the project will carry out the planned activity, are useful particularly when there is more than one project calendar assigned to different resources being used on the project. Project calendars are an output from the Develop Schedule process.

## Schedule Data

Schedule data is the raw data used to develop the project schedule model and includes the known milestones, activities, activity attributes and, if known, any identified constraints and assumptions. You use the schedule data to measure variance of planned versus actual. The schedule data is an output from the Develop Schedule process.

## Organizational Process Assets

The types of organizational process assets that will be useful as inputs into the Control Schedule process are any existing policies or procedures that the organization has that assist with measuring and reporting on project schedule progress, any manual or automated schedule control tools, and any established reporting templates that can be used.

# Tools and Techniques

The following tools and techniques can be used on the inputs into the Control Schedule process.

## Performance Reviews

*Performance reviews* are the key tool used to control the schedule, because the focus is on analyzing what you had planned to do in terms of project schedule performance and what you are actually doing. Several techniques can be used as part of applying performance reviews. One of these techniques, *trend analysis*, gathers data about your project performance to date and then, by using graphs that extrapolate from this information, what likely future performance will be. Another important tool or technique used for performance reviews is the *critical chain method,* which you also saw used as a tool in the Develop Schedule process. In the Control Schedule process, it is used to continually assess the allocated time buffers against what is actually occurring and to make adjustments as necessary.

# Project Management Software

Given the in-depth nature of variance analysis and its focus on actual versus planned durations and completion of activities, completing the work manually would be tedious and inefficient. This is where the use of project management software is very helpful.

---

## REAL WORLD

One of the key tasks I've always given to project administrators working on my projects is to take responsibility for using the project management software to keep track of both time and cost performance on the project. During one particularly complex project, I had our wonderful project administrator out on site nearly every day, checking what was actually being accomplished and recording this in the project management software against what we had planned to do. We were then able to use the project management software forecasting abilities to get early indicators of where we might end up if we continued at the same pace. This is one of the key benefits of using forecasting. A simple forecast of where you might end up is not a predetermination of the actual outcome; instead, it should be viewed as a warning of what may happen if you continue doing what you have been doing. If the results show that you will end up either over budget or over time, you have plenty of warning to implement strategies to make sure this doesn't happen.

---

# Resource Optimization Techniques

After the project is underway and resources are being used to complete activities, you may want to use resource optimization techniques and either resource leveling or resource smoothing to obtain a more efficient allocation of the resources.

# Modeling Techniques

Modeling techniques are used to forecast different schedule scenarios based on the different possibilities that could happen with the schedule. The most common one is what-if scenario analysis.

The what-if scenario analysis and Monte Carlo analysis are useful mathematical tools for forecasting future outcomes based on performance to date. A what-if scenario analysis uses known probabilities of work done to date and estimated probabilities of potential work paths to be done to calculate the likelihood of all possible scenarios. After this has been completed, you can determine the most likely scenarios and judge their impact, as well as determine the least likely scenarios and their impact. Monte Carlo analysis extrapolates from existing work performance data what likely future outcomes will be.

## Leads and Lags

In the Develop Schedule process, you also saw this tool used. The purpose of this is to be able to adjust leads and lags between activities to more efficiently achieve the expected activity duration and total project duration.

## Schedule Compression

In the process of examining planned versus actual time performance on the project, you may detect that some activities are taking longer than planned, and therefore that they threaten the total project duration. At this point, you may want to consider the application of schedule-compression techniques to shorten the duration of particular activities, a sequence of activities, or the total project. The two most commonly used schedule-compression techniques are crashing, which involves the use of more resources and usually costs more, and fast tracking, which involves the scheduling of activities in parallel that were previously scheduled in sequence.

---

▓ **Exam Tip**    On the exam, if any schedule-compression technique being used involves more cost, you can be certain that it is referring to crashing. Conversely, if the question poses a scenario where you are asked to compress a project schedule but do not have access to any more budget, you will not be able to select crashing as an option.

---

## Scheduling Tool

A scheduling tool is a specific piece of software dedicated to project scheduling only. It is often part of a more robust piece of project management software such as ProjectLibre, Primavera, or Microsoft Project.

---

▓ **Exam Tip**    Did you notice that the last five tools listed in the Control Schedule process are the same as the last five tools listed in the Develop Schedule process, with the exception that the Develop Schedule process uses *applying* leads and lags as a tool, whereas the Control Schedule process uses *adjusting* leads and lags as a tool?

---

# Outputs

The Control Schedule process produces the following outputs.

## Work Performance Information

As a result of investigating how your project is doing in terms of individual activity durations and overall project duration, you will develop work performance information. If you recall, work performance data was used as an input into this process, and with the application of the selected tools and techniques, that data has been refined into work performance information. The work performance information can be presented as schedule variance (SV) and schedule performance index (SPI) values for individual activities and work packages. The work performance information itself goes on to be used as an input into the Monitor and Control Project Work process.

---

■ **Exam Tip**   Work performance data is used to create work performance information, which in turn is used to produce work performance reports.

■ **Note**   Earned value management In Chapter 5, which focuses on cost management, you look in depth at the earned value management system and the associated formula for measuring current progress and forecasting likely future progress on a project. Two of the indicators you learn about are the schedule variance (SV) and schedule performance index (SPI) formulas. Both of these formulas and earned value management analysis focus on assessing current performance in relation to time and are useful for detecting variance from what was planned.

---

## Schedule Forecasts

Schedule forecasts are what you obtain by examining current performance and using this to extrapolate likely future performance. Chapter 5 looks in depth at the earned value management system. In this system, the formulas for calculating *estimate at completion* (EAC) and *estimate to complete* (ETC) are useful in forecasting the schedule. Schedule forecasts go on to be used as inputs into the Monitor and Control Project Work process.

■ **Note**    Estimate at completion As you will read in the next chapter, with its focus on the earned value management system, the estimate at completion (EAC) activity is one formula that can be calculated many ways. There are different formulas that take into account different parameters; if you want to use EAC and take into account the time performance to date, you select one of the formulas that uses the schedule performance index (SPI).

---

| REAL WORLD |
| --- |

Usually, immediately after you inform key stakeholders about how well the project is going to date, the next question they ask is how well it will go in the future. To answer this question, you need to forecast future performance of the project. In relation to the time or cost performance, the best way to forecast future performance is simply to analyze past performance. I have always used earned value management on projects I work on in order to give people an indication— because that is all it is—of the likely future outcomes based on past performance.

## Change Requests

If, during the process of examining actual versus planned performance in relation to project time, you discover any variances, one of your options is to submit a change request as per your documented and approved change-control process. Change requests go on to be used as inputs into the Perform Integrated Change Control process in the Integration Management knowledge area.

## Project Management Plan Updates

If, as a result of monitoring and controlling the project schedule, you do discover any variances, you may choose to update specific elements of the project management plan. Of these, the most common updates will be to the schedule management plan and the schedule baseline. Given the integrated nature of project management, though, any changes to the project schedule may also result in changes to the project cost baseline, project risks, project quality, and elements of the project scope. Project management plan updates are used in turn as inputs into the Develop Project Plan process.

# Project Document Updates

In addition to elements of the project management plan and its subsidiary plans, specific project documents may be updated as a result of information gathered during the Control Schedule process. You may want to update the project schedule data and, as a result, the project schedule.

## Organizational Process Asset Updates

Specific organizational process assets that may be updated as a result of the Control Schedule process are historical information, lessons learned, records of corrective actions, and updates to any organizational templates and policies in order to ensure that they are still relevant.

**Quick Check**

1.  What is the key focus of variance analysis tools and techniques used in the Control Schedule process?

2.  What is the relationship between work performance data and work performance information?

3.  What is the key earned value management formula used for schedule forecasts?

**Quick Check Answers**

1.  The focus of variance analysis tools and techniques used in the Control Schedule process is to look at what you had planned to achieve against what you are actually achieving and determine if there is a variance between the two.

2.  Work performance data is the raw data gathered that is filtered to become useful work performance information.

3.  The key earned value management formula used for schedule forecasts is the estimate at completion (EAC) formula when it incorporates the schedule performance index (SPI) into its calculation.

# Chapter Summary

- The Time Management knowledge area is focused on the development and checking of the project schedule.

- As with all the other knowledge areas, the Time Management knowledge area begins with an initial planning process, which in this instance produces the schedule management plan. The schedule management plan sets out how you will go about completing the planning, execution, and control of the project schedule.

- There is then a five-step iterative process that culminates in the development of a project schedule.

- The first of these five steps is to define the activities, which are a further level of decomposition of already-identified work packages from the Scope Management knowledge area.

- After the activities have been identified and documented in the Define Activities process, they can then be put in sequence with the relationships between the activities clearly identified and defined. This Sequence Activities process constitutes the beginning of the development of the schedule network diagram.

- The Estimate Activity Resources process then seeks to provide an estimate of the type and quantities of material, people, equipment, or supplies that will be required to complete each of the activities.

- After an estimate of the type and quantities of resources for each activity has been prepared, an estimate of the duration of each activity can then be completed. This is the main focus of the Estimate Activity Durations process.

- The Develop Schedule process takes the information from the previous four planning processes and combines it into the project schedule. Because it is a highly iterative process and subject to rolling-wave planning, it may focus more on the immediate future and leave further detail to be defined as the project progresses.

- After the planning activities have been completed and project execution is underway, the Control Schedule process seeks to monitor the schedule status of the project and what was planned against what is actually occurring by using the schedule baseline. Any variances from what was planned can be dealt with in a change request, corrective action, or preventive action recommendation.

# Exercises

The answers for these exercises are located in the "Answers" section at the end of this chapter.

1. Based on the information in the following table, complete a network diagram showing the project duration, and calculate the critical path or paths.

| Activity ID | Duration (Days) | Predecessor |
|---|---|---|
| A | 4 | - |
| B | 3 | A |
| C | 6 | A, B |
| D | 5 | B |
| E | 3 | C, D |
| F | 7 | D |
| G | 2 | D, E |
| H | 9 | F, G |

2. Using three-point estimating, what is the expected mean, standard deviation, and variance for each of the following scenarios?

| Optimistic | Most Likely | Pessimistic |
|---|---|---|
| 6 | 8 | 12 |
| 3 | 10 | 15 |
| 12 | 14 | 18 |
| 27 | 35 | 48 |

3. You have been asked by your project sponsor to provide a date range for which you are 99.7% certain the project will be delivered, with an optimistic duration of 35 days, a most likely duration of 45 days, and a pessimistic duration of 60 days. What is your answer to your project sponsor?

4. Match the estimating technique on the left with the appropriate description on the right.

| 1. Analogous estimating | a. An estimating technique that multiplies a known quantity by a known metric |
| 2. Parametric estimating | b. An estimating technique that takes the weighted average of the optimistic, most likely, and pessimistic estimates |
| 3. Bottom-up estimating | c. An estimating technique that gathers information from experts anonymously |
| 4. Delphi technique | d. An estimating technique using information from a similar activity |
| 5. Three-point estimating | e. An estimating technique that takes low-level detailed estimates and aggregates them |

# Review Questions

Test your knowledge of the information in Chapter 4 by answering these questions. The answers to these questions, and the explanation of why each answer choice is correct or incorrect, are located in the "Answers" section at the end of this chapter.

1.  What is the correct order of processes in the Time Management knowledge area?

    A.  Define Activities, Sequence Activities, Estimate Activity Resources, Estimate Activity Durations, Develop Schedule

    B.  Define Activities, Sequence Activities, Estimate Activity Durations, Estimate Activity Resources, Develop Schedule

    C.  Sequence Activities, Define Activities, Estimate Activity Resources, Estimate Activity Durations, Develop Schedule

    D.  Sequence Activities, Define Activities, Estimate Activity Durations, Estimate Activity Resources, Develop Schedule

2.  What is the document that provides additional information about activities identified on the activity list?

    A.  Project charter

    B.  Activity attributes

    C.  Resource breakdown structure

    D.  Scope statement

3.  What is the *best* definition of rolling-wave planning?

    A.  It is the breakdown of work packages into activities.

    B.  It is a form of progressive elaboration that focuses on defining work in the immediate future in more detail than work further off.

    C.  It is the process of first defining, then sequencing, then estimating durations in the preparation of the project schedule.

    D.  It is the process of comparing actual progress against planned progress.

4.  What is the name of the document that guides the definition, documentation, execution, and control of the project schedule?

    A.  Project management plan

    B.  Scope statement

    C.  Organizational process assets

    D.  Schedule management plan

5.  Why are activity resources generally estimated before activity durations?

    A.  Because that is the way the PMBOK Guide sets them out.

    B.  Because in order to estimate activity durations, you must know what sequence they occur in.

    C.  Because you need to know how many resources are available to complete an activity. This will affect how fast the activity can be completed.

    D.  They don't—it's better to estimate activity durations first, then estimate activity resources.

6.  What is the form of estimating that uses known quantities and multiplies them by known metrics?

    A.  Analogous estimating

    B.  Parametric estimating

    C.  Three-point estimating

    D.  The Delphi technique

7. You are obtaining information from a group of experts about your project durations, and each expert is being asked individually for their opinion without knowing who else is being interviewed. What sort of estimating technique are you using?

    A.  Alternatives analysis

    B.  Parametric estimating

    C.  Three-point estimating

    D.  The Delphi technique

8. Which of the following estimating techniques is part of the PERT technique?

    A.  Analogous estimating

    B.  Parametric estimating

    C.  Three-point estimating

    D.  Bottom–up estimating

9. If a successor activity cannot start until its predecessor activity has started, what sort of relationship is this?

    A.  Finish-to-start

    B.  Start-to-start

    C.  Finish-to-finish

    D.  Start-to-finish

10. What is the name of the process of considering whether an additional amount of time should be provided based on quantitative risk analysis?

    A.  Expert judgment

    B.  Parametric estimating

    C.  Reserves analysis

    D.  Monte Carlo analysis

11. The path, or paths, through a project schedule network that represent the most risk because there is no total float is called what?

    A.  Critical chain

    B.  Network diagram

    C.  Gantt chart

    D.  Critical path

12. If you are compressing the project schedule by using a technique that generally does not increase project costs, which of the following techniques are you using?

    A. Fast tracking

    B. Crashing

    C. Resource optimization

    D. Resource leveling

13. The amount of time a successor activity must wait after the completion of its predecessor activity is known as what?

    A. Lead

    B. Resource leveling

    C. Lag

    D. Float

# Answers

This section contains the answers for the Exercises and Review Questions in this chapter.

## Exercises

1. Based on the information in the following table, complete a network diagram showing the project duration, and calculate the critical path or paths.

| Activity ID | Duration (Days) | Predecessor |
|-------------|-----------------|-------------|
| A | 4 | - |
| B | 3 | A |
| C | 6 | A, B |
| D | 5 | B |
| E | 3 | C, D |
| F | 7 | D |
| G | 2 | D, E |
| H | 9 | F, G |

The project duration is 28 days.
The critical path is A-B-D-F-H.
The completed network diagram is shown in Figure 4-17.

***Figure 4-17.*** *A completed activity-on-node (AON) diagram*

2. Using three-point estimating, what is the expected mean, standard deviation, and variance of each of the following scenarios?

| Optimistic | Most Likely | Pessimistic | Meann | Standard Deviation | Variance |
|---|---|---|---|---|---|
| 6 | 8 | 12 | 8.33 days | 1 | 1 |
| 3 | 10 | 15 | 9.67 days | 2 | 4 |
| 12 | 14 | 18 | 14.33 days | 1 | 1 |
| 27 | 35 | 48 | 35.83 days | 3.5 | 12.25 |

3. You have been asked by your project sponsor to provide a date range for which you are 99.7% certain the project will be delivered, with an optimistic duration of 35 days, a pessimistic duration of 60 days, and a calculated mean of 45 days. What is your answer to your project sponsor?

To calculate the answer, first determine the standard deviation:

$$= \frac{60-35}{6}$$

$$= \frac{25}{6}$$

$$= 4.17$$

The question is asking for 99.7% certainty, which is three standard deviations either side of the mean, so multiply the standard deviation by 3:

$$4.17 \times 3 = 12.51$$

Therefore, the answer is $45 \pm 12.51$ or 32.49 – 57.21 days.

Match the estimating technique on the left with the appropriate description on the right.

| | |
|---|---|
| 1. Analogous estimating | d. An estimating technique using information from a similar activity |
| 2. Parametric estimating | a. An estimating technique that multiplies a known quantity by a known metric |
| 3. Bottom-up estimating | e. An estimating technique that takes low-level detailed estimates and aggregates them |
| 4. Delphi technique | c. An estimating technique that gathers information from experts anonymously |
| 5. Three-point estimating | b. An estimating technique that takes the weighted average of the optimistic, most likely, and pessimistic estimates |

# Review Questions

1. **Correct Answer: A**

   A. **Correct**: First define activities, then sequence them, then estimate resources prior to estimating durations, then develop the schedule.

   B. **Incorrect**: Estimate Activity Durations generally occurs after Estimate Activity Resources.

   C. **Incorrect**: Sequence Activities occurs after Define Activities.

   D. **Incorrect**: Sequence Activities occurs after Define Activities.

2. **Correct Answer: B**

   A. **Incorrect:** The project charter contains high-level information.

   B. **Correct**: The activity attributes document provides additional detail about identified activities.

   C. **Incorrect**: The resource breakdown structure provides a breakdown of categories and types of resources required on the project.

   D. **Incorrect**: The scope statement describes all the work to be done on the project.

3. **Correct Answer: B**

   A. **Incorrect:** The breakdown of work packages into activities is the process of decomposition.

   B. **Correct:** It is a form of progressive elaboration that focuses on defining work in the immediate future in more detail than work further off.

   C. **Incorrect**: The process of first defining, then sequencing, then estimating durations in the preparation of the project schedule broadly outlines the Time Management processes.

   D. **Incorrect**: The process of comparing actual progress against planned progress is variance analysis.

4. **Correct Answer: D**

   A. **Incorrect:** The project management plan is the overall plan containing many subsidiary plans and documents.

   B. **Incorrect:** The scope statement defines the work to be done on the project.

   C. **Incorrect**: The organizational process assets are process polices, templates, and methodologies the wider organization owns that can assist project management.

   D. **Correct**: The schedule management plan defines how the project schedule will be developed, executed, and controlled.

5.  **Correct: C**

    A.  **Incorrect:** The PMBOK Guide is not prescriptive.

    B.  **Incorrect:** This answer links two processes that are separated by the Estimate Activity Resources process.

    C.  **Correct**: You need to know how many resources are available to complete an activity because this will affect how fast the activity can be completed.

    D.  **Incorrect**: Generally, it's better to estimate activity resources first, then estimate activity durations.

6.  **Correct: B**

    A.  **Incorrect:** Analogous estimating uses a similar activity to estimate the resources or duration of a current activity.

    B.  **Correct:** Parametric estimating uses known quantities and multiplies them by known metrics.

    C.  **Incorrect**: Three-point estimating uses a weighted average of an optimistic, most likely, and pessimistic estimate.

    D.  **Incorrect**: The Delphi technique solicits information from experts anonymously.

7.  **Correct: D**

    A.  **Incorrect:** Alternatives analysis considers a range of alternative approaches in order to determine the most appropriate one.

    B.  **Incorrect:** Parametric estimating uses known quantities and multiplies them by known metrics.

    C.  **Incorrect**: Three-point estimating uses a weighted average of an optimistic, most likely, and pessimistic estimate.

    D.  **Correct**: The Delphi technique solicits information from experts anonymously.

8. **Correct: C**

   A. **Incorrect:** Analogous estimating uses a similar activity to estimate the resources or duration of a current activity.

   B. **Incorrect:** Parametric estimating uses known quantities and multiplies them by known metrics.

   C. **Correct**: Three-point estimating uses a weighted average of an optimistic, most likely, and pessimistic estimate and is part of the Program Evaluation and Review Technique (PERT).

   D. **Incorrect**: Bottom-up estimating aggregates low-level estimates and rolls them up to obtain higher-level estimates.

9. **Correct: B**

   A. **Incorrect:** A finish-to-start relationship means the successor cannot start until the predecessor finishes.

   B. **Correct:** A start-to-start relationship means a successor activity cannot start until its predecessor activity has started.

   C. **Incorrect**: A finish-to-finish relationship means the successor cannot finish until the predecessor finishes.

   D. **Incorrect**: A start-to-finish relationship means the successor cannot finish until the predecessor starts.

10. **Correct: C**

   A. **Incorrect:** Expert judgment is a technique for getting information from acknowledged experts.

   B. **Incorrect:** Parametric estimating uses known quantities and multiplies them by known metrics.

   C. **Correct**: Reserves analysis considers whether an additional amount of time should be provided based on quantitative risk analysis.

   D. **Incorrect**: Monte Carlo analysis uses sophisticated mathematical modeling to forecast future states from observed data.

11. **Correct: D**

   A. **Incorrect:** The critical chain method places time buffers around high-risk activities to mitigate any potential adverse impact on the project duration.

   B. **Incorrect:** The network diagram is a graphical representation of the project activities and the relationship between them.

   C. **Incorrect**: The Gantt chart is a graphical representation of the project schedule.

   D. **Correct**: The critical path is the path, or paths, through a project schedule network that represent the most risk because there is no total float.

12. **Correct: A**

   A. **Correct:** Fast tracking schedules activities in parallel that would normally be done in sequence.

   B. **Incorrect**: Crashing adds more resources to an activity to shorten its duration, but it usually costs money.

   C. **Incorrect**: Resource optimization is a technique of making the most efficient use of resources on a project.

   D. **Incorrect**: Resource leveling is a type of resource optimization.

13. **Correct: C**

   A. **Incorrect:** The lead is the amount of time a successor can start before completion of the predecessor activity.

   B. **Incorrect:** Resource leveling is a type of resource optimization.

   C. **Correct**: The lag is the amount of time a successor activity must wait after the completion of its predecessor activity.

   D. **Incorrect**: The float is the amount of time an activity can be delayed before it has an impact on successor activities or the total project duration.

# CHAPTER 5

# Cost Management

This chapter focuses on project cost management. Project cost management, like the other knowledge areas, begins with a process of planning that produces a cost management plan. Then there is an iterative process that produces and updates the cost estimates and cost baseline. After these have been developed, a monitoring and controlling process is used to measure actual versus planned cost performance and to manage any change requests.

You may need to pay particular attention in this chapter to the activities involved in calculating earned value management, because there is quite a bit of technical information you need to learn.

**The PMBOK® Guide Processes**
**Project Cost Management Knowledge Area**
The four processes in the Project Cost Management knowledge area are as follows:

- Plan Cost Management (planning process)

- Estimate Costs (planning process)

- Determine Budget (planning process)

- Control Costs (monitoring and controlling process)

## What Is Project Cost Management?

Project cost management is focused on the processes of developing a cost management plan, the processes of estimating costs for activities and the overall project, preparing your project budget or cost baseline, recording performance, and influencing and assessing any changes to the project budget.

---

**Exam Tip** Although presented as discrete processes, the two processes of estimating costs and determining budget are usually done concurrently.

---

The processes contained in this knowledge area present a logical and sequential flow of information from estimating costs through controlling changes to your project budget. Figure 5-1 shows the general flow through this linear process without the general initial Plan Cost Management process.

**Figure 5-1.** *The project cost baseline development process flow*

---

# REAL WORLD

I have always found that developing the project cost estimates and the approved cost budget is one of the most iterative parts of project management. You start out with high-level estimates based on incomplete information and constantly revise and refine both the information you have and the estimates based on the information. When you check how progress is going, you may need to revisit your estimates and revise individual cost estimates. Because of this iterative nature and the high expectations of stakeholders regarding project costs, I pay extra attention to the cost management processes.

# Plan Cost Management

▓ **More Info**   Plan Cost Management

You can read more about the Plan Cost Management process in the PMBOK Guide, 5th edition, in Chapter 7, section 7.1. Table 5-1 identifies the process inputs, tools and techniques, and outputs.

*Table 5-1.* *Plan Cost Management Process*

| Inputs ⇨ | Tools and Techniques ⇨ | Outputs |
|---|---|---|
| • Project management plan<br>• Project charter<br>• Enterprise environmental factors<br>• Organizational process assets | • Expert judgment<br>• Analytical techniques<br>• Meetings | • Cost management plan |

---

▓ **Exam Tip**    Did you notice that the inputs, tools, and techniques for the Plan Cost Management process are identical to the inputs, tools, and techniques for the Plan Schedule Management process? The only difference between the two processes is the single output.

---

The Plan Cost Management process is a planning process with a single output: the cost management plan. Like all other planning documents, the cost management plan guides your efforts in defining and controlling the project budget. It forms a subsidiary plan to the overall project management plan.

The Plan Cost Management process covers the following planning domain task:

- Task 3: Develop the cost management plan based on the project scope, schedule, resources, approved project charter and other information, using estimating techniques, in order to manage project costs.

# Inputs

The Plan Cost Management process uses some or all of the following inputs as part of the development of the cost management plan for the project.

## Project Management Plan

The distinct elements of the project management plan that are useful in developing your own cost management plan are the scope and schedule information contained in the scope baseline and schedule baseline, respectively. After it is created, the cost management plan becomes part of the project management plan. The project management plan is an output from the Develop Project Management Plan process.

## Project Charter

The project charter contains the approved initial budget for the project at the time of project initiation. It also contains known constraints, assumptions, and risks that may affect project costs and their management. The project charter is an output from the Develop Project Charter process.

## Enterprise Environmental Factors

Particular enterprise environmental factors that may assist with development of your cost management plan include the particular organizational culture and structure, any external market conditions that may affect project costs, and any published commercially available cost information that you may use to develop and check your cost estimates.

## Organizational Process Assets

Organizational process assets that may play an important part in the development of your cost management plan include any historical information and any established financial control procedures, policies, and templates for defining and controlling project costs and budget.

---

▓ **Exam Tip**    It is important to note that in your day-to-day work you may use the terms *cost* and *budget* interchangeably. However, for the purposes of this exam, you must understand that the two words have separate meanings. *Cost* refers to the actual costs of each activity or work package, which, when aggregated, form a total project cost. *Budget*, on the other hand, refers to costs over time.

---

## REAL WORLD

One way to keep your accounts people very happy is to be proactive with the development of your project budget. If you are able to tell them clearly when you expect to spend money and when you expect to have money come in, they can better plan the organization's cash flow requirements. It is important to realize that as a project manager, your project may impose serious cash flow problems on the wider organization, and the accounts people have to figure out how to make sure money is available when you need it. I have always found that giving the accounts people information early and often about when I plan to use money is a great way to manage this particular group of stakeholders.

# Tools and Techniques

The following tools and techniques are available to be used to develop the inputs into this process in order to produce the cost management plan.

# Expert Judgment

Expert judgment is used as a tool and technique in the Plan Cost Management process as again you rely on the experience, opinion, and expertise of individuals to assist with the development of a cost management plan. The experts you consult may be members of your project team, other employees in your organization, or people from outside your organization with particular experience in putting together an appropriate cost management plan.

# Analytical Techniques

Analytical techniques are an important tool in the development of your cost management plan because you or your financial department must analyze options and make decisions about how the project will be funded. You may be able to fund the project with cash reserves, bank loans, funding with equity from shareholders, or funding with debt from other sources. Each of these options has its own benefits and drawbacks. In making the decision, you can use a number of techniques such as payback period, return on investment, internal rate of return, discounted cash flow, and net present value. Each of these terms was discussed in more detail in the Develop Project Charter process as part of the project selection process.

---

## REAL WORLD

I have found that many project managers are completely oblivious to how the project is going to be funded. I believe an important skill that any project manager should have is an understanding of project financing methods and the implications of different finance sources for project costs. One of the first places to look for guidance about funding criteria and sources of potential funding is the project charter.

---

# Meetings

Meetings are a great way to bring together members of the project team who have expertise and skill in development of the cost management plan, because they are the people completing the work. You may also choose to invite selected stakeholders from outside the project team who have specialist knowledge and skills in this particular area. An example would be inviting members of your organization's financial or accounts department to contribute to the development of the cost management plan.

# Outputs

After the appropriate tools and techniques have been applied to the selected inputs, the Plan Cost Management process has the following output.

## Cost Management Plan

The Plan Cost Management process has only a single output: the cost management plan. The *cost management plan* is a subsidiary plan of the project management plan and is used as a guide for the other cost management processes. The purpose of the cost management plan is to provide guidance to the project manager and the project team on how the organization expects costs to be estimated, budgets to be determined, cost performance to be assessed, and any potential changes assessed, documented, and reported on. It also outlines the process of reporting progress in relation to forecast cost versus actual cost for the project and prescribes acceptable tools, techniques, processes, and any other relevant information relating to how costs will be managed on the project.

The cost management plan is then a key input into the Estimate Costs and Determine Budget processes, both of which are planning processes.

### Quick Check

1.  What is the main purpose of the cost management plan?

2.  What is the main reason for using analytical techniques during the Plan Cost Management process?

3.  What sort of organizational process assets would be useful as inputs into the Plan Cost Management process?

### Quick Check Answers

1.  The main purpose of the cost management plan is to provide guidance on further planning of project costs, estimating costs, developing a project budget, checking planned cost performance against actual cost performance, and managing any potential changes to the cost baseline.

2.  Analytical techniques are used as a tool to help assess the different options, and the pros and cons of each, for funding or financing the project.

3.  The types of organizational process assets that are useful as inputs into the Plan Cost Management process include any existing organizational financial control procedures, blank templates, established processes, gathered historical cost information, and any internal financial databases.

# Estimate Costs

▓ **More Info**   Estimate Costs

You can read more about the Estimate Costs process in the PMBOK Guide, 5th edition, in Chapter 7, section 7.2. Table 5-2 identifies the process inputs, tools and techniques, and outputs.

***Table 5-2.***  *Estimate Costs Process*

| Inputs ⇨ | Tools and Techniques ⇨ | Outputs |
|---|---|---|
| • Cost management plan<br>• Human resource management plan<br>• Scope baseline<br>• Project schedule<br>• Risk register<br>• Enterprise environmental factors<br>• Organizational process assets | • Expert judgment<br>• Analogous estimating<br>• Parametric estimating<br>• Bottom-up estimating<br>• Three-point estimating<br>• Reserve analysis<br>• Cost of quality<br>• Project management software<br>• Vendor bid analysis<br>• Group decision-making techniques | • Activity cost estimates<br>• Basis of estimates<br>• Project document updates |

The Estimate Costs process is a planning process that uses the cost management plan for guidance, takes the defined activities and work packages, and assigns a cost estimate for each one using a variety of tools and techniques. In order to easily track which estimates are for which particular work package, you can use the numbering systems from the work breakdown structure (WBS). This is a highly iterative process that is repeated throughout the life of the project.

The Estimate Costs process covers the following planning domain task:

- Task 3: Develop the cost management plan based on the project scope, schedule, resources, approved project charter and other information, using estimating techniques, in order to manage project costs.

In assessing the estimate for each activity, it is important to have a basic understanding of different types of costs that may be estimated.

*Variable costs* are costs that change with the amount of production. The more you produce, the more costs you incur. For example, if you increase the number of homes you are building, you will use more home-building materials. If you use more electricity as a result of greater amounts of work, then your costs will increase.

*Fixed costs* are costs that are fixed no matter how much you produce. For example, the rental you pay for your warehouse storage space is constant whether the warehouse is full or empty. Also, the costs you pay for any consents you require or equipment needed to complete the job are fixed costs.

*Direct costs* are costs attributable directly to the actions of the project. For example, the materials you use on your project are direct costs.

*Indirect costs* are costs that are not incurred directly by the project but that the project may have to account for. For example, the project may have to make provision for paying a share of corporate overheads such as office rental space and shared services. Your cost management plan may contain guidelines on what portion, if any, of indirect costs you must account for in your cost estimates. These are often referred to as *overheads*.

## REAL WORLD

Indirect costs, or overheads, are often overlooked by project managers when preparing their cost estimates. Unless there are clear guidelines from the organization about what portion, if any, of indirect costs the project must account for, many project managers simply do not think about this. Many organizations account for indirect costs in required margins or profits. Hopefully, your organizational process assets include guidance on how you are expected to manage this issue.

*Sunk costs* are costs spent on the project to date that cannot be recovered if the project were to stop. For example, the money you have spent developing code for a new piece of software is a sunk cost if you stop halfway through, because it has no recoverable value. Your cost management plan may contain guidelines on how sunk costs are treated in determining whether to continue on a troubled project.

All estimates are simply your best guess at the future, based on the information available to you. The better the information you have, the better the estimates will be. Thus, there is nearly always an element of uncertainty inherent in any estimate. It is often important to express this range of uncertainty inherent in any estimate. As a rule, the accuracy of cost estimates improves as the project progresses, and your organization may have, as part of its organizational process assets, guidelines on the necessary level of accuracy required before proceeding. Table 5-3 shows the typical description of a variety of estimate ranges.

***Table 5-3.*** *Range of Estimates*

| Estimate Type | Estimate Range |
|---|---|
| Order of magnitude estimate | -50% to +100% |
| Rough order of magnitude estimate | -25% to +75% |
| Conceptual estimate | -30% to +50% |
| Preliminary estimate | -20% to +30% |
| Definitive estimate | -15% to +20% |
| Control estimate | -10% to +15% |

# Inputs

The Estimate Costs process uses some or all of the following seven inputs.

## Cost Management Plan

The cost management plan is obviously a key input into the Estimate Costs process, because it provides the guidance for how you are going to complete this process. Without it, you would not be able to complete the process. The cost management plan is an output from the Develop Cost Management Plan process.

## Human Resource Management Plan

The *human resource management plan* is used as an input into the Estimate Costs process because it contains information about the project staff who will be working on the project and the charge-out rates, remuneration packages, and any other financial rewards to be paid to them. In order to develop the project cost, you need to know this information. The human resource management plan is an output from the Plan Human Resource Management process.

## Scope Baseline

The scope baseline is composed of the project scope statement, the work breakdown structure (WBS), and the WBS dictionary, and it contains a full and detailed description of all the work to be done on the project. By using this information, you can attribute costs to each of the work packages and also the activities taken from the project schedule, and aggregate these costs into a total project cost estimate. The scope baseline is an output from the Create WBS process.

## Project Schedule

The project schedule is an important input into the Estimate Costs process because it gives an indication of when the work packages and activities are to be completed. The sequencing, timing, and duration of distinct project work packages and activities affect the costs. The project schedule is an output from the Develop Project Schedule process, which in itself is the culmination of the other schedule management planning processes.

## Risk Register

The risk register is used as an input into the Estimate Costs process because it contains information around defined and documented uncertainty relating to specific work packages. This uncertainty is captured in the contingency reserve for each activity work package and needs to be taken into account in developing the project cost estimates. The risk register is an output from the Identify Risks process.

## Enterprise Environmental Factors

The specific types of enterprise environmental factors that are useful as inputs into the Estimate Costs process are external market conditions that will affect the prices of products and services being procured for the project, and any published commercially available estimating data.

---

### REAL WORLD

It is worthwhile to carefully subscribe to, and pay for access to, reputable published estimating databases. These databases are usually very accurate sources of information about the costs of particular materials and resources, and they are often separated into regional areas to determine variances at a local level. Many organizations, industry associations, and professional bodies compile these databases and allow access for a fee.

---

## Organizational Process Assets

The specific types of organizational process assets that are useful as inputs into the Estimate Costs process are any relevant templates and processes useful in the development of project cost estimates, including any historical information and lessons learned owned by the organization.

# Tools and Techniques

The following ten tools and techniques are used on the inputs to deliver the process outputs.

# Expert Judgment

The use of experts is an acknowledged tool in the preparation of project cost estimates. The experts, or people working on the project, have intimate knowledge of the work to be done and the likely cost of that work. In addition to project team members with expert judgment on the work to be done, you may also choose to consult external experts, such as those involved in the quantity surveying profession, who can provide expert advice on the expected costs of materials and resources to be used.

# Analogous Estimating

*Analogous estimating* is a quick means of estimating a likely cost for a particular material or resource by comparing your current requirements with the requirements of a previous project you have information on, and then looking at the similarities between the two instances to determine your current estimate. For example, if on a previous project you used a particular amount of concrete and it cost $1,500, and on this project you expect to use twice as much, you would assume that your cost estimate is $3,000, by using analogous estimating. Because you are using an analogy from previous experience, there is a certain degree of expected inaccuracy in this form of estimating.

# Parametric Estimating

*Parametric estimating* is generally considered to be more accurate than analogous estimating because it uses known quantities of materials for resources and multiplies them by known financial rates. For example, you may know that you require 50 hours of work to be done by a business analyst, and that a business analyst costs $80 an hour; therefore, multiplying 50 hours by $80 an hour, you will arrive at a cost estimate of $4,000 by using parametric estimating.

# Bottom-Up Estimating

*Bottom-up estimating* is generally considered to be quite an accurate form of estimating. You take cost estimates from lower-level information—for example, the bottom level of the WBS—and then add up, or roll up, to higher levels and aggregate those costs to report a total cost.

# Three-Point Estimating

You saw the use of three-point estimating in the Estimate Activity Durations process from the Schedule Management knowledge area. Here it is used again as a method of determining an estimate where there is a most likely (cM), an optimistic (cO), and a pessimistic (cP) cost estimate for an activity.

---

---

To get a *simple average,* which is used with a triangular distribution, you take these three figures and add them together and divide by 3. The formula is

$$\frac{cO + cM + cP}{3}$$

However, if you want to get a *weighted average* that gives greater weight to the most likely (cM) figure and is typical of a beta distribution, the formula to use is

$$\frac{\left(cO + (4xcM) + cP\right)}{6}$$

For example, if you have an optimistic cost estimate of $10, a most likely cost estimate of $16, and a pessimistic cost estimate of $25, the weighted average using three-point estimating is $16.50.

You can also calculate the standard deviation, which indicates how far from the average the optimistic and pessimistic figures are. A smaller standard deviation means they are closer to the average than a larger standard deviation. The formula for standard deviation is

$$\frac{cP - Co}{6}$$

For example, using the numbers from the previous example, the standard deviation is $2.50.

After you have determined the standard deviation, you can then express your certainty about a cost estimate range. You express this certainty as a confidence interval, where one standard deviation either side of the mean represents a confidence interval of 68%, two standard deviations either side of the mean gives a confidence interval of 95%, and three standard deviations either side of the mean gives a confidence interval of 99.7%.

For example, using the numbers from the previous example, you could say that you have a 95% certainty that the cost for the activity will be between $11.50 and $21.50.

---

**REAL WORLD**

---

In reality, when you are completing any sort of estimating process in the project, you will use a variety of estimating techniques. The type of estimating technique you choose to use will depend on how much information you have. At the beginning of a project, when information is generally less available, you may choose to use less accurate forms of estimating. As the project progresses and you have more information available, you may choose to use more accurate and time-consuming forms of estimating for work you have greater information about. In relation to rolling-wave planning, you will most likely use more accurate forms of estimating on the work to be done in the immediate future and less accurate forms of estimating on work to be done further off in the future.

## Reserve Analysis

*Reserve analysis* looks at the contingency reserves, or contingency allowances, provided for in the project cost estimates. The contingency reserve is an amount that reflects and allows for identified uncertainty in estimating particular costs. It is commonly known as "accounting for the known unknowns" in any project and is usually calculated during quantitative risk analysis performed as part of the Risk Management knowledge area. For example, you may determine that a particular activity has a 10% chance of experiencing a $1,750 cost overrun, and therefore you allow $175 ($1,750 × 10%) in the contingency reserve. By aggregating, or adding up, all the individual amounts allowed for in the contingency reserve analysis, you arrive at a total contingency reserve for the entire project.

The management reserve for unknown unknowns can also be calculated during risk assessment or by expressing the range of uncertainty in your estimates as a total amount. The management reserve is controlled by senior managers, and the project manager must apply to use it; it is not part of the approved budget.

---

**REAL WORLD**

---

In theory, the contingency reserve should be part of the approved project budget and under the control of the project manager, and the management reserve should be under the control of senior management or members of the steering group. In reality, you may find that your approved budget is just for known costs and that sponsors can sometimes be reluctant to approve reserve budgets, because they view it as endorsing inaccuracy and sloppy estimating practices. My argument is that I prefer to go forward on a "no surprises" basis and release the reserves once the identified uncertainty has been defined or passed.

## Cost of Quality

As part of the preparation of your quality management plan, you need to consider the issue of cost of quality. Any decisions made about what this means to you will affect cost on the project immediately and for the organization after the project is handed over. *Cost of quality* refers to the quality attributes of the project and the product over the life of the product. For example, you may need to take into account the cost of future product returns or warranty claims because of decisions made to manufacture lower quality to lower the project costs.

## Project Management Software

Project management software should be considered essential for any large and complex projects, because trying to collect and aggregate many cost estimates manually is simply not possible.

## Vendor Bid Analysis

The *vendor bid analysis* process is a way of double-checking the bids received from vendors to make sure they are neither overinflated nor underinflated. You can think of vendor bid analysis as your quality check on the prices people are submitting to you.

## Group Decision-Making Techniques

Good cost estimates are prepared by people familiar with the activities being estimated, and when you get a group of these people together, you need effective group decision-making techniques to make sense of the expert opinions supplied. These techniques are also used when estimating elements of the project schedule and include brainstorming, nominal group techniques, and the Delphi technique.

# Outputs

The Estimate Costs process produces some or all of the following outputs.

## Activity Cost Estimates

The *activity cost estimates* are the individual estimates for each activity identified. They are the entire focus of this process and are used to put together your cost baseline. The activity cost estimates are used as an input into the Determine Budget process.

## Basis of Estimates

The *basis of estimates* is a useful document because it outlines the assumptions made, the type of estimating technique used, any known constraints, and an indication of the range of uncertainty and of the confidence level of the final estimates for each activity and, indeed, the entire project. The basis of estimates is used as an input into the Determine Budget process.

▓ **Exam Tip**   Several supporting documents provide additional information to summary documents. For the requirements documentation, you have the requirements traceability matrix. For the WBS, you have the WBS dictionary. For the activity list, you have the activity attributes. For the activity cost estimates, you have the basis of estimates. The summary document and the document containing greater detail are both important to provide a full picture.

## Project Document Updates

The specific project documents that may be updated as a result of estimating costs include such things as the statement of work, which may be updated as a result of the cost estimates, and elements of the risk register that are refined and updated as a result of specific cost estimates.

**Quick Check**

1.   What is the difference between a simple average and a weighted average?

2.   What is the difference between a contingency reserve and a management reserve?

3.   What information does the basis of estimates contain?

**Quick Check Answers**

1.   A simple average divides the most likely (cM), the optimistic (cO), and the pessimistic (cP) cost estimates by 3, whereas a weighted average gives a higher weighting of 4 to the most likely cost estimate and then divides by 6.

2.   A contingency reserve is prepared for the known uncertainty, or known unknowns, on a project and should be under the control of the project manager. A management reserve is prepared for the unknown uncertainty, for unknown unknowns, and is generally under the control of senior management.

3.   The basis of estimates contains information about the assumptions made in preparing cost estimates, the types of estimating techniques used, and the amount of uncertainty in the final activity cost estimates.

# Determine Budget

▓ **More Info**    Determine Budget

You can read more about the Determine Budget process in the PMBOK Guide, 5th edition, in Chapter 7, section 7.3. Table 5-4 identifies the process inputs, tools and techniques, and outputs.

**Table 5-4.** *Determine Budget Process*

| Inputs ⇨ | Tools and Techniques ⇨ | Outputs |
|---|---|---|
| • Cost management plan<br>• Scope baseline<br>• Activity cost estimates<br>• Basis of estimates<br>• Project schedules<br>• Resource calendars<br>• Risk register<br>• Agreements<br>• Organizational process assets | • Cost aggregation<br>• Reserve analysis<br>• Expert judgment<br>• Historical relationships<br>• Funding limit reconciliation | • Cost baseline<br>• Project funding requirements<br>• Project document updates |

The Determine Budget process is a planning process that takes the individual activity cost estimates, aggregates them into a total project cost, and then applies the project schedule to determine the timing of when costs will be incurred in order to develop the project budget, or cost baseline.

The Determine Budget process covers the following planning domain task:

- Task 3: Develop the cost management plan based on the project scope, schedule, resources, approved project charter and other information, using estimating techniques, in order to manage project costs.

# Inputs

The inputs used in this process take the individual cost estimates and aggregate them into the project budget.

## Cost Management Plan

The cost management plan is used as a key input into the Determine Budget process because the cost management plan sets out the processes, policies, rules, and regulations that you will apply in order to determine a project budget. The cost management plan is an output from the Plan Cost Management process.

## Scope Baseline

The scope baseline is a very important input into this process because it outlines all the work to be done, and the work not to be done, as part of the project. By breaking down the scope baseline into its component parts via the WBS and subsequently down to activity level with the schedule of work, you can estimate individual activity costs. The scope baseline consists of the project scope statement, the WBS, and the WBS dictionary, and it is an output from the Create WBS process.

## Activity Cost Estimates

The activity cost estimates provide you with individual estimates of cost for identified activities by using a variety of tools and techniques from the Estimate Costs process. In order to put together your project budget, you take these individual activity estimates, aggregate them, and determine the time period in which those costs will be incurred. The activity cost estimates are an output from the Estimate Costs process.

## Basis of Estimates

The basis of estimates is an important input because it provides further information about each of the estimates you have determined for the individual activities. The basis of estimates is an output from the Estimate Costs process.

## Project Schedule

The project schedule is used as an input into the Determine Budget process because you need to know when each activity will be performed so that you can determine when the costs of activity will be incurred. This is the essence of developing a project budget: taking the project costs and applying them over time. The project schedule is an output from the Develop Schedule process.

## Resource Calendars

Resource calendars are used as an input into the Determine Budget process because they provide additional and more detailed information about when specific resources are available to work on the project. They are an output from the Acquire Project Team process.

## Risk Register

The risk register is used as an input into this process because it identifies risks associated with both individual activity cost estimates and elements of the project schedule that need to be taken into account when developing the project budget. It is an output from the Identify Risks process.

## Agreements

Any existing agreements are used by the project manager as an input into this process because they outline any agreement between parties to the project about costs, payments, and any other matters, such as retention payments, that need to be included in the project budget. For example, you may have an agreement for paying suppliers that requires payment regularly each month, or one that requires progress payments at certain project milestones. These agreements are an output from the Conduct Procurements process.

## Organizational Process Assets

The specific organizational process assets that can assist in the development of the project budget include any organizational policies and procedures relating to the development and presentation of the project budget, and any blank templates for preparing budgets and for reporting the budget.

# Tools and Techniques

The five tools and techniques of this process are all used on the separate inputs to deliver the process outputs.

## Cost Aggregation

*Cost aggregation* is the process of taking the individual estimates for each of the activities, aggregating upward to the work package level, and then rolling these estimates up to high-level, sub-deliverable level, and deliverable level to arrive at a bottom-up estimate for portions of the project or the entire project. Figure 5-2 shows how individual activities are added up, or aggregated.

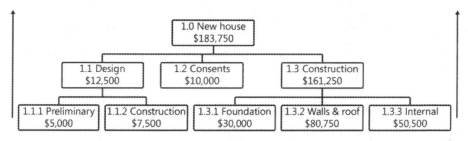

*Figure 5-2.* *An example of bottom-up cost aggregation*

# Reserve Analysis

*Reserve analysis* is a method of looking at both the contingency reserve and the management reserve required for the project and the timing of access to those reserves. Contingency reserves are identified for specific uncertain activities, or known unknowns; access to the contingency reserve will be when the activity is being performed. The contingency reserve is approved as part of the project budget and is under the control of the project manager.

Access to the management reserve, which is for unknown unknowns, could be required at any time in the project. Use of the management reserve requires approval from management; once approved, it is added to the cost baseline.

# Expert Judgment

Again, expert judgment is a key tool and technique in determining the budget. The experts should be from the project team and also from outside the project team: for example, from the organization's finance or accounts department.

# Historical Relationships

If the organization is mature enough to have been recording information about historical relationships and the reliability and range of uncertainty in its cost estimating process, it can use this information to further refine its current cost estimates or to acknowledge a quantifiable amount of uncertainty in those estimates.

# Funding Limit Reconciliation

As part of the Determine Budget process, you may find that there are *funding limit reconciliation* issues that need to be considered. For example, you may want to do more work but simply will not have the funds until a later time; therefore, you have to limit the activity on the project until funds to complete the work become available.

---

## REAL WORLD

It is important that you are able to determine how the project will be funded early on, and whether this funding process imposes any constraints on your project schedule. I have often found that there are constraints on when funds will be available, which is generally related to the financial years into which the funds are allocated. This is why the finance department of an organization is so interested in how much of your project budget you are spending, how much you are carrying over to the next financial year, and how much you want to bring forward into this financial year. You may not realize that someone has to find the finances to complete not only your project but all other projects the organization is completing.

---

# Outputs

The major outputs from the Determine Budget process are the following.

## Cost Baseline

The *cost baseline* is one of four baselines you will use to measure progress on the project. The other three are the scope baseline, the time baseline, and the quality baseline. The key element of the cost baseline is that it takes the aggregated individual estimates of cost for each activity and applies them to the time periods in which the costs will be accrued. This is the baseline against which you will measure project cost performance. Figure 5-3 shows an example of a cost baseline represented graphically. It shows the total amount of spend for each time period, in this case in months. Additionally, it shows the cumulative spend over the life of the project. This is represented by the line, which is often referred to as the *S-curve* because it is in the shape of the letter *S*. There is little spend at the beginning of a project, a lot of spend in the middle section of the project, and a decrease in spending toward the end of the project.

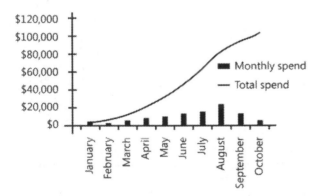

***Figure 5-3.*** *An example of a cost baseline*

---

▓ **Exam Tip**   Individual contingency reserve figures are added to the individual activity cost estimates. These are then aggregated and rolled up to work-package level, with the aggregated contingency reserve applied against individual work packages. The management reserve is added to the total cost baseline once management has approved its use. The only way you can use funds from the management reserve is to obtain approval by the documented and approved change-control process.

---

# Project Funding Requirements

The *project funding requirements* acknowledge when the funding for the project will be available: for example, annually, quarterly, or monthly. This recognizes that funding for a project often occurs in incremental amounts, whereas expenditure on a project may be continuous.

---

## REAL WORLD

Matching when funds will be available against when money will be spent is an important aspect of sound and prudent financial management for the project. You do not want to be in a situation where you have spent more than your ability to pay, because this may mean delays in paying creditors and ultimately delays to the project.

---

# Project Document Updates

The types of project documents that may be updated as a result of the Determine Budget process are the individual cost estimates, project schedule, and risk register.

### Quick Check

1. Why is the project schedule an important input into the Determine Budget process?

2. How would you describe cost aggregation?

3. Why are funding limit reconciliations and the project funding requirements important aspects of any project cost baseline?

### Quick Check Answers

1. The project schedule allows you to view the time period in which the project activities will be performed and their costs incurred.

2. Cost aggregation is the process of adding up individual activity cost estimates up to the work-package level, then the sub-deliverable level, and then the deliverable level.

3. Both the technique of funding limit reconciliation and the output of project funding requirements recognize that funds for the project may be incremental, whereas spending may be continuous, and therefore sometimes there are not enough funds to pay accrued expenses.

# Control Costs

⬛ **More Info**  Control Costs

You can read more about the Control Costs process in the PMBOK Guide, 5th edition, in Chapter 7, section 7.4. Table 5-5 identifies the process inputs, tools and techniques, and outputs.

***Table 5-5.***  *Control Costs Process*

| Inputs ⇨ | Tools and Techniques ⇨ | Outputs |
|---|---|---|
| • Project management plan<br>• Project funding requirements<br>• Work performance data<br>• Organizational process assets | • Earned value management<br>• Forecasting<br>• To-complete performance index (TCPI)<br>• Performance reviews<br>• Project management software<br>• Reserve analysis | • Work performance information<br>• Cost forecasts<br>• Change requests<br>• Project management plan updates<br>• Project document updates<br>• Organizational process asset updates |

⬛ **Exam Tip**  Did you notice that the outputs from the Control Costs process are the same as the outputs from the Control Schedule process, with the exception of the cost forecasts instead of schedule forecasts?

The Control Costs process is focused mainly on measuring actual against planned cost performance, forecasting likely future cost performance, and managing any changes to the cost baseline. The Control Costs process covers the following monitoring and controlling domain task:

- Task 1: Measure project performance using appropriate tools and techniques, in order to identify and quantify any variances and corrective actions.

# Inputs

The Control Costs process uses the following inputs.

## Project Management Plan

The project management plan and its subsidiary plans guide you in the process of controlling any potential changes to your cost baseline or any of the individual estimates that were prepared. As such, it is an important input into the Control Costs process. The project management plan is an output from the Develop Project Management Plan process.

## Project Funding Requirements

The project funding requirements are an important input into the Control Costs process because they enable you to determine when expenditures will be incurred and when funding for the project will be available, and to therefore assess actual versus planned project funding requirements and control any changes to these elements. The project funding requirements are an output from the Determine Budget process.

## Work Performance Data

By now you should have picked up that work performance data is an important input into several controlling processes. Work performance data is the information you gather about what is actually occurring on the project down to the level of which activities have started, the costs associated with completing those activities, and any estimates for completing the remainder of the work to be done. Work performance data is an output from the Direct and Manage Project Work process.

## Organizational Process Assets

The types of organizational process assets that are useful as inputs into the Control Costs process are any existing organizational policies, procedures, templates, or other elements relating to how costs will be monitored and reported on in your project.

# Tools and Techniques

The following tools and techniques can be used on the inputs into the Control Costs process.

## Earned Value Management

The earned value management (EVM) system provides an effective and efficient way of to establish what has occurred in the past and to use this information to forecast likely future scenarios by using a range of mathematical equations. It is better than simply taking one or two elements of past performance and expecting that performance to continue. For example, imagine that you are a project sponsor, and your project manager tells you that the project is 50% of the way through and has spent only 40% of the budget.

Is this a good situation? It may be, but without knowing how much of the actual work has been completed and how much value has been earned, you don't really know if this is a positive statement. This is exactly the scenario that EVM can get around.

EVM takes the original project cost baseline, the planned value of the work you had expected to have completed by now, the earned value of the work you have completed, and the actual cost of delivering that value, to determine the project cost and schedule performance to date and then forecast the likely costs at completion. It does this by using the following formulas:

- *Budget at completion (BAC):* The original forecast budget for the project. The BAC is also the total planned value (PV) for the project.

- *Planned value (PV):* The amount of value you should have earned by this time in the project. Because the total PV for a project equals the BAC, you can determine the PV by simply determining how far through the project you are in relation to time, and mapping this back to the approved cost baseline. Figure 5-4 demonstrates how to determine the PV from the BAC.

**Figure 5-4.** *The project cost baseline showing PV and BAC*

If you do not have a cost baseline from which to read PV, the easiest way to determine PV is to calculate the percentage of time that has been completed and multiply the BAC by this. If you have completed 7 months of a 10-month project and the BAC is $50,000, then your PV is 70% of $50,000, which equals $35,000. Obviously this method assumes a linear spend on the project instead of the S-curve you normally see.

- *Earned value (EV):* The value of the work that has been completed. This is not the actual cost of the work that has been completed but rather the original ascribed value from your approved cost baseline for the value of the work.

- *Actual cost (AC):* The actual realized cost incurred for the work done to date. You can get a record of this from your accounts system.

- Figure 5-5 shows the BAC, PV, EV, and AC on a single graph. Incidentally, it shows a project in trouble in terms of both time and cost: the AC is above the PV, and the EV is less than the PV.

**Figure 5-5.** *A record of project planned value, earned value, and actual cost*

---

▓ **Exam Tip**   On most questions, you will be challenged to extract the BAC, PV, EV, and AC from the scenario given. Take your time to ensure that you are extracting the correct figures.

---

## REAL WORLD

I've often found that when calculating the actual cost, it is important to remove from this calculation the value of any material held in stock. On some projects, you may decide to procure a lot of required materials early to avoid potential cost increases over time. Therefore, you will have paid for these materials, and this shows up in your accounts. However, incorporating this amount into your actual cost figure for the purposes of EVM will skew the results negatively. Therefore, I recommend that you do regular stock takes and remove the value of material held in stock from the actual cost figure you use for the EVM calculations.

- *Cost variance (CV):* The difference between the value of what you expected to have earned (EV) at this point and the AC at this point. A positive CV is good and shows that the project is under budget. A negative CV is bad and shows that the project is over budget. The formula is

  $CV = EV - AC$

- *Cost performance index (CPI):* One limitation of the CV equation is that it gives you a simple gross figure. You can't tell whether a $10,000 CV is significant on your project. If you are working on a $50,000 project, it is significant; if you are working on a $10 million contract, it may not be as significant. The CPI calculation tells you the magnitude of the variance. A CPI of more than 1 is good, because it means the project is under budget; a CPI of less than 1 is bad, because it means the project is over budget. For example, if you have a CPI of 1.1, it means for every dollar you spend on the project, you are getting a $1.10 return. The formula is

  $CPI = EV/AC$

- *Schedule variance (SV):* Tells you whether you are ahead or behind your planned schedule. It is the difference between the EV and the PV. A positive SV is good and means you are ahead of schedule; a negative SV is bad and means you are behind schedule. The formula is

  $SV = EV - PV$

- *Schedule performance index (SPI):* A ratio of the EV and PV that allows you to better determine the magnitude of any variance. An SPI of more than 1 is good, because it means the project is ahead of time; an SPI of less than 1 is bad, because it means the project is behind schedule. For example, if you have an SPI of 0.95, it means every day you spend working on the project, you are getting a 0.95 day return. The formula is

  $SPI = EV/PV$

---

░ **Exam Tip**   A quick and easy way to remember the formula for CV, CPI, SP, and SPI is that each of the formula starts with EV. If it is a formula relating to variance (CV or SV), then the next symbol is a minus sign. If it is a formula relating to a performance index (CPI or SPI), then the next symbol is a division sign. If the formula is in relation to cost (CV or CPI), then the final part of the formula is AC. If the formula is in relation to schedule (SV or SPI), then the final part of the formula is PV.

---

# Forecasting

*Forecasting* is the process of taking time and cost performance to date and using this information to forecast a likely future scenario. The time and cost performance measurements are the cost variance (CV), schedule variance (SV), cost performance index (CPI), and schedule performance index (SPI). You can use these measurements and the following formulas to forecast a likely project cost at completion, the amount of money required to complete the project, and the difference between what you originally thought it would cost and what you now think it will cost:

- *Estimate at completion (EAC):* There are many ways to calculate a forecast EAC. Keep in mind that in order to forecast a likely future cost or time frame for the project, you will be using historical information. Therefore, the quality of your EAC calculation depends entirely on the quality of the historical information you use. The following four formulas use different inputs to calculate the EAC. Each one gives a different answer for the same project.

  *EAC = BAC/CPI:* This is perhaps the simplest of the EAC calculations because it takes your original BAC and divides that by your CPI. Obviously, this is a useful calculation if your cost performance to date is indicative of your likely cost performance going forward; by the same measure, it will not be a great calculation to use if your cost performance to date is not indicative of your cost performance in the future.

  *EAC = AC+ ETC:* Simply adding your ETC to your AC spent to date is an effective way to determine your EAC. However, the method by which you determine your EAC calculation has a significant effect on whether this formula is accurate.

  *EAC = AC + (BAC – EV):* This formula takes the AC spent to date and adds to them the total BAC, subtracting the current EV.

  *EAC = AC + ((BAC – EV)/(CPI × SPI)):* This formula takes into account both your cost performance and your schedule performance and applies them to the value of the work you have left to complete.

---

▓ **Exam Tip** Memorize all these formulas, and as soon as you are allowed to start the exam, write them down.

---

225

■ **Note**    Cumulative vs. Non-Cumulative

When using either the CPI or SPI formula, you can choose whether to use cumulative or non-cumulative variations. The cumulative calculation calculates from the start of the project to where you are now in the project; obviously, if you use this, you are assuming that particular range is indicative and typical of your cost or schedule performance going forward. However, if for some reason you have experienced atypical variances in either time or cost on your project in the past, you may want to avoid using these when you use either CPI or SPI for forecasts. In this case, you should use non-cumulative CPI or SPI calculations taken from a specific period of time you feel is a more accurate representation of likely future performance.

---

## REAL WORLD

When using an EAC formula, as a general rule of thumb, I use the BAC divided by CPI calculation for the first third of the project because the information coming out at this point tends to be less accurate. After I get past the halfway point on a project, I use the AC + ((BAC-EV)/(CPI × SPI)) formula, because it takes into account all parameters and is generally more accurate.

- *Estimate to complete (ETC):* Your forecast of the remaining costs to be incurred on the project. The easiest way to calculate this is to subtract AC spent to date from your EAC. The formula is

  $ETC = EAC - AC$

- *Variance at completion (VAC):* The difference between what you originally thought the project was going to cost (BAC) and what you now think it will cost (EAC). A negative variance is bad, and a positive variance is good. The formula is

  $VAC = BAC - EAC$

▓ **Exam Tip**   There may be occasions when the acronyms used here to outline the EVM system are represented by an older set of four-letter acronyms, as follows:

Planned value (PV) = Budgeted cost of work scheduled (BCWS)

Actual cost (AC) = Actual cost of work performed (ACWP)

Earned value (EV) = Budgeted cost of work performed (BCWP)

▓ **Exam Tip**   On the exam, you will often be presented with a scenario that requires you to work out one set of figures before you can work out another set of figures. For example, you may be required to work out the EAC by using either CPI or SPI but will not be given the CPI figures or SPI figures. You will instead be given figures for EC, AC, and PV, and be expected to work out either the CPI or the SPI first. Also, when looking at a question that requires you to calculate any formula, be on the lookout for irrelevant information, because sometimes not all the information presented in the scenario is relevant.

## To-Complete Performance Index (TCPI)

The *to-complete performance index* (TCPI) tells you the rate at which you have to work to achieve either your EAC or your BAC, depending on which one you are targeting. A TCPI of less than 1 is good, whereas a TCPI of more than 1 is bad. If you are using the original BAC as your target, the formula is

$$TCPI = (BAC - EV) / (BAC - AC)$$

If you are using the EAC as the target, the formula for TCPI is

$$TCPI = (BAC - EV) / (EAC - AC)$$

▓ **Exam Tip**   When doing any calculations on the exam, round your answer to two decimals places, but be prepared for an answer that is slightly different due to minor differences in the approach to rounding of decimal places.

## Performance Reviews

Performance reviews are conducted via a variety of means, including EVM variances and trend analysis. You already have seen the use of EVM variances for the calculation of both the cost variance (CV) and schedule variance (SV) using EVM. These are the most frequently used methods of determining variance and performance.

In addition to EVM variances as a performance review tool, you can use trend analysis, which looks at past performance and extrapolates from that a likely future performance, usually by using graphs and linear regression.

## Project Management Software

Project management software is very useful in monitoring the performance of cost on a project because it can quickly do what would take a lot of time if done manually. Additionally, it can take both the original data and any data from calculations and display it graphically for easy interpretation and communication.

## Reserve Analysis

Reserve analysis in this monitoring and controlling process is the process of re-examining the original reserves calculated—both the contingency and management reserves—and checking whether the assumptions made when calculating them are still valid, and also releasing any unused portions of contingency reserves from the approved project budget in order to enable other projects to access the pool of funds.

# Outputs

The Control Costs process produces the following outputs.

## Work Performance Information

The easiest way to display work performance information based on the work performance data is by using the earned value calculations for CV, SV, CPI, SPI, and the TCPI. The work performance information goes on to be used as an input into the Monitor and Control Project Work process.

## Cost Forecasts

Cost forecasts are obtained from the EAC values. Cost forecasts go on to be used as an input into the Monitor and Control Project Work process.

| REAL WORLD |
| --- |

It is important to emphasize to project stakeholders that any EAC calculation is just that: your estimate about what it will cost to complete the project. When calculating the EAC, you are using historical information to try to forecast a likely future outcome. If project stakeholders consider your EAC figure an absolute amount that you will definitely achieve, this will create unrealistic expectations.

## Change Requests

One of the key outputs from any controlling process is change requests that arise as a result of either variances detected or additional information provided. Change requests may include preventive or corrective actions. All change requests are processed as per your documented and approved change-control process.

Change requests go on to be used as an input into the Perform Integrated Change Control process from the Integration Management knowledge area.

## Project Management Plan Updates

Specific parts of the project management plan that may be updated as a result of the Control Costs process include the cost baseline and the cost management plan. Project management plan updates are used in turn as an input into the Develop Project Plan process.

## Project Document Updates

Specific project documents that may be updated as a result of the Control Costs process include any documentation relating to how you build up your cost estimates, such as the cost baseline and the basis of estimates document.

## Organizational Process Asset Updates

Specific organizational process assets that may be updated as a result of the Control Cost process are historical information, records of financial information kept, lessons learned, records of corrective actions, and updates to any organizational financial templates and policies in order to ensure that they are still relevant.

### Quick Check

1.   What is the difference between work performance data and work performance information?

2.   If a project has a CPI of 1.1 and an SPI of .90, how is it performing in relation to time and cost?

3.   What is the key difference between each of the four formulas for estimate at completion?

### Quick Check Answers

1.   Work performance data is the raw information collected by checking on cost and time performance. Work performance information applies filters to this data to make it useful information.

2.   This project is under budget because the CPI is greater than 1, but behind schedule because the SPI is less than 1.

3.   Each of the four formulas uses different historical information about the project to forecast a likely future outcome.

# Chapter Summary

- The Cost Management knowledge area is focused on the development and checking of project costs and begins with a planning process that produces the cost management plan, which then guides the individual cost estimating process and development of the cost baseline. It also provides guidance on monitoring actual versus planned cost performance and managing any changes to the cost baseline.

- The Plan Cost Management process focuses on the production of the cost management plan, which is a subsidiary plan of the project management plan.

- The Estimate Costs process is a highly iterative process repeated throughout the project that uses a variety of estimating techniques to developed individual activity cost estimates.

- The Determine Budget process aggregates the individual activity cost estimates and determines exactly when the costs will be incurred to produce a time-phased project budget, or cost baseline.

- The Control Costs process assesses planned cost performance against actual cost performance and forecasts a likely future state by using the earned value management systems. Any changes to the project cost baseline or individual activity cost estimates are managed through the approved change-control process.

# Exercises

The answers for these exercises are located in the "Answers" section at the end of this chapter.

1. You are the project manager on a project to build ten identical offices. You expect to spend $50,000 per office to complete the work and take 20 months to finish. You are 12 months into the work and have completed five offices and spent $310,000 in total. Use this information to calculate the following:

     i. Budget at completion (BAC)

     ii. Actual cost (AC)

     iii. Planned value (PV)

     iv. Earned value (EV)

     v. Cost variance (CV)

     vi. Cost performance index (CPI)

     vii. Schedule variance (SV)

     viii. Schedule performance index (SPI)

     ix. Estimate at completion (EAC)

     x. Estimate to complete (ETC)

     xi. Variance at completion (VAC)

     xii. To-complete performance index (TCPI)

   (b) Based on the information gained from the calculations you have performed, how is the project performing in terms of both cost and time?

2. You are the project manager on a project to complete 15 miles of road. Your approved budget for the project is $930,000, and you have forecast that the project will take 35 weeks to complete. You are 13 weeks into the project and have constructed 7 miles of road at a cost of $58,000 per mile. Use this information to calculate the following:

     i. Budget at completion (BAC)

     ii. Actual cost (AC)

     iii. Planned value (PV)

     iv. Earned value (EV)

     v. Cost variance (CV)

     vi. Cost performance index (CPI)

    vii.   Schedule variance (SV)

    viii.   Schedule performance index (SPI)

    ix.   Estimate at completion (EAC)

    x.   Estimate to complete (ETC)

    xi.   Variance at completion (VAC)

    xii.   To-complete performance index (TCPI)

(b) Based on the information gained from the calculations you have performed, how is the project performing in terms of both cost and time?

# Review Questions

Test your knowledge of the information in Chapter 5 by answering these questions. The answers to these questions, and the explanation of why each answer choice is correct or incorrect, are located in the "Answers" section at the end of this chapter.

1.   What is the correct order of processes in the Cost Management knowledge area?

   A.   Plan Cost Management, Estimate Costs, Determine Budget, Control Costs

   B.   Plan Cost Management, Determine Budget, Estimate Costs, Control Costs

   C.   Plan Cost Management, Control Costs, Estimate Costs, Determine Budget

   D.   Plan Cost Management, Estimate Costs, Control Costs, Determine Budget

2.   What is the single output from the Plan Cost Management process?

   A.   Activity cost estimates

   B.   Cost baseline

   C.   Cost management plan

   D.   Cost forecasts

3.   All of the following could be included in the cost management plan *except*?

   A.   A description of the accuracy of estimating

   B.   The cost reporting formats to be used

   C.   A description of the units of measure used to estimate costs

   D.   The dates each activity will occur

4.  If you are estimating the cost for an activity by comparing the current activity with similar ones you have completed in the past, what sort of estimating technique are you using?

    A.  Analogous estimating

    B.  Parametric estimating

    C.  Three-point estimating

    D.  Bottom-up estimating

5.  If you are aggregating the individual activity cost estimates up to the work-package level, then the sub-deliverable level, and then the deliverable level to arrive at a total project cost estimate, what sort of estimating technique are you using?

    A.  Analogous estimating

    B.  Parametric estimating

    C.  Three-point estimating

    D.  Bottom-up estimating

6.  If you are applying to senior management to obtain extra funds for unforeseen costs on your project, what are you using?

    A.  Contingency reserve

    B.  Funding limit reconciliation

    C.  Management reserve

    D.  Cost aggregation

7.  If you have a project with a schedule performance index (SPI) of 1.05 and a cost performance index (CPI) of 0.92, how is your project performing?

    A.  The project is over budget and behind schedule.

    B.  The project is over budget and ahead of schedule.

    C.  The project is under budget and behind schedule.

    D.  The project is under budget and ahead of schedule.

8.  If the budget at completion for your project is $70,000, the earned value is $30,000, and the actual cost is $32,000, what is your estimate at completion?

    A.  $70,000.00

    B.  $65,625.00

    C.  $74,468.08

    D.  $62,000.00

9.    If the budget at completion for your project is $70,000, the
      earned value is $30,000, and the actual cost is $32,000, what is
      your variance at completion?

      A.   $0.00

      B.   $7,375.00

      C.   –$4 468.08

      D.   $8 000.00

10.   If the to-complete performance index calculated for the budget
      at completion for your project is 1.1, what does this mean?

      A.   Your project is doing well, and you can slow down and still
           achieve the budget at completion.

      B.   Your project is right on track to achieve the budget at
           completion.

      C.   You need to produce $1.10 worth of effort for every $1.00 spent
           to achieve the budget at completion.

      D.   You need to speed up the schedule but slow down spending.

11.   Which of the following is an example of work performance
      information?

      A.   Reserve analysis

      B.   Activity cost estimates

      C.   Project funding requirements

      D.   Schedule variance

# Answers

This section contains the answers to the questions for the Exercises and Review
Questions in this chapter.

## Exercises

1.    You are the project manager on a project to build ten identical
      offices. You expect to spend $50,000 per office to complete the
      work and take 20 months to finish. You are 12 months into the
      work and have completed five offices and spent $310,000 in
      total. Use this information to calculate the following:

      i.    Budget at completion (BAC): 10 offices × $50,000 each =
            $500,000

      ii.   Actual cost (AC): You have spent $310,000 in total, so this
            is your actual cost.

iii. Planned value (PV): You are 12 months into a 20-month work program, so you planned to have created value equivalent to 12/20, or 60%, of your total planned value, or budget at completion. Therefore, your planned value (PV) is $500,000 × 60% = $300,000.

iv. Earned value (EV): You have built five offices, each with a value to you of $50,000, so your earned value is 5 × $50,000 = $250,000.

v. Cost variance (CV): CV = EV – AC: $250,000 – $310,000 = –$60,000.

vi. Cost performance index (CPI): CPI = EV/AC: $250,000/$310,000 = 0.81.

vii. Schedule variance (SV): SV = EV – PV: $250,000 – $300,000 = –$50,000.

viii. Schedule performance index (SPI): SPI = EV/PV: $250,000/$300,000 = 0.83.

ix. Estimate at completion (EAC)

   a. EAC= BAC/CPI: $500,000/0.81 = $617,283.95

   b. EAC = AC + ETC: $310,000 + $307,283.95 = $617,283.95

   c. EAC = AC + (BAC – EV): $310,000 + ($500,000 – $250,000) = $560,000

   d. EAC = AC + ((BAC–EV)/(CPI × SPI)): $310,000 + (($500,000 – $250,000)/(0.81 × 0.83)) = $681,857.80

x. Estimate to complete (ETC): This answer depends on which EAC figure you choose to use in the formula ETC = EAC – AC. If you use the EAC from the BAC/CPI formula, the answer is $307,283.95.

xi. Variance at completion (VAC): This answer depends on which EAC you choose to use in the formula VAC = BAC – EAC. If you use the EAC from the BAC/CPI formula, the answer is –$117,283.95.

xii. To-complete performance index (TCPI): This answer depends on whether your target is your BAC or the EAC. If it is the EAC, the answer depends on which formula you use to calculate that. The following example uses BAC/CPI to calculate EAC:

   a. TCPI for EAC = (BAC – EV)/(EAC – AC) = 0.81

   b. TCPI for BAC = (BAC – EV)/(BAC – AC) = 1.31

(b) Based on the information gained from the calculations you have performed, how is the project performing in terms of both cost and time?

Based on the information calculated, the project is over budget because the cost variance (CV) is negative and the cost performance index (CPI) is less than 1. The project is behind schedule, because the schedule variance (SV) is negative and the schedule performance index (SPI) is less than 1.

2. You are the project manager on a project to complete 15 miles of road. Your approved budget for the project is $930,000, and you have forecast that the project will take 35 weeks to complete. You are 13 weeks into the project and have constructed seven miles of road at a cost of $58,000 per mile. Use this information to calculate the following:

   i. Budget at completion (BAC): $930,000

   ii. Actual cost (AC): You have built seven miles of road at a cost of $58,000, so your AC is 7 × $58,000 = $406,000.

   iii. Planned value (PV): You are 13 weeks into a 35-week work program, so you planned to have created value of 13/35, or 37%, of your total planned value, or budget at completion. Therefore, your PV is $930,000 × 37% = $344,100.

   iv. Earned value (EV): You are building 15 miles of road for $930,000, so each mile of road has a value of $930,000/15 = $62,000. You have built seven miles of road each with a value to you of $62,000, so your earned value is 7 × $62,000 = $434,000.

   v. Cost variance (CV): CV = EV – AC: $434,000 – $406,000 = $28,000.

   vi. Cost performance index (CPI): CPI = EV/AC: $434,000/$406,000 = 1.07.

   vii. Schedule variance (SV): SV = EV – PV: $434,000 – $344,100 = $89,900.

   viii. Schedule performance index (SPI): SPI = EV/PV: $434,000/$344,100 = 1.26.

   ix. Estimate at completion (EAC)

     a. EAC= BAC/CPI: $930,000 / 1.07 = $869,158.88

     b. EAC = AC + ETC: $406,000 + $464,158.88 = $870,158.88

     c. EAC = AC + (BAC – EV): $406,000 + ($930,000 – $434,000) = $902,000

     d. EAC = AC + ((BAC – EV)/(CPI × SPI)): $406,000 + (($930,000 – $434,000)/(1.07 × 1.26)) = $773,407.41

x.  Estimate to complete (ETC): This answer depends on which EAC figure you choose to use in the formula ETC = EAC – AC. If you use the EAC from the BAC/CPI formula, the answer is $463,158.88.

xi.  Variance at completion (VAC): This answer depends on which EAC you choose to use in the formula VAC = BAC – EAC. If you use the EAC from the BAC/CPI formula, the answer is $60,841.12.

xii.  To-complete performance index (TCPI): This answer depends on whether your target is your BAC or the EAC. If it is the EAC, the answer depends on which formula you use to calculate that. The following example uses BAC/CPI to calculate EAC:

a.  TCPI for EAC = (BAC – EV)/(EAC – AC) = 1.07

b.  TCPI for BAC = (BAC – EV)/(BAC – AC) = 0.95

(b) Based on the information gained from the calculations you have performed, how is the project performing in terms of both cost and time?

Based on the information from the earned value calculations, the project is ahead of schedule because the schedule variance (SV) is positive and the schedule performance index (SPI) is greater than 1. The project is also under budget, because the cost variance (CV) is positive and the cost performance index (CPI) is greater than 1.

# Chapter Review

1.  **Correct Answer: A**

    A.  **Correct:** First plan your approach to cost management, then estimate costs, then determine your budget, then control the costs.

    B.  **Incorrect:** Estimate Costs occurs before Determine Budget.

    C.  **Incorrect:** Control Costs occurs after Determine Budget.

    D.  **Incorrect:** Control Costs occurs after Determine Budget.

2.  **Correct Answer: C**

    A.  **Incorrect:** Activity cost estimates are an output from the Estimate Costs process.

    B.  **Incorrect:** The cost baseline is an output from the Determine Budget process.

    C.  **Correct:** The cost management plan is the sole output from the Plan Cost Management process.

    D.  **Incorrect:** Cost forecasts are an output from the Control Costs process.

3.  **Correct Answer: D**

    A.  **Incorrect:** A description of the accuracy of estimating would be included in the cost management plan.

    B.  **Incorrect**: A description of the cost reporting formats to be used would be included in the cost management plan.

    C.  **Incorrect**: A description of the units of measure used to estimate costs would be included in the cost management plan.

    D.  **Correct**: The dates each activity will occur would be included as part of your project schedule, not the cost management plan.

4.  **Correct Answer: A**

    A.  **Correct:** Analogous estimating uses similar activities from the past and extrapolates from them a likely current cost estimate.

    B.  **Incorrect**: Parametric estimating multiplies a known quality by a known dollar amount to arrive at a cost estimate.

    C.  **Incorrect**: Three-point estimating takes the weighted average of most likely, optimistic, and pessimistic cost estimates.

    D.  **Incorrect**: Bottom-up estimating aggregates lower-level cost estimates.

5.  **Correct Answer: D**

    A.  **Incorrect:** Analogous estimating uses similar activities from the past and extrapolates from them a likely current cost estimate.

    B.  **Incorrect**: Parametric estimating multiplies a known quality by a known dollar amount to arrive at a cost estimate.

    C.  **Incorrect**: Three-point estimating takes the weighted average of most likely, optimistic, and pessimistic cost estimates.

    D.  **Correct**: Bottom-up estimating aggregates lower-level cost estimates up to higher levels to arrive at a total project cost estimate.

6.  **Correct Answer: C**

    A.  **Incorrect:** The contingency reserve is for known unknowns on the project.

    B.  **Incorrect**: The funding limit reconciliation is an output from the Determine Budget process.

C. **Correct**: The management reserve is available for truly unforeseen costs that arise on a project and is controlled by senior management.

D. **Incorrect**: Cost aggregation is the technique of adding up lower-level costs to obtain higher-level cost estimates.

7. **Correct Answer: B**

A. **Incorrect:** The project would need a CPI less than 1 and an SPI less than 1 to be over budget and behind schedule.

B. **Correct**: A CPI less than 1 and an SPI greater than 1 indicate that the project is over budget and ahead of schedule.

C. **Incorrect**: The project would need a CPI greater than 1 and an SPI less than 1 to be under budget and behind schedule.

D. **Incorrect**: The project would need a CPI greater than 1 and an SPI greater than 1 to be under budget and ahead of schedule.

8. **Correct Answer: C**

A. **Incorrect:** $70,000 is the budget at completion.

B. **Incorrect**: You would arrive at this figure if you reversed the calculation for cost performance index (CPI).

C. **Correct**: If you calculate the cost performance index (CPI) first by dividing the earned value (EV) by the actual cost (AC), then divide the budget at completion (BAC) by the cost performance index (CPI), this is the answer you get.

D. **Incorrect**: This is the answer you get if you add the earned value (EV) to the actual cost (AC).

9. **Correct Answer: C**

A. **Incorrect:** There is a variance at completion, accordingly the formula VAC= BAC – EAC.

B. **Incorrect**: This is the answer you arrive at if you calculate estimate at completion (EAC) incorrectly.

C. **Correct**: Variance at completion (VAC) equals budget at completion (BAC) minus estimate at completion (EAC), which is –$4 468.08.

D. **Incorrect**: If you got this answer, you probably guessed or used the wrong equation.

10. **Correct Answer: C**

   A. **Incorrect:** A to-complete performance index (TCPI) of 1.1 is a bad thing and means you need to work faster or more efficiently to achieve your goal of either budget at completion (BAC) or estimate at completion (EAC).

   B. **Incorrect:** A to-complete performance index (TCPI) of 1.1 shows that the project is not on track.

   C. **Correct**: A to-complete performance index (TCPI) of 1.1 means you have to work harder or more efficiently to achieve the goal of the budget at completion (BAC).

   D. **Incorrect**: A to-complete performance index (TCPI) of 1.1 means you must pay attention to both schedule and spending; but neither one is in a good position, because the index is greater than 1.

11. **Correct Answer: D**

   A. **Incorrect:** Reserve analysis is the process of determining and monitoring contingency and management reserves.

   B. **Incorrect**: Activity cost estimates are an output of the Estimate Costs process.

   C. **Incorrect**: Project funding requirements are an output of the Determine Budget process.

   D. **Correct**: Schedule variance, cost variance, schedule performance index, and cost performance index are all examples of work performance information.

# CHAPTER 6

■ ■ ■

# Quality Management

This chapter focuses on the topic of project quality management. Project Quality Management, like the other knowledge areas, begins with a process of planning that produces a quality management plan. It then has an executing process, Perform Quality Assurance, which is focused on defining and checking the quality of the processes in the project. It also has a monitoring and controlling process, Control Quality, which is focused on defining and inspecting the quality of the project deliverables.

You may need to pay particular attention in this chapter to those activities and the range of different quality tools that are described, because many of them may be new to you.

**The PMBOK® Guide Processes**

**Project Quality Management Knowledge Area**

The three processes in the Project Quality Management knowledge area are as follows:

- Plan Quality Management (planning process)

- Perform Quality Assurance (executing process)

- Control Quality (monitoring and controlling process)

## What Is Project Quality Management?

Project Quality Management is focused on the processes of developing a quality management plan, defining and checking particular processes that affect the entire project, and inspecting the quality of project deliverables. The general process of quality management in the PMBOK Guide is aligned to the International Organization for Standardization (ISO) guide to quality management. Therefore, if you have experience with the standards, you will find this section easier to understand.

Let's start with the formal definition of what *quality* is. It is defined as the degree to which a set of inherent characteristics fulfills requirements. You should remember this definition because it may be different from how you define quality. It has two key elements: the first is a defined set of observed characteristics, which are then measured against the second element, a predefined set of requirements. The closer these two elements are, the higher the level of quality. As a result of defining the characteristics of quality and the requirements that will be met, you are seeking to satisfy customer and

© Sean Whitaker 2016
S. Whitaker, *Pass the PMP® Exam*, DOI 10.1007/978-1-4842-2074-0_6

241

stakeholder expectations. The responsibility for establishing a professional approach to quality management in an organization, and in a project, lies with management.

In addition to the exact definition of quality, there are some basic foundational concepts of quality management that you must be aware of.

A key foundational concept of the approach to quality management is that, generally speaking, it costs less to prevent a mistake than it does to correct a mistake. This concept of prevention over inspection informs much of the approach to quality management. You should always assume that you have the ability to prevent mistakes rather than spend time and money correcting them once they are discovered. In addition to costing time and money to fix mistakes, poor quality may result in the client not accepting the product, and therefore it can also adversely affect your reputation.

You need to be aware that quality management is not something that happens only once; it is ongoing throughout the life of the project, and it is iterative. Not only is quality management highly iterative, like other project management processes, but one of its central elements is the concept of *continuous improvement*, or *kaizen*. Continuous improvement is an iterative process of always seeking to improve your approach to, and results obtained from, quality management processes, and it has the goal of improving the quality of the project processes as well as the project deliverables.

---

▓ **Exam Tip**    *Kaizen* is a loose Japanese translation of the term *continuous improvement*. So on the exam, if you find either term, you will know what it means.

---

*Precision* and *accuracy* are two separate terms; you need to be aware of the definition of each. Precision relates to how tightly clustered results are. The closer the results are, the more precise the measurements being taken are. Accuracy, on the other hand, refers to how close the results are to the actual value. An example to illustrate the concepts is a shooting target and ten shots taken at the target. Accuracy refers to how close the shots are to the bullseye, which is the intended target. Precision refers to how tightly grouped the ten shots are, no matter how close to the bullseye they are. If they are tightly grouped, then they demonstrate a high level of precision. Obviously, the preferred mix is high degrees of both accuracy and precision.

In your workplace, you may use the two terms *quality* and *grade* interchangeably. However, for the purposes of the exam, it is important to realize they are distinct concepts. Quality is defined as the degree to which a set of inherent characteristics fulfills requirements. Grade, on the other hand, refers to the number of features a particular product has. For example, some manufacturers produce different brands to indicate the difference between low-grade and high-grade products. The products themselves are manufactured to the same quality standards, but some have fewer features, or are of a lower grade, than others.

Most people know *just in time (JIT)* as an inventory-control system in which suppliers provide materials just before they are required. It is often seen as an efficient way to manage organizational finances, because it does not require funds to be tied up in stock or materials being stored. However, JIT can also be used as a quality management approach; the absence of materials in stock forces an organization to maintain a high level of quality because it cannot depend on simply going to its warehouse for more stock when poor quality is produced.

*Total quality management* (TQM) is a particular approach to quality management that means everybody in an organization takes responsibility for quality within the organization or project. It is led by management, and everyone at all levels of the organization is expected, encouraged, and trained to participate in constantly improving all aspects of quality.

*Six Sigma* is a proprietary approach to quality management that offers credentials such as green belt and black belt. Six Sigma practitioners are focused on reducing quality defects to as close to zero as possible.

---

## REAL WORLD

When I was working in the telecommunications industry, we had to build telephone networks reliable enough that when someone dialed the emergency number for police, ambulance, or fire, it would connect 99,999 times out of every 100,000 attempts. This was known as *five nines* reliability; that is, 99.999% of the time, it had to work. This is an example of a Six Sigma approach.

---

▓ **Note**    Deming, Juran, and quality management

Much of the modern history of the profession of quality management is rooted in the seminal works of William Edwards Deming. Deming, through his approach to quality management, contributed greatly to the rise of the post–World War II Japanese economy based on competing on quality. Deming is also known for his collaboration with Walter Shewhart in producing and refining the Plan-Do-Check-Act cycle, which forms the basis not only of quality management but also of the profession of project management. At the same time that Deming was influencing Japanese industry, Joseph Juran was working in the same area; he is best known for his approach to quality as a management activity, the Pareto analysis, and the cost of quality analysis. If you want to know more about quality management, I highly recommend reading the work of these researchers.

---

# Plan Quality Management

---

▓ **More Info**    Plan Quality Management

You can read more about the Plan Quality Management process in the PMBOK Guide, 5th edition, in Chapter 8, section 8.1. Table 6-1 identifies the process inputs, tools and techniques, and outputs.

---

***Table 6-1.*** *Plan Quality Management Process*

| Inputs ⇨ | Tools and Techniques ⇨ | Outputs |
|---|---|---|
| • Project management plan | • Cost-benefit analysis | • Quality management plan |
| • Stakeholder register | • Cost of quality | • Process improvement plan |
| • Risk register | • Seven basic quality tools | • Quality metrics |
| • Requirements documentation | • Benchmarking | • Quality checklists |
| • Enterprise environmental factors | • Design of experiments | • Project document updates |
| • Organizational process assets | • Statistical sampling | |
| | • Additional quality planning tools | |
| | • Meetings | |

The Plan Quality Management process is a planning process with a range of outputs including, most important, the *quality management plan*. Similar to the other planning documents, the quality management plan will guide your efforts in defining and controlling the quality of both the project processes and the deliverables. It forms a subsidiary plan to the overall project management plan. Another important output from the Plan Quality Management process is the process improvement plan, which is also a subsidiary of the project management plan and details how you will define and continuously improve all the processes on your project.

The Plan Quality Management process covers the following planning domain task:

- Task 8: Develop the quality management plan and define the quality standards for the project and its products, based on the project scope, risks, and requirements, in order to prevent the occurrence of defects and control the cost of quality.

# Inputs

The Plan Quality Management process uses some or all of the following inputs as part of the development of the quality management plan for the project.

## Project Management Plan

The distinct elements of the project management plan that are useful in developing your own quality management plan are the scope, schedule, and cost baselines, because they contain information against which to measure quality. The project management plan is an output from the Develop Project Management Plan process.

# Stakeholder Register

Given that the purpose of quality management is to deliver processes and products that meet customer and stakeholder expectations, the *stakeholder register*—which describes stakeholders, their interest in the project, the impact they have on the project, and their expectations in relation to the project generally and quality specifically—can be considered a very important input into the Plan Quality Management process.

The stakeholder register is an output from the Identify Stakeholders process in the Stakeholder Management knowledge area.

# Risk Register

The risk register documents and assesses specific risks that may have an impact on any quality management issues and decisions you are making. The risk register is an output from the Identify Risks process in the Risk Management knowledge area.

# Requirements Documentation

Given that the definition of quality is the degree to which a set of inherent characteristics fulfills requirements, it is important to use the requirements documentation as an input because it describes and documents the requirements. Requirements documentation is an output from the Collect Requirements process in the Scope Management knowledge area.

# Enterprise Environmental Factors

Particular enterprise environmental factors that may assist with the development of your quality management plan include any external local or central government regulations pertaining to quality specifications, and any other industry rules or guidelines.

---

## REAL WORLD

One of the key enterprise environmental factors affecting the quality management plans that I have worked on are external standards that different products and deliverables must meet. These are often set by industry organizations or government departments and may change during the duration of your project. Local governments may set building or manufacturing quality standards or health and safety standards, or industry or professional bodies may set employment standards. There are many examples of external enterprise environmental factors relating to quality. If you are getting accredited as an ISO 9001–compliant organization or obtaining the PMP credential because it is a government or industry requirement for you to work as a project manager, this is an example of an enterprise environmental factor at work.

---

## Organizational Process Assets

Organizational process assets that may be important inputs into the development of your quality management plan include relevant organizational policies and guidelines relating to the organization's approach and expectations of quality, and any historical information or lessons learned from previous projects relating to quality.

# Tools and Techniques

The following tools and techniques are available to be used to develop the inputs into this process in order to produce the quality management plan.

## Cost-Benefit Analysis

*Cost-benefit analysis* is used as a tool in the Plan Quality Management process because you need to look at the costs of meeting quality requirements, which generally increase as you seek to improve quality and avoid re-work and decreasing stakeholder satisfaction. The pursuit of quality is always a trade-off between the costs involved and the benefits obtained; therefore, using cost-benefit analysis is an important tool for producing a quality management plan.

## Cost of Quality

*Cost of quality* considers the total cost of quality over the life of the product, which is well beyond the life of the project and examines the cost of low quality, subsequent warranty claims, any negative effect on brand or reputation, and loss of future work.

---

▨ **Exam Tip**    Cost of quality is mirrored by, and sometimes referred to as, *cost of poor quality*. Whatever the term used, it is the concept of assessing what the implications are for producing or not producing quality products far beyond the life of the project.

---

## Seven Basic Quality Tools

The catchall phrase *seven basic quality tools* refers to the graphical representation of tools used to measure, assess, and determine causes of quality issues. They are a convenient and graphical way to represent what can often be quite complex text-based or numerical information to allow quick communication and assessment of quality issues.

---

▨ **Exam Tip**    Each of the seven basic quality tools refers to a particular type of diagram.

---

The *cause-and-effect diagram*, which is also called the *Ishikawa* or *fishbone diagram*, is used to describe a known defect and assess the variety of possible causes. It enables you to consider multiple causes for a single problem. Figure 6-1 shows a cause-and-effect diagram with one level of analysis done. You start by identifying a particular defect and then look at all the possible causes of that defect; if you want to, you can also seek further root causes of each identified cause. After you have identified the potential causes, you can then use more quantifiable analysis, such as counting the number of times that cause is responsible for the defect, and come up with a prioritized list of causes.

---

░ **Exam Tip** This is one of those instances where multiple terms mean the same thing on the exam. This diagram may be referred to as the *cause-and-effect*, *Ishikawa*, or *fishbone diagram*.

---

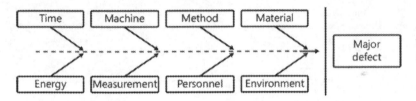

**Figure 6-1.** *A cause-and-effect, Ishikawa, or fishbone diagram*

*Flowcharts* are a convenient way to show the flow of information, or the sequence of steps, in a particular process. Figure 6-2 shows an example of a flowchart.

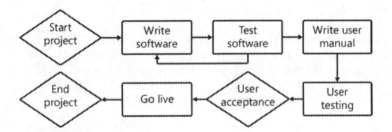

**Figure 6-2.** *Flowchart*

## REAL WORLD

Each shape used in a flow chart has a specific meaning attached to it. For example, the rectangle shape indicates a process, and the diamond shape indicates a decision point. Every shape used has a different meaning so that you can look at the flowchart and get information quickly.

---

░ **Exam Tip**    On the exam, you may see the acronym SIPOC used. If so, it is referring to a particular type of flowchart used for documenting the flow of goods and information between and customers. The acronym SIPOC stands for Suppliers, Inputs, Process, Outputs. and Customers.

---

*Checksheets* are a convenient way to document quality problems or issues and their frequency of occurrence. Checksheets are sometimes called *tally sheets*. Figure 6-3 shows an example of a checksheet.

| Health and Safety Breaches (last 12 Months) | | | | | |
|---|---|---|---|---|---|
| Reason | Mon | Tue | Wed | Thu | Fri |
| Training not adequate | | I | | I | II |
| Safety gear not worn | IIII | | III | | |
| Site not secure | II | II | | II | |
| Lack of communication | IIIII | | | | |

***Figure 6-3.***  *Checksheet*

Checksheets can provide a simple but useful way of capturing events and trends as they occur. Looking at the example in Figure 6-3, it could be determined that the majority of the team's health and safety breaches occur after a weekend. If this is deemed to be true, the project manager could put measures in place to ensure that health and safety matters are on the forefront on the team's mind after each weekend.

---

░ **Exam Tip**    The difference between a checksheet and a checklist is that a checksheet provides a way to capture the occurrences of an event, whereas a checklist documents what steps need to be completed to carry out a certain process. Checksheets are a tool in the Plan Quality Management process. Quality checklists are an output from Plan Quality Management and are used as an input into Control Quality.

---

A *Pareto diagram* is a way of using a histogram to document the frequency of particular events in descending order and then add up the cumulative percentage of the quality defects in order to assess which subset of defects causes the greatest number of problems. The purpose of this Pareto analysis is to focus your attention and energy on those 20% of problems that are causing 80% of the issues. Figure 6-4 shows an example of a Pareto diagram.

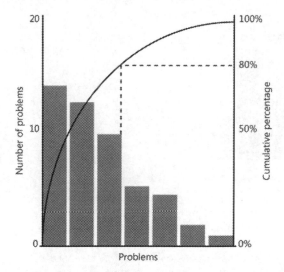

**Figure 6-4.** *Pareto diagram*

---

▨ **Note**    Pareto principle

Joseph Juran first used the term *Pareto principle* to refer to what is now more commonly referred to as the *80:20 rule*. It was called the Pareto principle because in the early part of the 20th century, an economist by the name of Wilfried (or Vilfredo, if you are Italian) Pareto observed that 80% of the land in Italy was owned by 20% of the people. This 80:20 rule has come to be used in a wide variety of disciplines to describe any situation where a small amount of a population is responsible for many of the observations made.

---

*Histograms*, or bar charts, are a simple way of representing frequency, or occurrence, of particular events. Figure 6-5 shows an example of a histogram.

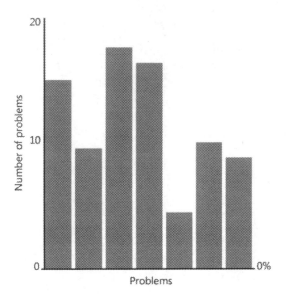

*Figure 6-5.* *Histogram*

*Control charts* are an effective way of recording data and determining whether a manufacturing process is still in control or is about to go out of control. Information is gathered and plotted on the control chart around an expected average, or mean. Using standard deviations, you can then set the upper and lower control limits, three standard deviations either side of the mean. Beyond these *control limits*, the upper and lower *specification limit* is set. Any data point that appears outside of the specification limit will not be accepted by the customer. Any data point that appears outside of the control limit but within a specification limit indicates that the process is out of control and investigation should commence immediately as to the cause. Any information or data gathered in the control limits is acceptable.

The exception to this rule is when seven consecutive data points appear either side of the mean. This is called the *rule of seven*: it is statistically improbable that you will get seven consecutive points on either side of the mean. An easy way to understand the rule of seven is to consider a coin being tossed and the chances of it landing with either heads or tails facing up. You would expect a random distribution of heads and tails but would consider it statistically improbable that you would get seven consecutive heads or tails. If you do note seven consecutive data points above or below the mean, it signals that you should investigate the cause, because the process may be about to go out of control. Figure 6-6 shows an example of a control chart. Note the appearance of seven consecutive data points above the mean, indicating the rule of seven.

*Figure 6-6.* *Control chart*

*Scatter diagrams* simply record the relationship between two variables in graphical form. Figure 6-7 shows an example of a scatter diagram.

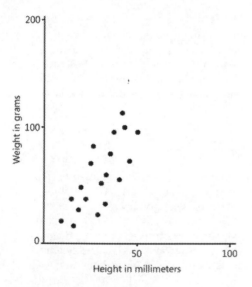

*Figure 6-7.* *Scatter diagram*

---

▒ **Note**    Ishikawa and quality management

The development of the seven basic quality tools is attributed to the work of Kaoru Ishikawa, a Japanese professor and one of the great quality management advocates and developers.

---

# Benchmarking

*Benchmarking* is the process of comparing your quality practices to those of other projects or other organizations and seeing how you compare.

# Design of Experiments

*Design of experiments* is a tool to assist with developing useful and reliable experiments to test quality. Key considerations in the design of experiments include the identification and control of variables and the understanding of how the testing process itself may affect observed outcomes. A well-designed experiment can independently control different variables to determine which ones are causing problems.

# Statistical Sampling

*Statistical sampling* is used when there are either too many quality checks to do or quality checks involve destructive testing. For example, you may want to do testing on lines of software code being written, but there are more than 100,000 lines of code. Instead of checking every line of code, you can select 100 lines of code and check them for accuracy. One constraint of statistical sampling is the assumption that the result from a small population is representative of the entire population.

# Additional Quality Planning Tools

Along with the tools and techniques listed previously, *additional quality planning tools* can be used to plan your particular approach to quality management. These include brainstorming and nominal group techniques, both of which you have seen as tools and techniques and other areas. In addition to these two tools, you can use force field analysis, affinity diagrams, process decision program charts, interrelationship diagrams, tree diagrams, prioritization matrices, activity network diagrams, and matrix diagrams. All of these quality management and control tools are covered in more depth in the Perform Quality Assurance process.

Another quality planning tool that can be used is failure mode and effect analysis (FMEA). FMEA is a widely used technique that examines the consequence of failure in any part of the system and uses those observations to ensure that failure does not actually occur or that, if it does, the impact is anticipated and mitigated. In this process, you could use this tool to determine the likely effect of failure of the product and prepare to ensure that it doesn't happen.

# Meetings

Meetings are a useful way to bring together members of the project team and other stakeholders so that they can contribute to the development of the quality management plan.

# Outputs

After applying the appropriate tools and techniques to the selected inputs, the Plan Quality Management process has the following outputs.

## Quality Management Plan

The Plan Quality Management process has the *quality management plan* as its primary output. Similar to other management plans, the quality management plan provides a description of the overall approach to quality management, guidelines for all project processes and how they will be implemented, and a description of expected quality, testing, and inspection of project deliverables. The detail contained in the quality management plan reflects the size and complexity of the project, and the plan should be updated and reviewed regularly to ensure that it is still accurate. The quality management plan is then a key input into the Perform Quality Assurance and Control Quality processes.

---

▓ **Exam Tip**    According to the PMBOK Guide, every project should have a quality management plan. The quality management plan can be formal and documented, or it can be an informal set of policies and guidelines. It reflects the size and complexity of the project but should always be done.

---

```
┌─────────────────────────────────────────────────────────────┐
│                       REAL WORLD                              │
└─────────────────────────────────────────────────────────────┘
```

Many organizations, after they reach a certain size, appoint a particular person to manage quality in the organization and also within projects. I believe this is an important step for an organization to take, because a focus on quality is often a much more important element than a focus on cost. A simple way to remember why quality is so important to your project is that if you don't care about quality, your competitor will. I remember on one large project I was managing that I wanted the quality of the project to be the legacy that I left rather than coming in under budget and ahead of time. We still focused on measuring cost and time performance, and we did come in under budget and ahead of time, but the element I was proudest of was the extra quality we were able to deliver.

## Process Improvement Plan

The *process improvement plan* is a subsidiary of the project management plan that focuses specifically on analyzing quality processes and describing ways in which continuous improvement can be applied to these processes. The process improvement plan is used as an input into the Perform Quality Assurance process.

---

※ **Exam Tip**　Note that the process improvement plan is not used as an input into the Control Quality process because its primary focus is on project processes, which are the main focus of the Perform Quality Assurance process.

---

# Quality Metrics

The development and documentation of specific *quality metrics* is necessary in order to be able to measure progress against what has been planned. The more specific the quality metric, the more detailed the measurement and reporting can be. The most common quality metrics developed include performance measurements relating to schedule, cost, defects, failure, and reliability. The quality metrics are used as an input into the Perform Quality Assurance and the Control Quality processes.

# Quality Checklists

The *quality checklist* is a specific type of checklist you can use to determine whether defined steps of the quality process have been performed. A quality checklist should both document the steps to be taken and incorporate acceptance criteria from the project requirements and scope baseline. The quality checklists are used as an input into the Control Quality process.

# Project Document Updates

The specific project documents that may be updated as a result of completing the Plan Quality Management process are the stakeholder register and the responsibility assignment matrix.

### Quick Check

1. What is the key function of a quality management plan?

2. What does it mean when a data point is outside the control limit but within the specification limit?

3. Under what circumstances would you use statistical sampling?

### Quick Check Answers

1. The key function of a quality management plan is to describe your particular approach to quality in your project, the relevant policies, your approach to quality assurance and process improvement, quality metrics, and how you will control and measure quality of the project deliverables.

2. If a data point is outside the control limit but within the specification limit, this indicates that the process may be out of control and requires immediate investigation.

3. You would use statistical sampling to determine the level of quality when there are too many samples to investigate individually or when investigating the quality of the sample involves destructive testing.

# Perform Quality Assurance

---

░ **More Info**  Perform Quality Assurance

You can read more about the Perform Quality Assurance process in the PMBOK Guide, 5th edition, in Chapter 8, section 8.2. Table 6-2 identifies the process inputs, tools and techniques, and outputs.

---

*Table 6-2.* *Perform Quality Assurance Process*

| Inputs ⇨ | Tools and Techniques ⇨ | Outputs |
|---|---|---|
| • Quality management plan<br>• Process improvement plan<br>• Quality metrics<br>• Quality control measurements<br>• Project documents | • Quality management and control tools<br>• Quality audits<br>• Process analysis | • Change requests<br>• Project management plan updates<br>• Project document updates<br>• Organizational process asset updates |

The Perform Quality Assurance process is an executing process that uses the quality management plan for guidance and is focused on implementing processes across the entire project and checking that these processes are being adhered to and continuously improved. The processes that you define and audit won't only be processes around quality management. For example, you could decide to have a process about setting up and choosing the right projects, culminating in a signed project charter, all of which would be covered in the Develop Project Charter process. The Perform Quality Assurance process checks that you have followed this process correctly.

The Perform Quality Assurance process covers the following executing domain task:

• Task 3: Implement the quality management plan using the appropriate tools and techniques, in order to ensure that work is performed in accordance with required quality standards.

---

▓ **Exam Tip**   A simple way to remember the difference between quality assurance and quality control is that quality assurance uses audits and focuses on processes, whereas quality control focuses on inspections and the project deliverables.

---

| **REAL WORLD** |
|---|

The ISO 9000 standard is an excellent example of quality assurance at work. This standard requires processes to be in place and regular audits to occur to ensure that the processes are being followed. The standard does not focus on the quality of the product being produced. Thus, some unscrupulous companies have ISO 9000 accreditation but produce low-quality products.

# Inputs

The Perform Quality Assurance process uses some or all of the following inputs.

## Quality Management Plan

The quality management plan is obviously a key input into the Perform Quality Assurance process because it guides how the process is carried out. The quality management plan is an output from the Plan Quality Management process.

## Process Improvement Plan

The *process improvement plan* is used as an input into this process because it is focused on detailing the processes that will be put in place and how they will be checked and improved. The process improvement plan is an output from the Plan Quality Management process.

## Quality Metrics

The *quality metrics* are specific variables that can be measured as part of checking whether you are implementing and adhering to particular quality processes. The quality metrics are an output from the Plan Quality Management process.

## Quality Control Measurements

*Quality control measurements* are generated by the Control Quality process and are used in the Perform Quality Assurance process to analyze and evaluate the particular quality standards relating to the quality processes that are supposed to have been followed.

## Project Documents

The specific types of *project documents* that are useful as inputs into the Perform Quality Assurance process are any documents relating to requirements or quality processes, or those that define stakeholder expectations.

---

▓ **Exam Tip**   Did you notice that neither environmental enterprise factors nor organizational process assets are used as inputs into this process?

---

# Tools and Techniques

The following tools and techniques are used on the inputs to deliver the Perform Quality Assurance process outputs.

## Quality Management and Control Tools

The Perform Quality Assurance process uses all the tools and techniques featured throughout the Quality Management knowledge area. It uses the seven basic tools of quality already covered in the Plan Quality Management process, as well as statistical sampling, inspection, benchmarking, design of experiments, cost-benefit analysis, and cost of quality.

Additionally, you can use the following *seven new quality tools* and techniques. Each of these quality management and control tools is used to document and represent particular measurements taken during the Perform Quality Assurance process.

---

▓ **Note**   Seven new quality tools

The seven new quality tools come from the book *Seven New QC Tools: Practical Applications for Managers* by Yoshinobu Nayatani, Toru Eiga, Ryoji Futami, and Hiroyuki Miyagawa (Productivity Press, 1994). These seven tools and the basic seven tools all represent data in graphical format for easy interpretation and communication.

---

*Affinity diagrams*, or KJ Methods diagrams, can be used during a brainstorming session to create cause-and-effect diagrams because they group data in logical relationships. Figure 6-8 shows an example of an affinity diagram.

**Figure 6-8.** *Affinity diagram*

A *process decision program chart* (PDPC) displays in graphical and hierarchical form the steps in a process in order to understand issues that may positively or negatively affect the sequence of activities to reach a goal. In this sense, it is a cross between a flowchart and a breakdown structure. Figure 6-9 shows an example of a PDPC.

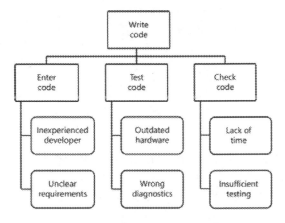

**Figure 6-9.** *Process decision program chart*

*Interrelationship digraphs* are useful to graphically show multiple cause-and-effect relationships among various factors. Figure 6-10 shows an example of an interrelationship digraph.

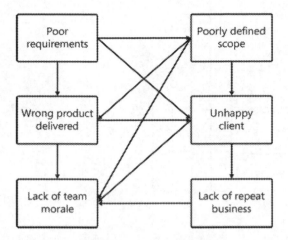

*Figure 6-10.* *Interrelationship digraph*

A *tree diagram* is a very useful graphical representation of hierarchical relationships and parent-to-child relationships. You have seen the tree diagram as a work, risk, and organizational breakdown structure. In managing quality, the tree diagram can be used to describe nested relationships between steps in the quality assurance process. Figure 6-11 shows an example of a tree diagram.

*Figure 6-11.* *Tree diagram*

*Prioritization matrices* use a variety of weighted criteria to determine the priority of quality actions to enable the key issues to be determined. Figure 6-12 shows an example of a prioritization matrix.

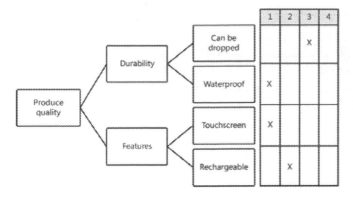

**Figure 6-12.** *Prioritization matrix*

*Activity network diagrams* are used to show relationships between activities to be completed. You have already seen these diagrams used in the managing the project schedule and determining the tasks on the critical path with activity-on-node (AON) diagrams. In quality management, they are used to show the sequence of, and interrelationships between, various quality activities. Figure 6-13 shows an example of an activity network diagram.

**Figure 6-13.** *Activity network diagram*

*Matrix diagrams* are used to indicate whether a relationship exists between two variables. Figure 6-14 shows an example of a matrix diagram.

|  | Customer A | Customer B | Customer C | Customer D |
|---|---|---|---|---|
| **Durability** | High | High | Moderate | High |
| **Features** | Low | High | High | Moderate |
| **Price** | Low | Moderate | Low | High |
| **Size** | Small | Med | Large | Small |

**Figure 6-14.** *Matrix diagram*

## Quality Audits

A *quality audit* is an independent process that seeks to determine whether the defined project processes are being carried out as per the quality management plan. Quality audits are carried out using the quality management plan as a guideline and should generally be done by people not involved with the project who can independently assess whether the required processes are in place and whether they are being followed.

---

### REAL WORLD

On one particularly large project I was managing, we had it as part of the contract that regular audits would occur on all our project processes. We had an independent assessor appointed from one of the large global auditing companies, and every six months, that assessor would show up in person and spend several days requesting proof that we had processes in place and that we followed those processes correctly. The assessor would then produce a report detailing areas of both compliance and noncompliance. As the project manager, it was my responsibility to ensure that any areas of noncompliance were addressed promptly. The costs for completing these quality audits were part of the overall project budget.

---

▓ **Exam Tip**   Wherever you find an audit being used as a tool, it will be checking that processes are in place, that they are being followed as per the requirements, and that any deviation from the processes is documented and dealt with. Audits do not check the quality of any deliverables or products.

---

## Process Analysis

*Process analysis* takes the steps in the process improvement plan and executes them in order to identify and improve existing processes.

# Outputs

The Perform Quality Assurance process produces some or all of the following outputs.

# Change Requests

*Change requests* are generated as a result of information discovered by audits and process analysis that then requires changes to be considered as per the agreed change management process. The change requests are used as an input into the Perform Integrated Change Control process.

# Project Management Plan Updates

The specific parts of the project management plan that may be updated as a result of the Perform Quality Assurance process are the quality management plan, the process improvement plan, the schedule management plan, and the cost management plan.

# Project Document Updates

The specific project documents that may be updated as a result of the Perform Quality Assurance process include such things as project-specific policies and guidelines relating to preparation and execution of processes.

# Organizational Process Asset Updates

The specific organizational process assets that may be updated as a result of the Perform Quality Assurance process are any templates, policies, or guidelines relating to quality audits, and training and appointment of independent auditors.

### Quick Check

1. What is the difference between quality assurance and quality control?

2. What is it that both the seven basic quality tools and the seven new quality tools are attempting to do?

3. What is the purpose of a quality audit?

### Quick Check Answers

1. The difference between quality assurance and quality control is that quality assurance is focused on the processes of the project, whereas quality control is focused on the project deliverables.

2. All of the quality tools described seek to take what can be quite complex text, verbal, or numerical information and collate and present it in an easy-to-understand graphical form.

3. The purpose of the quality audit is to independently check that required processes are in place and are being followed.

# Control Quality

▓ **More Info**    Control Quality

You can read more about the Control Quality process in the PMBOK Guide, 5th edition, in Chapter 8, section 8.3. Table 6-3 identifies the process inputs, tools and techniques, and outputs.

*Table 6-3.* *Control Quality Process*

| Inputs ⇨ | Tools and Techniques ⇨ | Outputs |
|---|---|---|
| • Quality management plan<br>• Quality metrics<br>• Quality checklists<br>• Work performance data<br>• Approved change requests<br>• Deliverables<br>• Project documents<br>• Organizational process assets | • Seven basic quality tools<br>• Statistical sampling<br>• Inspection<br>• Approved change requests review | • Quality control measurements<br>• Validated changes<br>• Verified deliverables<br>• Work performance information<br>• Change requests<br>• Project management plan updates<br>• Project document updates<br>• Organizational process asset updates |

The Control Quality process is a monitoring and controlling process that uses the quality management plan and checks that the project deliverables will meet the documented requirements and stakeholder expectations.

The Control Quality process covers the following monitoring and controlling domain task:

- Task 3: Verify that project deliverables conform to the quality standards established in the quality management plan by using appropriate tools and techniques, in order to meet project requirements and business needs.

# Inputs

The following inputs are used in the Control Quality process.

## Quality Management Plan

The quality management plan is a critical input into the Control Quality process because it sets out and describes how this process will occur. The quality management plan is an output from the Plan Quality Management process

## Quality Metrics

The quality metrics are a required input into the Control Quality process because they describe the attributes that are expected in the project deliverables and how these attributes will be measured. Quality metrics are an output from the Plan Quality Management process

## Quality Checklists

Quality checklists provide a documented and structured list of steps, attributes, and guidelines that can be used to ensure that all the quality control work is done correctly. Quality checklists are an output from the Plan Quality Management process.

## Work Performance Data

In order to measure whether the project is being delivered as per the desired quality requirements, you need work performance data. Work performance data is an output from the Direct and Manage Project Work process.

## Approved Change Requests

Approved change requests can have an impact on the project deliverables and may require modifications, such as defect repairs, and thus are an important input into this process. Approved change requests are an output from the Perform Integrated Change Control process.

## Deliverables

Given that the control quality process is focused on checking the quality of the deliverables, having the deliverables as an input into the process can be viewed as quite critical.

## Project Documents

The specific types of project documents that may be used as inputs into this process include any contracts that specify deliverable requirements and attributes, and any relevant quality audit reports.

## Organizational Process Assets

The specific organizational process assets that can assist with the Control Quality process are any guidelines, processes, policies, or blank templates that the organization has relating to quality control.

# Tools and Techniques

The following tools and techniques for this process can be used on the separate inputs to deliver the process outputs.

## Seven Basic Quality Tools

The seven basic quality tools were described in detail earlier in the Plan Quality Management process. They can be used in the Control Quality process to graphically represent and analyze any of the data gathered.

---

▓ **Exam Tip**    By now you have probably realized that the seven basic quality tools can be used as tools or techniques in any of the quality management processes.

---

## Statistical Sampling

As part of completing a check on the quality of the deliverables, you may choose to use statistical sampling as a tool or technique, if the number of deliverables is too great to test each one individually or if the sampling would involve destructive testing.

## Inspection

Inspection is one of the key tools of the Control Quality process. It is a physical examination of the deliverable to measure and determine whether it complies with the required standards. As a result of completing inspection, you will generally produce a variety of measurements indicating compliance or noncompliance with the required deliverable standards.

## Approved Change Request Review

It is one thing to have approved change requests; it is another to ensure that they have been implemented as per the change documentation. The way to do this is via the use of an *approved change request review*.

```
┌─────────────────────────────────────────────────────────┐
│                      REAL WORLD                           │
└─────────────────────────────────────────────────────────┘
```

I have often seen assumptions made about approved change requests being carried out. Some people seem to think that simply because the change has been requested and considered and a decision has been made to approve it, the change is automatically carried out. Unfortunately, this isn't always the case. This is one of the reasons you should record all change requests, their status, any decisions made, and any required follow-up actions on your change-request log. Furthermore, assigning someone to be responsible for not only carrying out the change but also checking that it was carried out correctly is an important factor in making sure all of your approved change requests are implemented.

# Outputs

The major outputs from the Control Quality process are the following.

## Quality Control Measurements

The *quality control measurements* are the documents you produce as a result of carrying out the Quality Control processes and activities. They should be concise and presented in an appropriate format for easy communication, presentation, and tracking. Quality control measurements go on to be used as an input into the Perform Quality Assurance process.

## Validated Changes

The *validated changes* output involves checking that approved change requests and any required modifications have been inspected and comply with the change-request documentation. Validated changes go on to be used as an input into the Monitor and Control Project Work process.

---

▓ **Exam Tip**    The process of validation occurs after the process of verification. The process of validation is an important one to understand, as well as how it is different from the process of verification. Verification is about confirmation that the product, service, or result produced complies with agreed specifications or requirements. It is primarily an internal process performed by the delivering organization prior to submitting the product, service, or result for validation, which involves the customer as well. Validation also involves a check that the product, service, or result meets stakeholder requirements. Verification occurs before validation.

---

## Verified Deliverables

You will recall that deliverables are one of the inputs into the Control Quality process. After they have been subjected to the appropriate tools and techniques to check that they conform to the required standards, if they are accepted, *verified deliverables* become an output from the process. Verified deliverables go on to be used as an input into the Validate Scope process.

## Work Performance Information

You will recall that work performance data is used as an input into the Control Quality process. This is the raw data collected about work performance to date. After it is subjected to the appropriate tools and techniques, it becomes work performance information. Work performance information then goes on to be used as an input into the Monitor and Control Project Work process.

## Change Requests

As a result of carrying out the Control Quality process, there may be a reason to raise a change request to deal with defect repairs, required modifications, or corrective or preventive actions. All change requests should be prepared, submitted, and assessed as per the documented and defined change-control process. Change requests go on to be used as an input into the Perform Integrated Change Control process.

## Project Management Plan Updates

Specific parts of the project management plan that may be updated as a result of the Control Quality process are the quality management plan and the process improvement plan.

## Project Document Updates

Specific project documents that may be updated as a result of the Control Quality process are any relevant quality standards or agreements relating to any aspect of the quality management process.

## Organizational Process Asset Updates

Specific organizational process assets that may be updated include lessons learned databases and any blank templates for any aspect of the organization's quality management process.

**Quick Check**

1. What is the main focus of the Control Quality process?

2. Which three inputs into the Control Quality process are outputs from the same process in a more refined state?

3. How does inspection differ from audits?

**Quick Check Answers**

1. The main focus of the Control Quality process is to check that the project deliverables meet the required and documented standards. This is in contrast to the Perform Quality Assurance process, which is focused on the processes of the project.

2. The three inputs are approved change requests, deliverables, and work performance data. Each is used as an input into the Control Quality process and, after the application of appropriate tools, is further refined so that approved change requests become validated changes, deliverables become verified deliverables, and work performance data becomes work performance information.

3. Inspection is one of the tools of the Control Quality process and involves physical examination of the deliverables produced by the project to determine whether they conform to the required standards. On the other hand, audits are used as a tool in the Perform Quality Assurance process to check whether processes are in place and that they are being followed correctly.

# Chapter Summary

The Quality Management knowledge area is focused on the development of the quality management plan and then using this quality management plan to carry out quality assurance to check the project processes and quality control to check the project deliverables.

- The quality tools and techniques are common to all three quality processes.

- The Plan Quality Management process produces the quality management plan for the project, which sets out guidelines and processes for checking both the processes and deliverables for the project.

- The Perform Quality Assurance process focuses on checking that processes are in place and are being followed. It uses a variety of tools and techniques, including audits.

- The Control Quality process is focused on checking project deliverables and approved change requests for conformity to requirements.

# Exercise

The answer for this exercise is located in the "Answers" section at the end of this chapter.

1. Match up the quality tool on the left with the description on the right.

| Quality Tool | Definition |
| --- | --- |
| 1. Histogram | A. A diagramming technique showing relationships and sequencing of quality activities so you can determine the critical path of activities |
| 2. Tree diagram | B. A diagram that groups similar concepts under relevant headings that can then be used to generate cause-and-effect diagrams |
| 3. Pareto diagram | C. A process of comparing your quality activities to those of other projects or organizations |
| 4. Flowchart | D. A standardized and documented list of quality activities to be carried out and confirmed as completed |
| 5. Prioritization matrix | E. A graphical representation of data points measured against an expected mean with control limits set three standard deviations either side of the mean |
| 6. Affinity diagram | F. A diagram showing the sequence of steps in a process using standardized shapes to represent different activities |
| 7. Matrix diagram | G. A bar chart showing frequency of discrete data |
| 8. Scatter diagram | H. A graphical representation showing multiple cause-and-effect relationships among various factors |
| 9. Ishikawa diagram | I. A diagrammatic way of representing effects and their possible causes |
| 10. Activity network diagram | J. A diagram that shows how multiple variables interact with each other |
| 11. Control chart | K. A diagram showing the individual and cumulative frequency of events to determine which 20% of events cause 80% of the problems |
| 12. Process decision program chart | L. A diagram showing the weighted scoring of variables to determine the priority of activities |

(*continued*)

| Quality Tool | Definition |
|---|---|
| 13. Interrelationship digraph | M. A graphical way to show the hierarchy of steps in a process in order to understand the sequence of activities to reach a goal |
| 14. Benchmarking | N. A diagram with data points showing the correlation between two variables, each represented on a vertical or horizontal axis |
| 15. Statistical sampling | O. A process of testing that takes a small population and extrapolates the result to a larger population |
| 16. Checksheet | P. A diagram of hierarchical relationships and parent-to-child relationships |

# Review Questions

Test your knowledge of the information in Chapter 6 by answering these questions. The answers to these questions, and the explanations of why each answer choice is correct or incorrect, are located in the "Answers" section at the end of this chapter.

1. What are the three processes in the Quality Management knowledge area?

   A. Control Quality, Perform Quality Assurance, Plan Quality Management

   B. Plan Quality Management, Control Assurance, Perform Quality Control

   C. Perform Quality Control, Determine Quality, Plan Quality Management

   D. Plan Quality Management, Assure Quality, Control Quality

2. Which of the following is *not* one of the seven basic quality tools?

   A. Benchmarking

   B. Scatter diagram

   C. Control chart

   D. Pareto diagram

3.  What does it mean if a single data point appears above the upper specification limit on a control chart?

    A.  The process is in control, and the customer is happy.

    B.  The process may be out of control, and consideration should be given to checking the process in the near future.

    C.  A single data point outside the upper specification is okay. You only need to be concerned if there are seven consecutive data points outside either of the specification limits.

    D.  The process is out of control and requires immediate action, because the customer will not accept any deliverables outside the specification limit.

4.  What is the best definition of quality?

    A.  Quality is whatever the customer says is right.

    B.  Quality is the degree to which a product can be used for its intended purpose.

    C.  Quality is the degree to which a set of inherent characteristics fulfills requirements.

    D.  Quality is the number features the product has.

5.  What is the best definition of the principle of kaizen?

    A.  Defining quality processes and checking that they are being used

    B.  Continuously improving

    C.  Checking the quality of the product

    D.  Having a quality management plan

6.  If you are considering the impact of potential future warranty claims as part of your quality management plan, what are you considering?

    A.  Cost of quality

    B.  Quality assurance

    C.  Benchmarking

    D.  Prevention over inspection

7. If you are using a diagram to determine the potential causes of quality issues, what are you using?

   A. Control chart

   B. Histogram

   C. Checksheet

   D. Fishbone diagram

8. If you are testing and measuring a small sample and extrapolating those results to be indicative of a total population, what tool or technique are you using?

   A. Benchmarking

   B. Statistical sampling

   C. Design of experiments

   D. Brainstorming

9. If you are conducting an audit to check whether processes are being followed correctly, what process are you involved in?

   A. Plan Quality Management

   B. Control Quality

   C. Perform Quality Assurance

   D. Perform Quality Audit

10. What are the variables and allowable variations called that should be measured as part of the Perform Quality Assurance and Control Quality processes?

    A. Quality control measurements

    B. Quality checklists

    C. Quality metrics

    D. Cost of quality

11. Which quality process uses inspection as a tool or technique?

    A. Plan Quality Management

    B. Control Quality

    C. Perform Quality Assurance

    D. Perform Quality Inspection

# Answers

This section contains the answers for the Exercises and Review Questions in this chapter.

## Exercises

1. Match up the quality tool on the left with the description on the right.

| Quality Tool | Definition |
| --- | --- |
| 1. Histogram | G. A bar chart showing frequency of discrete data |
| 2. Tree diagram | P. A diagram of hierarchical relationships and parent-to-child relationships |
| 3. Pareto diagram | K. A diagram showing the individual and cumulative frequency of events to determine which 20% of events cause 80% of the problems |
| 4. Flowchart | F. A diagram showing the sequence of steps in a process using standardized shapes to represent different activities |
| 5. Prioritization matrix | L. A diagram showing the weighted scoring of variables to determine the priority of activities |
| 6. Affinity diagram | B. A diagram that groups similar concepts under relevant headings that can then be used to generate cause-and-effect diagrams |
| 7. Matrix diagram | J. A diagram that shows how multiple variables interact with each other |
| 8. Scatter diagram | N. A diagram with data points showing the correlation between two variables, each represented on a vertical or horizontal axis |
| 9. Ishikawa diagram | I. A diagrammatic way of representing effects and their possible causes |
| 10. Activity network diagram | A. A diagramming technique showing relationships and sequencing of quality activities so you can determine the critical path of activities |
| 11. Control chart | E. A graphical representation of data points measured against an expected mean with control limits set three standard deviations either side of the mean |
| 12. Process decision program chart | M. A graphical way to show the hierarchy of steps in a process in order to understand the sequence of activities to reach a goal |

(*continued*)

273

| Quality Tool | Definition |
|---|---|
| 13. Interrelationship digraph | H. A graphical representation showing multiple cause-and-effect relationships among various factors |
| 14. Benchmarking | C. A process of comparing your quality activities to those of other projects or organizations |
| 15. Statistical sampling | O. A process of testing that takes a small population and extrapolates the result to a larger population |
| 16. Checksheet | D. A standardized and documented list of quality activities to be carried out and confirmed as completed |

# Review Questions

1.  **Correct Answer: A**

    A.  **Correct**: The three processes in the Quality Management knowledge area are Plan Quality Management, Perform Quality Assurance, and Control Quality.

    B.  **Incorrect**: There is no process called Control Assurance.

    C.  **Incorrect**: There is no process called Perform Quality Control or Determine Quality.

    D.  **Incorrect**: There is no process called Assure Quality.

2.  **Correct Answer: A**

    A.  **Correct**: Benchmarking is a tool that is used in quality management, but it is not one of the seven basic quality tools.

    B.  **Incorrect**: The scatter diagram is one of the seven basic quality tools, which include cause-and-effect diagrams, flowcharts, checksheets, Pareto diagrams, histograms, control charts, and scatter diagrams.

    C.  **Incorrect**: The control chart is one of the seven basic quality tools.

    D.  **Incorrect**: The Pareto diagram is one of the seven basic quality tools.

3.  **Correct Answer: D**

    A.  **Incorrect**: A data point outside the specification limit does not mean that the process is in control; the customer will not pay for anything that is outside the specification limit.

    B.  **Incorrect**: A data point outside the specification limit indicates that the process is definitely out of control.

    C.  **Incorrect**: A single data point outside the specification limit indicates that something is wrong. The rule of seven applies to consecutive data points within the control limits.

    D.  **Correct**: Any data point outside the specification limits indicates that the process is out of control and should be investigated immediately.

4.  **Correct Answer: C**

    A.  **Incorrect**: Quality doesn't necessarily relate to what the customer says is right, unless what the customer says is right is captured in the requirements.

    B.  **Incorrect**: Quality is more than the degree to which a product can be used for its intended purpose.

    C.  **Correct**: Quality is the degree to which a set of inherent characteristics fulfills requirements—remember this definition for the exam.

    D.  **Incorrect**: The number of features a product has or does not have refers to grade, not quality.

5.  **Correct Answer: B**

    A.  **Incorrect**: Defining quality processes and checking that they are being used is the process of quality assurance.

    B.  **Correct**: Kaizen is the loose Japanese translation of the term *continuously improving*.

    C.  **Incorrect**: Checking the quality of the product is the process of quality control.

    D.  **Incorrect**: Have a quality management plan is the process of planning quality management.

6. **Correct Answer: A**

   A. **Correct**: Cost of quality, mirrored by the cost of low quality, considers the impacts of quality decisions over the entire life of the product.

   B. **Incorrect**: Quality assurance is the process of defining processes and checking that you are using them as planned.

   C. **Incorrect**: Benchmarking is the process of comparing your efforts against other projects or organizations.

   D. **Incorrect**: Prevention over inspection is a key concept of the overall approach to project quality management.

7. **Correct Answer: D**

   A. **Incorrect**: A control chart maps data points against an expected mean, upper and lower control limits set three standard deviations either side of the mean, and upper and lower specification limits.

   B. **Incorrect**: A histogram, or bar chart, is a graphical way of representing frequency or total occurrences of data.

   C. **Incorrect**: A checksheet is a standardized description of processes, steps and information to be completed or gathered.

   D. **Correct**: A fishbone diagram, also called an Ishikawa diagram or cause-and-effect diagram, shows a graphical representation of potential causes of a particular event.

8. **Correct Answer: B**

   A. **Incorrect**: Benchmarking is the process of comparing your efforts against other projects or organizations.

   B. **Correct**: Statistical sampling means taking a small sample of a total population for testing and then assuming those results apply to the entire population. It is used when there are simply too many tests to be done or when the testing involves destructive testing.

   C. **Incorrect**: Design of experiments is the process of designing, and considering the implications and effects on the results, of experiments to determine quality.

   D. **Incorrect**: Brainstorming is a technique that gathers a group of people together and encourages them to think laterally about a particular issue.

9. **Correct Answer: C**

   A.   **Incorrect**: Plan Quality Management is the initial planning process and delivers the quality management plan.

   B.   **Incorrect**: Control Quality uses inspection to determine the quality of the product.

   C.   **Correct**: Perform Quality Assurance is the process of establishing processes and checking that you are following them by conducting audits.

   D.   **Incorrect**: Perform Quality Audit is a made-up process name.

10. **Correct Answer: C**

   A.   **Incorrect**: Quality control measurements are the measurements taken that allow you to assess whether quality metrics are being achieved.

   B.   **Incorrect**: A quality checklist is a standardized description of processes, steps, and information to be completed or gathered.

   C.   **Correct**: Quality metrics are defined during the Plan Quality Management process and set out the variables and allowable variations that should be measured as part of the Perform Quality Assurance and Control Quality processes.

   D.   **Incorrect**: Cost of quality considers the impact of quality decisions over the entire life of the product.

11. **Correct Answer: B**

   A.   **Incorrect**: Plan Quality Management is the initial planning process and delivers the quality management plan. It does not use inspection as a tool or technique.

   B.   **Correct**: The Control Quality process is focused on checking the quality of the product or deliverable and uses inspection as a tool.

   C.   **Incorrect**: Perform Quality Assurance is the process of establishing processes and checking that you are following them by conducting audits. It does not use inspection as a tool or technique.

   D.   **Incorrect**: Perform Quality Inspection is a made-up process name.

# CHAPTER 7

■ ■ ■

# Human Resource Management

This chapter focuses on Project Human Resource Management. Similar to the other knowledge areas, it begins with a planning process, which in this case produces a human resource management plan. It then has three executing processes that focus on carrying out the contents of the human resource management plan. The three executing processes focus on acquiring your project team members, developing those project team members, and managing them.

You may need to pay particular attention in this chapter to the different theories relating to management, motivation, and development of people, because many of them may be new to you.

**The PMBOK® Guide Processes**

**Project Human Resource Management Knowledge Area**

The four processes in the Project Human Resource Management knowledge area are as follows:

- Plan Human Resource Management (planning process)

- Acquire Project Team (executing process)

- Develop Project Team (executing process)

- Manage Project Team (executing process)

---

■ **Exam Tip**   Did you notice that this knowledge area is the only one without a monitoring and controlling process? It is assumed that functional managers will carry out monitoring and controlling activities associated with human resources, because they generally have final authority over human resources working on your project. Even in a strong matrix structure, although the project manager has authority, the people allocated to the project eventually go back to the functional manager.

---

© Sean Whitaker 2016
S. Whitaker, *Pass the PMP® Exam*, DOI 10.1007/978-1-4842-2074-0_7

# What Is Project Human Resource Management?

Project Human Resource Management is focused on the processes of developing a human resource management plan, which allows you to identify how you will recognize which people you want as part of your project team; when you will require them and for how long; and how you will get those people and develop, reward, motivate, and manage them. It covers all aspects relating to your project team, including you as a project manager.

---
**REAL WORLD**
---

I have always found the term *human resource* to be a little too technical and clinical for my liking. Machines are resources, and there is an element of expected decay, obsolescence, and replacement with the term. People are not resources. So, if you are having the same trouble, I suggest using the much friendlier term *project people management* for this section. Of course, for the exam, you need to use *Project Human Resource Management*.

---

▓ **Exam Tip**   In considering all the issues and topics relevant to human resource management, there are a host of ancillary topics around interpersonal skills, leadership, ethics, and organizational and motivational theories that you must also know for the exam. This chapter covers a wide range of topics relating to all these different aspects of Project Human Resource Management.

---

# Plan Human Resource Management

---

▓ **More Info**   Plan Human Resource Management

You can read more about the Plan Human Resource Management process in the PMBOK Guide, 5th edition, in Chapter 9, section 9.1. Table 7-1 identifies the process inputs, tools and techniques, and outputs.

---

*Table 7-1.* *Plan Human Resource Management Process*

| Inputs ⇨ | Tools and Techniques ⇨ | Outputs |
|---|---|---|
| • Project management plan<br>• Activity resource requirements<br>• Enterprise environmental factors<br>• Organizational process assets | • Organizational charts and position descriptions<br>• Networking<br>• Organizational theory<br>• Expert judgment<br>• Meetings | • Human resource management plan |

The Plan Human Resource Management process is a planning process with a single output: the human resource management plan.

The Plan Human Resource Management process covers the following planning domain task:

- Task 5: Develop the human resource management plan by defining the roles and responsibilities of the project team members, in order to create a project organizational structure and provide guidance regarding how resources will be assigned and managed.

# Inputs

The Plan Human Resource Management process uses some or all of the following inputs as part of the development of the human resource management plan for the project.

## Project Management Plan

The key elements of the project management plan that are useful as inputs into the Plan Human Resource Management process are a description of the work to be completed to determine what skills will be required and elements from the project schedule and schedule management plan that are useful for determining time constraints. The project management plan is an output from the Develop Project Management Plan process.

## Activity Resource Requirements

Activity resource requirements contain information about the specific activities to be completed and the resources, particularly human resources, needed to complete the work. Activity resource requirements are an output from the Estimate Activity Resources process.

## Enterprise Environmental Factors

The specific enterprise environmental factors that are useful as inputs into this process are the external organization culture, existing employees, existing organizational employment and personnel policies, and external marketplace conditions affecting availability and cost of hiring people.

## Organizational Process Assets

The specific organizational process assets that may be important inputs into the development of your human resource management plan include any specific organizational policies, process, or guidelines for the recruitment, reward, and retention of people, and any historical information about what has and has not worked on previous projects.

# Tools and Techniques

The following tools and techniques are available to be used to develop the inputs into this process in order to produce the human resource management plan.

## Organizational Charts and Position Descriptions

A foundational concept of the Plan Human Resource Management process is the need to define a role for everyone on the project and define the responsibilities for each role. In order to do this, you can use *organizational charts and position descriptions* to clearly show what roles there are, how they are linked by reporting lines, and their expected experience, technical skills, duties, and responsibilities.

Before we go any further, let's focus on describing all the roles that can exist in a typical project. In addition to the individual and defined project team member roles, the primary roles in the world of project management are the project manager, sponsor, functional manager, program manager, and portfolio manager.

The *project manager* is one of the key roles in the successful delivery of any product, service, or result because this role takes full responsibility for the project. The project manager works closely with the program manager, because the project manager's project may be part of a program, and also works closely with the portfolio manager, because the project is part of a portfolio. The role of project manager is obviously central to the profession of project management. The project manager is the person assigned to lead the project team and take responsibility for the delivery of the project's objectives. This is different from the work of a *functional manager*, who takes responsibility for a functional unit within an organizational structure. In some instances, a project manager may report to a functional manager, but other times the role may report to a program or portfolio manager.

---

■ **Exam Tip**    Not all organizations have program managers or portfolio managers, nor should they. Those roles are generally reserved for large, mature organizations. But for the exam, unless you are specifically told otherwise in the question, you should assume that the scenario has all three roles in an organization.

---

A competent project manager must have a wide range of skills and experience to be successful. These include specific skills for the industry in which the manager is working, and general management skills; the manager must also demonstrate a high degree of expertise in and knowledge about project management, the ability to self-motivate and achieve results through high performance, and great personal effectiveness while leading the project. It is key to the success of the project manager that this person possess not only the right technical skills but also the right interpersonal skills, which are covered in a later section.

---

▓ **Exam Tip**    On the exam, you must always assume that the role of the project manager is proactive and in control of the project. The project manager takes complete responsibility for the project, which may differ from your experience.

---

## REAL WORLD

In my opinion, the easiest way to describe the role of the project manager is to replace the title *project manager* with *general manager of a project*. We all know what a general manager does, and a project manager really is the general manager of a project and must take the same senior role.

In addition to the role of project manager, there are also the roles of *project coordinator* and *project expeditor*. A project coordinator has less power and authority than a project manager, and a project expeditor has little or no power and authority.

---

▓ **Exam Tip**    For the exam, look for any project role description that differs on the basis of the amount of power and authority. High levels of both refer to a project manager; mid levels refer to a project coordinator; and low levels refer to a project expeditor.

---

The project team is made up of the staff who have been assigned or recruited to the project to provide technical skills. It includes at its core the project manager, the direct members of the project team, and also the members of the wider project team. The difference between direct members of the project team and members of the wider project team relates to whether they are assigned full-time or part-time to the project. If you are working in a matrix organizational structure, team members come from different functional areas. If it is a strong matrix organization, the team members report solely to the project manager; if it is a weak matrix organization, the team members still report to the functional managers.

The exact composition of any project team depends on the organizational culture, organizational structure, scope of work, geographic location of the work to be done, and availability of team members. There are four categories of project team. The first is the *dedicated project team*, where the majority of the team members are working full-time on the project. Second is the *part-time project team*, where functional managers have more power and authority and assignment to the project is generally part-time for both the project manager and the project team members. A third type of project team is created from the *partnership between two or more organizations* that agree to assign staff to the project team. This offers flexibility and the ability to secure resources and technical experience that any one organization may not have. The fourth and final form of project team is the *virtual team*, which is increasingly used with the broadening geographical spread of team members throughout the world. Bringing together a virtual team and getting it to perform well is a challenge for any project manager and requires special attention to overcome potential obstacles.

## REAL WORLD

It is increasingly common in the real world for team members to be drawn from differing geographical locations. These locations can be different parts of a city, different parts of a country, or even different countries. In addition to the problems presented by a lack of colocation and face-to-face communication when developing a high-performing team, a number of other problems can potentially adversely affect the outcome of the project. A project manager working in or with a virtual team needs to be mindful and aware of the potential problems that can arise and address them early and consistently throughout the life of the project.

A *program manager* leads a program of projects. A *program of projects* is a group of projects that are linked in some way. They may share resources, or they may be contributing to a greater deliverable. The role of the program manager is to manage competing interests between the projects. A *portfolio manager* has responsibility for a *portfolio of projects*—all the projects an organization is undertaking—and is usually in charge of project-selection processes to ensure that all projects align with organizational strategy and meet documented financial and nonfinancial criteria.

A *project sponsor* is the person responsible for providing the initial statement of work, approving the financial spend on the project, signing the project charter and approving any changes to it, and being the project champion. The person in this role is internal to the organization and sits on the *project steering committee* or group. The role of the project steering committee or group is to provide high-level support, oversight, and, if required, governance.

---

▓ **Exam Tip**   Don't get the roles of project sponsor and client mixed up. The project sponsor is always internal, whereas the client may be internal or external but is the recipient of the deliverable.

---

## REAL WORLD

Many people assume that the client is responsible for financing a project. This isn't true. The client pays the bills after the costs have been incurred. Someone in the organization, usually the project sponsor, must approve the organization's incurring the costs, such as wages or salaries and materials purchased to complete the work, and financing these costs until such time as the client pays the bills.

Figure 7-1 shows the hierarchy of roles from project steering committee down to members of the wider project team.

*Figure 7-1.* *The descending hierarchy of groups and individuals in a project*

The functional manager is a role that a project manager needs to be mindful of, because the majority of organizations are organized around functional areas, even if they are acting as matrix organizations. The functional manager is usually a general manager or team leader of a particular group of technical experts, and this manager assigns staff members to the project for the duration of the project. The project manager must negotiate with the functional manager for the people; who has the most power in the relationship will affect availability of people for the project. This issue is discussed in more depth in an upcoming section.

Now that the typical roles in an organization have been covered, you can use organizational charts and position descriptions to help produce the human resource management plan. There are several graphical and text-based formats for doing this. The most popular are organizational charts, matrix charts such as the *RACI* chart, and text-based descriptions, such as those often used for job descriptions.

The *organizational chart* is another example of a breakdown structure such as the work breakdown structure (WBS). It takes a high-level concept—in this case, the organization—and breaks it down into its component roles. It starts at the top with the chief executive officer (CEO) or general manager and breaks down the organization into lower-level roles such as line manager, team leader, team member, and specific technical roles. In addition to using the chart to break down organization-wide roles, you can also use it to break down project roles, in which case you have the project manager at the top and lower-level project roles beneath this. Figure 7-2 shows an example of an organizational chart.

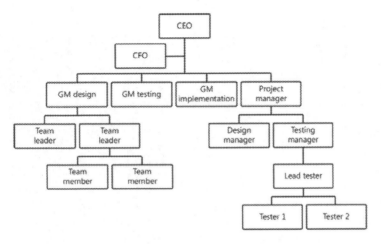

**Figure 7-2.** *An example of an organizational chart*

Another popular way to display not only roles but also the responsibilities of different roles is a matrix-based chart called a *RACI chart*. A RACI chart is a type of *responsibility assignment matrix* (RAM). A RACI chart describes who is responsible (R), who is accountable (A), who will be consulted (C), and who will be informed (I) about different activities. Being *responsible* for an activity means producing or actually completing the work, whereas being *accountable* for an activity means having to answer for the work being done or not being done on time. A single person can be both responsible and accountable for an activity, and if your project is large enough to have many team members, you can split the responsibility and accountability as a means of ensuring better management of activities. Figure 7-3 shows an example of a RACI chart.

| Activity | Team member | | | |
|---|---|---|---|---|
| | David | Thomas | Jayne | Mark |
| Collect requirements | R/A | C | C | I |
| Design prototype | C | A | R | |
| Test | | I | R | A |

*Figure 7-3.* *An example of a RACI chart showing team member responsibility and accountability*

---

## REAL WORLD

I have used several forms of the RACI chart on different projects. Some smaller projects simply have an RA chart. I also did some work for a large company that had its own variant, an RASCI chart, with the S standing for *support*, to indicate which team members were providing technical support.

---

# Networking

*Networking* is the action of interacting with and building relationships with other people for political and influencing purposes. Networking can be undertaken in both informal and formal ways. Networking is important because getting the people you want when you want them usually involves negotiation with other managers.

---

## REAL WORLD

I have always found that networks are a great way to increase your influence and reputation. At the heart of any network connection is a strong personal relationship and reputation. Take time to build genuine relationships, and your networking efforts will pay off more.

---

# Organizational Theory

As part of your efforts to produce an appropriate human resource management plan for your project, you need to have a good grasp of organizational theory and how it impacts on human resource management and project success. The way in which an organization is structured can influence its culture, its strategy, its personnel recruitment, and the projects it chooses to do. Different organizational structures have different strengths and weaknesses when it comes to successful project management. The main types of organizational structures are the functional organization, the matrix organization, and the projectized organization. The organizational structure is usually demonstrated in the organizational breakdown structure or organization chart.

In a *functional organizational* structure, there is a chief executive officer (CEO) or similar at the top. Under the CEO are general managers, or functional managers, of each functional area. Below the general managers are team leaders. There may also be shared services, such as human resources and finance, directly reporting to the CEO as well. In this sort of organizational structure, staff report directly to the functional manager, who is responsible for assigning them to work or deciding on their remuneration packages and ensuring that they are part of the team; thus, the functional manager has all the power and authority. If an organization wants to undertake a project, generally the project is staffed by members from one functional area, and there can be little cooperation and coordination between the different functional areas. A project manager working in this sort of organizational structure will have great difficulty in obtaining the people and finances needed to complete the project without first getting approval from the functional manager. Figure 7-4 shows an example of a functional organizational structure.

***Figure 7-4.*** *An organizational chart showing a functional organizational structure*

A *matrix organization* is one in which a functional structure exists, but the organization has decided to do projects by using people and resources from different functional areas. The project manager is assigned a team and access to resources from these different functional areas, and both the project manager and functional manager have power and authority in deciding the allocation and use of people.

In a *weak matrix* organization, most of the power and authority resides with the functional manager. Due to the project manager's low levels of power and authority in a weak matrix organizational structure, the role may more appropriately be described as a project expeditor or project coordinator. In a *strong matrix* organization, most of the power and authority is with the project manager. Between strong and weak forms of the matrix organization is the *balanced matrix*, where power and authority is shared between functional managers and project managers. Figure 7-5 shows an example of a matrix organization with the dotted lines around roles indicating which people are assigned to the project.

**Figure 7-5.** *An organization chart showing a matrix organizational structure*

*Projectized organizations* are organized according to the projects they undertake. In this instance, the project manager acts almost as a functional manager, but instead of having a team of specialists and a functional area, the project manager has the project team, which may consist of several different technical specialties. In this instance, the project manager acts as general manager of the project and has full power and authority. Figure 7-6 shows an example of a projectized organization.

**Figure 7-6.** *Projectized organizational structure*

---

# REAL WORLD

In the real world, you often have to negotiate with functional managers for access to resources and money. Your ability to be a skilled communicator, influencer, and negotiator will come to the fore in this instance to enable you to get the resources you require when you need them.

---

Table 7-2 shows the allocation of power and authority between functional managers and project managers in the different types of organizational structures.

*Table 7-2.* *Organizational Structures, Authority, and Power*

| Functional | Weak Matrix | Balanced Matrix | Strong Matrix | Projectized |
|---|---|---|---|---|
| • Project manager may be part-time and has very little power and authority<br>• Functional manager has most authority over people and budget | • Project manager may be part-time and has low levels of power and authority<br>• Functional manager has most authority over people and budget | • Project manager may be part-time or full-time and has equal levels of power and authority with functional manager<br>• Functional manager has equal levels of authority with project manager over people and budget | • Project manager is full-time and has more power and authority than functional manager<br>• Functional manager has less authority over people and budget than project manager | • Project manager is full-time and has high to almost total power and authority<br>• Functional manager has very little, if any, authority over people and budget |

---

▓ **Exam Tip**    It is important for the exam that you understand the differences in power and authority in each of the different organizational structures. In the absence of any further information provided in the question, any questions in relation to this topic assume first that you are working in a matrix form of organizational structure and second that it is a strong matrix.

---

# Expert Judgment

Expert judgment from functional managers, current and potential team members, the project sponsor, and other stakeholders will be useful as you put together your human resource management plan.

# Meetings

Meetings are a useful way to bring together members of the project team and other stakeholders so that they can contribute to the development of the human resource management plan.

# Outputs

After applying the appropriate tools and techniques to the selected inputs, the Plan Human Resource Management process has the following output.

## Human Resource Management Plan

The Plan Human Resource Management process has the human resource management plan as its sole output. Similar to other management plans, the human resource management plan provides a description of the overall approach to human resource management and details specific guidelines on acquiring, developing, training, motivating, rewarding, and managing your project team members. In addition to the text describing all of these aspects, the human resource management plan also includes diagrams such as organizational charts and RACI charts.

An important sub-plan of the human resource management plan is the *staffing management plan*, which describes when and how project team members are to be recruited. The staffing management plan identifies whether project team members are to be recruited from internal or external sources, and the process by which they will be described, contacted, assessed, and appointed.

The human resource management plan is a subsidiary of the project management plan and is used as an input into the three human resource management executing processes. It is also used as an input into the Estimate Costs process, because it provides information about personnel costs, and it is used as an input into the Identify Risks process.

### Quick Check

1. What is the purpose of the human resource management plan?

2. What is the primary role of the project sponsor?

3. If you always have to ask the functional manager for permission to use staff to work on your project, what sort of matrix organization are you working in?

### Quick Check Answers

1.  The main purpose of the human resource management plan is to guide your actions in identifying, obtaining, rewarding, training, motivating, and managing your project team members.

2.  The primary role of the project sponsor is to provide financial support, provide project charter approval, appoint the project manager, and provide political support for the project.

3.  In this instance you are working in a weak matrix, because the functional manager has the power and authority.

# Acquire Project Team

▒ **More Info**  Acquire Project Team

You can read more about the Acquire Project Team process in the PMBOK Guide, 5th edition, in Chapter 9, section 9.2. Table 7-3 identifies the process inputs, tools and techniques, and outputs.

*Table 7-3.* *Acquire Project Team Process*

| Inputs ⇨ | Tools and Techniques ⇨ | Outputs |
|---|---|---|
| • Human resource management plan<br>• Enterprise environmental factors<br>• Organizational process assets | • Preassignment<br>• Negotiation<br>• Acquisition<br>• Virtual teams<br>• Multicriteria decision analysis | • Project staff assignments<br>• Resource calendars<br>• Project management plan updates |

The Acquire Project Team process is an executing process that uses the human resource management plan for guidance to check and confirm the availability of project team members and have them assigned to, or recruited to, the project for the period of time their services are required. If you can't get the human resources you require with the skills you need them to have at the time you need them, this will greatly affect the chances of project success. Additionally, in acquiring project team members, you need to be aware of any local or national employment legislation, collective bargaining agreements, typical employment contracts, and any other relevant guidelines.

The Acquire Project Team process covers the following executing domain task:

- Task 1: Acquire and manage project resources by following the human resource and procurement management plans, in order to meet project requirements.

# Inputs

The Acquire Project Team process uses some or all of the following inputs.

## Human Resource Management Plan

The human resource management plan is obviously a key input into the Acquire Project Team process because it provides a description of how you will carry out acquiring the people you need for your project team. More specifically, the human resource management plan includes a description of the roles and responsibilities required during the life of the project to complete the project activities, and the project organizational chart showing the number and reporting lines of people on the project team.

One of the most important parts of the human resource management plan to be used as an input into the Acquire Project Team process is the staffing management plan, because it specifically addresses how project team members are to be acquired. The human resource management plan is an output from the Plan Human Resource Management process. The staffing management plan is a subsidiary plan of the human resource management plan.

## Enterprise Environmental Factors

The specific types of enterprise environmental factors that will be useful in acquiring your project team are any local government or industry regulations affecting the employment of project personnel. Other enterprise environmental factors may also include general organizational structure issues.

## Organizational Process Assets

The specific types of organizational process assets that will assist you in acquiring your project team members include any relevant organizational policies, processes, and guidelines relating to the acquisition and employment of people. Additionally, historical information and lessons learned from previous projects are also useful organizational process assets.

# Tools and Techniques

The following tools and techniques are used on the inputs to deliver the Acquire Project Team process outputs.

# Preassignment

*Preassignment* is the advanced allocation of project team members to your project. This can happen as a result of both internal and external processes in which specific people are assigned to the project as a result of the skills and experience they may have or because of particular contractual arrangements.

---

## REAL WORLD

I've found that as a general rule, up to half of my project team members are allocated on a preassigned basis due to their particular skills and knowledge. This can be a good thing, because you know you have people with the right skills allocated to your project from the beginning. There can be a high degree of uncertainty in the process of trying to acquire people for your project via either negotiation with functional managers or an external recruitment process.

---

# Negotiation

*Negotiation* for project team members occurs in several ways. First, you need to negotiate with functional managers to get the staff you want when you want them. Your ability to negotiate in the circumstances reflects your power and authority. If you are working in a weak matrix environment, you have little power and authority, and the allocation of project team members to your project will be at the discretion of the functional manager. However, if you are working in a strong matrix organization, you have the power and authority to get the project team members you need when you need them.

The process of negotiation also occurs with external providers of project team members, or during the process of recruiting a project team member and the negotiation of a particular employment contract.

Given the importance of negotiation in acquiring project team members in a timely and cost-effective manner, it is important that you have good negotiation skills.

# Acquisition

The term *acquisition* in this instance means an external process of advertising for, interviewing, and negotiating employment contracts with project team members. Often this process is best left to professionals with experience in advertising and recruitment.

# Virtual Teams

The use of *virtual teams* is becoming increasingly common throughout the world as technology allows people to work together in ways they previously couldn't. These virtual teams can be separated by different floors in a building, can be in different cities, or can even be in different countries. The advantages of a virtual team are that it allows you to use the skills and experience of people who may not be able to co-locate in the same area, and also to cater to individual preferences in terms of work hours or work locations. The use of virtual teams is also a legitimate option when a project may incur large travel expenses in order to host face-to-face meetings. A drawback of virtual teams is that it is difficult to maintain effective communication by using any sort of technology, such as e-mail, telephone, or video conference.

## Multicriteria Decision Analysis

The process of acquiring project team members can also use *multicriteria decision analysis* so that you can take into account a variety of criteria in order to make the best decision about who should be selected to work on the project. In this instance, you choose the criteria that are relevant; these criteria can be such things as cost, experience, and availability. You give each of these a weight and then score individual candidates, multiply their scores by the weightings, and arrive at a total score. By ranking each candidate by their total score, you can determine your preferred candidates.

# Outputs

The Acquire Project Team process produces some or all of the following outputs.

## Project Staff Assignments

A key output from the Acquire Project Team process is, of course, the *project staff assignments*. Project staff assignments provide documentation of project team members' names, roles and responsibilities, contact details, and other relevant information that allows all interested stakeholders to view who is part of the project team, their roles, and how to contact them. The project staff assignments go on to be used as an input into the Manage Project Team and Develop Project Team processes.

## Resource Calendars

Resource calendars are a useful output from the Acquire Project Team process because they document when people are available to work on the project. At a high level, they include such things as weekends or public holidays; at a lower and more specific level, they include when personnel actually work according to their individual work agreements and any known holidays they are taking. The resource calendars go on to be used as an input into the Develop Project Team process, as well as the Estimate Activity Resources, Estimate Activity Durations, Develop Schedule, and Determine Budget processes.

## Project Management Plan Updates

The specific parts of the project management plan that may be updated as a result of the Acquire Project Team process are the human resource management plan and any documents affected by the human resource management plan.

### Quick Check

1. Why is the human resource management plan an important input into the Acquire Project Team process?

2. What is meant by the term *preassignment*?

3. Why are negotiation skills useful during the Acquire Project Team process?

4. What is the advantage gained in using multicriteria decision analysis?

### Quick Check Answers

1. The human resource management plan and the staffing management plan provide specific guidance on how the process of acquiring your project team members will be carried out.

2. Preassignment involves having team members allocated to your project before the project begins as a result of specific skills and experience or as a result of contractual negotiations.

3. Negotiation skills are important because when you are recruiting project team members, you may have to negotiate with their functional managers or, if you are recruiting team members from the open employment marketplace, you will have to negotiate employment contracts with them directly.

4. Using multicriteria decision analysis allows you to rank prospective team members based on important attributes to decide who should be recruited.

# Develop Project Team

▒ **More Info**   Develop Project Team

You can read more about the Develop Project Team process in the PMBOK Guide, 5th edition, in Chapter 9, section 9.3. Table 7-4 identifies the process inputs, tools and techniques, and outputs.

**Table 7-4.** *Develop Project Team Process*

| Inputs ⇨ | Tools and Techniques ⇨ | Outputs |
|---|---|---|
| • Human resource management plan<br>• Project staff assignments<br>• Resource calendars | • Interpersonal skills<br>• Training<br>• Team-building activities<br>• Ground rules<br>• Co-location<br>• Recognition and rewards<br>• Personnel assessment tools | • Team performance assessments<br>• Enterprise environmental factor updates |

The Develop Project Team process is an executing process that uses the human resource management plan to improve individual and team performance so that team members can contribute to a greater chance of project success. The goal is to develop a high-performing team, and a key concept is that the project manager has responsibility for this, must lead by example, and must actively seek to continuously develop the team. Thus, it is important that project managers actively develop and practice their leadership skills and knowledge of how to build a high-performing team.

The Develop Project Team process covers the following executing domain task:

- Task 2: Manage task execution based on the project management plan by leading and developing the project team, in order to achieve project deliverables.

# Inputs

The following inputs are used in the Develop Project Team process.

## Human Resource Management Plan

The human resource management plan is a critical input into the Develop Project Team process because it sets out and describes how the process of developing a high-performing team will occur. The human resource management plan is an output from the Plan Human Resource Management process.

## Project Staff Assignments

The project staff assignments describe who the individual project team members are and their current roles, experience, and ability. This information is useful for identifying team members and deciding who needs training. Project staff assignments are an output from the Acquire Project Team process.

## Resource Calendars

Resource calendars, which identify when the project team members are available to work, are an important input into the Develop Project Team process because they let you know when people are available to participate in team-building activities. Resource calendars are an output from the Acquire Project Team process.

# Tools and Techniques

The following tools and techniques of this process can be used on the separate inputs to deliver the process outputs.

## Interpersonal Skills

*Interpersonal skills* are key skills for any project manager to have so that the manager can effectively contribute to the development of the team. Team development is not a mechanical exercise; it is one built on relationships between people. Thus, interpersonal skills, or *soft skills*, are useful in building these relationships and contributing toward a high-performing project team.

A project manager must develop and learn a wide range of interpersonal skills to use at the appropriate times. These include the following 11 skills:

- Leadership

- Team building

- Motivation

- Communication

- Influencing

- Decision making

- Political and cultural awareness

- Negotiation

- Trust building

- Conflict management

- Coaching

You now look at each of these skills in more detail.

## Leadership

*Leadership* is the purposeful influencing of followers. A leader must have a clear vision of where they want to take their followers. In relation to a project, a *vision* can be a successful project in terms of time, cost, and quality. Because leadership is essentially a relationship between leader and follower, it must be built like any other human relationship on respect and trust, which are key elements of effective leadership.

Project managers are responsible for developing their own leadership abilities and must realize that different situations call for different leadership styles or the demonstration of a different set of leadership competencies. Because leadership is situational, the type of leadership required over time can change. Figure 7-7 shows how different leadership styles can change from a more autocratic style at the beginning of a project to a more participatory or supporting style toward the end of the project. This model indicates that a leader trusts the team members and gives away some power. Both trust and the ability to give away power are important attributes of a good leader.

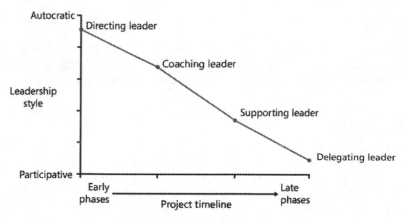

**Figure 7-7.** *The types of project leadership required at different points in a project*

*Fielder's contingency theory* states that a leader's effectiveness is contingent on two sets of factors: whether the leader is task-oriented or relationship-oriented and whether the environment is stressful or calm. A task-oriented leader is more effective in stressful situations, and a relationship-oriented leader is more effective in calm situations.

Being in a position of leadership gives power to the project manager, and a good project manager recognizes the responsibility that comes with power. If used well, power can be a great way to lead project team members, inspire people, and motivate people. If used incorrectly by a project manager, power can create hostility, demotivate an entire team, and cause staff to leave. A project manager can use five forms of power to assist in leadership of and negotiation for the project team.

- *Formal or legitimate power* is based on the position you hold as a manager. It should be viewed as an interim form of power. People may respect you initially because you are the manager, but your subsequent actions could cause this form of power to become invalid; therefore, it is not the best form of power to use.

- *The power to reward people* is a good form of power because you use it to incentivize good performance and discourage poor performance. It should not be used to blackmail or manipulate people.

- *The power to impose penalties or punishment* on people is never the best form of power to use, because it always generates negative feedback in both explicit and subtle ways.

- *Expert power* is an excellent form of power to use because it is ascribed to you by others due to your respected position as a technical expert. You are viewed as the expert in a particular area and, as such, people look up to you.

- *Referent power* is a result of your own personality and whether you are liked and respected by other people.

## Team Building

The ability to build teams is a key interpersonal skill for any project manager and leader. This topic is covered in more detail in a later section in this chapter. Team-building activities go together with good leadership to build a high-performing team.

## Motivation

The ability to motivate people and understand what motivates different people is a key interpersonal skill for a project manager to have. Different people are motivated by different things, and it is important that a project manager have an understanding of different motivation theories. The following are the most popular motivation theories that a project manager should be aware of:

- *Maslow's hierarchy of needs* describes a situation whereby people perform at their best when they have the opportunity to be what Maslow refers to as *self-actualized*. This is the top of the needs pyramid he describes. However, people want to fulfill the bottom needs first and cannot fulfill higher needs until lower ones are fulfilled, and the current need always takes precedence. So if people are concerned about their physiological well-being—for instance, if they can't afford groceries—then they will not be able to gain acceptance and esteem. Figure 7-8 shows the levels in Maslow's hierarchy of needs.

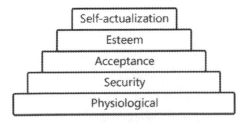

*Figure 7-8.* *Maslow's hierarchy of needs*

- *Vroom's expectancy theory* states that the expectation of receiving a reward for a certain accomplishment will motivate people to work harder, but it only works if the accomplishment is perceived to be achievable. People will make a conscious decision to work harder if they believe there are achievable outcomes. For a project manager, this means some people will respond to rewards offered in return for higher productivity, but those rewards need to be available, specific, measurable, and relevant to the individual. If not, they can prove to be a disincentive.

- *Herzberg's motivation-hygiene theory* states that hygiene factors (such as company policies, good supervision, and safe and pleasant working conditions) do not motivate, but their absence makes staff unsatisfied. Motivation factors (such as achievement, work, responsibility, and advancement) motivate, but only if hygiene factors are in place. For the project manager leading a project team, this means if the working conditions are unpleasant or unsafe, offering greater responsibility to people in return for more work will not succeed. They will first want the basic workplace environment conditions improved.

- *McClelland's human motivation, achievement, or three needs theory* states that people will work not for more money but instead for achievement, power, and affiliation. A manager should use these three needs to motivate employees.

## REAL WORLD

It is often thought that money is the prime motivator for people. This is true only to the point where you pay people enough to take the issue of money off the table. The specific amount differs between regions and countries, but at a certain point, people have enough money to take care of their essential and basic needs and have some discretionary income to be able to afford nonessential things. Above a certain amount of money, people are motivated by more intrinsic things such as prestige, responsibility, recognition, and authority. I have always found that when working with experienced, educated professionals, as I often do in a project, these latter factors are much more productive ways to motivate people.

- *McGregor's theory X and theory Y* describe a manager's attitude toward staff or team members. A theory X manager believes that team members are inherently unmotivated to work, require constant supervision, and can't be trusted. A theory Y manager believes that people want to work, can be trusted, and are naturally ambitious and self-motivated.

- Following on from McGregor's theory X and theory Y comes *Ouchi's theory Z*, which tries to increase worker loyalty and raise worker productivity by offering a job for life and providing support for the employee both in and out of the workplace.

---

## REAL WORLD

I'm sure we have all dealt with managers who exhibit some theory X attributes. It is important to realize that it has been proven that management in a theory X style is extremely counterproductive and leads to lower productivity, decreased staff morale, and increased staff turnover. As you develop your own managerial style, I encourage you to model yourself after those managers you have admired most; they probably displayed theory Y attributes.

---

▨ **Note**    Motivation Theories

As part of your own professional development, you may want to read the seminal works by the authors mentioned in this section and the works of authors influenced by these people.

▨ **Exam Tip**    Make sure you know the basics of each of these theories for the exam. Don't get confused by an answer with just any old surname in it. If you know the basics, you will be able to differentiate between a right answer, a wrong answer, and a made-up answer.

---

# Communication

Excellent communication skills are an essential interpersonal skill for a project manager, because communication forms the basis of any relationship. Chapter 8 covers communication skills in more detail.

# Influencing

The ability to proactively influence people is an important interpersonal skill that a project manager must have. It is achieved through being genuine, leading by example, establishing networks, and adjusting communication styles to suit the audience.

■ **Exam Tip** A project manager must always be proactively influencing all aspects of the project, potential change requests, and stakeholder expectations.

---

## REAL WORLD

There is a fine line between influencing and manipulation. Manipulation usually has a secret agenda and seeks to force people to do something they wouldn't normally do. Influencing is a political act that is built on relationships, mutual understanding, and an attempt to elicit cooperation from others.

---

# Decision Making

Decision-making skills are essential for any project manager. In making decisions, project managers normally use four basic decision styles, depending on time constraints, trust between team members, quality of information, and ability to get acceptance. These decision styles are *command, consultation, consensus,* and, if all else fails, *coin flip*. In addition to these reactive means of making a decision, there is a more formal six-phase decision-making model developed by Morris and Sashkin. In this model, the six phases in making a decision are as follows:

1. Problem definition

2. Problem solution generation

3. Ideas to action

4. Solution action planning

5. Solution evaluation planning

6. Evaluations of the outcome and process

# Political and Cultural Awareness

Political and cultural awareness should be a focus for project managers because they need to develop and demonstrate the skillful use of politics and power in order to be successful. Additionally, having an awareness of various cultures and their differences enables a project manager to operate more effectively.

## Negotiation

Advanced negotiation skills are key skills used in several areas in the profession of project management. The goal of any negotiation is an agreement from which all parties to the agreement will benefit. A win-win outcome is the optimal outcome from a negotiation. Complex negotiations may require specialist skills that the project manager may want to learn, or the project manager may want to bring in experts to complete the negotiations.

## Trust Building

Trust building within the team and also with stakeholders is a key interpersonal skill of any project manager. Trust is a reciprocal relationship built on authenticity. A lack of trust in your relationships with team members and other stakeholders will adversely affect your chances of project success.

## Conflict Management

Conflict management is covered in more detail in the Manage Project Team process in the next section. The key goal of conflict management is to resolve conflict permanently and openly wherever possible.

## Coaching

Coaching is an important interpersonal skill for the project manager to have and display. It involves providing wisdom and experience to others to enable them to develop professional and personally.

---

■ **Exam Tip**    All negotiations should be entered into in good faith. It is never acceptable to coerce weaker parties in a negotiation into an agreement that may be against their best interests.

---

# Training

In order to fully develop individuals on your team, you need to offer *training* in both technical and nontechnical (or *soft*) skills. Training can occur using internal or external trainers and can occur in a classroom environment, on the job, or, increasingly, via remote or online means. Training needs can be agreed on with team members at regular intervals such as during their performance appraisals, or training can be provided reactively in response to observed needs.

▓ **Exam Tip**   You should always assume that you will have to provide training to team members and that you have made a commitment to providing training at all times. This is particularly important if you come across a question on the exam where a team member does not have the right skills to complete an activity. Your first option is always to get them the required training.

## Team-Building Activities

*Team-building activities* can take many forms, but all have the goal of enhancing the sense of a single team among everyone working on the project. They can be informal or formal, planned or spontaneous, structured or free-flowing. It is important to realize that team-building activities are not a one-time event; they are instead a continual and ongoing process.

---
### REAL WORLD
---

I have always found that having a constant series of both organized and spontaneous team-building activities that appeal to team members is not only an important way to increase a sense of camaraderie and productivity, but also a great way to develop a unique sense of a team identity and culture.

The *Tuckman five-stage model* is a convenient way to describe the stages a team goes through: forming, storming, norming, performing, and adjourning. Although many models show these as linear stages in team development, this isn't always the case; any of the behaviors can be observed at any time. Also, teams can cycle between and within an area, and providing awareness of the model and stages to team members can help propel your team to the performing stage more quickly. The key point about the model is that your goal is to get your team to the performing stage and keep them there with proactive team management.

Figure 7-9 shows the different stages of the Tuckman five-stage model against performance and time. Although the diagram may indicate an unstoppable linear progression, the reality is that team dynamics can be highly unstable and teams are always in danger of slipping backward into storming behaviors.

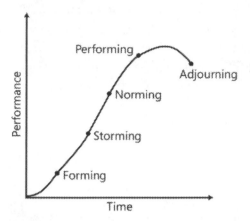

*Figure 7-9.* *The Tuckman five-stage model of team development*

When a group meets for the first time, or when new people join a group, there is a period of *forming* as everybody tries to figure out who the other members are, what common interests they share, where they sit in the hierarchy, and what their role in the team will be.

Fairly soon after a new team forms or a new person joins the team, you witness *storming* behaviors. This is the phase in which the team has to work out what direction they will all be going in, which ideas take priority, and which ideas will be cast aside. This phase is often one of conflict and argument; it can also include passive-aggressive behavior as people on the team jostle for position and power. You will also find storming behaviors in the life of an established team when conditions change. Although storming is essential, the core issues must be resolved to allow the team to fully move beyond it.

*Norming* is the process when team members explicitly and implicitly define and accept team behaviors and norms. Norming should be the outcome of the storming phase. During the process of norming, if the issues from the storming phase haven't been dealt with, it will be very hard for people to settle down into a normalized culture.

*Performing* describes the state where the team has moved through the other phases and begins to achieve a high sense of synergy. This is not a static state, however; it's threatened by things such as conflict, team stability, team culture, and external influences. The goal is to keep the team at this stage with constant attention and effort.

*Adjourning* is the final stage for groups, particularly in project management. It occurs when individuals leave the project as their jobs end or when the team disbands after completing the project. Recognizing and planning for this stage is an important part of the project manager's job.

| REAL WORLD |
| --- |

As a project manager, I have been lucky enough to understand teams and their development and have often watched people go through the stages described in the Tuckman five-stage model of team development. My main focus as a project manager has been to make people aware of what was going on and assist them to move to the performing stage. However, I must admit to also being involved in storming behaviors and being totally oblivious to it until the benefit of hindsight revealed it to me. This is one of the main reasons I now often use an independent outsider to assist with regular team-building and assessment activities.

## Ground Rules

Having a clear set of *ground rules* for expected and accepted group behaviors is an important element of successful team building. Ground rules are more often accepted and enforced by team members if they have had input into the rules' creation. Common ground rules are related to work hours, cooperation, conflict resolution, and participation.

## Co-location

*Co-location* means trying to get as many of the project team members in face-to-face contact with each other as possible by placing them in the same physical location permanently or on a regular basis, such as in team meeting rooms. The purpose of co-location is to enhance team building through better and more effective communication and relationship building. People do these things better when they can see each other. The practice of co-locating people in the same space is often called the creation of a *war room*.

## Recognition and Rewards

The purpose of *recognition* and *rewards* is to promote acceptable behaviors and discourage unacceptable behaviors from project team members. As covered already, several motivation theories point out that money is not the best way to recognize or reward performance or behavior. There are other ways of recognizing and rewarding people that are much more effective. Team members appreciate recognition, either publically or privately, for good work, and they feel valued when the right rewards are given. It is up to project managers to ensure that they are catering to individual needs with appropriate recognition and rewards.

## Personnel Assessment Tools

A key element of any effort to develop individual team members is a defined way to assess individual performances and training needs. *Personnel assessment tools* assist in formalizing the process of assessing an individual and planning for their future professional development. A common means of doing this is via the regular performance appraisal meeting and the use of the 360-degree feedback method. In this method, feedback is sought from an individual's peers, superiors, and those who report to that individual and then provided in a structured setting in a positive way.

---

### REAL WORLD

A poorly carried out 360-degree review can backfire very badly. I recall witnessing a junior manager carrying out his first 360-degree review on a project manager. As part of the team, I was sent a questionnaire that only asked what the project manager's weaknesses were and what that manager had done wrong that had to be improved. The very way the questions were phrased set a poor tone, and I heard that the project manager walked out of the assessment and refused to take part in another with that manager due to the stream of negative feedback.

---

# Outputs

The major outputs from the Develop Project Team process are the following.

## Team Performance Assessments

The primary output from the Develop Project Team process are the *team performance assessments*, which are prepared by the project manager and document the training activities undertaken and still to be undertaken, any team-building activities undertaken or planned and their outcome, and individual performance assessments. These assessments are measured against any predefined performance expectations. These predefined performance expectations can include such metrics as staff turnover, length of employment, improvement in individual and team competency, and measures of team cohesiveness.

Team performance assessments go on to be used as an input into the Manage Project Team process.

# Enterprise Environmental Factor Updates

The enterprise environmental factors updates that occur as a result of the Develop Project Team process include general organizational personnel employment policies and guidelines.

**Quick Check**

1. Who has responsibility for the ongoing development of the team and individuals on the team?

2. Why is it important that the project manager have a well-developed set of interpersonal skills?

3. If you are witnessing arguments between team members, what phase of the Tuckman five-stage team development model is the team at?

4. What is the most important aspect to recognize when rewarding people for work done or offering rewards as the incentive to do work?

5. What are the two best forms of power a project manager can use?

**Quick Check Answers**

1. The project manager has ultimate responsibility for leading the team and taking care of group and individual development needs.

2. The successful development of a team requires the project manager to use a range of interpersonal skills.

3. The team is at the storming stage.

4. The most important thing to recognize when using rewards is to make them appropriate and meaningful to the individual or team.

5. The two best forms of power the project manager can use are expert, in which the manager is viewed as an expert because of their technical ability, and reward, in which they can provide incentives for good work.

# Manage Project Team

---

▓ **More Info**    Manage Project Team

You can read more about the Manage Project Team process in the PMBOK Guide, 5th edition, in Chapter 9, section 9.4. Table 7-5 identifies the process inputs, tools and techniques, and outputs.

---

***Table 7-5.***  *Manage Project Team Process*

| Inputs ⇨ | Tools and Techniques ⇨ | Outputs |
|---|---|---|
| • Human resource management plan<br>• Project staff assignments<br>• Team performance assessments<br>• Issue log<br>• Work performance reports<br>• Organizational process assets | • Observation and conversation<br>• Project performance appraisals<br>• Conflict management<br>• Interpersonal skills | • Change requests<br>• Project management plan updates<br>• Project document updates<br>• Enterprise environmental factor updates<br>• Organizational process asset updates |

The Manage Project Team process is an executing process that uses the human resource management plan, team performance assessments, and work performance reports to monitor team and individual performance, resolve conflicts, and optimize team performance. If as a result of carrying out this process any changes are required, then a change request is generated.

The Manage Project Team process covers the following executing domain task:

- Task 2: Manage task execution based on the project management plan by leading and developing the project team, in order to achieve project deliverables.

# Inputs

The following inputs are used in the Manage Project Team process.

# Human Resource Management Plan

The human resource management plan is a critical input into the Manage Project Team process because it provides vital information about how human resources (people) will be managed, controlled, and assessed. The human resource management plan is an output from the Plan Human Resource Management process.

# Project Staff Assignments

Project staff assignments provide a list of the project team members, their roles, and contact details, all of which are important when managing project team members. Project staff assignments are an output from the Acquire Project Team process.

# Team Performance Assessments

Team performance assessments, which are an output from the Develop Project Team process, contain information about the performance of both individuals and the entire project team. They can include an assessment of how well the team is performing as a whole and also individual assessments, such as key performance indicators (KPIs) from a person's job description, an assessment of interpersonal skills, and an assessment of contribution to the organization's goals. They can identify future training needs and contribute to professional development both while the team members are on the project and also after they leave.

# Issue Log

The *issue log* is used as an input into this process because it may describe and document relevant issues relating to management of individual team members or the team as a whole. The issue log is an output from the Manage Stakeholder Engagement process.

# Work Performance Reports

*Work performance reports*, which are an output from the Monitor and Control Project Work process, provide information about how the project team members are actually performing compared to the forecasts made about their performance. Because the project team members are responsible for all aspects of the project that generate other success metrics such as time, cost, quality, and scope, it is important that the work they are expected to do generates these performance measurements. The work performance reports focus on the performance of the team and individuals.

## Organizational Process Assets

The specific types of organizational process assets that may be useful in managing the project team include any processes or guidelines for acknowledging good work or dealing with poor performance, any financial incentive structures that may be applied to high performance, and any other relevant organizational guidelines on managing team members.

# Tools and Techniques

The following tools and techniques of this process can be used on the separate inputs to deliver the process outputs.

## Observation and Conversation

*Observation* and *conversation* are important tools to use because they allow the project manager, who has ultimate responsibility for managing a project team, to observe team member performance and talk with team members about current performance and planned future performance.

---

**REAL WORLD**

---

I have always found that one of the easiest ways to keep team members engaged is regular and ongoing direct communication using face-to-face conversations. You will be surprised what information can be exchanged and how quickly relationships can be built with a simple 10-minute conversation.

---

## Project Performance Appraisals

*Project performance appraisals* can occur on a regularly scheduled basis or on a more spontaneous basis in response to either good or poor performance. They can be conducted formally or informally but should always be viewed as an opportunity to increase good performance and offer assistance, training, and feedback to improve poor performance.

## Conflict Management

Although conflict can at times be a positive and beneficial tool for soliciting lateral thinking, in most instances conflict is perceived as a negative influence on team performance and needs to be addressed promptly, openly, and with a view to resolving the core issues in order to ensure that it does not adversely affect team performance. The most common causes of conflict between project team members are time constraints, project priorities, resource availability, differences in technical opinions, administrative processes, project cost and budget, and individual personalities.

It is the role of the project manager to take responsibility first of all for setting in place ground rules for accepted and expected behaviors in working with the team. If conflict does arise, the project manager must take responsibility for dealing with it. There are five main ways to deal with conflict, each with a different outcome:

- *Withdrawal or avoiding* simply avoids dealing with conflict. This is definitely not the best way to deal with conflict.

- *Smoothing, or accommodating*, tries to resolve conflict by getting parties to agree to disagree and put work ahead of conflict. This approach doesn't deal with the root causes, and therefore the conflict may flare up again at any time.

- *Compromise, or reconciliation*, is a conflict-resolution technique that involves each party giving something up in order to resolve the conflict. Thus, instead of being a win-win solution, the result can often be a lose-lose situation. This approach should be viewed as a second-best option to confronting or problem-solving.

- *Forcing, or directing*, involves one party to the conflict pushing their viewpoint on another person and trying to have that person adopt it, through the use of various forms of power.

- *Collaboration, or problem-solving*, is the best option for dealing with any conflict, because it seeks to deal with the conflict in a permanent manner involving multiple viewpoints and resolve it openly through consensus.

---

░ **Exam Tip**   You should always assume that conflict is inevitable in any project and that you will have to deal with it. As the project manager, it is your responsibility to always deal with conflict in an open manner that seeks to resolve the core reasons for the conflict. Simply ignoring conflict or sweeping it under the carpet is not an acceptable solution, because this will eventually manifest in a number of ways, all of which are detrimental to your team's performance and ultimately to the success of the project.

---

## Interpersonal Skills

A project manager's interpersonal skills are very useful in managing the project team—particularly leadership, influencing, and decision-making skills. These were covered in depth in the Develop Project Team process.

# Outputs

The major outputs from the Manage Project Team process are the following.

## Change Requests

As a result of carrying out the Manage Project Team process, you may discover variations between what you had planned in terms of team performance and what is actually occurring. Additionally, you may wish to amend any planned acquisition or development activities in order to optimize team performance. Any of these options will involve the creation of a change request; the change request will be an input into the Perform Integrated Change Control process, where it will be considered as part of the documented change-control process.

## Project Management Plan Updates

The specific parts of the project management plan that may be updated as a result of the Manage Project Team process are the human resource management plan and the staffing management plan.

## Project Document Updates

Specific project documents that may be updated as a result of carrying out this process are such things as the issue log and project staff assignments.

## Enterprise Environmental Factor Updates

The specific enterprise environmental factors that may be updated include any organizational employee performance appraisal and feedback policies and guidelines.

## Organizational Process Asset Updates

The specific organizational process assets that may be updated include any standard templates or processes relating to management of personnel, any templates, and any historical information or lessons-learned documentation.

### Quick Check

1. What is the main focus of the Manage Project Team process?

2. Why are observation and conversation important tools in successfully managing a project team?

3. What is the best method to use for successful conflict management?

**Quick Check Answers**

1. The main focus of the Manage Project Team process is to analyze team performance against forecast team performance and undertake actions to ensure high team performance by providing feedback and, if necessary, submitting change requests to optimize team performance.

2. Because the management of team performance relies heavily on a project manager's ability to accurately observe what is occurring with individual and team performance, the two tools of observation and conversation are excellent means of gathering information from team members.

3. The best method to ensure successful conflict management is to take a confronting or problem-solving approach that will permanently resolve any conflict being dealt with.

# Chapter Summary

- The Human Resource Management knowledge area is focused on the areas around planning which people you need, obtaining the people you need when you need them, taking responsibility to continually train and develop your project team members, and monitoring individual and team performance.

- The Plan Human Resource Management process produces the human resource management plan, which guides the three subsequent executing processes.

- The first of the three executing processes in the Human Resource Management knowledge area, the Acquire Project Team process, uses the human resource management plan to obtain the project team members you require with the appropriate skills at the time when you need them.

- The Develop Project Team process, which is an executing process, reflects a commitment to understanding the professional development and ongoing training needs of individual team members and the overall team. The goal of this process is to achieve a high-performing project team via a variety of tools and techniques.

- The Manage Project Team process is focused on using the human resource management plan, which outlines the expected levels of individual and team performance, and checking team performance against it. Providing feedback and making changes and corrective actions is an important part of the Manage Project Team process.

# Exercises

The answers for these exercises are located in the "Answers" section at the end of this chapter.

1.  Match the management theory on the left with the description on the right.

| Human Resource Management Tool | Definition |
| --- | --- |
| 1. McGregor's theory X and theory Y | A. A theory stating that certain basic workplace factors must be in place before less tangible factors can be used to motivate staff |
| 2. Tuckman five-stage model of team development | B. A theory that describes the attitude of managers toward staff and separates them into those who believe staff are self-motivated and trustworthy and those who belief staff are lazy and untrustworthy |
| 3. Vroom's expectancy theory | C. A theory stating that people will perform at their best when self-actualized but want to fulfill lower-level needs first |
| 4. Herzberg's motivation-hygiene theory | D. A theory stating that the expectation of receiving a reward for a certain accomplishment will motivate people to work harder, but it only works if the accomplishment is perceived to be achievable |
| 5. McClelland's human motivation, achievement, or three needs theory | E. A theory that people will work not for more money, but instead for achievement, power, and affiliation |
| 6. Maslow's hierarchy of needs | F. A process of describing phases that a team can pass through on the way to becoming a high-performing team |

2.  Arrange the following organizational structures in relation to the power and authority of the project manager, from weakest to strongest.

    - Strong matrix

    - Functional

    - Balanced matrix

    - Weak matrix

    - Projectized

3.  Take a look at the following list of words. They represent a type of power a project manager can have, a decision-making style a project manager can use, or a conflict-management style that can be used. Sort each of them into one of these three categories.

    - Consensus

    - Forcing

    - Referent

    - Punishment

    - Coin flip

    - Command

    - Compromise

    - Consultation

    - Withdrawal

    - Reward

    - Collaboration

    - Problem-solving

    - Formal

    - Expert

    - Smoothing

# Review Questions

Test your knowledge of the information in Chapter 7 by answering these questions. The answers to these questions, and the explanation of why each answer choice is correct or incorrect, are located in the "Answers" section at the end of this chapter.

1.  Which of the following is not an executing process in the Human Resource Management knowledge area?

    A.  Manage Project Team

    B.  Develop Project Team

    C.  Acquire Project Team

    D.  Plan Human Resource Management

2. What is the correct order of project role descriptions when ranking from most to least power?

   A. Project manager, project coordinator, project expediter

   B. Project manager, project expediter, project coordinator

   C. Project coordinator, project manager, project expediter

   D. Project coordinator, project expediter, project manager

3. If you are working in an organization where you continually have to ask another manager if you can spend money allocated to your project and obtain personnel to work on your project, what sort of organizational structure are you working in?

   A. Projectized organization

   B. Functional organization

   C. Strong matrix organization

   D. Balanced matrix organization

4. What is the best definition of a program of projects?

   A. All projects that the organization is undertaking

   B. An individual project

   C. A group of projects that a portfolio manager oversees

   D. A group of projects that are related in some way

5. What is the primary role of the project sponsor?

   A. To be ultimately accountable for the project

   B. To directly manage the performance of the project manager

   C. To provide financial and political support for the project

   D. To be the primary liaison with the client

6. If you are placing advertisements in local newspapers seeking to recruit project team members, which tool or technique are you using?

   A. Negotiation

   B. Preassignment

   C. Acquisition

   D. Recruitment

7. What information does a resource calendar contain?

    A. The pay rates of project team members

    B. A description of the role of each team member and contact details

    C. The days and times when the project team members are available to work on the project

    D. A description of the work to be done on the project

8. As a project manager, you have access to different forms of power. When managing your team, what is the worst form of power to use?

    A. Punishment

    B. Expert

    C. Referent

    D. Legitimate

9. What is the generally correct order of stages, or phases, a team will go through according to the Tuckman five-stage model of team development?

    A. Forming, storming, norming, performing, adjourning

    B. Norming, storming, forming, performing, adjourning

    C. Storming, norming, forming, performing, adjourning

    D. Storming, forming, norming, performing, adjourning

10. Which of the following is the lowest level in Maslow's hierarchy of needs?

    A. Physiological

    B. Security

    C. Esteem

    D. Self-actualization

11. You have exhausted all other techniques for making a decision and are making a random decision between two possible options. What style of decision-making technique are you using?

    A. Dice throw

    B. Coin flip

    C. Random assignment

    D. Lucky guess

12. Two project team members are disagreeing strongly about the relevant engineering standards to apply to the design of a particular element in your project. You ask them to carry on working and ignore the problem. What conflict-resolution technique are you using?

    A. Problem-solving

    B. Collaboration

    C. Forcing

    D. Avoiding

# Answers

This section contains the answers for the Exercises and Review Questions in this chapter.

## Exercises

1. Match the management theory on the left with the description on the right.

| HR Management Tool | Definition |
|---|---|
| 1. McGregor's theory X and theory Y | B. A theory that describe the attitude of managers toward staff and separates them into those who believe staff are self-motivated and trustworthy and those who belief staff are lazy and untrustworthy |
| 2. Tuckman five-stage model of team development | F. A process of describing phases that a team can pass through on the way to becoming a high-performing team |

*(continued)*

| HR Management Tool | Definition |
| --- | --- |
| 3. Vroom's expectancy theory | D. A theory stating that the expectation of receiving a reward for a certain accomplishment will motivate people to work harder, but it only works if the accomplishment is perceived to be achievable |
| 4. Herzberg's motivation-hygiene theory | A. A theory stating that certain basic workplace factors must be in place before less tangible factors can be used to motivate staff |
| 5. McClelland's human motivation, achievement, or three needs theory | E. A theory that people will work not for more money, but instead for achievement, power, and affiliation |
| 6. Maslow's hierarchy of needs | C. A theory stating that people will perform at their best when self-actualized but want to fulfill lower-level needs first |

2. Arrange the following organizational structures in relation to the power and authority of the project manager, from weakest to strongest.

    2. Functional

    4. Weak matrix

    3. Balanced matrix

    1. Strong matrix

    5. Projectized

3. Take a look at the following list of words. They represent a type of power a project manager can have, a decision-making style a project manager can use, or a conflict-management style that can be used. Sort each of them into one of these three categories.

| Types of Power | Decision-Making Styles | Conflict Management |
| --- | --- | --- |
| Formal | Command | Withdrawal |
| Reward | Consultation | Forcing |
| Punishment | Consensus | Smoothing |
| Expert | Coin flip | Collaboration |
| Referent | | Compromise |
| | | Problem-solving |

# Chapter Review

1.  **Correct Answer: D**

    A.  **Incorrect:** The Manage Project Team process is an executing process.

    B.  **Incorrect:** The Develop Project Team process is an executing process.

    C.  **Incorrect:** The Acquire Project Team process is an executing process.

    D.  **Correct:** The Plan Human Resource Management process is a planning process.

2.  **Correct Answer: A**

    A.  **Correct:** A project manager has the most power, followed by a project coordinator and then a project expediter.

    B.  **Incorrect:** A project coordinator has more power than a project expediter.

    C.  **Incorrect:** A project manager has more power than a project coordinator.

    D.  **Incorrect:** A project manager has more power than both a project coordinator and a project expediter.

3.  **Correct Answer: B**

    A.  **Incorrect:** In a projectized organization, a project manager has all the power and authority in relation to control of people and budgets.

    B.  **Correct:** In a functional organization, it is the functional manager who controls project costs and personnel.

    C.  **Incorrect:** In a strong matrix organization, the project manager has more power than a functional manager.

    D.  **Incorrect:** In a balanced matrix organization, the project manager and functional manager have equal amounts of power over staff and budget.

4.  **Correct Answer: D**

    A.  **Incorrect:** A portfolio best describes all the projects an organization is undertaking.

    B.  **Incorrect:** A program is more than just a single project.

    C.  **Incorrect:** A portfolio manager oversees a portfolio.

D. **Correct:** A program of projects is related in some way, and it is the role of the program manager to sort out potential conflicts between projects in a program.

5. **Correct Answer: C**

A. **Incorrect:** The project manager is ultimately accountable for the project, not the project sponsor.

B. **Incorrect:** It is not generally the project sponsor's role to manage the performance of the project manager, although this can occasionally occur.

C. **Correct:** The primary role of the project sponsor is to provide financial and political support for the project from initiation through closure.

D. **Incorrect:** The primary liaison with the client is generally the project manager, unless there are contractual reasons for it to be somebody else.

6. **Correct Answer: C**

A. **Incorrect:** Negotiation is the process of negotiating with other managers for people to work on your project, or negotiation as part of employment contracts.

B. **Incorrect:** Preassignment is the process of having people directly allocated to your project.

C. **Correct:** Acquisition is the tool or technique that actively seeks to recruit project team members.

D. **Incorrect:** Recruitment may be a particular term used by some in the industry, but it is not the standardized PMBOK Guide term.

7. **Correct Answer: C**

A. **Incorrect:** The resource calendar does not contain the pay rates of project team members.

B. **Incorrect:** It is not the resource calendar, but the project staff assignments, that contain a description of the role of each team member and their contact details.

C. **Correct:** A resource calendar outlines when project team members are available to work on the project.

D. **Incorrect:** A description of the work to be done on the project is found in the scope statement.

323

8. **Correct Answer: A**

   A. **Correct:** The use of punishment generally results in negative consequences on team performance; thus it is the worst form of power to use.

   B. **Incorrect:** Expert power is gained from being an acknowledged technical expert in a particular area, and it is a positive form of power to use.

   C. **Incorrect:** Referent power is gained from your personality and charisma, and it is a positive form of power to use.

   D. **Incorrect:** Legitimate power is attributed to the person due to the job description. It is not a long-lasting form of power.

9. **Correct Answer: A**

   A. **Correct:** First people come together in the forming phase, and then they go through storming behaviors before settling on norming. Then a team can enter the performing stage and finally the adjourning stage.

   B. **Incorrect:** Norming behaviors come after storming behaviors, and forming behaviors come before storming behaviors.

   C. **Incorrect:** Norming behaviors come after storming behaviors.

   D. **Incorrect:** Storming behaviors come after forming and before norming.

10. **Correct Answer: A**

   A. **Correct:** Physiological needs like food and water must be satisfied first.

   B. **Incorrect:** Security is the second-lowest level in Maslow's hierarchy of needs.

   C. **Incorrect:** Esteem is the second-highest level in Maslow's hierarchy of needs.

   D. **Incorrect:** Self-actualization is the highest level in Maslow's hierarchy of needs and can only be realized after lower-level needs have been filled.

11. **Correct Answer: B**

   A. **Incorrect:** Dice throw is a made-up term and not one of the four basic decision-making techniques.

   B. **Correct:** Coin flip is one of the four basic decision-making techniques.

   C. **Incorrect:** Random assignment does not relate to decision-making techniques.

   D. **Incorrect:** Lucky guess is a made-up term and not one of the four basic decision-making techniques.

12. **Correct Answer: D**

   A. **Incorrect:** If you were using problem-solving, you would require the team members to work it out and resolve the dispute, not simply ignore it.

   B. **Incorrect:** If you were using collaboration as a conflict-resolution technique, you would ask the team members to work constructively together and, as necessary, to make compromises to achieve an agreeable outcome.

   C. **Incorrect:** Forcing would at least impose a solution and would be an attempt to resolve the conflict.

   D. **Correct:** This is a classic example of avoiding resolving the conflict.

# CHAPTER 8

■ ■ ■

# Communications Management

This chapter focuses on Project Communications Management. Similar to the other knowledge areas, it begins with a process of planning, which produces a communications management plan. It then has an executing process, Manage Communications, focusing on carrying out the communications management plan, and a monitoring and controlling process, Control Communications, focused on checking whether project communications are meeting stakeholder communication requirements.

**The PMBOK® Guide Processes**

**Project Communications Management Knowledge Area**

The three processes in the Project Communications Management knowledge area are as follows:

- Plan Communications Management (planning process)

- Manage Communications (executing process)

- Control Communications (monitoring and controlling process)

## What Is Project Communications Management?

Project communications management is focused on the processes of developing a communications management plan, gathering and distributing project information according to the communications management plan, and checking that you are completing the communications activities in accordance with the plan.

Project communications are absolutely critical for a smooth and successful running of any project, whether you are gathering information or disseminating information. You should assume that a project manager will spend 90% of their time communicating in different ways to different stakeholders. Of this time spent communicating, 50% will be spent communicating with project team members because they are the most important of the stakeholders.

© Sean Whitaker 2016
S. Whitaker, *Pass the PMP® Exam*, DOI 10.1007/978-1-4842-2074-0_8

▓ **Exam Tip**   You should always assume that communication in its many forms is at the heart of many issues in project management. If you get a question outlining a problem, and one of the potential answers involves better or improved communication, this may be the correct choice.

---

## REAL WORLD

I managed a construction project that I soon realized was actually a communications project. At the outset, we focused on building the deliverable and reporting on time and cost progress. Very few of the stakeholders were interested in the construction project itself; they were interested in how it would affect their business and the intended outcome. After about four months of work on what was a two-and-a-half-year-long project, I was taken aside by the project sponsor and told that despite the project being under budget and ahead of time, many stakeholders considered the project a failure because I wasn't communicating effectively with them. I discovered that many of these stakeholders weren't interested in updates about time and cost. They had other communication needs. The project sponsor was correct, and overnight we changed our focus from a construction project to a communications project. We began focusing on what people actually wanted to hear, how they wanted to hear it, when they wanted to hear it, and who they wanted to hear it from. Within a relatively short time, the project was judged a success.

---

▓ **Exam Tip**   The project manager should not be in control of every communication, but the project manager should control the communications process.

# Plan Communications Management

▓ **More Info**   Plan Communications Management

You can read more about the Plan Communications Management process in the PMBOK Guide, 5th edition, in Chapter 10, section 10.1. Table 8-1 identifies the process inputs, tools and techniques, and outputs.

*Table 8-1.* *Plan Communications Management Process*

| Inputs ⇨ | Tools and Techniques ⇨ | Outputs |
|---|---|---|
| • Project management plan<br>• Stakeholder register<br>• Enterprise environmental factors<br>• Organizational process assets | • Communications requirements analysis<br>• Communications technology<br>• Communications models<br>• Communications methods<br>• Meetings | • Communications management plan<br>• Project document updates |

The Plan Communications Management process is a planning process with the communications management plan as its primary output. In order to successfully develop a successful communications management plan, you need to gather and analyze information about individual stakeholders and their communication needs.

The Plan Communications Management process covers the following planning domain tasks:

- Task 6: Develop the communications management plan based on the project organization structure and stakeholder requirements, in order to define and manage the flow of project information.

- Task 12: Conduct kick-off meeting, communicating the start of the project, key milestones, and other relevant information, in order to inform and engage stakeholders and gain commitment.

# Inputs

The Plan Communications Management process uses some or all of the following inputs as part of the development of the communications management plan for the project.

## Project Management Plan

The key elements of the project management plan that are useful as inputs into the Plan Communications Management process are information about project constraints; timeframes; and scope, risk, and stakeholder expectations. The project management plan is an output from the Develop Project Management Plan process.

## Stakeholder Register

The stakeholder register is an essential input into the Plan Communications Management process. It provides information about stakeholders and most likely an assessment of their power, interest, impact, or influence on the project. This information can be used to assist in the development of a robust and appropriate communications management plan that can contribute to the effective management of stakeholder engagement and expectations. The stakeholder register is an output from the Identify Stakeholders process.

## Enterprise Environmental Factors

The specific enterprise environmental factor that is useful as an input into this process is the broader organizational structure, because that affects how well communications are managed.

## Organizational Process Assets

The specific organizational process assets that may be an important input into the development of your communications management plan include any lessons learned and historical information about successful or unsuccessful communications from past projects, and any blank templates or guidelines for the preparation of the communications management plan.

# Tools and Techniques

The following tools and techniques are available to be used to develop the inputs into this process in order to produce the communications management plan.

## Communications Requirements Analysis

The purpose of *communications requirements analysis* is to obtain a detailed description of individual stakeholders and their communications needs. In order to identify the communications requirements of individual stakeholders, you can use a variety of techniques to identify the stakeholders. These techniques allow you to either solicit their requirements from them directly or gather information from other sources about their requirements. The important thing is to gather and document the stakeholder communication requirements so you can then plan how you will meet them.

In order to appreciate the number of potential communications channels that can exist as part of identifying stakeholders on a project, you can use a formula that shows the exponential growth and total number of potential communications channels with every additional stakeholder that is identified. The formula is

$$n(n-1)/2 \frac{n(n-1)}{2}$$

where $n$ equals the number of stakeholders, including yourself.

For example, if you have four stakeholders in your project, you have six potential communications channels:

$$\frac{4 \times (4-1)}{2} = 6$$

If you have five stakeholders in your project, you have ten potential communications channels:

$$\frac{5 \times (5-1)}{2} = 10$$

If you have 20 stakeholders, you have 190 potential communication channels:

$$\frac{20 \times (20-1)}{2} = 190$$

The number of communications channels is an important consideration in your communications requirements analysis. Figure 8-1 shows how these communication channels are formed between stakeholders.

 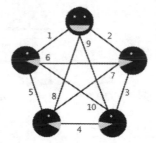

*Figure 8-1.* *How to show the number of communications channels in a project*

# Communications Technology

The choice of *communications technology* depends on several different factors, including urgency, the availability of specific forms of technology, the ease of use of that technology, the project environment, whether the project team members and stakeholders are able to communicate face to face or virtually by using technology, and the sensitivity and confidentiality of information. All of these factors influence which technologies you choose to use and favor in your communications management plan. It is becoming increasingly common to rely on virtual forms of technology, but nothing is as good as face-to-face communication.

# Communications Models

Having an awareness of a *communications model,* which outlines how communications can work, is an important skill for a project manager to have. Communications is not just a simple matter of your deciding which information you want to communicate and assuming that those with whom you want to communicate will understand what you are trying to say. According to the Shannon and Weaver communication model, there is a continual looping process in action, as Figure 8-2 shows. The sender encodes a message according to their own preferences, prejudices, and particular worldview. The sender then transmits this message via whichever communications technology, or medium, they have selected to use. As the message is transmitted, it must pass through a particular medium, and in doing so it will encounter noise. In this instance, noise does not always relate just to acoustic noise, but also includes any other aspects present in the selected medium that may interfere with or change the message being transmitted. It can include the physical environment, participant energy levels, cultural differences, accents, and individual prejudices.

The receiver then receives the message and decodes it according to their own preferences and prejudices. If the receiver then attempts to send the message on to another person or back to the original sender, it must go through the same obstacles again.

You can begin to recognize how errors in communication can happen very easily even with the best of intent. It is vital that project managers recognize the challenges to effective communication and to try to minimize the potential disruption to the messages they are trying to send.

**Figure 8-2.** *A communications model showing how a sender encodes and sends a message through a medium to a receiver*

You can mitigate some of the potential negative effects on communication in this model by practicing and being aware of the following five techniques:

- *Active listening:* With this technique, the listener takes active steps to ensure that the message was understood correctly. The result is that the listener is more engaged and there is a much better transfer of information between sender and receiver.

```
┌─────────────────────────────────────────────────────────────┐
│                       REAL WORLD                              │
└─────────────────────────────────────────────────────────────┘
```

Throughout my career as a project manager, the ability to listen and understand what people are actually communicating has played an important role in the success of projects I have managed. I remember when I was younger and perhaps a little more headstrong, and I would take shortcuts when receiving information from people, assuming I understood what they were trying to communicate. This, of course, led to many misunderstandings and inefficiencies and mistakes that affected the chances of project success. I have since learned that being an active listener is more important than being an active talker.

- *Effective listening:* Similar to active listening, this technique also involves the listener or receiver monitoring non-verbal and physical communication.

- *Feedback:* This consists of cues from the receiver to the sender that indicate whether the message has been understood.

- *Nonverbal:* This is communication in the form of body language, posture, and similar. You may be surprised to know that most communication is nonverbal and that we are very skilled at picking up nonverbal communication.

- *Paralingual:* This type of communication is vocal but not verbal, and includes tone of voice, inflections, and volume—how the words are said rather than what is said.

## Communications Methods

You can use three broad categories of types of *communications methods*:

- *Interactive communication:* Where all parties in the communications conduct a multidirectional exchange of information concurrently. The most common examples of interactive communication include team meetings, phone calls, and videoconferencing.

- *Push communication:* A form of communication that is sent to recipients. It is an effective means of communication to ensure that information is distributed as planned and includes e-mail messages, reports, memos, press releases, and letters.

- *Pull communication:* Used when recipients can choose to access information at their own discretion. Common examples of pull communication include intranet and Internet sites and e-learning sites.

333

In addition to these categories of communications, there are also different ways in which communications can be delivered. These can be formal or informal and verbal or written. Table 8-2 shows the possible combinations of these communications forms and examples of each.

***Table 8-2.*** *Types of Communication*

| Method | Examples |
| --- | --- |
| Informal written | Notes, e-mail messages, memos |
| Formal written | Contracts, legal notices |
| Informal verbal | Meetings, discussions, phone calls, conversations |
| Formal verbal | Speeches, mass communications, presentations |

# Meetings

Meetings are generally a useful way to bring together members of the project team and other stakeholders so that they can contribute to the development of the communications management plan. Effective meetings feature the use of predistributed agendas, defined start and finish times, agreed ground rules, and a focus on decision-making.

A particular type of meeting that is useful for communicating the end of project planning and the beginning of project execution is the kick-off meeting. The kick-off meeting is held with project team members and relevant stakeholders in attendance, usually on site, and it signifies the start of execution. It is a particularly effective form of communication because it signals to the team and stakeholders that the project is progressing, and it contributes to increased team morale.

# Outputs

After applying the appropriate tools and techniques to the selected inputs, the Plan Communications Management process has the following outputs.

## Communications Management Plan

The Plan Communications Management process has the *communications management plan* as its primary output. Similar to other management plans, the communications management plan provides a guide for completing the communications management activities in the project.

Your communications management plan identifies individual stakeholders, what information they require, when they require that information, how they will receive information, from whom the information will be received, and any other issues affecting communications. Your communications management plan may also outline key messages, general communication strategies, how you will review and update the plan, and an overview of the intended outcomes from the communications management plan. The communications management plan is a subsidiary of the project management plan and is used as an input into the other two communications management processes.

---

## REAL WORLD

Keep in mind that a lack of communication is a communication in itself. Some stakeholders will take a lack of communication as a sign of arrogance and indifference. I have always found that the absence of communication leads to opinions based on assumptions and gossip. Correcting these opinions takes more energy and time than it would have taken to distribute the correct information in the first place.

---

## Project Document Updates

The specific project documents that may be updated as a result of the Plan Communications Management process are the stakeholder register and requirements documentation, scope statement, issue log, and any other relevant documents.

### Quick Check

1.  What is the primary purpose of the communications management plan?

2.  If you are working in an organization with nine stakeholders, including yourself, how many potential communications channels are there?

3.  What is the significance of the kick-off meeting?

### Quick Check Answers

1.  The main purpose of the communications management plan is to guide your actions in defining what communications the project is going to receive and send, how it will identify stakeholders communications requirements, and how information will be tracked and measured.

2.  If you have 9 stakeholders, including yourself, there are 36 potential communications channels.

3.  The kick-off meeting is used to gather project team members and other relevant stakeholders together and communicate to them that enough planning has occurred for project execution to begin.

# Manage Communications

---

▧ **More Info**    Manage Communications

You can read more about the Manage Communications process in the PMBOK Guide, 5th edition, in Chapter 10, section 10.2. Table 8-3 identifies the process inputs, tools and techniques, and outputs.

---

*Table 8-3.* *Manage Communications Process*

| Inputs ⇨ | Tools and Techniques ⇨ | Outputs |
|---|---|---|
| • Communications management plan<br>• Work performance reports<br>• Enterprise environmental factors<br>• Organizational process assets | • Communications technology<br>• Communications models<br>• Communications methods<br>• Information management systems<br>• Performance reporting | • Project communications<br>• Project document updates<br>• Project management plan updates<br>• Organizational process asset updates |

The Manage Communications process is an executing process that gathers project information so that it can be distributed and stored according to the communications management plan.

The Manage Communications process covers the following executing domain task:

- Task 6: Manage the flow of information by following the communications plan, in order to keep stakeholders engaged and informed.

# Inputs

The Manage Communications process uses some or all of the following inputs.

## Communications Management Plan

The communications management plan is an essential component of the Manage Communications process because it provides direction and guidelines on how to complete this process. The communications management plan is an output from the Plan Communications Management process.

# Work Performance Reports

Work performance reports are a specific presentation of work performance information. The timely dissemination of work performance reports to the right stakeholders is one of the factors influencing project success. All project reports should be tailored to be suitable to their intended audience. Work performance reports are an output from the Monitor and Control Project Work process.

# Enterprise Environmental Factors

The specific types of enterprise environmental factor that are useful in managing project communications are any broad organizational cultural issues, any relevant government or industry standards, and any licensed software being used to gather and disseminate information.

# Organizational Process Assets

The specific types of organizational process assets that will assist in managing project communications are any blank templates, historical information and lessons learned, and project-specific policies and guidelines relating to communications management.

# Tools and Techniques

The following tools and techniques are used on the inputs to deliver the Manage Communications process outputs.

# Communications Technology

The particular type of communication technology you choose to use to facilitate project communication is an important consideration because each stakeholder will respond differently to the technology chosen. It is up to the project manager to ensure that the correct type of communication technology is selected to ensure that individual project communication requirements can be met. Remember that what works well for one stakeholder may not work for another stakeholder.

## REAL WORLD

On a project I was managing, we generally disseminated project progress information by way of written and graphical reports. One senior manager continued to ask questions about information that was clearly contained in these reports. Answering these questions took time, so we gave this issue some thought. Ultimately we realized that instead of written reports, this person preferred brief face-to-face updates. So we initiated a regular process of "accidentally" stopping by this manager's office and giving him a brief update.

## Communications Models

An awareness of how communications work, according to a basic communications model, is important for project managers to understand so they can avoid potential obstacles and difficulties in transmitting messages. A more thorough description of communications models was covered earlier in this chapter in the Plan Communications Management process.

## Communications Methods

Your choice of push communications, pull communications, or interactive communications as a communications method depends on the stakeholder communications requirements. Communications methods were covered in more detail earlier in this chapter in the Plan Communications Management process.

## Information Management Systems

*Information management systems* are ways of managing and distributing your project information in hard copy and electronic form. Examples of hard copy distribution formats include press releases, memos, and project documents and plans. Increasingly, management and distribution of project information is handled by electronic means such as web sites, web publishing, and intranet portals.

## Performance Reporting

Effective *performance reporting* is a key element in ensuring that a project is successful and that stakeholder communication requirements are met. The way in which you collect and report performance information should be in response to how individual stakeholders want to receive that information. All performance reports should be concise, succinct, and targeted at their intended audience. Performance reports may include simple text reports, or they may be more complex reports featuring a lot of narrative and descriptive text, diagrams, and tables. The content of a performance report can be on any relevant element and metric of the project. You may also choose to report certain elements such as cost and time to one group of stakeholders, while reporting aspects of quality to another group of stakeholders.

# Outputs

The Manage Communications process produces some or all of the following outputs.

# Project Communications

*Project communications* are the key output from the Manage Communications process. They can take many forms, based on the communications management plan. You may choose to send project communications in different formats, at different times and frequencies, and with different content, according to individual stakeholder communication requirements. Project communications go on to be used as an input into the Control Communications process.

# Project Document Updates

The specific types of project documents that may be updated as a result of completing the Manage Communications process are issue logs, stakeholder registers, project schedules, and budget.

# Project Management Plan Updates

The specific part of the project management plan that may be updated as a result of the Manage Communications process is the communications management plan, along with any document affected by the communications management plan, such as the stakeholder management plan. Additionally, as a result of reporting project performance, parts of the scope management plan, time management plan, and quality management plan may be updated.

# Organizational Process Asset Updates

The specific organizational process assets that may be updated as a result of this process include any generic project performance reports, templates, stored project records, and lessons learned documentation.

**Quick Check**

1. What is the main purpose of the Manage Communications process?

2. What format should be selected, and what content should be included, when reporting project performance?

3. In the basic communication model, what can happen to an intended communication between sender and receiver?

### Quick Check Answers

1. The main purpose of the Manage Communications process is to gather project information and distribute and store it in accordance with the communications management plan, which will also reflect individual stakeholder communication requirements.

2. When reporting project performance, your choice of format and content will be directly influenced by the intended audience and their communication needs.

3. In the basic communication model, a message that is sent can encounter noise in the chosen medium. This noise could be actual audio sound, or it could be any other aspect that impedes, or interferes with, the message being sent.

# Control Communications

░ **More Info**    Control Communications

You can read more about the Control Communications process in the PMBOK Guide, 5th edition, in Chapter 10, section 10.3. Table 8-4 identifies the process inputs, tools and techniques, and outputs.

***Table 8-4.***  *Control Communications Process*

| Inputs ⇨ | Tools and Techniques ⇨ | Outputs |
|---|---|---|
| • Project management plan<br>• Project communications<br>• Issue log<br>• Work performance data<br>• Organizational process assets | • Reporting systems<br>• Expert judgment<br>• Meetings | • Work performance information<br>• Change requests<br>• Project management plan updates<br>• Project document updates<br>• Organizational process asset updates |

The Control Communications process is focused on monitoring and controlling project communications to ensure that they are in accordance with the communications management plan and individual stakeholder communication requirements.

The Control Communications process covers the following monitoring and controlling domain tasks:

- Task 1: Measure project performance using appropriate tools and techniques, in order to identify and quantify any variances and corrective actions.

- Task 5: Review the issue log, and update if necessary, and determine corrective actions by using appropriate tools and techniques, in order to minimize the impact on the project.

- Task 6: Capture, analyze, and manage lessons learned using lessons learned management techniques, in order to enable continuous improvement.

# Inputs

The following inputs are used in the Control Communications process.

## Project Management Plan

The project management plan contains information about how each part of the project will be executed, monitored, and closed, and as such it provides a valuable input into any monitoring and controlling process. The specific part of the project management plan that is most useful for the Control Communications process is the communications management plan. The project management plan is an output from the Develop Project Management Plan process, and the communications management plan is an output from the Plan Communications Management process.

## Project Communications

Project communications include all forms of communication about project progress, and also any communications that seek to generate political support from stakeholders for the project. As such, project communications can be in many forms and can contain different amounts and types of information. The most common forms of project communications relate to project performance reports about the most popular project metrics: cost, time, and quality. Project communications are an output from the Manage Communications process.

## Issue Log

The issue log is a useful input into the Control Communications process because it documents and describes issues relating to communication. Additionally, the issue log provides information about who is responsible for resolving and monitoring the issue. Therefore, the issue log is useful both as a repository of project issues and as a communications tool that shows stakeholders that issues are being dealt with. The issue log is an output from the Manage Stakeholder Engagement process.

## Work Performance Data

Work performance data is the raw information gathered about how well the project is doing in relation to cost, time, quality, and any other relevant metrics that are being measured. Work performance data is turned into work performance information in the Control Communications process, and this work performance information in turn is turned into work performance reports in the Monitor and Control Project Work process. Work performance data is an output from the Direct and Manage Project Work process.

---

▓ **Exam Tip**    Remember the sequence that work performance data becomes work performance information, which becomes work performance reports.

---

## Organizational Process Assets

The specific organizational process assets that are of use in the Control Communications process are any templates, policies, and guidelines for project communications that the organization has.

# Tools and Techniques

The following tools and techniques of this process can be used on the separate inputs to deliver the Control Communications process outputs.

## Reporting Systems

*A reporting system* is any method you choose to gather, store, and distribute or disseminate information. Reporting systems can be manual, although they are increasingly electronic and based on software. Reporting systems can be based on text or graphs and pictures. Whatever method you choose, it must be appropriate to the needs of you and your project team, as well as the stakeholders.

## Expert Judgment

The use of expert judgment in monitoring and controlling communications is a valuable tool, because it makes available to you the experience, wisdom, and skills of groups or individuals on the project team or within the wider group of project stakeholders, or of external consultants or subject matter experts. It is often important to bring in people external to the project who can add a sense of objectivity to how well the communications on the project are being monitored and controlled, and how effective and appropriate they are. This is the real strength in using expert judgment as a tool in this process.

## Meetings

The Control Communications process is a monitoring and controlling process and, as such, requires careful attention. One of the better ways of giving it the attention it deserves is through the use of meetings as a tool, where the project team is able to discuss progress with project communications and make decisions about any improvements. Meetings are a form of communication themselves and so should always be run in an effective way to encourage attendance and involvement.

# Outputs

The outputs from the Control Communications process are the following.

## Work Performance Information

Work performance information is work performance data that has been organized and summarized in a way that can be used for work performance reports. Work performance information typically organizes raw data and reports on project status in relation to time and cost progress on the project. Work performance information is used as an input into the Monitor and Control Project Work process.

## Change Requests

As a result of carrying out any monitoring and controlling process, including the Control Communications process, you may come across variations between what you planned to do in the communications management plan and what is actually occurring. You may also have situations in which corrective or preventive actions are required to ensure that you stay on track. The best way to ensure that any variations or preventive or corrective actions are captured is through a change request. Change requests then go on to be processed according to your approved change-control process in the Perform Integrated Change Control process.

## Project Management Plan Updates

As a result of monitoring and controlling project communications, you may choose to update parts of your project management plan to ensure that all of your planning efforts result in good communication and support your communication efforts.

## Project Document Updates

The specific project documents that may be updated as a result of the Control Communications process include any issues logs, performance reports, and other relevant communications documents.

## Organizational Process Asset Updates

The specific organizational process assets that will be updated include any existing templates, guidelines, lessons learned, or historical databases relating to project communications management.

### Quick Check

1. What is the main purpose of the Control Communications process?

2. Why are reporting systems an important tool or technique in the Control Communications process?

3. What is the relationship between work performance data, work performance information, and work performance reports?

### Quick Check Answers

1. The main purpose of the Control Communications process is to assess whether project communications are being carried out as per the communications management plan and whether variations or corrective or preventive actions need to be taken to ensure that you stay on track.

2. Reporting systems are the primary tool used in the Control Communications process because they are the manual or electronic means by which you choose to gather and distribute information about project progress to stakeholders.

3. Work performance data is the raw data that is refined and becomes work performance information, which in turn is further refined to become work performance reports.

# Chapter Summary

- The Communications Management knowledge area is focused on the successful use of project communications to report project performance, gain political support, and provide stakeholders with their communications requirements.

- The Plan Communications Management process produces the communications management plan, which guides the subsequent communications management processes.

- The Manage Communications process, which is an executing process, uses the communications management plan to gather, store, and distribute project information to stakeholders in the most effective way.

- The Control Communications process, which is a monitoring and controlling process, is like other monitoring and controlling processes in that it assesses actual performance against that forecast in the communications management plan and, if variations or corrective or preventive actions are required, raises a change request.

# Exercises

The answers for these exercises are located in the "Answers" section at the end of this chapter.

1. Match up the communication tool on the left with the description on the right.

| Communication Tool | Definition |
| --- | --- |
| 1. Communications technology | A. A tool that recognizes that communications can be interactive, push, or pull |
| 2. Communications requirements analysis | B. A tool that describes how communication moves from sender to receiver through a particular medium |
| 3. Communications models | C. A tool for gathering and documenting the communication requirements of project stakeholders |
| 4. Communications methods | D. A tool that decides the particular form of technology to be used to disseminate information |
| 5. Performance reporting | E. A tool for collecting and disseminating appropriate reporting on project progress to stakeholders |
| 6. Information management systems | F. A tool for the management, storage, and distribution of project information in either hard copy or electronic form |

2. You are the project manager on a project that initially identified seven stakeholders, including yourself. You have since identified an additional six stakeholders. How many extra potential communication channels are there?

# Review Questions

Test your knowledge of the information in Chapter 8 by answering these questions. The answers to these questions, and the explanation of why each answer choice is correct or incorrect, are located in the "Answers" section at the end of this chapter.

1. Which of the following processes produces the communications management plan?

    A. Develop Project Management Plan

    B. Plan Communications Management

    C. Manage Communications

    D. Develop Communications Management Plan

2. The decision to use a written document to provide project updates is an example of what sort of tool or technique?

    A. Communication technology

    B. Communication models

    C. Expert judgment

    D. Meetings

3. What is the name of the tool that analyzes the individual communication requirements for each of the stakeholders?

    A. Communication models

    B. Information management systems

    C. Communications requirements analysis

    D. Communications technology

4. You are managing a project with 17 stakeholders, including yourself. How many potential communication channels are there?

    A. 17

    B. 136

    C. 272

    D. 34

5. You have decided to send a handwritten update to project stakeholders on project progress. Some stakeholders complain that they are unable to read your handwriting. This is an example of what?

   A. Bad handwriting

   B. Noise

   C. Interference

   D. Feedback

6. You have set up an intranet site for project team members to be able to download project progress updates. This is an example of which method of communication?

   A. Interactive

   B. Push

   C. Pull

   D. Manual

7. How does the project kick-off meeting act as a means of communication?

   A. The kick-off meeting does not act as a means of communication.

   B. The kick-off meeting signals to the team that enough planning has been completed to begin execution.

   C. The kick-off meeting is completed to start project initiation, and therefore it informs the team that the project is about to start.

   D. The kick-off meeting signals the beginning of project closure and communicates to the team that the job is done.

8. What is the correct sequence of the following terms?

   A. Work performance report, work performance data, work performance information

   B. Work performance information, work performance data, work performance report

   C. Work performance data, work performance report, work performance information

   D. Work performance data, work performance information, work performance report

9.  If you are engaged in consciously paying attention to body language and trying to understand the communication from a sender, what are you involved in?

    A.  Active listening

    B.  Effective listening

    C.  Providing feedback

    D.  Paralingual communication

# Answers

This section contains the answers for the Exercises and Review Questions in this chapter.

## Exercises

1.  Match up the communication tool on the left with the description on the right.

| Communication Tool | Definition |
|---|---|
| 1. Communications technology | D. A tool that decides the particular form of technology to be used to disseminate information |
| 2. Communications requirements analysis | C. A tool for gathering and documenting the communication requirements of project stakeholders |
| 3. Communications models | B. A tool that describes how communication moves from sender to receiver through a particular medium |
| 4. Communications methods | A. A tool that recognizes that communications can be interactive, push, or pull |
| 5. Performance reporting | E. A tool for collecting and disseminating appropriate reporting on project progress to stakeholders |
| 6. Information management systems | F. A tool for the management, storage, and distribution of project information in either hard copy or electronic form |

2.  You are the project manager on a project that initially identified seven stakeholders, including yourself. You have since identified an additional six stakeholders. How many extra potential communication channels are there?

This question is asking you what the difference is between 7 stakeholders and 13 stakeholders in relation to the number of potential communication channels. You need to calculate $n(n - 1)/2$ for each and find the difference. The answer is not simply subtracting 7 from 13 and applying the formula to it—that would give you a very wrong answer, but be aware that on the exam that answer may be one of the options.

For 7 stakeholders, you have 21 communication channels; and for 13 stakeholders, you have 78 communication channels. Therefore, the correct answer is the difference between these two numbers, which is 57 extra potential communication channels

# Chapter Review

1. **Correct Answer: B**

   A.  **Incorrect:** The Develop Project Management Plan process produces the project management plan.

   B.  **Correct:** The main output from the Plan Communications Management process is the communications management plan.

   C.  **Incorrect**: The Manage Communications process uses the communications management plan to gather, store, and distribute project information and communications.

   D.  **Incorrect**: Develop Communications Management Plan is a made-up process name.

2. **Correct Answer: A**

   A.  **Correct:** Any decision you make about the technology used, whether manual or electronic, for the dissemination of project information, is a decision about communication technology.

   B.  **Incorrect:** Communication models explain what might happen between sender and receiver.

   C.  **Incorrect**: Expert judgment is a tool used to assist with monitoring how well communications are going.

   D.  **Incorrect**: Meetings are a tool used to help the project team understand and contribute to effective project communications.

3.  **Correct Answer: C**

    A.  **Incorrect:** Communications models explain what may happen to communications between sender and receiver.

    B.  **Incorrect:** Information management systems are used to gather and store project information.

    C.  **Correct**: Communications requirements analysis is the technique used to determine individual stakeholder communication requirements.

    D.  **Incorrect**: Communications technology is a technique used to determine what form the communication will take.

4.  **Correct Answer: B**

    A.  **Incorrect:** This is simply the number of stakeholders, not the number of potential communication channels.

    B.  **Correct:** If you use the formula $n(n-1)/2$, you will calculate that there are 136 potential communications channels.

    C.  **Incorrect**: This is the answer you get if you only use the first part of the correct formula.

    D.  **Incorrect**: This is the number of stakeholders multiplied by 2.

5.  **Correct Answer: B**

    A.  **Incorrect:** In the strictest sense of the word, it is an example of bad handwriting. But according to the basic communications model, it is an example of interference with the message, and that is the definition of noise.

    B.  **Correct:** Any element that can interfere with the message is considered to be noise.

    C.  **Incorrect**: This is not the correct answer because noise creates interference.

    D.  **Incorrect**: Feedback is used by the receiver to send confirmation of the message received back to the sender.

6. **Correct Answer: C**

   A.   **Incorrect:** Interactive communication is where more than one person is involved in the communication at the same time.

   B.   **Incorrect:** Push communication involves the sender sending the communication to the receiver.

   C.   **Correct**: This is an example of pull communication, because the receivers download the information at their discretion.

   D.   **Incorrect**: Manual communication refers to forms of communication that are not conducted electronically.

7. **Correct Answer: B**

   A.   **Incorrect:** The kick-off meeting does act as a means of communication by communicating to the team that enough planning has been done to begin execution.

   B.   **Correct:** The use of the kick-off meeting as both a functional meeting to discuss execution and as a team morale-building exercise means it is an effective form of communication.

   C.   **Incorrect**: The kick-off meeting is completed after enough planning has been done to begin project execution, not at the beginning of project initiation.

   D.   **Incorrect**: The kick-off meeting does not begin the process of project closure.

8. **Correct Answer: D**

   A.   **Incorrect:** Work performance reports come after work performance data and work performance information.

   B.   **Incorrect:** Work performance data comes before work performance information.

   C.   **Incorrect**: Work performance information comes before work performance reports.

   D.   **Correct**: This is the correct order: work performance data, which is the raw data gathered about project performance, in turn is filtered and refined as understandable work performance information, which in turn is selected to be included in work performance reports.

9. **Correct Answer: B**

    A.    **Incorrect:** Active listening means the receiver is actively engaged in trying to understand the message from the sender and does not necessarily involve paying attention to things like body language.

    B.    **Correct:** Effective listening takes active listening one step further and has the receiver monitoring nonverbal cues such as body language.

    C.    **Incorrect**: Feedback doesn't necessarily involve the interpretation of body language.

    D.    **Incorrect**: Paralingual communication involves recognizing and observing vocal but nonverbal communication clues such as expressions, inflections, tone, and volume of voice.

# CHAPTER 9

■ ■ ■

# Risk Management

This chapter focuses on the topic of Project Risk Management; like the other knowledge areas, it begins with a process of planning, which produces a risk management plan. It then has four further planning process—Identify Risks, Perform Qualitative Risk Analysis, Perform Quantitative Risk Analysis, and Plan Risk Responses—that iteratively develop and refine the risk register. It has a single monitoring and controlling process, Control Risks, which measures the actual risks versus the forecast risks and, if required, generates change requests.

**The PMBOK® Guide Processes**
**Project Risk Management Knowledge Area**
The six processes in the Project Risk Management knowledge area are as follows:

- Plan Risk Management (planning process)

- Identify Risks (planning process)

- Perform Qualitative Risk Analysis (planning process)

- Perform Quantitative Risk Analysis (planning process)

- Plan Risk Responses (planning process)

- Control Risks (monitoring and controlling process)

## What Is Project Risk Management?

Project Risk Management is focused on the processes of developing a risk management plan and a risk register that outlines and identifies how you will deal with project risks or uncertainties. In order to do this effectively, you need to be able to define all potential risks, their causes, and their potential impact, and formulate strategies for dealing with them. After they are identified, you then monitor what you had forecast would occur in relation to risk and what is actually occurring, while looking out for new or changed risks.

Figure 9-1 shows the general linear and highly iterative process of planning for risk and developing the risk register.

© Sean Whitaker 2016
S. Whitaker, *Pass the PMP® Exam*, DOI 10.1007/978-1-4842-2074-0_9

**Figure 9-1.** *A sequential and iterative reprocess for risk management*

All projects experience some degree of risk throughout the project life cycle. How you choose to identity and respond to risk reflects the level of *risk tolerance* that your project team or the wider organization has. If you have a low tolerance for risk, then you will either devote more time and energy to dealing with risks or choose not to undertake projects with high levels of risk. Conversely, if you have a high tolerance for risks, you will either devote less time to proactively planning for risks or choose to take on projects with high degrees of risk, perhaps seeking a high return. It is very important that the project manager spend time assessing the level of risk tolerance that key stakeholders such as your organization and the customer have, because this will affect how much time and effort goes into your risk management planning.

---

■ **Exam Tip**   If you are familiar with ISO 31000 Standard for Risk Management, much of this section will be familiar to you.

---

*Risk* is simply a measure of uncertainty that can affect the project either positively or negatively. For example, all the estimates you have done have some degree of uncertainty—either positive or negative—and this uncertainty represents risk that you need to account for and seek to manage.

---

■ **Exam Tip**   If you are having trouble understanding exactly what risk management is all about, simply substitute the word *uncertainty* for the word *risk*. Risk management focuses on acknowledging that there is uncertainty throughout the entire project and on planning how to deal with that uncertainty.

If you come across a question on the exam that hints at any amount of uncertainty, you should assume that you must perform some level of risk identification and analysis.

---

Risk, or uncertainty, can be positive or negative. If a factor is a potential positive risk, then it is viewed as an opportunity to be maximized through proper selection of risk-response strategies. If it is a negative risk, then it is a threat to the project, and your risk-response strategies should seek ways to minimize it. Most people tend to think of risks as purely negative events, and although the majority of risks may indeed be potentially negative, there are many positive risks. For example, there can be a risk that you will deliver the project under budget by careful procurement of goods and services, in which case you should seek to ensure that you maximize the chances of this risk occurring.

```
┌─────────────────────────────────────────────────────────┐
│                     REAL WORLD                            │
└─────────────────────────────────────────────────────────┘
```

As a very general rule of thumb, I try to have about two-thirds of my project risk register focused on negative risks, or threats, and about one-third focused on positive risks, or opportunities. This is a very loose rule, and you may find that your projects differ depending on their industry, size, and complexity. The key point is to make sure you consider both negative and positive risks on your project.

# Plan Risk Management

▦ **More Info**   Plan Risk Management

You can read more about the Plan Risk Management process in the PMBOK Guide, 5th edition, in Chapter 11, section 11.1. Table 9-1 identifies the process inputs, tools and techniques, and outputs.

*Table 9-1.*  *Plan Risk Management Process*

| Inputs ⇨ | Tools and Techniques ⇨ | Outputs |
|---|---|---|
| • Project management plan<br>• Project charter<br>• Stakeholder register<br>• Enterprise environmental factors<br>• Organizational process assets | • Analytical techniques<br>• Expert judgment<br>• Meetings | • Risk management plan |

The Plan Risk Management process is a planning process with the risk management plan as its sole output. In order to develop a successful risk management plan, you first need to understand the general level of risk your project faces, as well as the project team's or organization's tolerance for risk. Because risk or uncertainty can occur in any part of the project, you need all the other management plans contained in the project management plan to ensure that you assess and consider all potential sources of risk.

The Plan Risk Management process covers the following planning domain task:

- Task 10: Develop the risk management plan by identifying, analyzing, and prioritizing project risks, and defining risk response strategies, in order to manage uncertainty and opportunity throughout the project life cycle.

# Inputs

The Plan Risk Management process uses some or all of the following inputs as part of the development of the risk management plan for the project.

## Project Management Plan

The project management plan is useful as an input into the Plan Risk Management process because risk can occur at any point from any other aspect of the project. Thus, the already-developed subsidiary plans and baselines contained in the project management plan highlight areas of uncertainty that can be used to develop the risk management plan. The project management plan is an output from the Develop Project Management Plan process.

## Project Charter

The project charter, depending on the form it takes, may contain initial descriptions and assessments of known or anticipated risks for the project that provide valuable information for the development of the risk management plan. The project charter is an output from the Develop Project Charter process.

## Stakeholder Register

The stakeholder register identifies stakeholders in the project, records their roles and contact details, and documents their expectations, all of which are important in including stakeholders in the process of managing risk. The stakeholder register is an output from the Identify Stakeholders process.

## Enterprise Environmental Factors

The specific enterprise environmental factor that is useful as an input into this process is the broader organizational tolerance for risk. Organizations with a low tolerance for risk put much more effort and energy into managing risk on a project, whereas organizations with a higher tolerance for risk and uncertainty expend less effort in managing risk and may take on higher-risk projects. International standards such as ISO 31000 may also affect how this process is carried out and, as such, constitute enterprise environmental factors.

## Organizational Process Assets

The specific organizational process assets that may play an important input in the development of your risk management plan include any templates, processes, or guidelines that the organization has for the development of a risk management plan and managing risk. Other important organizational process assets are, of course, lessons learned and historical information about successful or unsuccessful risk identification and management from past projects.

# Tools and Techniques

The following tools and techniques are available to be used to develop the inputs in this process in order to produce the risk management plan.

## Analytical Techniques

The main purpose of analytical techniques is to determine the approach to risk management on your project. This involves checking with stakeholders about their particular appetite and attitude toward risk on the project, and also completing a high-level assessment of risk exposure for the project. Typical analytical techniques are a *stakeholder risk profile analysis,* which can be completed by interviewing individual stakeholders about their attitudes and expectations of risk that is suitable for the project. Strategic risk scoring sheets are also used to provide a high-level view of the types and level of risk the project will encounter.

## Expert Judgment

*Expert judgment* is an excellent tool to use when planning your approach to risk management. Using the knowledge and experience of subject matter experts is invaluable not only in your overall risk management plan but also in identifying and completing an analysis of risks. Suitable experts who may provide judgment include senior management, stakeholders with relevant experience, and external subject matter experts such as risk professionals, industry groups, and professional associations.

---

### REAL WORLD

If your project is likely to be subject to a high number of complex risks, you may want to consider employing the services of a risk management professional. Just as the profession of project management requires a particular skill set, the profession of risk management also employs a particular skill set. I highly recommend using risk management professionals for dealing with complex risk issues.

---

## Meetings

Meetings are a great way to bring together project team members, stakeholders, and other experts in order to consider how risk will be managed on the project. There are a number of ways you can run these meetings in order to efficiently get the information you require. They can be run formally with defined agendas and examination of reports, or they can be run as creative brainstorming sessions. The style of meeting you choose will reflect the participants and your intended outcomes.

| REAL WORLD |
| --- |

I have often found that meetings are a great way to not only solicit technical input from people with relevant experience but also generate buy-in and commitment. This is especially important in the area of risk management, because giving team members and relevant stakeholders the opportunity to contribute to the management of project risk helps keep them involved and also allows them to understand the importance of being proactive rather than reactive when managing risk.

# Outputs

After applying the appropriate tools and techniques to the selected inputs, the Plan Risk Management process has the following output.

## Risk Management Plan

The Plan Risk Management process has the *risk management plan* as its sole output. Similar to other management plans, the risk management plan provides a guide for completing the project's risk management activities. The risk management plan will probably contain information about the following:

- The risk methodology and approach to be taken on the project.

- The individual roles and responsibilities within the team and the wider group of stakeholders.

- Any approved budgets for managing risk, which should then be included in the cost performance baseline.

- An initial analysis of the individual risk categories using a *risk breakdown structure* (RBS). Figure 9-2 shows an example of a risk breakdown structure.

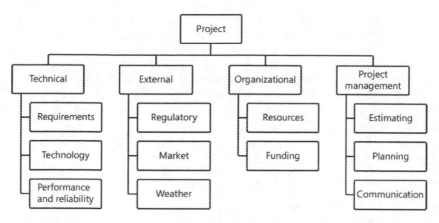

***Figure 9-2.*** *The development of risk categories using a risk breakdown structure*

---

▓ **Exam Tip** The RBS is one of four breakdown structures. The other three are the organizational breakdown structure, work breakdown structure, and resource breakdown structure. Each of the breakdown structures takes a high-level concept and breaks it down into its component parts.

---

- A standardized definition of risk probability and impact, which is particularly useful for qualitative analysis because the analysis can be subjective. Figure 9-3 shows an example of a standardized definition of risk probability and impact.

| | Very low or 1 | Low or 2 | Moderate or 3 | High or 4 | Very high or 5 |
|---|---|---|---|---|---|
| **Scope** | No noticeable change to scope | Minor changes to scope | Significant change to scope | Changes to scope unacceptable to sponsor or client | Changes the complete purpose of the project |
| **Time** | No noticeable change to time | Less than 10% increase in time | 10–20% increase in time | 20–30% increase in time | Greater than 30% increase in time |
| **Cost** | No noticeable change to cost | Less than 10% increase in cost | 10–20% increase in cost | 20–30% increase in cost | Greater than 30% increase in cost |

***Figure 9-3.*** *Standardized definitions of risk probability and impact*

- A probability and impact matrix is useful again for qualitative risk analysis, because it allows you to focus risk activities on positive or negative risks that present the greatest opportunity or threat. Figure 9-4 shows an example of a probability and impact matrix showing that the highest risks are any with a combined probability and impact greater than 45%; these are colored dark grey.

| Impact Probability | 10% | 30% | 50% | 70% | 90% |
|---|---|---|---|---|---|
| 90% | 9% | 27% | 45% | 63% | 81% |
| 70% | 7% | 21% | 35% | 49% | 63% |
| 50% | 5% | 15% | 25% | 35% | 45% |
| 30% | 3% | 9% | 15% | 21% | 27% |
| 10% | 1% | 3% | 5% | 7% | 9% |

*Figure 9-4. Probability and impact matrix*

- Any predefined formats, processes, guidelines, or templates for risk registers or tracking or reporting risks.

The risk management plan is a subsidiary of the project management plan and is used as an input into the other five risk management processes.

### Quick Check

1.  What is the main focus of the Plan Risk Management process?

2.  Why is it important to also consider positive risk?

3.  What other areas of the project management plan can risk affect?

### Quick Check Answers

1.  The main focus of the Plan Risk Management Process is to formulate your particular approach to how you will manage risks on your project. This is documented in the risk management plan.

2.  Many people naturally consider risk a negative event; however, there are many positive risks, which can lead to a project being under budget, ahead of time, delivering greater quality, and delivering higher-than-expected stakeholder expectations.

3.  Risk management can affect every other aspect of the project, because there is generally always uncertainty in all elements of your project.

# Identify Risks

■ **More Info**   Identify Risks

You can read more about the Identify Risks process in the PMBOK Guide, 5th edition, in Chapter 11, section 11.2. Table 9-2 identifies the process inputs, tools and techniques, and outputs.

**Table 9-2.**  *Identify Risks Process*

| Inputs ⇨ | Tools and Techniques ⇨ | Outputs |
|---|---|---|
| • Risk management plan | • Documentation reviews | • Risk register |
| • Cost management plan | • Information-gathering | |
| • Schedule management plan | techniques | |
| • Quality management plan | • Checklist analysis | |
| • Human resource management plan | • Assumption analysis | |
| • Scope baseline | • Diagramming techniques | |
| • Activity cost estimates | • SWOT analysis | |
| • Activity duration estimates | • Expert judgment | |
| • Stakeholder register | | |
| • Project documents | | |
| • Procurement documents | | |
| • Enterprise environmental factors | | |
| • Organizational process assets | | |

The Identify Risks process is a planning process that uses a wide variety of inputs and tools and techniques to identify all the risks to the project. It is performed through the life of the project, and the risk register is always updated with newly identified risks or current risks that are reassessed by using the other risk planning processes.

The Identify Risks process covers the following planning domain task:

- Task 10: Develop the risk management plan by identifying, analyzing, and prioritizing project risks, and defining risk response strategies, in order to manage uncertainty and opportunity throughout the project life cycle.

In addition to being performed throughout the life of the project, risk identification should be completed by all project team members and stakeholders with experience in the area. This enables you to draw on their skills and experience, and it also creates buy-in to the process of risk management. It is important to realize that the process of identifying risks is not a stand-alone process but one that involves many stakeholders in a constant state of communication to obtain their expertise and experience.

---

| **REAL WORLD** |

Despite your best efforts, you will probably miss certain risks. On a project I was working on, we spent a lot of time and money identifying risks for a particularly complex piece of work that was to occur over a five-day period. We used historical information, consulted experts, reviewed documents and plans, involved the project team members, and conducted tests to prepare what we thought was a completely comprehensive risk register. Within the first two hours of the five-day piece of work, a problem arose that we had not identified. We were able to respond to the situation well in this instance, and we used this information for a new risk register for a similar piece of work to be completed 12 months later. The main lesson we learned is that you need to be ready for the unexpected and not assume that your risk register captures every risk.

---

You should recognize from the range of inputs into the Identify Risks process that risk can occur in any other part of the project.

# Inputs

The Identify Risks process uses some or all of the following inputs.

## Risk Management Plan

The risk management plan is an essential input into the Identify Risks process because it contains information about your particular approach or methodology to identifying risks generally, and more specifically it contains information derived from the risk breakdown structure regarding already-identified risk categories. It also contains a description of the particular risk tolerance for the project, which will assist you in determining the effort you put into identifying particular risks. The risk management plan is an output from the Plan Risk Management process.

## Cost Management Plan

The cost management plan contains cost estimates for all elements of the project, and these estimates should reflect the amount of uncertainty in the estimating process. Each of these areas of uncertainty, either negative or positive, represents a risk on the project. The cost management plan is an output from the Plan Cost Management process.

---

**Exam Tip**   All estimates are by their very nature uncertain. They are educated guesses of what the future will be, based on information in hand today. As such, any baselines, such as cost and time, that are built up using estimates will have a range of uncertainty, both negative and positive. On the exam, if you find the word *uncertainty* or *estimate*, you should assume that risk is present.

---

## Schedule Management Plan

The schedule management plan refers to areas of uncertainty or risk in the development of the project schedule. This information can be used to identify risks associated with the project time frame. The schedule management plan is an output from the Plan Schedule Management process.

## Quality Management Plan

The quality management plan identifies areas of uncertainty in the delivery of quality on the project. The quality management plan is an output from the Plan Quality Management process.

## Human Resource Management Plan

The human resource management plan identifies areas of uncertainty with the definition, recruitment, retention, and development of project team members, all of which represent risks for the project and should be taken into account during the Identify Risks process. The human resource management plan is an output from the Plan Human Resource Management process.

## Scope Baseline

The scope baseline, made up of the scope statement, the work breakdown structure (WBS), and the WBS dictionary, defines the work to be done on the project and also outlines any areas of uncertainty in the project scope that require further definition. These areas of uncertainty represent risk for the project and should be used to identify individual risks related to the project scope. The scope baseline is an output from the Create WBS process.

## Activity Cost Estimates

Individual activity cost estimates include cost estimates for individual project activities. In addition to the actual dollar amount of the estimate, there is information about the information used and assumptions made in preparing the estimates, which provides insight into the range of uncertainty in the estimate. This uncertainty represents risk for the project and should be included in the development of the risk register. Activity cost estimates are an output from the Estimate Costs process.

## Activity Duration Estimates

Activity duration estimates contain information about the individual time estimates prepared for project activities. This estimating information should contain an indication of the range of uncertainty surrounding the estimate, which represents risk to the project. Activity durations estimates are an output from the Estimate Activity Duration process.

## Stakeholder Register

The stakeholder register is extremely useful in identifying individual risks for two reasons. First, the stakeholder register allows you to interview individual stakeholders about their particular attitude toward risk. Second, each stakeholder can assist with identifying project risks from their own unique point of view. The stakeholder register is an output from the Identify Stakeholders process.

## Project Documents

The specific types of project documents that are useful in the Identify Risks process are things such as work performance reports, network diagrams, and assumption logs, because they provide information about how the project is performing, the sequence of planned activities, and the assumptions made about different estimates, respectively.

## Procurement Documents

Procurement documents are a key input into the Identify Risks process because they outline any contractual obligations that may contribute to uncertainty, and the value of this uncertainty. Procurement documents are an output from the Plan Procurement Management process.

## Enterprise Environmental Factors

The specific types of enterprise environmental factors that are useful in managing project risk are any broader organizational attitude and tolerance for risk, and any external risk standards the organization is using.

## Organizational Process Assets

The specific types of organizational process assets that will assist in managing project risk are any blank templates, historical information and lessons learned, and any project-specific policies and guidelines relating to risk management.

# Tools and Techniques

The following tools and techniques are used on the inputs to deliver the Identify Risks process outputs.

## Documentation Reviews

*Documentation reviews* refer to a structured analysis and review of all relevant project documents and the information they contain to detect any areas of uncertainty or risk on the project. The types of documents reviewed are any part of the project management plan or baselines, documents providing descriptions of any part of the project, and documents outlining the assumptions made in preparing estimates. Documentation reviews are generally carried out by the project manager and project team members.

## Information-Gathering Techniques

There are many different ways to gather information in relation to project risk. Each has its own benefits and delivers a varying degree of accuracy and thoroughness. Examples of useful *information-gathering techniques* for the Identify Risks process include the following:

- *Brainstorming*: This is an excellent way to encourage creative thinking about particular risk issues. The intended outcome is a comprehensive list of all potential risks.

- *Interviewing*: Interviewing experts and people with experience in similar projects and the associated risks is an excellent way to quickly obtain relevant information.

- *Delphi technique*: This is an extremely useful tool to use to solicit information from experts anonymously, to avoid peer pressure and groupthink. This is particularly useful when you are seeking to encourage a wide range of opinions and assessments of potential project risks.

---

## REAL WORLD

One of the few times I've been involved as a participant in a Delphi technique was in the identification of risks on a large, complex IT project. To me as a participant, it was a complex process requiring significant thought, input, and review of other anonymous participants' opinions. After the results were gathered and disseminated to participants, though, I could see that there had been an extremely comprehensive identification and assessment of all the potential risks that could affect this particular project.

---

# Checklist Analysis

*Checklist analysis* uses historical information gathered from previous projects and presents a list of activities and items that must be checked off to ensure that they have been done as part of a thorough risk identification process.

# Assumption Analysis

Any and all assumptions made about any aspect of the project represent uncertainty and therefore risk for the project. Therefore, gathering the assumptions log and testing its accuracy, stability, consistency, and completeness are essential parts of identifying project risks.

# Diagramming Techniques

The use of *diagramming techniques* is an excellent way to graphically represent the process of identifying individual risks. Several diagramming techniques are particularly useful in the identification of risks. They include the cause-and-effect, Ishikawa, or fishbone diagram, which is extremely useful for getting to the root cause of project risks. You saw the use of this diagramming technique in Chapter 6, to determine the root cause of quality issues. Figure 9-5 shows a cause-and-effect diagram being used to identify risks associated with cost overruns on a project.

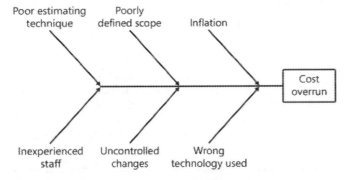

**Figure 9-5.** *A cause-and-effect diagram for risk identification*

Another useful diagramming technique is a flowchart, which can show how events are related to each other in a system. By analyzing how different activities or events are interrelated, you can recognize how risk can flow from one part of the project to another.

A third type of diagramming technique that is useful for the identification of risks is an influence diagram, which is a simple graphical representation of cause-and-effect relationships between sequential activities.

## SWOT Analysis

A key element of any risk identification process is the use of *SWOT analysis. SWOT* stands for *strengths, weaknesses, opportunities, and threats.* The idea is to identify and document each of these four areas and then focus on your strengths while making provision for your weaknesses, prepare to take advantage of the opportunities that present themselves, and plan how to respond to identified threats. All of these are key elements in identifying risks.

---

**REAL WORLD**

---

I have successfully used SWOT analysis on many occasions to put a framework around a brainstorming session. Getting people to focus on current strengths, weaknesses, opportunities, and threats is an extremely easy way to start them thinking about uncertainty in the project.

---

## Expert Judgment

The use of experts and their experience and skills in identifying risks is a key tool to be used during this process, because the identification of risks can be quite a complex process. By using the experience of project team members who may have done this sort of project before or external consultants with expertise in this particular area, you have a greater chance of identifying all the risks on the project.

# Outputs

The Identify Risks process has the following single output.

## Risk Register

The risk register is the single output from the Identify Risks process. The development of the risk register is highly iterative, and the risk register itself should be treated as a live document and reviewed regularly. It should be reviewed at all levels from testing the assumptions made right through to the qualitative and quantitative analysis applied to the identified risks. The actual risk register can take many forms depending on your organizational risk tolerance and any existing templates and guidelines. Figure 9-6 shows a generic form of risk register indicating risk identification, qualitative analysis, quantitative analysis, and risk responses.

| Risk Identification | | | | Qualitative Analysis | | | Quantitative Analysis | | | Risk Response Planning |
|---|---|---|---|---|---|---|---|---|---|---|
| Category | Event | Consequence | +/- | P | I | P x I | P | I$ | P x I$ | Response |
| | | | | | | | | | | |

*Figure 9-6.* *A generic risk register*

---

# REAL WORLD

In addition to providing extremely valuable technical information about your assessment of risk on the project, the preparation and constant revisiting of the risk register keeps risk at the forefront of your project team's minds. I have found time and effort invested in risk management to be useful not only from a technical point of view in managing risk, but also for obtaining buy-in and helping people to recognize the importance of proactive risk management.

---

▒ **Exam Tip**   The risk register is perhaps the most iterative document in the project, because it is constantly undergoing review and being updated. On the exam, you should always assume that the risk register is being referred to frequently.

---

### Quick Check

1. Why is the risk register considered a highly iterative document?

2. Who should be involved in the identification of risks?

3. What are three types of information-gathering techniques that can be used to identify risks?

### Quick Check Answers

1. The risk register is a highly iterative document because you will always be updating it as information becomes available, assumptions made are tested and refined, and new risks are identified and old ones closed.

2. The project manager will take ultimate responsibility for the Identify Risks process. But the entire project team and relevant external experts should also be involved in the process.

3. Many types of information-gathering techniques are useful for many aspects of project management. Techniques specifically mentioned as useful for the Identify Risks process include brainstorming, the Delphi technique, interviewing, and root-cause analysis.

# Perform Qualitative Risk Analysis

▓ **More Info**  Perform Qualitative Risk Analysis

You can read more about the Perform Qualitative Risk Analysis process in the PMBOK Guide, 5th edition, in Chapter 11, section 11.3. Table 9-3 identifies the process inputs, tools and techniques, and outputs.

***Table 9-3.***  *Perform Qualitative Risk Analysis Process*

| Inputs ⇨ | Tools and Techniques ⇨ | Outputs |
|---|---|---|
| • Risk management plan<br>• Scope baseline<br>• Risk register<br>• Enterprise environmental factors<br>• Organizational process assets | • Risk probability and impact assessment<br>• Probability and impact matrix<br>• Risk data quality assessment<br>• Risk categorization<br>• Risk urgency assessment<br>• Expert judgment | • Project document updates |

The Perform Qualitative Risk Analysis process is a planning process focused on assigning a qualitative, or subjective, analysis of probability and impact to all identified risks. The Perform Qualitative Risk Analysis process covers the following planning domain task:

- Task 10: Develop the risk management plan by identifying, analyzing, and prioritizing project risks, and defining risk response strategies, in order to manage uncertainty and opportunity throughout the project life cycle.

▓ **Exam Tip**  The key difference between qualitative and quantitative assessment is that qualitative assessment is subjective—that is, it uses opinion and experience—and is done quickly. On the other hand, quantitative assessment involves actual data and figures to support a more objective assessment. For example, you may do a qualitative assessment that the chance of it snowing in winter during your construction project is 7 out of 10 (1 being that it definitely will not snow, and 10 being that it definitely will snow) and that the impact if it does snow is 6 out of 10 (1 being no impact at all, and 10 being a catastrophic impact). This gives a total qualitative assessment of 42 out of a possible 100. You may then decide to spend some time and money doing quantitative risk analysis on this risk and contact the local weather bureau, which tells you that there is a 0.831 chance of it snowing on those dates; in addition, your team members tell you that if it does snow, you will suffer a $10,000 loss. This gives you a total quantitative assessment of $8,310. You can see that quantitative assessment takes more time and money to get the information, but it is more accurate.

---

The process of qualitative risk analysis is generally done on all identified risks because it is quick and easy. It is simply a matter of assigning a subjective assessment of the probability of the risk occurring and also assigning a subjective assessment of the impact of the risk, using defined scales. The scales used can be numerical, such as 1–10, or text based, such as low, very low, high, and so on.

When these two factors are multiplied together, the result is an individual qualitative risk score for each identified risk, which you can use to prioritize the risks and choose to focus on those that rank the highest. Additionally, you will go on to perform quantitative risk analysis only on those risks that score the highest.

# Inputs

The following inputs are used in the Perform Qualitative Risk Analysis process.

## Risk Management Plan

Obviously one of the key inputs into any of the other risk management planning processes is the risk management plan because it contains information about how each risk management process, including the Perform Qualitative Risk Analysis process, will be performed. The risk management plan is an output from the Plan Risk Management process.

## Scope Baseline

The scope baseline is an important input into the Perform Qualitative Risk Analysis process because it describes all the work to be done and the work not to be done on the project. With this description of the work, you get a full picture of the elements of the scope that are clear and defined, along with those elements of the scope that are still uncertain and ill-defined and that represent risk on the project that needs to be analyzed. The scope baseline is an output from the Create WBS process.

## Risk Register

The risk register is a key input into the Perform Qualitative Risk Analysis process because, in its first iteration, it is a list of all the risks that have been identified. The continual development of the risk register includes qualitative risk analysis performed not only once, but on an ongoing basis as new information, new risks, and assumptions are refined. The risk register is an output from the Identify Risks process.

## Enterprise Environmental Factors

The specific types of enterprise environmental factors that are useful as inputs into the Perform Qualitative Risk Analysis process are any external industry standards, such as ISO 31000, and any external information held by risk professionals, such as risk databases and information about the analysis of individual risks.

## Organizational Process Assets

The specific organizational process assets that are of use in the Perform Qualitative Risk Analysis process are any historical information the organization has about similar risks and their probability and impact, and any pre-prepared templates and processes to assist in the qualitative analysis of individually identified risks.

# Tools and Techniques

The following tools and techniques of this process can be used on the separate inputs to deliver the Perform Qualitative Risk Analysis process outputs.

## Risk Probability and Impact Assessment

The primary tool used in the Perform Qualitative Risk Analysis process is *risk probability and impact assessment*. The key here is to assess each identified risk and assign to it a probability of the risk occurring and an assessment of the impact if the risk does occur, by using a standardized scale that should be included in the risk management plan. Because it is a qualitative analysis, several kinds of numerical scales or text descriptions can be used to standardize the responses assessing probability and impact.

Because the assessments of probability and impact being made are qualitative and therefore somewhat subjective, it is important during this process to document assumptions that are made based on the information available at the time the assessment is done. Throughout the course of the project, you will revisit these assumptions, and you will gain further information, which may change either the assessment of risk probability or its impact.

---

## REAL WORLD

---

There are many different ways to assess qualitative probability and impact on projects. In my career, I have used simple numerical scales from 1 to 5, and text-based descriptions such as likely, unlikely, and highly likely.

---

## Probability and Impact Matrix

A *probability and impact matrix* standardizes and identifies risks after they have had a probability and impact assessment performed on them so that individual risks can be ranked very quickly. Figure 9-4, shown earlier in this chapter in the "Plan Risk Management" section, presented an example of a probability and impact matrix as a key component of the risk management plan.

## Risk Data Quality Assessment

A key element when performing any sort of risk assessment is the quality of the information being used. Obviously, if poor-quality information is being used, your subsequent assessment will be poor. Therefore, it is important to use a *risk data quality assessment* technique to evaluate the quality of the data being used to make the assessment.

---

### REAL WORLD

In my experience, the quality of information that you use to identify and analyze risks definitely gets better over time, especially if you are doing particular types of work for the first time and you are constantly learning and refining the information you have on hand.

---

## Risk Categorization

A useful way of representing and presenting the qualitative risk analysis is with *risk categorization* techniques, which you can use to sort risks into categories for easy monitoring and reporting. An excellent example of risk categorization is the risk breakdown structure (RBS) shown earlier, in Figure 9-2. You may also choose to categorize risks by project phase or by relevance to particular stakeholders. However you choose to categorize risks, you should be able to present them in a document or graphically.

## Risk Urgency Assessment

A *risk urgency assessment* is a tool that takes into account not only an assessment of the probability and impact of the risk, but the urgency of the risk. Urgency has to do with whether the risk is likely to occur in the near future, in which case you have a high degree of urgency compared to risks that may not manifest until a later point in time. Risks that may occur in the near future need the greatest attention paid to them. Risks that may occur further off in the project timeframe can have less attention paid to them.

## Expert Judgment

Again, the use of expert judgment is an exceptionally good way to bring a robust level of analysis to your Perform Qualitative Risk Analysis process. Your choice of experts, and the way in which you choose to solicit information from them, will be an important factor in the quality of the advice given.

---

### REAL WORLD

It is always important to give a high degree of consideration when selecting people to consult with as experts. The types of things you may want to consider are their level of experience, willingness to share this experience, availability, and ability to share information concisely, and any costs associated with the use of those experts.

---

# Outputs

The sole output from the Perform Qualitative Risk Analysis process is the following.

## Project Document Updates

The specific project documents that will be updated are the risk register and the assumptions log. Any time you complete any new qualitative risk assessments or revise existing qualitative risk assessments based on refined or new information, you need to update the risk register. In addition to updating the risk register with new or revised information, you must update the assumptions log to reflect the new assumptions that have been made.

### Quick Check

1.  What is the main difference between qualitative risk assessment and quantitative risk assessment?

2.  What sort of probability and impact assessment is best used for the Perform Qualitative Risk Analysis process?

3.  How does risk urgency assessment differ from risk probability and impact assessment?

### Quick Check Answers

1.  The main difference between qualitative risk assessment and quantitative risk assessment is that qualitative risk assessment uses subjective assessments of probability and impact, whereas quantitative risk assessment uses objective assessments of probability and impact, usually quantifying them in terms of money or time.

2. There is no one best type of probability and impact assessment to use in the Perform Qualitative Risk Analysis process. The decision whether to use numerical scales or text-based descriptions of qualitative risk analysis is entirely up to you and depends on what is appropriate for your project.

3. Risk urgency assessment takes into account the timeframe in which the risk may manifest, with risks that may manifest in the near future having a higher urgency than risks that may occur in the longer term. Risk probability and impact assessment is applied to all risk and simply assesses the probability of the risk occurring and the impact if it does occur.

# Perform Quantitative Risk Analysis

▓ **More Info**    Perform Quantitative Risk Analysis

You can read more about the Perform Quantitative Risk Analysis process in the PMBOK Guide, 5th edition, in Chapter 11, section 11.4. Table 9-4 identifies the process inputs, tools and techniques, and outputs.

**Table 9-4.** *Perform Quantitative Risk Analysis Process*

| Inputs ⇨ | Tools and Techniques ⇨ | Outputs |
|---|---|---|
| • Risk management plan<br>• Cost management plan<br>• Schedule management plan<br>• Risk register<br>• Enterprise environmental factors<br>• Organizational process assets | • Data gathering and representation techniques<br>• Quantitative risk analysis and modeling techniques<br>• Expert judgment | • Project document updates |

The Perform Quantitative Risk Analysis process is a planning process focused on the development of a quantitative, or objective, assessment of individual risk probability and impact, often by using a metric based on money or time.

The Perform Quantitative Risk Analysis process covers the following planning domain task:

- Task 10: Develop the risk management plan by identifying, analyzing, and prioritizing project risks, and defining risk response strategies, in order to manage uncertainty and opportunity throughout the project life cycle.

Performing quantitative risk analysis generally takes more effort than performing qualitative risk analysis and assessment, and therefore it is generally performed on risks that are identified as having a higher probability and impact on the project. The intended outcome of the quantitative risk assessment process is to assign a dollar or time amount to specific risks if they occur. You can then aggregate all these individual quantitative estimates to build contingency reserves for time or cost. Because of the complexity of the tools and techniques and information required for successful quantitative risk analysis, it is often done by risk professionals who have experience and access to relevant historical information that can be used in the analysis.

# Inputs

The following inputs are used in the Perform Quantitative Risk Analysis process.

## Risk Management Plan

The risk management plan outlines the particular way in which you will approach the process of quantitative risk analysis and, as such, it is an extremely important input to assist in the completion of this process. The risk management plan is an output from the Plan Risk Management process.

## Cost Management Plan

The cost management plan is a useful input into the Perform Quantitative Risk Analysis process because it outlines how financial reserves will be developed and managed. One of the key metrics used in quantitative risk analysis is the use of dollar amounts; cumulatively, the individual dollar amounts can be added up to become a cost reserve for the project. The cost management plan is an output from the Plan Cost Management process.

## Schedule Management Plan

Like the cost management plan, the schedule management plan provides guidelines for the development and management of a schedule reserve, which is calculated with quantitative risk analysis by using time as a metric. The schedule management plan is an output from the Plan Schedule Management process.

## Risk Register

The risk register, from the moment it first appears and throughout its subsequent iterations, is an essential input into the Perform Quantitative Risk Analysis process because the outputs from this process update the risk register with specific information about individual risk assessment. The risk register is an output from the Identify Risks process.

## Enterprise Environmental Factors

The specific enterprise environmental factors that are useful in the Perform Quantitative Risk Analysis process are any external industry standards such as ISO 31000 and any risk databases held by risk professionals.

## Organizational Process Assets

The specific organizational process assets that are of use in the Perform Quantitative Risk Analysis process are any historical information the organization has regarding previous experience with performing quantitative risk analysis and, of course, any blank templates or guidelines the organization has for completing the Perform Quantitative Risk Analysis process.

# Tools and Techniques

The following tools and techniques of this process can be used on the separate inputs to deliver the Perform Quantitative Risk Analysis process outputs.

## Data Gathering and Representation Techniques

A key technique to assist with the execution of the Perform Quantitative Risk Analysis process is the use of *data gathering and representation techniques*. The purpose of using these techniques is to obtain relevant and accurate data that can then be assessed to develop the quantitative metrics of risk probability and impact. These data gathering and representation techniques include the following:

- *Interviewing techniques* that draw on the experience and skills of experts. The type of information that you seek from experts is their own quantitative assessment of probability and impact of particular risks. You may end up with a range of responses and thus may want to consider the use of three-point estimating, which was covered in the cost and time estimating processes in Chapter 4 and Chapter 5.

- *Established statistical probability distributions*. There are many types of probability distributions, but the most commonly used are normal distributions, beta distributions, triangular distributions, and uniform distributions, each with its own statistical distribution of data that can be used to quantify a particular risk probability or impact and the associated range of data. The type of distribution you use should be based on professional experience and historical information, in order to make sure it is valid.

# Quantitative Risk Analysis and Modeling Techniques

In *quantitative risk analysis and modeling techniques,* sophisticated statistical and mathematical approaches are applied to the calculation and range of risk probability and impact. A variety of techniques can be used, but because of their sophistication, they are usually carried out using software. Of the available types of quantitative risk analysis and modeling techniques, the following are the most popular and useful for quantitative risk analysis:

- *Sensitivity analysis:* A technique that looks at different aspects of the project and how they have an impact on project risk, to determine which parts of the project are most sensitive to risk. It may, for example, determine that issues around cost are more sensitive to risk and, more specifically, that cost issues related to inflationary pressures on materials over time are most at risk. Sensitivity analysis is a highly complex set of calculations using software and, as such, generally requires specialized knowledge and expertise to carry out.

- *Tornado diagrams:* Often used to present the results of sensitivity analysis. A tornado diagram is a histogram or bar chart where the data categories are listed vertically instead of horizontally, with the largest category at the top and the other categories in order of descending size, giving the diagram the appearance of a tornado. Figure 9-7 shows an example of a tornado diagram presenting the results of sensitivity analysis to show which parts of the project are most sensitive to risk, judged by the quantitative impact they will have on the net present value (NPV) of the project.

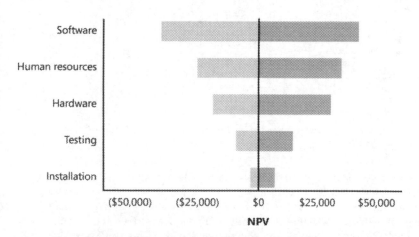

**Figure 9-7.** *A example of tornado diagram showing how different risks may impact the project's net present value*

- *Expected monetary value analysis (EMV):* A way to allocate quantitative numerical probability and impact to particular options and from this to arrive at the expected monetary value of each option. Depending on the calculated outcome, you can then quantify your decision. The usual way of graphically representing the EMV analysis is with the use of decision trees. In Figure 9-8, a decision tree shows the calculation of EMV regarding whether to upgrade existing customer ordering software or to develop a completely new piece of software.

| Decision Definition | Decision node | Chance node | Net path value |
|---|---|---|---|
| Decision to be made | Input: cost of each option<br><br>Output: decision made (true, false) | Input: scenario probability, reward if it occurs<br><br>Output: expected monetary value (EMV) | Computed: (Payoffs minus Costs) along path |

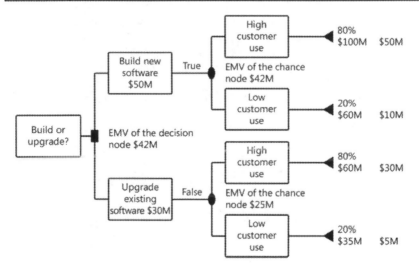

***Figure 9-8.*** *A decision tree analysis for assessing the expected monetary value of building new software or upgrading existing software*

Figure 9-8 shows that for either decision, there is an 80% chance of high customer use and a 20% chance of low customer use. If you decide to build new software, it will cost $50 million, and if there is high customer use, you will make $100 million, so there is an 80% chance of making a net figure of $50 million. By the same token, if you decide to build new software at a cost of $50 million, and there is low customer use, you will only make $60 million, so there is a 20% chance of making a net figure of $10 million. You then add these two calculations together

$$(0.8 \times \$50m) + (0.2 \times \$10m)$$

to get an EMV of $42 million.

The other option is to upgrade the existing software, which will cost $30 million and has an 80% chance of making a net figure of $30 million and a 20% chance of making a net figure of $5 million. Therefore, the EMV for this decision is

$$(0.8 \times \$30m) + (0.2 \times \$5m) = \$25m$$

By using this form of quantitative risk analysis, you can recognize that the best decision is to take the option with the greater EMV, which is to build new software. What is also apparent in this example is that the quality of the calculated outcome is only as good as the quality of the information going into the model. This is another example of why it is important to document the assumptions you make, so that if any of this changes in the future, you can quickly recalculate.

---

■ **Exam Tip**   You may have to calculate a decision tree on the exam, so remember to calculate the probability of each by the net value—cost minus income.

---

- *Modeling and simulation*: Includes Monte Carlo analysis, which is the most common type. In the Monte Carlo technique, all potential outcomes are modeled and computed many times, with different input values, to assess the most likely outcomes—that is, those with the highest probability—and to come up with a probability distribution (normal, uniform, or beta) associated with each of these outcomes. By using Monte Carlo analysis, you can find the likely probability of many different risks, and this allows you and your team to determine which risks will have the greatest or least chance of occurring. It is a highly sophisticated form of mathematical modeling and requires the use of software.

---

■ **Exam Tip**   If a question on the exam refers to mathematical modeling of risks, it is referring to one of these techniques.

---

# Expert Judgment

Given the complexity of performing accurate quantitative risk analysis, the use of subject matter experts with relevant experience in this area is very important. Expert judgment is important not only for the quantitative calculations but also for the interpretation of the data produced.

# Outputs

The single output from the Perform Quantitative Risk Analysis process is the following.

## Project Document Updates

The specific project document that will be updated is the risk register. The types of information that will feature in the risk register updates include all the calculations generated by the quantitative risk analysis, which includes quantitative probabilities of individual risks, quantitative impacts of individual risks in terms of both cost and time, and subsequently a prioritized list of quantified risks.

### Quick Check

1. What is the main purpose of quantitative risk analysis?

2. Why is it important to consider the use of experts during the Perform Quantitative Risk Analysis process?

3. What is the main value of using quantitative risk analysis and modeling techniques such as sensitivity analysis and expected monetary value analysis?

### Quick Check Answers

1. The main purpose of quantitative risk analysis is to quantify in either cost or time values the particular probability and impact of individual risks, and the development of reserves for both cost and time.

2. The Perform Quantitative Risk Analysis process can be a highly sophisticated process using complex statistical and mathematical modeling. As such, to extract maximum benefit from quantitative risk analysis, it may be necessary to use people with experience in both the preparation and interpretation of quantitative risk data.

3. The main value in using quantitative risk analysis and modeling techniques is that it gives you a standardized and defined means of analyzing and presenting data in a way that can be understood easily.

# Plan Risk Responses

▓ **More Info**   Plan Risk Responses

You can read more about the Plan Risk Responses process in the PMBOK Guide, 5th edition, in Chapter 11, section 11.5. Table 9-5 identifies the process inputs, tools and techniques, and outputs.

*Table 9-5.* *Plan Risk Responses Process*

| Inputs ⇨ | Tools and Techniques ⇨ | Outputs |
|---|---|---|
| • Risk management plan<br>• Risk register | • Strategies for negative risks or threats<br>• Strategies for positive risks or opportunities<br>• Contingent response strategies<br>• Expert judgment | • Project management plan updates<br>• Project document updates |

The Plan Risk Responses process is a planning process that is focused on the development of proactive responses to risks.

The Plan Risk Responses process covers the following planning domain task:

- Task 10: Develop the risk management plan by identifying, analyzing, and prioritizing project risks, and defining risk response strategies, in order to manage uncertainty and opportunity throughout the project life cycle.

The development of proactive responses is a very effective way of both minimizing the potential effects of negative risk and maximizing the potential benefits of positive risk on a project. Each of the risk responses seeks to influence the risk prior to its possible occurrence and also to influence the risk if it does occur. In addition to planning responses to identified risk, the Plan Risk Responses process proactively considers responses to unplanned or unforeseen risks.

# Inputs

The following inputs are used in the Plan Risk Responses process.

## Risk Management Plan

The risk management plan contains information about the processes you have decided are most appropriate for the development of risk responses; as such, it is an essential input into the Plan Risk Responses process. The risk management plan is an output from the Plan Risk Management process.

## Risk Register

Obviously, in order to develop risk responses, you need a list of all the identified risks, their potential consequences, and either the qualitative or quantitative risk analysis for each. All this information is contained in the risk register, which makes it an essential input into the Plan Risk Responses process. The risk register is an output from the Identify Risks process.

# Tools and Techniques

The following tools and techniques of this process can be used on the separate inputs to deliver the Plan Risk Responses process output.

## Strategies for Dealing with Negative Risks or Threats

There are four key strategies for dealing with negative risks or threats in relation to the development of appropriate risk responses:

- *Avoid:* Make plans to avoid the risk occurring. For example, if you have identified that there is a risk of earthquake damage in a building you plan to construct, an avoid strategy is to relocate the building to an area that is more geologically stable.

- *Transfer:* Assign someone else the responsibility and ultimately the consequences of the risk. The most common form of transfer is insurance. For example, after identifying that your building may be subject to damage from an earthquake, you may decide to take out insurance for this event.

- *Mitigate:* Accept that the risk may occur, but attempt to put in place a risk response that minimizes the negative effects of the risk. For example, you may decide to build your multistory building in a known earthquake zone but choose to mitigate the effects of an earthquake on the building by using base isolators and materials that are impact resistant.

- *Accept:* Simply accept the consequence of the risk occurring. For example, you may choose not to take out insurance, shift a planned building, or use earthquake-resistant building technology, and simply accept that if an earthquake hits, you will take responsibility for repairs.

You can have multiple strategies for each risk; often this is the wisest approach because different strategies can be enacted at different points on the timeline of a risk potentially occurring. You will also choose the most appropriate risk strategy, or strategies, for your particular risk and your particular risk tolerance.

## Strategies for Dealing with Positive Risks or Opportunities

Four key *strategies for dealing with positive risks or opportunities* seek to maximize the chance of a positive risk occurring and if it does occur, to maximize the positive impact on the project:

- *Exploit:* Seek to ensure that the positive risk has the maximum chance of occurring. For example, you may decide to allocate your top designers to a particular client's project to ensure that the positive risk of a happy client is enhanced.

- *Share:* Take on board a third party with particular skills and experience to help maximize the occurrence and the impact of a positive risk. For example, you may choose to go into a joint venture with a company with complementary skills in order to increase the chances of securing a particular contract.

- *Enhance:* Be prepared to increase the chances of the positive risk occurring and, if it does occur, its positive impact. For example, you may choose to buy more lottery tickets in order to enhance the chances of your winning.

- *Accept:* Make no changes to the project management plan, and simply accept the chances of the positive risk occurring and the impact it will have.

## Contingent Response Strategies

Each of the strategies for dealing with negative risk or positive risk discussed previously is developed for clearly identified risks. However, despite your best efforts, you are highly unlikely to identify all the risks that may occur on a project; thus it is prudent to have in place *contingent response strategies,* which are planned responses to unplanned risk. The contingent response strategies outline the actions your project team will take if a set of predefined conditions occurs. This set of predefined conditions can refer to particular metrics relating to the project budget or project schedule. Your contingent response strategies are included in your *contingency plan.*

A further means of dealing with unplanned risks occurring is a *workaround.* The difference between a workaround and contingent response strategies is that a workaround is an unplanned and reactive response to an unplanned risk occurring, whereas a contingent response strategy is a planned and prepared response to an unplanned risk occurring. A workaround is a plan to get around a problem or risk that has arisen and not necessarily fix it. A great way to implement a workaround is to gather experienced people in a single location and get them to brainstorm a solution as fast as possible. The workaround may be a temporary solution to allow you to continue working on the project; therefore, you should be prepared to revisit the situation with a more permanent solution. Always include your experience with workarounds in your lessons learned so that future projects may anticipate the risk and include it in their risk register.

## Expert Judgment

Given the complexity of executing a well-defined series of planned risk responses, it is prudent to use expert judgment as a tool in developing your risk responses. The experts you choose to use will be people with experience and skills in anticipating and dealing with the identified risks.

# Outputs

The outputs from the Plan Risk Responses process are the following.

## Project Management Plan Updates

The specific parts of the project management plan that will be updated as a result of your consideration of potential risk responses will include all aspects of the project management plan, such as the schedule, cost, quality, and procurement management plans, as well as the human resource management plan and scope, schedule, and cost baselines. The consideration of different and appropriate risk responses often requires you to revisit these foundational documents as a result of the risks identified and the planned responses.

## Project Document Updates

The specific project documents that will be updated will of course be the risk register and the assumptions log. It is essential that both of these documents are kept up to date and reflect the latest information about particular risks, the analysis of individual risks, and the planned risk responses.

### Quick Check

1.   What is the main purpose of the Plan Risk Responses process?

2.   What are the four risk response strategies for positive risks?

3.   What are the four risk response strategies for negative risks?

4.   What is the purpose of having contingent response strategies in place?

### Quick Check Answers

1.   The main purpose of the Plan Risk Responses process is to give proactive consideration to the actions you will put in place prior to a risk occurring, and actions you will take as a risk occurs, in order to minimize the impact from negative risks and maximize the impact from positive risks.

2. The four risk response strategies for positive risks are enhance, share, exploit, and accept.

3. The four risk response strategies for negative risks are transfer, mitigate, avoid, and accept.

4. The purpose of contingent response strategies is to ensure that you have a proactive response planned to unplanned risk occurring.

# Control Risks

▓ **More Info**   Control Risks

You can read more about the Control Risks process in the PMBOK Guide, 5th edition, in Chapter 11, section 11.6. Table 9-6 identifies the process inputs, tools and techniques, and outputs.

*Table 9-6.*  *Control Risks Process*

| Inputs ⇨ | Tools and Techniques ⇨ | Outputs |
|---|---|---|
| • Project management plan<br>• Risk register<br>• Work performance data<br>• Work performance reports | • Risk reassessment<br>• Risk audits<br>• Variance and trend analysis<br>• Technical performance measurement<br>• Reserve analysis<br>• Status meetings | • Work performance information<br>• Change requests<br>• Project management plan updates<br>• Project document updates<br>• Organizational process asset updates |

The Control Risks process is focused on monitoring and controlling the project risk management activities being undertaken to ensure that they are in accordance with the risk management plan and the information contained in the risk register.

The Control Risks process covers the following monitoring and controlling domain task:

• Task 4: Monitor and assess risk by determining whether exposure has changed and evaluating the effectiveness of response strategies, in order to manage the impact of risks and opportunities on the project.

Like all the other monitoring and controlling processes, the Control Risks process checks the implementation of the plan. In this case, you are checking what is occurring against what you planned to occur in relation to risk management. You will be looking out for any variance between the risks you planned for and the risks that are occurring, any new risks, and any new information affecting already-identified risks, and evaluating the overall risk process.

# Inputs

The following inputs are used in the Control Risks process.

## Project Management Plan

The project management plan contains information about how each part of the project will be executed, monitored, and closed, in relation to risk. The specific part of the project management plan that is most useful for the Control Risk process is the risk management plan. The project management plan is an output from the Develop Project Management Plan process, and the risk management plan is an output from the Plan Risk Management process.

## Risk Register

The risk register is the key document in this process, because you are checking the information contained in the risk register against what is actually occurring. You are checking that you identified all the risks; that you correctly estimated their consequences, probability, and impact; and that your documented responses were appropriate. You are also using the risk register to check for any risks you may have missed. The risk register is an output from the Identify Risks process.

## Work Performance Data

In order to assess how you are doing against what you had planned to do, you require work performance data. Work performance data will in turn become work performance reports in the Monitor and Control Project Work process. Work performance data is an output from the Direct and Manage Project Work process.

---

▦ **Exam Tip**   Remember the sequence that work performance data becomes work performance information, which becomes work performance reports.

---

## Work Performance Reports

Work performance reports are the result of analyzing the work performance information and presenting it in a coherent and easy-to-understand manner in order to give you a comprehensive picture of how well, or how poorly, the project is doing. Work performance reports are an output from the Monitor and Control Project Work process.

# Tools and Techniques

The following tools and techniques of this process can be used on the separate inputs to deliver the Control Risks process outputs.

## Risk Reassessment

*Risk reassessment* is an ongoing process of checking whether there are new risks, whether already-identified risks are still current, whether the analysis of their probability and impact is still accurate, and whether the planned risk responses are still appropriate. The contents of the risk register are highly fluid and subject to a high degree of change as the project progresses and more information is known about existing risks. Thus you should treat the risk register as a live document in constant need of checking and reassessment.

---

■ **Exam Tip**   Risk reassessment should be viewed as a continual activity led by the project manager and involving the project team.

---

## Risk Audits

Generally, audits are a great way to check that processes are working as planned and whether there is any room for improvement. In the Control Risks process, *risk audits* are used to check whether the planned risk responses are appropriate, how well the risk management processes are being implemented, and whether they are appropriate. It is the project manager's responsibility to ensure that risk audits are carried out at appropriate times and with defined objectives. The results of the risk audit contribute to the ongoing continuous improvement of your project processes.

## Variance and Trend Analysis

*Variance and trend analysis* is used in other areas as a technique to identify and document what is occurring against what was planned and then extrapolate from that any identifiable trends that may indicate future performance. When it is used in the Control Risks process, you are looking for any divergence from the risk management plan and risk register and examining this to determine whether it indicates any trends that you can proactively plan for. For example, you may spot that you have consistently underestimated the magnitude of risks around costs of a certain material and use variance and trend analysis to reforecast the future impact and probability of these risks.

## Technical Performance Measurement

*Technical performance measurement* means putting in place acceptable parameters around potentially negative risk events—generally those affecting scope, time, and cost—and then checking that the work being performed is within these technical performance

387

measurements. Work being performed outside the defined technical performance measurements represents risk on the project and may require change requests to be prepared and considered, to change parameters if the planed risk response cannot bring performance back into line. For example, you may have set a range of acceptable costs for development of a new product, but when measuring the actual costs, you find them to be greater than planned; therefore, the risk of a cost overrun on the project is greater.

## Reserve Analysis

During the Perform Quantitative Risk Analysis process, you used objective measurements to develop contingency reserves for either cost or time. During the Control Risks process, you check whether these calculations are still accurate and the reserves you have planned for are still appropriate. It may be that new information has come to light that means the reserve for either cost or time needs to be changed. As a project progresses and estimates become more accurate, it is typical for the range of contingency calculated by using qualitative risk analysis to decrease. For example, you may find that extra information gained about an estimate for the range of time taken to perform a certain activity means the estimate can be refined and reduced, because you have performed the activity several times. You can then reduce the time reserve allocated to this activity.

## Status Meetings

You should either make risk management a normal part of regular project meetings or schedule meetings with a special focus on risk management to ensure that you and the team remain focused on risk management activities throughout the life of the project. The purpose of these *status meetings* is to examine all aspects of risk management on the project and ensure that they are still appropriate and effective. Additionally, having regular meetings where risk management is a topic of discussion creates greater awareness and buy-in from team members, which in turn results in better risk management.

# Outputs

The outputs from the Control Risks process include the following.

## Work Performance Information

As a result of carrying out the Control Risks process, you will end up with valuable work performance information about risk management activities. This information will take the form of revised information about risk responses and their effectiveness, the use of planned time and cost contingency reserves, and any defined technical performance measurements. Work performance information is used as an input into the Monitor and Control Project Work process.

# Change Requests

As a result of completing the Control Risks process and conducting risk audits, variance and trend analysis, technical performance measurements, or reserve analysis, you may discover information that requires a formal change to be made to a part of the project; this is done via a change request. Change requests then go on to be processed according to your approved change-control process in the Perform Integrated Change Control process.

# Project Management Plan Updates

Because risk management affects all other areas of the project, you may update many different parts of the project management plan and its baselines. You will most definitely update the risk management plan.

# Project Document Updates

The specific project documents that will be updated include the risk register and the assumptions log.

# Organizational Process Asset Updates

The specific organizational process assets that will be updated include any historical information about risk management and any templates, processes, or guidelines the organization has in relation to project management.

### Quick Check

1. What is the main purpose of the Control Risks process?

2. Why is risk reassessment an important tool or technique in the Control Risks process?

3. How does the Control Risks process contribute to the development of contingency reserves for time and cost?

### Quick Check Answers

1. The main purpose of the Control Risks process is to determine whether the risk management activities as planned in the risk management plan are being completed as per the plan, whether the risks identified in the risk register are manifesting as forecast, and whether the qualitative and quantitative assessments and planned risk responses are still appropriate.

2. In addition to checking whether risk management activities are being completed as per the plan, a key element of the Control Risks process is a complete reassessment of the assumptions made, the risks identified, and whether any new risks have been identified.

3.     The Control Risks process allows you to examine the time and cost contingency reserves you have developed; as part of the reassessment of risks, you may choose to redefine the reserves allowed for time and cost. Usually this process results in a reduction in the reserves for both time and cost. As more information is known, the better the estimate is, and less risk or uncertainty is associated with time and cost.

# Chapter Summary

- The Risk Management knowledge area is focused on the successful use of project risk to report project performance, gain political support, and provide stakeholders with their risk requirements.

- The Plan Risk Management process produces the risk management plan, which guides the subsequent risk management processes.

- The Identify Risks process, which is a planning process, uses the risk management plan to begin the iterative process of developing the risk register by using a variety of tools and techniques to identify all potential negative and positive risks.

- The Perform Qualitative Risk Analysis process is a planning process that seeks to assign a subjective probability and impact assessment to each of the identified risks so that they can be prioritized.

- The Perform Quantitative Risk Analysis process is a planning process that assigns a quantitative and objective analysis, usually based on statistics and factual data, to the individual probability and impact of identified risks, which can lead to the creation of contingency reserves for time and cost.

- The Plan Risk Responses process is a planning process that outlines a proactive response to all identified risks on the project.

- The Control Risks process, which is a monitoring and controlling process, is like other monitoring and controlling processes in that it assesses actual performance against that forecast in the risk management plan, checks whether the risks identified and assessed in the risk register are still accurate, and checks whether there are any new risks.

# Exercises

The answers for these exercises are located in the "Answers" section at the end of this chapter.

1. Match up the risk response strategy on the left with the correct description on the right.

| Risk Response Strategy | Definition |
| --- | --- |
| 1. Avoid | A. You are working on an IT project and decide that you will bear the consequences if something goes wrong on the project. |
| 2. Enhance | B. You decide to partner with another organization that has skills and experience you don't, in order to present a better response to a contract on offer. |
| 3. Transfer | C. You have considered several options for the location of a new manufacturing plant and decide to locate it in a region with plenty of experienced workers, to get around the risk of not having enough people to do the work. |
| 4. Mitigate | D. You are working on a complex IT project and decide to put in place backup data storage so that you can quickly restart should anything occur to the data you are working on during the project. |
| 5. Accept | E. You take out insurance against wet weather delaying your construction project. |
| 6. Exploit | F. You pull your top project manager off other projects and assign that person to a new bridge construction project to ensure that it has the greatest chance of success. |
| 7. Share | G. You put all your project staff through a workshop to improve their communications management strategy to minimize the risk of not managing stakeholder expectations effectively. |

2. Consider the following five examples of risk analysis, and decide whether they are qualitative or quantitative methods.

    A. You ask your team members to provide their opinion about whether the chance of a storm affecting your construction project next April is very low, low, neither low nor high, high, or very high.

B.   You pay the local meteorological bureau to provide you with the exact probability of there being a storm in April of a magnitude that would affect your construction project.

C.   You gather a team of seven subject matter experts and ask them to provide their opinion of probability and impact of the risk of the selected technology on your IT project. You ask them to select from a standardized scale of probabilities ranging from 0.1, meaning very low probability or impact, up to 0.9, meaning very high probability and impact. You then multiply these two numbers together to obtain a risk score.

D.   The quantity surveyor working for your cost-estimating team has calculated that over the next two years of your project, there is a risk of a 10.3% increase in hardware costs, and that this increase could cost you a total of $173,000. The surveyor recommends purchasing this hardware now and finding a place to store it to avoid this risk.

E.   You have calculated that there is a very high chance that a senior staff member will leave your project within the next three months, and that replacing them will cost $25,000. You decide to offer the staff member a salary increase of $15,000 to get them to stay with the project.

3.   Consider the decision tree shown in Figure 9-9, outlining a choice about whether to build a new factory or upgrade an existing factory to take advantage of increased demand for your product. Using expected monetary value analysis, what is the best decision to make?

| Decision Definition | Decision node | Chance node | Net path value |
|---|---|---|---|
| Decision to be made | Input: cost of each option<br><br>Output: decision made (true, false) | Input: scenario probability, reward if it occurs<br><br>Output: expected monetary value (EMV) | Computed: (Payoffs minus Costs) along path |

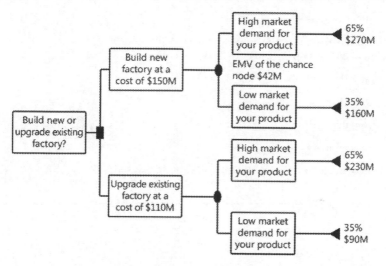

***Figure 9-9.*** *A decision tree showing the expected monetary value of building a new factory or upgrading an existing factory*

# Review Questions

Test your knowledge of the information in Chapter 9 by answering these questions. The answers to these questions and the explanation of why each answer choice is correct or incorrect are located in the "Answers" section at the end of this chapter.

1.  Which of the following processes produces the risk management plan?

    A.  Develop Project Management Plan

    B.  Plan Risk Management

    C.  Manage Risk

    D.  Develop Risk Management Plan

2. The particular attitude that an organization has to the amount of risk it is prepared to accept for the project is known as what?

   A. Risk analysis

   B. Risk tolerance

   C. Risk aversion

   D. Risk avoidance

3. Uncertainty that presents opportunities to deliver a project ahead of time is known as what?

   A. Risk threshold

   B. Positive risk

   C. Negative risk

   D. Risk analysis

4. Which of the following documents will contain a description of risk categories?

   A. Risk register

   B. Risk analysis

   C. Risk management plan

   D. Risk progress report

5. You have prepared a grid that shows a standardized representation of probability and impact in order to prioritize individual risks. What is this known as?

   A. Risk breakdown structure

   B. Ishikawa diagram

   C. Probability and impact matrix

   D. Risk register

6. You are in the process of identifying individual risks to your project and are using a technique to discover the underlying causes that lead to a particular risk. What technique are you using?

   A. Brainstorming

   B. Delphi technique

   C. Interviewing

   D. Root cause analysis

7. You have called your team together for a meeting in which you ask them to analyze the strengths, weaknesses, opportunities, and threats your project faces. What tool or technique are you using?

   A. Delphi technique

   B. Brainstorming

   C. SWOT analysis

   D. Root cause analysis

8. After carrying out a particular risk process, you end up with a prioritized list of risks, ranking them from highest to lowest priority. Which of the following risk processes produces this list?

   A. Plan Risk Management

   B. Identify Risks

   C. Perform Qualitative Risk Analysis

   D. Perform Quantitative Risk Analysis

9. In carrying out the risk management processes, you will often update particular project documents. What is the most common project document to be updated as a result of completing risk management processes?

   A. Risk register

   B. Risk management plan

   C. Assumptions log

   D. Project management plan

10. You have developed a range of statistical data that demonstrates the characteristics of a beta distribution and are using this information to analyze the probability of a risk occurring. Which risk management process are you carrying out?

    A. Identify Risks

    B. Perform Qualitative Risk Analysis

    C. Perform Quantitative Risk Analysis

    D. Plan Risk Responses

11. If you are using a piece of software to carry out the simulation of the probability of a particular risk occurring over many iterations, what tool are you using?

    A. Expected monetary value analysis

    B. Interviewing

    C. Sensitivity analysis

    D. Monte Carlo analysis

12. The decision to delay the beginning of construction until the end of winter to ensure that team members do not have to contend with the risk of dangerous working conditions is what sort of risk response strategy?

    A. Mitigation

    B. Transference

    C. Avoidance

    D. Acceptance

13. You have identified a potential risk to your project but have decided that you will not conduct an assessment of the probability or impact, or have a proactive response in place. What sort of risk response strategy is this?

    A. Mitigation

    B. Enhancement

    C. Transference

    D. Acceptance

14. You are carrying out a reassessment of the cost reserves built up by using quantitative risk assessment for the procurement of materials for your project, due to new information that reduces the uncertainty in the initial estimates. Which risk management process are you carrying out?

    A. Identify Risks

    B. Perform Quantitative Risk Analysis

    C. Plan Risk Responses

    D. Control Risks

# Answers

This section contains the answers for the Exercises and Review Questions in this chapter.

## Exercises

1.  Match up the risk response strategy on the left with the description on the right.

| Risk Response Strategy | Definition |
| --- | --- |
| 1. Avoid | C. You have considered several options for the location of a new manufacturing plant and decide to locate it in a region with plenty of experienced workers, to get around the risk of not having enough people to do the work. |
| 2. Enhance | G. You put all your project staff through a workshop to improve their communications management strategy to minimize the risk of not managing stakeholder expectations effectively. |
| 3. Transfer | E. You take out insurance against wet weather delaying your construction project. |
| 4. Mitigate | D. You are working on a complex IT project and decide to put in place backup data storage so that you can quickly restart should anything occur to the data you are working on during the project. |
| 5. Accept | A. You are working on an IT project and decide that you will bear the consequences if something goes wrong on the project. |
| 6. Exploit | F. You pull your top project manager off other projects and assign that person to a new bridge construction project to ensure that it has the greatest chance of success. |
| 7. Share | B. You decide to partner with another organization that has skills and experience you don't, in order to present a better response to a contract on offer. |

2.  Consider the following five examples of risk analysis, and decide whether they are qualitative or quantitative risk analysis methods.

    A.  You ask your team members to provide their opinion about whether the chance of a storm affecting your construction project next April is very low, low, neither low nor high, high, or very high.

Answer: This is an example of qualitative risk analysis because it is using subjective assessment and opinion on a fixed scale.

B. You pay the local meteorological bureau to provide you with the exact probability of there being a storm in April of a magnitude that would affect your construction project.

Answer: This is an example of quantitative risk analysis because you are using actual statistical data instead of subjective opinion to calculate probability.

C. You gather a team of seven subject matter experts and ask them to provide their opinion of probability and impact of the risk of the selected technology on your IT project. You ask them to select from a standardized scale of probabilities ranging from 0.1, meaning very low probability or impact, up to 0.9, meaning very high probability and impact. You then multiply these two numbers together to obtain a risk score.

Answer: This is an example of qualitative risk analysis, because, despite the use of experts using numbers with decimal points in them, it is still an opinion-based assessment on a fixed, predetermined scale.

D. The quantity surveyor working for your cost estimating team has calculated that over the next two years of your project there is a risk of a 10.3% increase in hardware costs, and that this increase could cost you a total of $173,000. The surveyor recommends purchasing this hardware now and finding a place to store it to avoid this risk.

Answer: This is an example of quantitative risk analysis because it uses clear, calculated numbers based on facts to determine probability and impact.

E. You have calculated that there is a very high chance that a senior staff member will leave your project within the next three months, and that replacing them will cost $25,000. You decide to offer a salary increase of $15,000 to get them to stay with the project.

Answer: This is an example of qualitative risk analysis because you have made a subjective assessment of the probability.

3. Consider the decision tree outlining a choice about whether to build a new factory or upgrade an existing factory to take advantage of increased demand for your product. Using expected monetary value analysis, what is the best decision to make? (See the updated decision tree in Figure 9-10.)

| Decision | Decision node | Chance node | Net path value |
|---|---|---|---|
| Decision to be made | Input: cost of each option<br><br>Output: decision made (true, false) | Input: scenario probability, reward if it occurs<br><br>Output: expected monetary value (EMV) | Computed: (Payoffs minus Costs) along path |

**Figure 9-10.** *A decision tree showing the expected monetary value of building a new factory or upgrading an existing factory*

Expected monetary value of building a new factory:

$$(0.65 \times \$120M) + (0.35 \times \$10M) = \$81.5M$$

Expected monetary value of upgrading the existing factory:

$$(0.65 \times \$120M) + (0.35 \times -\$20M) = \$71M$$

Therefore, you would choose to build a new factory because it has the higher expected monetary value.

# Chapter Review

1.  **Correct Answer: B**

    A.  **Incorrect:** The Develop Project Management Plan produces the project management plan.

    B.  **Correct:** The Plan Risk Management process has the risk management plan as its primary output.

    C.  **Incorrect:** Manage Risk is a made-up process name.

    D.  **Incorrect:** Develop Risk Management plan is a made-up process name.

2.  **Correct Answer: B**

    A.  **Incorrect:** Risk analysis is the process of analyzing either quantitatively or qualitatively the probability and impact of particular risks.

    B.  **Correct:** Risk tolerance describes the amount of risk an organization is prepared to accept on a project.

    C.  **Incorrect:** Risk aversion is a state of mind whereby an organization would prefer not to undertake high-risk activities.

    D.  **Incorrect:** Risk avoidance is similar to risk aversion and indicates an outcome of assessing risk tolerance.

3.  **Correct Answer: B**

    A.  **Incorrect:** The risk threshold is the level of risk tolerance that an organization is comfortable with.

    B.  **Correct:** Any uncertainty that presents opportunities constitutes positive risk.

    C.  **Incorrect:** Negative risk is any uncertainty that represents a threat to the project.

    D.  **Incorrect:** Risk analysis is the process of analyzing either quantitatively or qualitatively the probability and impact of particular risks.

4.  **Correct Answer: C**

    A.  **Incorrect:** The risk register contains a list of identified risks, probability and impact assessment, and any planned risk responses. It may use risk categories to group individual risks together, but it does not generally contain a description of the risk categories.

B.  **Incorrect:** Risk analysis is the process of analyzing either quantitatively or qualitatively the probability and impact of particular risks.

C.  **Correct:** The risk management plan contains a lot of information about the particular approach you will take to manage risk on your project; included in this information is a description of the risk categories.

D.  **Incorrect:** Any risk progress reports prepared will focus on risk activities completed against risk activities planned, not on a description of risk categories.

5.  **Correct Answer: C**

A.  **Incorrect:** The risk breakdown structure shows the risk categories in graphical form.

B.  **Incorrect:** An Ishikawa diagram shows the probable causes of particular risk effects.

C.  **Correct:** The probability and impact matrix is a grid that shows a standardized list of both probability on one axis and impact on another axis; after the two values are multiplied together, it presents a graphical analysis of risk priorities.

D.  **Incorrect:** The risk register presents a list of identified risks, probability and impact assessment, and proactive risk responses.

6.  **Correct Answer: D**

A.  **Incorrect:** Brainstorming is a technique to gather as much information as possible from project team members or subject matter experts.

B.  **Incorrect:** The Delphi technique is a method of anonymously interviewing and gathering data from experts.

C.  **Incorrect:** Interviewing is a technique used to formally gather data from subject matter experts in a structured format.

D.  **Correct:** Root cause analysis seeks to discover the underlying cause or causes of a particular risk.

7. **Correct Answer: C**

   A. **Incorrect:** The Delphi technique is a method of anonymously interviewing and gathering data from experts.

   B. **Incorrect:** Brainstorming is a technique to gather as much information as possible from project team members or subject matter experts.

   C. **Correct:** *SWOT* stands for *strength, weaknesses, opportunities, and threats.*

   D. **Incorrect:** Root cause analysis seeks to discover the underlying cause or causes of a particular risk.

8. **Correct Answer: C**

   A. **Incorrect:** The Plan Risk Management process produces the risk management plan.

   B. **Incorrect:** The Identify Risks process produces an iteration of the risk register.

   C. **Correct:** The Perform Qualitative Risk Analysis process uses subjective assessment of probability and impact to give each identified risk a score so it can be ranked and prioritized.

   D. **Incorrect:** The Perform Quantitative Risk Analysis process uses actual statistical data to calculate probability and impact and produces contingency reserves for either time or cost.

9. **Correct Answer: A**

   A. **Correct:** The risk register is a highly iterative document that is constantly updated by most of the risk management planning processes.

   B. **Incorrect:** The risk management plan may be updated as a result of completing risk management activities, particularly the Control Risks process, but the frequency of updates will be less than the updates to the risk register.

   C. **Incorrect:** The assumptions log will be checked and reassessed often, but not as often as the risk register.

   D. **Incorrect:** The project management plan, its subsidiary plans, and its baselines may be updated, but certainly not as often as the risk register.

10. **Correct Answer: C**

   A. **Incorrect:** The Identify Risks process does not use any form of either qualitative or quantitative risk analysis.

   B. **Incorrect:** The Perform Qualitative Risk Analysis process uses subjective data rather than statistical data to complete its assessment of probability and impact.

   C. **Correct:** The Perform Quantitative Risk Analysis process uses statistical data and probability distributions such as the beta distribution to calculate quantitative risk.

   D. **Incorrect:** The Plan Risk Responses process is focused on the development of appropriate responses to identified risks.

11. **Correct Answer: D**

   A. **Incorrect:** The expected monetary value analysis analyzes particular options, and the probability and net impact of those options, to determine which has the higher expected monetary value.

   B. **Incorrect:** Interviewing is a technique for gathering information from team members and subject matter experts in a formal setting.

   C. **Incorrect:** Sensitivity analysis is a way of determining which parts of the project are most sensitive to risk.

   D. **Correct:** Monte Carlo analysis is a sophisticated type of mathematical and statistical analysis. It carries out simulations of events occurring, to determine the likely probability and impact.

12. **Correct Answer: C**

   A. **Incorrect:** Mitigation is a response that seeks to minimize the impact of risk if it occurs.

   B. **Incorrect:** Transference makes the impact of the risk someone else's responsibility.

   C. **Correct:** The example represents a strategy of avoiding an identified risk.

   D. **Incorrect:** Acceptance would mean doing nothing and accepting the consequences.

13. **Correct Answer: D**

    A. **Incorrect:** Mitigation is a response that seeks to minimize the impact of risk if it occurs.

    B. **Incorrect:** Enhancement is a risk response strategy for positive risks that seeks to enhance the probability and impact of the risk.

    C. **Incorrect:** Transference makes the impact of the risk someone else's responsibility.

    D. **Correct:** Acceptance is a strategy whereby you make no provision at all should the risk occur and simply accept the consequences.

14. **Correct Answer: D**

    A. **Incorrect:** The Identify Risks process seeks to identify individual risks for inclusion on the risk register.

    B. **Incorrect:** The Perform Quantitative Risk Analysis process conducts a quantitative assessment of probability and impact of individual risks.

    C. **Incorrect:** The Plan Risk Responses process prepares a proactive response to identified risks.

    D. **Correct:** The Control Risks process includes the reassessment of reserves to determine if the uncertainty within them has changed.

# CHAPTER 10

■ ■ ■

# Procurement Management

This chapter focuses on the topic of Project Procurement Management; like the other knowledge areas, it begins with a process of planning, which in this case produces a procurement management plan. It then uses this plan to carry out the procurement work, which involves making decisions about whether to procure goods, services, or resources from external sources and, if so, how to advertise and award the contract, and what form of contract to use. Procurement management also involves monitoring contractual terms for performance and includes a process for making sure all contracts are formally closed.

**The PMBOK® Guide processes**

**Project Procurement Management knowledge area**

The four processes in the Project Procurement Management knowledge area are as follows:

- Plan Procurement Management (planning process)

- Conduct Procurements (executing process)

- Control Procurements (monitoring and controlling process)

- Close Procurements (closing process)

## What Is Project Procurement Management?

---

■ **Exam Tip**   If you are familiar with the ISO 31000 Standard for Procurement Management, much of this section will be familiar to you. Additionally, much of this topic is based on formal government procurement processes.

---

Project procurement management is focused on planning for and making decisions about whether to procure goods and services needed on the project from external sources, which form of contact to choose, how to select sellers to deliver the work, and how to check that the work is being done in accordance with the agreed contracts.

© Sean Whitaker 2016
S. Whitaker, *Pass the PMP® Exam*, DOI 10.1007/978-1-4842-2074-0_10

The Plan Procurement Management process results in a procurement management plan, which guides the other procurement management processes. The organization looking to procure goods or services then performs a make-or-buy analysis to determine whether it should complete the work internally or source the goods and services from external sources. After the decision has been made to go to external sources, the buying organization then decides what form of contract it will use, how it will inform potential sellers of its needs, and how it will select the successful seller.

When the contract has been signed, both parties take responsibility for checking that the agreed contract terms are being followed and that any changes to the contract are formally documented.

Finally, all contracts must be closed. Contractual closure does not mean project closure, because contracts can be closed at any time during a project. Remember, contractual closure must be performed before project closure.

In any contract there are *buyers*, the party looking to acquire the goods or services, and there are *sellers*, the parties with goods or services to sell. There can be multiple sellers, but generally there is a single buyer.

---

▧ **Exam Tip**   On the exam, unless otherwise stated, you should assume that you are the buyer in any contract. But read the question thoroughly to ensure that you understand whether you are the buyer or seller, because your answer to the question may be different depending on which position you are in. You can also be both buyer and seller at different points in the project. Take your time reading the question to understand the perspective from which you are answering the question.

---

# Plan Procurement Management

---

▧ **More Info**   Plan Procurement Management

You can read more about the Plan Procurement Management process in the PMBOK Guide, 5th edition, in Chapter 12, section 12.1. Table 10-1 identifies the process inputs, tools and techniques, and outputs.

---

*Table 10-1. Plan Procurement Management Process*

| Inputs ⇨ | Tools and Techniques ⇨ | Outputs |
|---|---|---|
| • Project management plan<br>• Requirements documentation<br>• Risk register<br>• Activity resource requirements<br>• Project schedule<br>• Activity cost estimates<br>• Stakeholder register<br>• Enterprise environmental factors<br>• Organizational process assets | • Make-or-buy analysis<br>• Expert judgment<br>• Market research<br>• Meetings | • Procurement management plan<br>• Procurement statement of work<br>• Procurement documents<br>• Source-selection criteria<br>• Make-or-buy decisions<br>• Change requests<br>• Project document updates |

The Plan Procurement Management process is a planning process with the procurement management plan and procurement statement of work as its main outputs. The purpose of this process is, as with other planning processes, to enable you and your team to proactively plan your particular approach to procurement requirements on the project.

The Plan Procurement Management process covers the following planning domain task:

- Task 7: Develop the procurement management plan based on the project scope, budget, and schedule, in order to ensure that the required project resources will be available.

# Inputs

The Plan Procurement Management process uses some or all of the following inputs as part of the development of the procurement management plan for the project.

## Project Management Plan

The project management plan is a key input into the Plan Procurement Management process because it contains vital information about the scope of work and elements of the scope of work that need to be considered for external procurement. These potential procurement elements are described in the scope baseline, which includes the scope statement, work breakdown structure (WBS), and WBS dictionary. The project management plan is an output from the Develop Project Management Plan process.

# Requirements Documentation

The requirements documentation includes information about specific project requirements that can be taken into consideration when looking at whether to make a requirement internally or procure it from external sources and, if the decision is made to procure it from external sources, what sort of contract is best to use. Requirements documentation is an output from the Collect Requirements process.

# Risk Register

The risk register is an important input into the Plan Procurement Management process because it identifies specific risks around the decision to make goods or services internally versus the decision to procure them from external sources, and the risks associated with individual contract types. The risk register is an output from the Identify Risks process.

# Activity Resource Requirements

Activity resource requirements contain information about the resources required to complete individually identified activities; this information can be useful when making decisions about whether to procure goods and services externally and the type of contract to use. Activity resource requirements are an output from the Estimate Activity Resources process.

# Project Schedule

The project schedule is a key input into the Plan Procurement Management process because it outlines the planned deliverable dates of particular activities and tasks, and this information is used when negotiating contracts. The project schedule is an output from the Develop Schedule process.

# Activity Cost Estimates

Activity cost estimates include the cost estimates of individual activities, which can then be used to anticipate what likely contractual responses will be and assess whether they are reasonable and accurate. Activity cost estimates are an output from the Estimate Costs process.

# Stakeholder Register

The stakeholder register identifies individual stakeholders and their interest in the project. Thus it is useful in terms of managing stakeholder expectations around which goods and services will be procured externally and the type of contract selected. The stakeholder register is an output from the Identify Stakeholders process.

| REAL WORLD |
| --- |

The type of contract selected will have an impact on the stakeholders, particularly if stakeholders are to be intimately involved in the administration and execution of the contract. Many types of contracts set up an adversarial relationship with stakeholders, whereas other more modern forms of contract establish a relationship based on trust between stakeholders. Thus, having an in-depth knowledge of how your stakeholders will perceive and react to different contractual decisions is an important consideration in your procurement management process. A style of contract that works for one group of stakeholders may not work for another group of stakeholders. Also, keep in mind that many stakeholders will have preferred vendors and long-established types of contracts with them.

## Enterprise Environmental Factors

The specific enterprise environmental factors that are useful as inputs into the Plan Procurement Management process include any marketplace conditions that determine whether there will be a lot of interest in your procurement decisions, the specific types of products and services available in a particular marketplace, the size of the marketplace and whether you can stay local or have to go wider in your search for suppliers, and the expected terms and conditions for contract types with particular industries.

## Organizational Process Assets

The specific organizational process assets that may be important inputs into the Plan Procurement Management process include any formal procurement policies the organization has that state what goods and services will be procured, how the decisions will be made, what sort of contract types are preferred, and who has responsibility in negotiating and administering the contracts.

| REAL WORLD |
| --- |

I have found that most organizations have clear procurement policies that specify when external procurement can be or must be used, and the type of contract that the organization prefers. You should always endeavor to familiarize yourself with any procurement policies your organization has.

---

**Exam Tip** You must always conduct procurement in accordance with the relevant organizational procurement guidelines. Don't be tempted to act outside of the guidelines: if the guidelines are wrong, you can seek to change them; but until they are changed, you must adhere to them.

---

# Tools and Techniques

The following tools and techniques are available to be used to develop the inputs in this process in order to produce the procurement management plan.

## Make-or-Buy Analysis

The *make-or-buy analysis* is a comprehensive description of the decision-making process an organization goes through when deciding whether it should make the goods or services it requires itself or seek to acquire goods or services from external sources. There are a number of ways of making the decision and a number of factors to take into account.

Of the factors that can be taken into account when making a make-or-buy decision, the following are the most important:

- The organization's risk profile and risk tolerance

- Ownership of intellectual property

- Availability of suitable sellers

- Availability of internal resources capable of delivering a good or service

- Timeframes for delivery of a good or service

- Length of time the resource required for the good or service is needed on the project

- Ability to support ongoing changes and technical support

The make-or-buy process should follow established procedures that take into account the relevant factors. You can even assign weights to various factors to enable you to score factors differently.

In making make-or-buy decisions, you may also want to use more quantitative methods such as the decision tree analysis used in Chapter 9 in the Quantitative Risk Analysis section.

# Expert Judgment

Expert judgment is an excellent tool to use when planning your approach to procurement management. Using the knowledge and experience of subject matter experts will be invaluable not only in your overall procurement management plan, but also in identifying and completing an analysis of procurements. Suitable experts who may provide judgment include senior management, stakeholders with relevant experience, external subject matter experts such as procurement professionals, industry groups, and professional associations.

One particularly useful type of expert that you should consider using in your procurement management decisions is the legal expert. Your procurement decisions will be supported by legally enforceable contracts, so it is highly recommended that you involve experts with legal experience in the formation, negotiation, execution, and administration of any procurement contracts.

---

### REAL WORLD

I have always found that referring decisions about contracts to legal experts is a good investment. The wording of contracts can be complicated, and it often takes somebody with particular experience in an area to be able to effectively negotiate a contract that is easy to understand and enforce and doesn't place an undue amount of work on one or the other of the parties involved. Certainly any changes or variations to contracts should involve people with legal expertise.

---

# Market Research

*Market research* is carried out to determine the capability and availability of potential sellers in the market and their interest in responding to your procurement requests. Additionally, any market research you carry out may reveal additional ways of delivering goods and services; as such, it is an important tool in the Plan Procurement Management process.

# Meetings

Meetings are a great way to bring together project team members, stakeholders, and other experts to consider how procurement will be managed on the project. There are a number of ways you can run these meetings in order to efficiently obtain the information you require. They can be run formally with defined agendas and examination of reports, or they can be run as creative brainstorming sessions. The style of meeting you choose to use will reflect the participants and your intended outcomes.

# Outputs

After the appropriate tools and techniques have been applied to the selected inputs, the Plan Procurement Management process has the following outputs.

## Procurement Management Plan

The Plan Procurement Management process has the *procurement management plan* as its major output. Similar to other management plans, the procurement management plan provides a guide for completing the procurement management activities in the project. The procurement management plan will probably contain information about the types of contracts to be used, whether independent estimates will be used to check responses received, any methods for identifying and selecting sellers, and any other important procurement information that can be used in the other three procurement processes. The procurement management plan goes on to be used as an input into the Conduct Procurements process. Given that it is also a subsidiary plan of the project management plan, is used as an input into the Control Procurements process and Close Procurements process.

## Procurement Statement of Work

The *procurement statement of work* is an output that describes each good or service that will be procured externally in enough detail to allow potential sellers to determine whether they are interested in and able to provide the goods or services sought. You should spend as much time as possible defining the procurement statement of work because it will form the basis of your procurement contracts, and any omissions or areas that are not sufficiently defined may cause conflict in the administration of the contract.

---

▓ **Exam Tip**  You can think of the procurement statement of work as a type or subset of the project scope of work specifically focused on the work to be done as part of a contract for goods and services.

---

## Procurement Documents

A variety of key *procurement documents* are produced as a result of the Plan Procurement Management process. They are useful in soliciting responses from prospective sellers and will form the basis of the contracts that will eventually be agreed on. Some of the more common types of procurement documents include the following:

- Request for information (RFI)
- Expression of interest (EOI)
- Invitation for bid (IFB)

- Request for proposal (RFP)
- Request for quotation (RFQ)
- Tender

---

## REAL WORLD

If you have ever been involved in any formal seller-selection process, you will find this section very straightforward. However, if you have not been involved in formal contractual negotiation processes, pay particular attention. It is not uncommon for a project manager to receive negotiated contracts without being involved in the make-or-buy decisions, seller selection, and contractual negotiations.

---

## Source-Selection Criteria

The point of *source-selection criteria* is to enable the buyer to rate individual seller responses. They can include both objective and subjective criteria. The source-selection criteria reflect the criteria that are important to you and your decision-making process for selecting sellers. In addition to the prices submitted, you may also want to take into account a variety of other factors and give them a particular weight to reflect their importance. Examples of the types of criteria you may want to take into account include how well the seller understands your needs beyond what you may have described in the procurement statement of work, their technical ability to deliver the requested solution, the financial stability of the organization, their previous experience doing this type of work, and references from other buyers who may have used this seller. You can use the source-selection criteria during the Conduct Procurements process.

---

## REAL WORLD

There are certain occasions when your only source-selection criterion will be the lowest price; however, in many instances you will want to take into account other criteria in selecting a seller. Typically, you should look at their experience, their financial stability, the staff members who are allocated to do the work, and other factors such as health and safety and environmental record.

---

## Make-or-Buy Decisions

The output from the make-or-buy analysis will be *make-or-buy decisions*. These documented decisions outline how you decided to either make the goods or services internally or go to external sources. Make-or-buy decisions are used as an input into the Conduct Procurements process.

# Change Requests

As a result of carrying out the Plan Procurement Management process, you may want to change some elements and subsidiary plans or baselines of the project management plan via a change request. All change requests go on to be used as inputs into the Perform Integrated Change-control process.

# Project Document Updates

The types of project documents that may be updated as a result of completing the Plan Procurement Management process are the project scope, requirements documentation, risk register, and stakeholder register.

### Quick Check

1. What is the main focus of the Plan Procurement Management process?

2. What are some of the factors you take into account when conducting a make-or-buy analysis?

3. What are some typical factors included in source-selection criteria?

### Quick Check Answers

1. The main focus of the Plan Procurement Management process is to make decisions and provide a documented guideline for the rest of the procurement management processes. This information is contained in the procurement management plan, which is a subsidiary of the project management plan.

2. The types of factors that can be taken into account when conducting a make-or-buy analysis include the risk profile of the organization, the issue of ownership of intellectual property, the timeframe in which the work must be done, the current capability of internal resources, and the cost differential between choosing to make a good or service internally and procuring it externally.

3. In addition to including the price in the source-selection criteria, you may choose to include how well the seller understands your needs, their proposed response and the life-cycle cost, their technical ability to deliver the solution, the staff they have allocated to do the work and their experience, any warranties they offer on the work being completed, the financial capacity and stability of the performing organization, their past performance in doing this type of work, references from others who have used them, and who owns the rights to the work done.

# Conduct Procurements

---

▓ **More Info**    Conduct Procurements

You can read more about the Conduct Procurements process in the PMBOK Guide, 5th edition, in Chapter 12, section 12.2. Table 10-2 identifies the process inputs, tools and techniques, and outputs.

---

*Table 10-2.* *Conduct Procurements Process*

| Inputs ⇨ | Tools and Techniques ⇨ | Outputs |
|---|---|---|
| • Procurement management plan | • Bidder conference | • Selected sellers |
| • Procurement documents | • Proposal evaluation techniques | • Agreements |
| • Source-selection criteria | • Independent estimates | • Resource calendars |
| • Seller proposals | • Expert judgment | • Change requests |
| • Project documents | • Advertising | • Project management plan updates |
| • Make-or-buy decisions | • Analytical techniques | • Project document updates |
| • Procurement statement of work | • Procurement negotiations | |
| • Organizational process assets | | |

The Conduct Procurements process is an executing process that seeks to carry out the initial identification of prospective sellers, effectively pass on to them information about the work required, get responses from the sellers, evaluate and select the best seller for the job, and sign an agreement or contract.

The Conduct Procurements process covers the following executing domain task:

- Task 1: Acquire and manage project resources by following the human resource and procurement management plans, in order to meet project requirements.

# Inputs

The Conduct Procurements process uses some or all of the following inputs.

## Procurement Management Plan

The procurement management plan is an important input into the Conduct Procurements process because it outlines exactly how the Conduct Procurements process will be carried out. The procurement management plan is an output from the Plan Procurement Management process.

# Procurement Documents

The procurement documents are an output from the Plan Procurement Management process and include a range of different documents for soliciting information from prospective sellers. As such, they are an important input into the Conduct Procurements process.

# Source-Selection Criteria

Source-selection criteria are used during the Conduct Procurements process to enable an evaluation of sellers against predetermined criteria that are important to the organization buying the goods or services. Source-selection criteria are an output from the Plan Procurement Management process.

# Seller Proposals

*Seller proposals* are documents received from interested sellers in response to a particular procurement documents package that you have put out to the market. They are in the form prescribed in the procurement documents and contain enough information for the buyer to evaluate the response and decide whether the seller is to go on to the next stage in the procurement process.

---

▨ **Exam Tip**   Did you notice that seller proposals are not an output from any other process? Instead, they are an independent input into this process.

---

# Project Documents

The specific types of project documents that are useful as inputs into the Conduct Procurements process include risk-related contract decisions captured by the risk register, which is an output from the Plan Risk Responses process.

# Make-or-Buy Decisions

The documented make-or-buy decisions are used as an input into the Conduct Procurements process to enable verification of the decisions made about which goods or services to procure externally. Make-or-buy decisions are an output from the Plan Procurement Management process.

# Procurement Statement of Work

The procurement statement of work is required as an input into the Conduct Procurements process because it forms the basis of any procurement documents to go out to the market for sellers to review and respond to. The procurement statement of work should be as detailed as possible, because sellers' responses will only be as detailed as the procurement statement of work. The procurement statement of work is an output from the Plan Procurement Management process.

---

## REAL WORLD

A poorly worded procurement statement of work will lead to assumptions about what work is included and what is excluded from the contract, and these assumptions can lead to requests to change the contract or to contractual disputes. It is a good idea to make the procurement statement of work as detailed as possible to avoid these potential problems.

---

## Organizational Process Assets

The specific types of organizational process assets that assist in the Conduct Procurements process include any historical information about market conditions, databases of prospective or prequalified sellers, and any other information about previous experience with sellers.

---

## REAL WORLD

Many organizations keep lists or databases of prequalified sellers that have already gone through a selection process and met defined requirements to be able to provide goods or services to the organization. Usually the organization will simply issue procurement requests to these prequalified sellers and only go to the wider market when none of the prequalified sellers is able to provide the required good or service.

---

# Tools and Techniques

The following tools and techniques are used on the inputs to deliver the Conduct Procurements process outputs.

## Bidder Conference

A *bidder conference* is any type of formal meeting between the buyer and all prospective sellers for the purpose of exchanging further information and answering questions. Bidder conferences are generally fairly formal with rules to ensure fairness to all sellers participating in the process. They are also increasingly held virtually, with Internet forums being used to solicit questions and provide answers.

It is extremely important that you keep all bidder conferences fair and equitable to all sellers involved in the process. This means if a seller asks you a question, you must provide the answer to all bidders. As a general rule, you should refuse to go into private talks with any seller during this process unless it is for commercially confidential information. This is not merely a good suggestion but also often a legal, commercial, or organizational requirement in many countries, and failure to follow it could result in your decision being challenged in court.

## Proposal Evaluation Techniques

*Proposal evaluation techniques* include a range of methods for evaluating and scoring the different responses received from individual sellers. They can use the source-selection criteria to provide a weighted-attribute selection model. They can also take into account any other important elements useful in differentiating and distinguishing between seller responses.

## Independent Estimates

*Independent estimates* are used as a technique to ensure that the seller responses in relation to cost are reasonable. You will want to carry out your own independent estimates to ensure that sellers are not bidding either far too high or too low, both of which indicate potential problems. Sellers bidding high can indicate either collusion between sellers or more commonly, incorrect information contained in the procurement statement of work, or information that is being misinterpreted.

A range of prices lower than your independent estimates could indicate once again that the procurement statement of work and procurement documents provided are inaccurate, or that an organization is deliberately bidding low in order to win the work. The risk in this case is that the organization may go out of business trying to complete the work or that it is relying on variations to the contract to make the job profitable.

## Expert Judgment

Expert judgment is an excellent tool to use in evaluating seller proposals. The range of experts you will use during this process include people with experience in the procurement response process, contract negotiation and administration process, legal process, finance process, and any other relevant areas of expertise.

## Advertising

*Advertising* is a tool you may choose to use in order to take your procurement proposals to a wider market. You may choose to advertise in specific industry publications or more broadly in public newspapers. The type of advertising you choose will reflect the audience you are trying to reach.

## Analytical Techniques

Analytical techniques involve a detailed analysis of the seller responses to examine them for completeness and accuracy to ensure that the seller is able to carry out the work. You may choose to bring in independent experts to carry out audits of the seller responses and even of the sellers' organizations, particularly in relation to financial capability and stability.

## Procurement Negotiations

*Procurement negotiations* can be simple and straightforward, or they can be highly complex affairs requiring teams of experts and a long period of time to work out. The end result is a contract that both parties are happy to commit themselves to.

---

**REAL WORLD**

---

Like project management, the world of contract negotiation requires a distinct set of skills and experience. I have found that if you are entering into complex negotiations, you should enlist the help of experts with both technical expertise and negotiation expertise.

---

# Outputs

The Conduct Procurements process has the following outputs.

## Selected Sellers

After carrying out the Conduct Procurements process and advertising for sellers, carrying out bidder conferences, evaluating seller responses, and negotiating contracts, you will choose the *selected sellers* to provide the goods or services required for the project.

## Agreements

A procurement *agreement* is generally reflected in a contract between the organizations involved in buying or selling the goods or services for the project. It is important to keep in mind that a contract is a legally binding document with conditions that must be understood by both parties. Most agreements or contracts feature the following content in their terms and conditions:

- Description of the parties to the contract

- The outline of the work to be done as part of the contract

- The timeframe for delivery

- How and where the work is to be performed

- The agreed price

- A description of incentives used

- The terms of payment

- Penalties for nonperformance

- Termination clauses

- Dispute resolution procedures

- Ownership of intellectual property

- Audit, inspection, and acceptance criteria

- How variations will be handled

## REAL WORLD

I've found that many project managers do not take the time to read a contract in its entirety. I strongly recommend that if you have any contracts for work on a project, either as a buyer or seller, you take the time to read the entire contract and understand the terms and conditions it contains. If you do not understand certain parts of the contract, you should seek clarification from experts who do.

There are several forms of contract you can use. The differences between the forms reflect the risk apportioned to the buyer or the seller. Table 10-3 lists the types of contracts and indicates where risk is apportioned.

*Table 10-3.* *Types of Contracts*

| Type of Contract | Description | Risk Apportionment |
|---|---|---|
| Fixed-price contract (also known as lump sum contract) | A form of contract that includes an agreed, fixed price for the delivery of goods and services. There are several variations, as follows:<br>1. Firm fixed-price contract (FFP) with no provision at all for cost overruns<br>2. Fixed-price incentive fee contract (FPIF), which offers an incentive fee for meeting cost or time targets<br>3. Fixed-price with economic price adjustment contract (FP-EPA), which is often used on longer contracts and allows prices to be amended to reflect changes in inflation rates or exchange rates | Seller has the risk. If the cost to deliver the goods or services is greater than the fixed price, the seller bears the extra costs. |
| Cost-reimbursable contract | A form of contract that requires the seller to pass on the actual cost of the work to be done. There are several variations, including the following:<br>• Cost plus fixed-fee contract (CPFF), which reimburses the seller for actual costs incurred and provides an additional fixed fee<br>• Cost plus incentive fee contract (CPIF), which reimburses the seller for actual costs incurred and offers an incentive fee for meeting or exceeding agreed cost or time targets | Risk is split between buyer and seller, depending on the actual form and wording of the contract. |
| Time and material contract (T&M) | A form of contract where the seller charges for all time spent and materials used with no agreed maximum. This form of contract is typically used on projects that are either small and of low complexity or emergency works, or where there is a poorly defined scope of work. | Buyer has the risk because there is no agreed maximum price. |

A method for determining where risk lies between buyer and seller cost is to use the calculation for point of total assumption (PTA), particularly when using fixed-price incentive fee (FPIF) forms of contract. The *point of total assumption* is the point in the contract where the seller assumes total responsibility for all cost increases. In order to calculate this, you need a contract that has an agreed maximum ceiling price, target cost to the seller, target price to the buyer, and agreed ratio between buyer and seller of the percentages of costs over the target cost each party is responsible for.

For example, consider a fixed-price incentive fee contract with a seller that sets a maximum price the buyer will pay (ceiling price) for the contract of $50,000, a target cost to the seller of $42,000, and a target price to the buyer of $46,000. There is also an agreement that the buyer will pay 60% of the cost overrun above the target cost. Using these figures, you can use the following formula to calculate the point of total assumption:

$$Point\ of\ total\ assumption\ =\ Target\ cost + \left( \frac{(Ceiling\ price - Target\ price)}{Buyer's\ \%\ share\ of\ cost} \right)$$

For this example:

Point of total assumption = $42,000 + (($50,000 – $46,000)/0.6)
$$= \$42{,}000 + (\$4\,000/0.6)$$
$$= \$42{,}000 + \$6{,}666.67$$
$$= \$48{,}666.67$$

The point at which the seller assumes total responsibility for all cost increases is $48,666.67. After this price is reached, the buyer has no further obligation.

## Resource Calendars

A resource calendar is a useful output from the Conduct Procurements process because it documents the resources committed to delivering the goods and services as part of the contract and the dates on which those resources are or are not available. The resource calendar goes on to be used as an input into the Estimate Activity Resources, Estimate Activity Duration, Develop Schedule, Determine Budget, and Develop Project Team processes.

## Change Requests

As a result of carrying out the Conduct Procurements process, you may discover that changes need to be made to the project management plan, subsidiary plans, or baselines to reflect work that has been negotiated and agreed to. Any change requests will be used as inputs into the Perform Integrated Change-control process.

## Project Management Plan Updates

The specific parts of the project management plan that may be updated as a result of carrying out the Conduct Procurements process are the cost baseline, scope baseline, and schedule baseline, to reflect any amendments made as a result of contractual negotiations.

# Project Document Updates

The specific project documents that will be updated include requirements documentation, the risk register, and any historical information.

### Quick Check

1. What is the main focus of the Conduct Procurements process?

2. Why is it important to keep bidder conferences fair to all prospective sellers?

3. Why is it important to carry out your own independent estimates?

4. Who should be involved in procurement negotiations?

5. What form of contract most favors a buyer in terms of risk?

6. Under what conditions would you generally choose to use a time and materials contract?

### Quick Check Answers

1. The Conduct Procurements process is focused on carrying out the process documented in the procurement management plan. This involves going to prospective sellers with information about the required goods and services, carrying out a fair and transparent process for selecting the sellers to do the work, and negotiating contracts.

2. In order to solicit professional and fair responses to your procurement process, it is important to treat all potential sellers or bidders equitably and provide them all with the same information.

3. There are several benefits to carrying out your own independent estimates. The first is to ensure that the estimates you are being provided with by potential sellers are neither too high nor too low, perhaps indicating incorrect or insufficient information contained in the procurement statement of work. Another benefit of carrying out your own independent estimates is to independently check the accuracy of responses received from sellers.

4. The project manager should take responsibility for carrying out procurement negotiations, with the assistance of people with technical, legal, financial, and negotiation skills.

5. The form of contract that most favors a buyer in terms of risk is a fixed-price contract, because in this instance the risk is with the seller, particularly if they have developed estimates based on inaccurate or incomplete information.

6. You would generally choose to use a time and materials form of contract when the work is small and ill defined, or under emergency conditions where the work must be completed quickly and there is not time to negotiate any other form of contract.

# Control Procurements

▓ **More Info**   Control Procurements

You can read more about the Control Procurements process in the PMBOK Guide, 5th edition, in Chapter 12, section 12.3. Table 10-4 identifies the process inputs, tools and techniques, and outputs.

*Table 10-4.*  *Control Procurements Process*

| Inputs ⇨ | Tools and Techniques ⇨ | Outputs |
|---|---|---|
| • Project management plan<br>• Procurement documents<br>• Agreements<br>• Approved change requests<br>• Work performance reports<br>• Work performance data | • Contract change-control system<br>• Procurement performance reviews<br>• Inspections and audits<br>• Performance reporting<br>• Payment systems<br>• Claims administration<br>• Records management system | • Work performance information<br>• Change requests<br>• Project management plan updates<br>• Project document updates<br>• Organizational process asset updates |

The Control Procurements process is a monitoring and controlling process focused on the sometimes complex process of checking that your procurement process and contracts entered into comply with both your procurement management plan and the terms and conditions contained within the negotiated contracts and agreements.

▓ **Exam Tip**   It is the responsibility of all parties to a contract to carry out work to ensure that the terms and conditions of the contract are being fulfilled.

The Control Procurements process covers the following monitoring and controlling domain task:

- Task 7: Monitor procurement activities according to the procurement plan, in order to verify compliance with project objectives.

# Inputs

The following inputs are used in the Control Procurements process.

## Project Management Plan

The project management plan is a key input into the Control Procurements process, especially the procurement management plan, which is a subsidiary plan. Specific elements of the project management plan that are useful include the scope management plan, the schedule management plan, and the cost management plan. The project management plan is an output from the Develop Project Management Plan process.

## Procurement Documents

The specific procurement documents that are useful as inputs into the Control Procurements process include any documents from the Conduct Procurements process that result in legal agreements being signed. You need these documents in addition to the individual agreements to understand the full breadth of agreements you are monitoring. Procurement documents are an output from the Plan Procurement Management process.

## Agreements

You require any and all binding agreements between parties to all contracts in order to understand the terms and conditions and performance criteria you are monitoring. Agreements are an output from the Conduct Procurements process.

## Approved Change Requests

Approved change requests can affect and modify any agreed terms and conditions of agreements or contracts. They are often referred to as *variations*, and it is important that as part of the Control Procurements process you check not only that the changes have been approved or agreed to, but also that they are being carried out as per the agreed change. Approved change requests are an output from the Perform Integrated Change-control process.

## Work Performance Reports

Work performance reports are the result when work performance information interprets work performance data. Work performance reports are useful in determining whether the terms and conditions of individual agreements are being met by parties to the agreement. Work performance reports are an output from the Control Project Work process.

## Work Performance Data

Work performance data that specifically relates to whether quality standards are being met is important in any assessment of whether contractual obligations are being met. Work performance data is an output from the Direct and Manage Project Work process.

# Tools and Techniques

The following tools and techniques of this process can be used on the separate inputs to deliver the Control Procurements process outputs.

## Contract Change-Control System

A *contract change-control system*, which includes the processes, guidelines, and tracking systems for reporting all requested changes, all variations, and the decisions made about them, is essential when monitoring the performance or lack of performance of any procurement agreements.

---

▓ **Exam Tip**   Any and all changes to a contract need to be recorded in formally and in writing to reflect the formal nature of a contract.

---

## Procurement Performance Reviews

As part of the normal course of administering a negotiated contract, it is common for the buyer to carry out *procurement performance reviews*. This involves comparing the seller's performance against the agreed and documented criteria in the contract. The purpose of the procurement performance reviews is to determine whether there is any variance between what was agreed to and what is actually occurring.

---

▓ **Exam Tip**   A procurement performance review is essentially the quality assurance process for any negotiated contracts. It focuses on the agreed processes contained within the negotiated contract and not the actual deliverable.

---

# Inspections and Audits

Other key tools and techniques that can be used in the Control Procurements process are inspections and *audits*. Inspections are used to check deliverables, whereas audits are used to check that any agreed processes are being followed. As with other areas that use audits as a tool, it is often a good idea for them to be completed by independent personnel.

# Performance Reporting

*Performance reporting* takes information gathered as part of procurement performance reviews, inspections, and audits and presents it to management so that the seller's performance against agreed contractual objectives can be easily communicated. There are a number of methods and formats for reporting performance, including text, graphics, color coding, and pictures.

# Payment Systems

*Payment systems* are used to record invoices received and payments made to the seller, and to ensure that they are in accordance with the agreed payment terms in the contract.

---

▓ **Exam Tip**   All payments made as part of a negotiated and agreed contract should be strictly in accordance with the contract. Don't be tempted to make payments outside of the agreed terms.

---

# Claims Administration

*Claims administration* is used when there is a dispute about the amount charged or the work done as part of a contract. It is generally a result of poorly worded contracts or a poorly defined scope of work. Claims can be made by either the buyer or the seller in a contract and are usually made for something to be done outside of the agreed procurement statement of work. If agreement is reached, then the claim ceases and a change is made to the contract. Resolving claims often requires the use of dispute-resolution techniques.

---

▓ **Exam Tip**   The word *claim* refers to a disputed cost or change. If you use this word in everyday language to mean something else, you must remember that for the exam, this is the correct definition.

---

```
┌─────────────────────────────────────────────────────────────┐
│                       REAL WORLD                              │
└─────────────────────────────────────────────────────────────┘
```

The process of claims administration is unfortunately a very common and often complex reality of dealing with contracts, generally arising as a result of poorly negotiated or ambiguously worded contracts. Avoiding this potential minefield is a simple process of taking extra time when writing up the original contract and being as explicit as possible about as many potential scenarios as possible to avoid extra time spent disagreeing about what the costs were and whether work performed constituted an agreed change to the contract.

## Records Management System

A comprehensive *records management system* is essential for dealing with and recording all contract-related agreements and variations. The records management system is a subset of the project management information system.

```
┌─────────────────────────────────────────────────────────────┐
│                       REAL WORLD                              │
└─────────────────────────────────────────────────────────────┘
```

Given that contracts are formal, written legal documents, you should ensure that your records management system reflects the importance of this and captures information in such a way that it can be retrieved, that it is accurate, and that it will be useful if any disputes escalate to litigation.

# Outputs

The Control Procurements process has the following outputs.

## Work Performance Information

As with other monitoring and control processes, the Control Procurements process has work performance information as a major output. The work performance information compiles information gathered as a result of using the Control Procurements tools and techniques and presents it in a way that the intended audience can easily obtain relevant information about the project performance, specifically in relation to contractual administration and compliance. Work performance information can also be used by one contractual party to inform the other party of any areas of noncompliance. Work performance information is used as an input into the Control Project Work process.

# Change Requests

Change requests are a common output from any monitoring and control process. For the Control Procurements process, change requests relate to both internal project processes and also to change requests for the negotiated contracts.

---

## REAL WORLD

It is very important that you document any and all changes, no matter how small, to any contract.

---

# Project Management Plan Updates

As a result of carrying out the Control Procurements process, you may update specific elements of the project management plan, which obviously include the procurement management plan and other plans and baselines such as the scope baseline, cost baseline, and schedule baseline.

# Project Document Updates

The specific types of project documents that may be updated as a result of carrying out the Control Procurements process are generally focused on procurement documentation, such as the initial description of work, processes relating to the selection of sellers, and any documents relating to how contracts are monitored.

# Organizational Process Assets Updates

The specific organizational process assets that will be updated as a result of the Control Procurements process are any historical information databases, correspondence files, records of payments made, and internal documentation regarding seller performance.

### Quick Check

1. What is the main focus of the Control Procurements process?

2. What is the benefit of having a payment system in place?

3. Why is it important to keep well-documented records of any claims made?

**Quick Check Answers**

1.  The Control Procurements process is focused on checking that the procurements process is being carried out as per the procurement management plan, and also that the terms and conditions of any contracts being used are being met by both parties.

2.  Having a payment system in place ensures that all payments required as part of the agreed contractual terms and conditions are paid on time and records are kept.

3.  If a claim has been made, that means there is a disagreement about performance on a contract. Disagreements can escalate and require dispute resolution. Having well-documented records will assist during any dispute-resolution process.

# Close Procurements

▓ **More Info**   Close Procurements

You can read more about the Close Procurements process in the PMBOK Guide, 5th edition, in Chapter 11, section 12.4. Table 10-5 identifies the process inputs, tools and techniques, and outputs.

*Table 10-5.* *Close Procurements Process*

| Inputs ⇨ | Tools and Techniques ⇨ | Outputs |
|---|---|---|
| • Project management plan<br>• Procurement documents | • Procurement audits<br>• Procurement negotiations<br>• Records management system | • Closed procurements<br>• Organizational process asset updates |

The Close Procurements process is a closing process focused on ensuring that all contracts used in the project are either closed according to the documented terms and conditions, or closed as a result of nonperformance.

The Close Procurements process covers the following closing domain tasks:

•   Task 1: Obtain final acceptance of the project deliverables from relevant stakeholders, in order to confirm that project scope and deliverables were achieved.

•   Task 3: Obtain financial, legal, and administrative closure using generally accepted practices and policies, in order to communicate formal project closure and ensure transfer of liability.

# Inputs

The following inputs are used in the Close Procurements process.

## Project Management Plan

The project management plan outlines the particular way in which you will carry out the closure of all contracts. Because contracts typically reflect many different aspects of the project, many subsidiary plans and baselines of the project management plan are required in order to successfully close procurements or contracts. The project management plan is an output from the Develop Project Management Plan process.

## Procurement Documents

Obviously, in order to close any procurements, you require the relevant procurement documents that outline either the agreed terms and conditions for normal contractual closure or the processes for terminating a contract due to nonperformance. You also want procurement documents that relate to how well the contractual terms have been met, how well the deliverables have been delivered, what payments have already been made and whether there are retention payments, and any other relevant material. Procurement documents are an output from the Plan Procurement Management process.

# Tools and Techniques

The following tools and techniques of this process can be used on the separate inputs to deliver the Close Procurements process outputs.

## Procurement Audits

*Procurement audits* are structured reviews of how both the buyer and seller have carried out the procurement process. From the buyer's point of view, the procurement audit checks that the procurement process has been carried out as planned and documented in the procurement management plan, right through to whether the seller met the terms and conditions of a negotiated contract. From the seller's point of view, the procurement audit ill determines whether the procurement process as planned and documented has been followed for everything from responding to initial procurement requests through to product delivery and warranty requirements.

---

▓ **Exam Tip** Both buyer and seller should carry out procurement audits to ensure that there are no disagreements about which parts of the contract have been met and which haven't, and also for the benefit of developing and documenting any lessons learned for future procurement processes.

---

431

# Procurement Negotiations

Despite your best efforts at documenting and describing contractual processes that include a clear final resolution and closure process, it is not uncommon for all parties to a contract to have to enter into some form of *procurement negotiations* to terminate the contract fully. In this instance, procurement negotiations can result in negotiated settlements that place agreed obligations and agreements on both buyer and seller as to final payments, warranty obligations, and other matters to enable the contract to be fully closed. If any disagreements arise as a result of misunderstandings or poorly worded contracts, and negotiated settlements cannot be achieved through direct negotiation by all parties to a contract, some form of escalation and external dispute resolution may have to be used, such as mediation, arbitration, or litigation.

*Negotiation* is when two or more parties attempt to agree on a solution between themselves. *Mediation* is when the disagreeing parties bring in an independent person to help them reach an agreement. *Arbitration* is when the parties agree to allow an independent person to hear both sides of the story and make a binding decision. *Litigation* is when the parties resolve their disputes through the civil courts system.

---

■ **Exam Tip**    Contracts should spell out very clearly what the process is for negotiated settlements or dispute resolution. They should include a section on how mediation and arbitration will be carried out and also when and where litigation can occur.

---

# Records Management System

The records management system is a way to record and store all records relating to procurement on a project. It is a part of the project management information system, and it should reflect the formal and legal nature of the procurement process.

```
REAL WORLD
```

Many countries have statutory requirements for how long contractual documents must be stored. It pays to check the local requirements are and make sure you meet them.

# Outputs

The outputs from the Close Procurements process are the following.

## Closed Procurements

The key outputs from the Close Procurements process are *closed procurements*, which include formal documented proof that the contract terms have been met, settlement has been agreed, and thus the contract is now closed. Given that contracts are formal, legal, written documents, you should have formal, legal, written proof that a contract has been closed. Contractual closure does not mean project closure. Contracts can be closed at any time in a project. You will want to be sure that before you close a project, all contracts are closed.

---

▓ **Exam Tip** All contracts on a project must be closed. They can be closed as part of normal and agreed processes, or they can be closed as a result of unusual circumstances. This also applies to the situation in which your project is suddenly terminated; you must still ensure that documentation records that contracts were closed under abnormal circumstances. You may get a question on the exam that presents a scenario in which you have been told to close a project immediately and but perhaps do not have the authority, money, or time to close contracts formally. This may certainly be the case in relation to formal contract closure, but you should still record that contracts have been closed as a result of abnormal circumstances.

---

## Organizational Process Assets Updates

As a result of carrying out the Close Procurements process, you may want to update particular organizational process assets, including any templates, processes, or guidelines relating to how procurement is carried out and how deliverables are accepted; historical databases; and lessons-learned documentation to use in future procurements.

### Quick Check

1. What is the main focus of the Close Procurements process?

2. Why is it sometimes necessary to use negotiated settlements to close contracts?

3. What is the purpose of the records management system?

**Quick Check Answers**

1.  The main purpose of the Close Procurements process is to ensure that all contracts being used on the project are formally closed and recorded as being so.

2.  Not all contracts end without some form of difference of opinion about what constitutes full and final closure or termination. In these instances, a contract is often terminated or closed as a result of negotiated settlement between both parties.

3.  The primary purpose of the records management system is to store any documents relating to the procurement process for future use.

# Chapter Summary

- The Procurement Management knowledge area is focused on the development of a plan to guide decisions around external procurement of goods and services and the execution, monitoring, and control of this plan.

- The Plan Procurement Management process provides a procurement management plan and the procurement statement of work, both of which provide guidance for the subsequent processes for the work to be done as part of agreements.

- The Conduct Procurements process is an executing process that seeks to carry out the procurement management plan in relation to the identification of sellers, the distribution of information about the procurement statement of work to sellers, the selection of sellers to carry out the work, and the type of contract that will be used.

- The Control Procurements process is a monitoring and control process that seeks to check both that the procurement process is being carried out as per the procurement management plan and that the contracts are being carried out as per the agreed terms and conditions.

- The Close Procurements process, which is a closing process, seeks to ensure that all contracts entered into as part of a project are formally closed, either as part of normal procedure or as a result of nonperformance or disagreement.

# Exercises

The answers for these exercises are located in the "Answers" section at the end of this chapter.

1. Unscramble the table below to match up the contract type with its description and the description of risk apportionment.

| Type of Contract | Description | Risk Apportionment |
|---|---|---|
| Fixed-price contract | A form of contract that requires the seller to pass on the actual cost of the work to be done | Seller has the risk, and if the cost to deliver the goods or services is greater than the fixed price, the seller bears the extra costs. |
| Cost-reimbursable contract | A form of contract where the seller charges for all time spent and materials used with no agreed maximum | Buyer has the risk, because there is no agreed maximum price. |
| Time and material contract (T&M) | A form of contract that includes an agreed, fixed price for the delivery of goods and services | Risk is split between buyer and seller, depending on the actual form and wording of the contract. |

2. You are the project manager working on a construction project using a fixed-price incentive fee (FPIF) form of contract with a selected seller. The agreed contract sets a total ceiling price of $325,000, a target cost to the seller of $280,000, and a target price to you as buyer of $310,000. There is also an agreement that you will pay 70% of the cost overruns above the target cost. What is the point of total assumption?

# Review Questions

Test your knowledge of the information in Chapter 10 by answering these questions. The answers to these questions and the explanation of why each answer choice is correct or incorrect are located in the "Answers" section at the end of this chapter.

1. Which of the following processes produces the procurement management plan?

   A. Close Procurements

   B. Plan Procurement Management

   C. Conduct Procurements

   D. Develop Procurement Management Plan

2. The organization seeking to procure external resources to provide goods or services on a project is known as what?

   A. Procurement specialist

   B. Seller

   C. Lawyer

   D. Buyer

3. You are the seller of a potential good or service and are responding to an RFP document where there is a poorly defined scope of work. What type of contract would you prefer to enter into?

   A. Fixed-price

   B. Fixed-price incentive fee

   C. Cost-reimbursable

   D. Time and materials

4. The document that describes and defines the portion of the project scope to be included in the related contract is known as what?

   A. Procurement management plan

   B. Organizational process assets

   C. Scope statement

   D. Procurement statement of work

5. A technique that considers a variety of factors in order to determine whether the particular project work is best done by the project team or by external sources is known as what?

   A. Expert judgment

   B. Market research

   C. Proposal evaluation techniques

   D. Make-or-buy analysis

6. All of the following could be included as part of your source-selection criteria except what?

   A. Intellectual property rights

   B. Technical capability

   C. Financial capacity

   D. Organizational process assets

7. You have decided to engage the services of a quantity surveyor to review the prices received from sellers responding to your procurement requests. What tool or technique are you using?

    A. Delphi technique

    B. Independent estimates

    C. Analytical techniques

    D. Bidder conferences

8. You and your team are in the process of negotiating a contract for a particular service required on your project. Which process are you in?

    A. Plan Procurement Management

    B. Conduct Procurements

    C. Control Procurements

    D. Close Procurements

9. The seller you have engaged to carry out a contract for the provision of services on your project has started submitting multiple change requests, which are escalating into claims. What is the most likely cause of this?

    A. Incomplete risk register

    B. Poorly worded procurement statement of work

    C. Incomplete project management plan

    D. Lack of quality management

10. Who is responsible for carrying out audits on contracts?

    A. Only the buyer

    B. Only the seller

    C. An independent legal professional

    D. Both buyer and seller

11. Which tool or technique would be most useful for storing information about procurement documentation and records?

    A. Records management system

    B. Project management information system

    C. Contract change-control system

    D. Procurement performance reviews

12. All of the following conditions can lead to early termination of a contract except what?

    A. Mutual agreement by both parties

    B. Default of one party

    C. Convenience of the buyer if provided for in the contract

    D. An incomplete procurement statement of work

13. Which of the following is not a form of alternative dispute resolution?

    A. Mediation

    B. Arbitration

    C. Litigation

    D. Audit

# Answers

This section contains the answers for the Exercises and Review Questions in this chapter.

## Exercises

1. Unscramble the table below to match up the contract type with its description and the description of risk apportionment.

| Type of Contract | Description | Risk Apportionment |
|---|---|---|
| Fixed-price contract | A form of contract that includes an agreed, fixed price for the delivery of goods and services | Seller has the risk, and if the cost to deliver the goods or services is greater than the fixed price, the seller bears the extra costs. |
| Cost-reimbursable contract | A form of contract that requires the seller to pass on the actual cost of the work to be done | Risk is split between buyer and seller, depending on the actual form and wording of the contract. |
| Time and material contract (T&M) | A form of contract where the seller charges for all time spent and materials used with no agreed maximum | Buyer has the risk, because there is no agreed maximum price. |

2.  You are the project manager working on a construction project using a fixed-price incentive fee (FPIF) form of contract with a selected seller. The agreed contract sets a total ceiling price of $325,000, a target cost to the seller of $280,000, and a target price to you as buyer of $310,000. There is also an agreement that you will pay 70% of the cost overruns above the target cost. What is the point of total assumption?

$$Point\ of\ total\ assumption\ =\ Target\ cost\ +$$
$$((Ceiling\ price - Target\ price)/$$
$$Buyer's\ \%\ share\ of\ cost\ overrun)$$

Therefore, the point of total assumption is

$$= \$280{,}000 + ((\$325{,}000 - \$310{,}000)/0.7)$$
$$= \$280{,}000 + (\$15{,}000/0.7)$$
$$= \$280{,}000 + \$21{,}428.57$$
$$= \$301{,}428.57$$

# Chapter Review

1.  **Correct Answer: B**

    A.  **Incorrect:** The Close Procurements process is focused on the administrative and legal closure of all contracts.

    B.  **Correct:** The Plan Procurement Management process has the procurement management plan as its primary output.

    C.  **Incorrect:** Conduct Procurements uses the procurement management plan.

    D.  **Incorrect:** Develop Procurement Management Plan is a made-up process name.

2.  **Correct Answer: D**

    A.  **Incorrect:** A procurement specialist may be an expert that you choose to use as part of your decision to procure from external sources.

    B.  **Incorrect:** The seller is the organization or individual who is responding to a request from a buyer for the provision of goods and services.

    C.  **Incorrect:** A lawyer can act for either buyer or seller.

D.  **Correct**: The buyer is the organization that is requiring goods or services to be performed and is asking for external sources to do the work via a negotiated contract.

3.  **Correct Answer: D**

A.  **Incorrect:** A fixed-price contract would represent the greatest risk to the seller in the face of a poorly defined scope of work.

B.  **Incorrect:** A fixed-price incentive fee contracts does little to remove the risk to the seller with a poorly defined scope of work.

C.  **Incorrect**: A cost-reimbursable form of contract may be preferable to a fixed-price form of contract where there is a poorly defined scope of work, but it still represents more risk to the seller that a time and materials contract.

D.  **Correct**: Given that there is a poorly defined scope of work, you would want to enter into the type of contract that represented the least risk to you, the seller, and this is the time and materials contract.

4.  **Correct Answer: D**

A.  **Incorrect:** The procurement management plan provides guidelines for carrying out the entire procurement management process.

B.  **Incorrect:** Organizational process assets include templates, historical information, and other guidelines of use in carrying out the procurement management process, but they do not describe or define the work to be done as part of the contract.

C.  **Incorrect**: The project scope statement defines and describes all the work to be done as part of the project; the procurement statement of work is a subset of the project scope statement specifically related to the work to be done as part of a contract.

D.  **Correct**: The procurement statement of work describes and defines the portion of the project scope to be completed as part of a negotiated contract.

5.   **Correct Answer: D**

   A.   **Incorrect:** Expert judgment is used as a tool and may contribute to the make-or-buy analysis, but it is not the best answer.

   B.   **Incorrect:** Market research is a technique that examines the number of potential sellers and their interest in responding to your procurement documents.

   C.   **Incorrect**: Proposal evaluation techniques are used after sellers have responded to your requests, in order to determine which sellers advance in the procurement process.

   D.   **Correct**: Make-or-buy analysis is the technique that takes into account a variety of factors to determine whether you should complete the work in house or outsource it.

6.   **Correct Answer: D**

   A.   **Incorrect:** Intellectual property rights are an important consideration in your source-selection criteria, to determine who ultimately owns the work performed as part of a contract.

   B.   **Incorrect:** Technical capability will be considered as part of your source-selection criteria, in order to ensure that the selected seller has the technical capability to perform the required work.

   C.   **Incorrect**: Financial capacity will be considered as part of your source-selection criteria, to ensure that the sellers selected are of sufficient financial strength to be able to complete the work.

   D.   **Correct**: Organizational process assets may help you with the procurement management processes, but they would not be included as part of your source-selection criteria.

7. **Correct Answer: B**

   A. **Incorrect:** The Delphi technique is a tool used to solicit information from participants anonymously in order to reach consensus.

   B. **Correct:** Independent estimates are a technique used to determine whether prices received from sellers are accurate.

   C. **Incorrect**: Analytical techniques are a tool used to evaluate a variety of elements and seller responses, not just prices.

   D. **Incorrect**: Bidder conferences are used to provide information to prospective sellers on a fair and equitable basis.

8. **Correct Answer: B**

   A. **Incorrect:** The Plan Procurement Management process is focused on the production of the procurement management plan and the procurement statement of work, which will assist with the Conduct Procurements process, which negotiates contracts.

   B. **Correct:** The Conduct Procurements process uses the project management plan and seeks to negotiate contracts with potential sellers.

   C. **Incorrect**: The Control Procurements process monitors the negotiated contracts but does not actually negotiate them.

   D. **Incorrect**: The Close Procurements process closes contracts after they have been negotiated and the terms and conditions have been fulfilled.

9. **Correct Answer: B**

   A. **Incorrect:** An incomplete risk register may expose your project to unforeseen risks. But that would not contribute to multiple change requests and an escalating number of claims.

   B. **Correct:** The scenario is most likely the result of a poorly worded procurement statement of work, creating ambiguity and disagreement about the work to be performed as part of the contract.

C.   **Incorrect**: An incomplete project management plan may affect several other areas of your project but would not be directly responsible for multiple contractual change requests and claims.

D.   **Incorrect**: A lack of quality management on your project may cause a number of problems but would not be the most likely cause of multiple contractual change requests and claims.

10.   **Correct Answer: D**

A.   **Incorrect:** The seller is also responsible for carrying out audits on contracts to ensure that both they and the buyer are meeting the agreed terms and conditions.

B.   **Incorrect:** The buyer also has responsibility for carrying out audits of the contracts because they initiated the process and have obligations as well.

C.   **Incorrect**: An independent legal professional may be engaged by either buyer or seller, but the ultimate responsibility lies with both buyer and seller.

D.   **Correct**: Both buyer and seller are responsible for carrying out audits on contracts, because they are both parties to the contract and have responsibilities under the negotiated terms and conditions.

11.   **Correct Answer: A**

A.   **Correct:** The records management system is a subset of the project management information system devoted to storing information about procurement documentation and records.

B.   **Incorrect:** The project management information system includes the records management system, which is the better answer this question because it specifically focuses on storing information about procurement documentation and records.

C.   **Incorrect**: The contract change-control system records information about requested contractual changes and the status.

D.   **Incorrect**: Procurement performance reviews gather information about whether each party to a contract is carrying out their obligations and responsibilities. Information gathered from procurement performance reviews is stored in a records management system.

12.  **Correct Answer: D**

 A.  **Incorrect:** Both parties can, by way of mutual agreement, agree to terminate the contract early.

 B.  **Incorrect:** The default of one party to a contract is considered sufficient cause for early termination of a contract.

 C.  **Incorrect:** Some forms of contract have written into them that early termination can occur if it is convenient to the buyer. These contracts normally include some form of compensation to the seller.

 D.  **Correct:** An incomplete procurement statement of work may lead to disagreements, change requests, and claims, but not generally to an early termination of the contract except under extreme circumstances.

13.  **Correct Answer: D**

 A.  **Incorrect:** Mediation is a form of alternative dispute resolution that seeks to have both parties reach an agreement.

 B.  **Incorrect:** Arbitration is a form of alternative dispute resolution that brings in a third party to make a decision that is binding on both parties.

 C.  **Incorrect:** Litigation is a form of alternative dispute resolution that involves some form of court involvement.

 D.  **Correct:** An audit is used to determine whether parties to a contract are carrying the contract out as per the agreed terms and conditions.

# CHAPTER 11

■ ■ ■

# Stakeholder Management

This chapter focuses on the topic of Project Stakeholder Management, which begins
with an initiating process, Identify Stakeholders, to identify the stakeholders. Next, the
process involves developing the stakeholder register that is used in the Plan Stakeholder
Management process; this additional process involves developing the stakeholder
management plan. The Manage Stakeholder Engagement process carries out the
stakeholder management plan, and the Control Stakeholder Engagement process
checks planned activities against what is actually occurring in relation to stakeholder
management.

**The PMBOK® Guide processes**
**Project Stakeholder Management knowledge area**
The four processes in the Project Stakeholder Management knowledge area are as
follows:

- Identify Stakeholders (initiating process)

- Plan Stakeholder Management (planning process)

- Manage Stakeholder Engagement (executing process)

- Control Stakeholder Engagement (monitoring and controlling
  process)

## What Is Project Stakeholder Management?

Project stakeholder management is focused on all the processes involved in identifying as
many stakeholders as possible on a project, understanding their expectations and levels
of engagement, planning how to proactively engage and influence them, checking that
what you are doing is in accordance with the stakeholder management plan, and acting
on any deviations or variances.

A *stakeholder* is any person, group, or organization who can affect or be affected
by your project. Stakeholders can have an impact on your project in both positive and
negative ways. All projects have stakeholders interested in the outcomes and impact of
the project. It is your job as project manager to identify all of these stakeholders and their

© Sean Whitaker 2016
S. Whitaker, *Pass the PMP® Exam*, DOI 10.1007/978-1-4842-2074-0_11

expectations, keep them engaged, and ensure that stakeholder satisfaction becomes a key project deliverable. The easiest way to do this is to ensure that stakeholder management is a continuous dialogue rather than a one-off event or a series of sporadic events.

A main objective of the stakeholder management process is to get stakeholders to support your project or at least not to oppose it.

In order to effectively understand and manage stakeholders' engagement and expectations, you must be both proactive and influencing. Being *proactive* means anticipating and planning, and it is the opposite of being reactive. By being proactive, you will minimize surprises that stakeholders can bring to the project.

To carry out effective influencing, you need to first ensure that you understand where stakeholders currently sit in relation to their expectations and engagement and know where you want them to be. *Influencing* means using a variety of skills and techniques to modify, enhance, or reduce particular aspects of stakeholder engagement and expectations. These skills and techniques include effective communication, highly developed interpersonal skills, and the correct display of technical ability. A skilled project manager chooses which combination to use in order to maximize stakeholder influencing.

---

■ **Exam Tip**   The success or failure of your efforts to identify and manage stakeholders will have a high degree of impact on whether your project is a success or failure. On the exam, you should treat any questions that refer to stakeholders as ones that require you to proactively define, manage, and influence their engagement and expectations.

---

| REAL WORLD |
| :---: |

I have often found that the actual or perceived success or failure of a project rests on how satisfied stakeholders are rather than technical measurements of cost or time. This is a sign of just how important it is to keep your stakeholders engaged and to ensure that their expectations are managed.

# Identify Stakeholders

---

■ **More Info**   Identify Stakeholders

You can read more about the Identify Stakeholders process in the PMBOK Guide, 5th edition, in Chapter 13, section 13.1. Table 11-1 identifies the process inputs, tools and techniques, and outputs.

---

*Table 11-1. Identify Stakeholders Process*

| Inputs ⇨ | Tools and Techniques ⇨ | Outputs |
|---|---|---|
| • Project charter<br>• Procurement documents<br>• Enterprise environmental factors<br>• Organizational process assets | • Stakeholder analysis<br>• Expert judgment<br>• Meetings | • Stakeholder register |

The Identify Stakeholders process is an initiating process with the stakeholder register as its sole output. The stakeholder register contains key information about stakeholders that can be used in the other stakeholder management processes.

The Identify Stakeholders process covers the following initiating domain tasks:

- Task 3: Perform stakeholder analysis using appropriate tools and techniques, in order to align expectations and gain support for the project.

- Task 8: Inform stakeholders of the approved project charter, in order to ensure common understanding of the key deliverables, milestones, and their roles and responsibilities.

# Inputs

The Identify Stakeholders process uses some or all of the following inputs as part of the development of the stakeholder register for the project.

## Project Charter

The project charter contains information about internal and external stakeholders identified as part of project initiation, such as the customer, the project sponsor, and any other easily identified stakeholders. The project charter is an output from the Develop Project Charter process.

## Procurement Documents

The procurement documents are used as an input into the Identify Stakeholders process if a contract forms the basis of the project, because the parties to the contract are key stakeholders. Procurement documents are an output from the Plan Procurement Management process.

## Enterprise Environmental Factors

The specific enterprise environmental factors that are useful as inputs into this process are organizational culture and structure, any relevant government or industry standards, and any external cultural aspects of dealing with particular individuals or groups of stakeholders.

## Organizational Process Assets

The specific organizational process assets that may be important inputs into the development of your stakeholder register are any blank stakeholder register templates the organization has and lessons learned that your organization has gathered from previous projects.

# Tools and Techniques

The following tools and techniques are available to be used to develop the inputs in this process in order to produce the stakeholder register.

## Stakeholder Analysis

There are a number of ways to carry out stakeholder analysis; each of them seeks to identify the stakeholders' interests, expectations, power, influence, and level of engagement in the project. *Stakeholder analysis* begins with the use of information-gathering techniques such as brainstorming, interviewing, and other data-gathering techniques to identify stakeholders. The information gathered as part of carrying out stakeholder analysis will enable you to clearly describe the power, interest, influence, impact, and engagement stakeholders have on your project; then you can develop a robust stakeholder management strategy.

After you have gathered data about stakeholders, there are a number of ways to present this data. A very popular way of graphically showing the level of impact or engagement a stakeholder has on your project is with a matrix displaying either power and interest, power and influence, or influence and impact on the x-axis and y- axis, respectively. Figure 11-1 shows an example of a power and interest matrix.

|  |  | Level of interest | |
|---|---|---|---|
|  |  | Low | High |
| **Power** | Low | Monitor | Keep informed |
|  | High | Keep satisfied | Key players, manage closely |

*Figure 11-1.* *A categorization of stakeholder power and interest using a matrix*

---

■ **Exam Tip**   Figure 11-1 is often called a *Gardner grid or matrix*, named after one of the original authors who developed it.

---

Another way to represent levels of stakeholder influence on your project is to use the *salience model*, which maps stakeholders' power, urgency, and legitimacy to place the stakeholders into one of seven possible categories, each of which begins with the letter *D*. Figure 11-2 shows an example of a salience model and the seven possible categories of stakeholder. It shows, for example, that a stakeholder with high levels of power and urgency but a low level of legitimacy is categorized as dangerous, whereas a stakeholder with legitimacy and power but a low level of urgency is categorized as dominant.

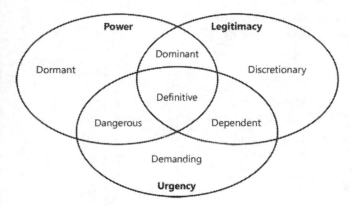

*Figure 11-2. Salience model*

---

▓ **Exam Tip**  The salience model was developed by Ronald Mitchell, Bradley Agle, and Donna Wood. If an exam question refers to any form of diagram by these authors, you will know it is referring to the salience model.

---

# Expert Judgment

Expert judgment is a key tool to be used in the Identify Stakeholders process, because using experts with experience in the identification and assessment of stakeholders will ensure that you have a more complete stakeholder register. Particular experts you may want to consult with include the project sponsor, senior management, the key stakeholders themselves, other people who have worked in similar areas with relevant experience, and any subject matter experts in the area in which you are working.

---

▓ **Exam Tip**  Recall that when soliciting information from experts, you can use a wide variety of information-gathering techniques such as interviews, consultation, meetings, surveys, workshops, and focus groups.

---

## Meetings

Meetings are an important tool for gathering, exchanging, and analyzing information gathered about stakeholders and their power, interest, influence, impact, engagement, and expectations.

# Outputs

After applying the appropriate tools and techniques to the selected inputs, the Identify Stakeholders process has the following sole output.

## Stakeholder Register

The Identify Stakeholders process has the stakeholder register as its sole output. The stakeholder register will probably contain information on the following:

- A classification of stakeholder categories so you can distinguish between different stakeholders and their expectations and engagement

- Information about individual stakeholders and their contact details

- A description of the interest that each stakeholder has in the project

- An assessment of the stakeholders' power, impact, influence, engagement, and interest in the project

- A description of the strategy to be employed to gain their support and keep them satisfied

- A description of the frequency and method by which you will revisit the stakeholder register

---

### REAL WORLD

Take great care with information that you record in your stakeholder register, and always keep in mind that a stakeholder may one day view the register; ensure that the information you include about your assessment of the stakeholders' influence, impact, or engagement on the project will not adversely affect your project if the stakeholder reads the register. For example, on a project I worked on, one extremely difficult senior manager was part of the project control group and constantly failed to read reports, undermined project team members, and had a difficult interpersonal style. He also had the ability to greatly influence the project. As we documented his interest and impact on the project in the stakeholder register, we had to be careful how we described his interaction with the team, because if we had written what we really thought, it would have caused significant problems if he had viewed it.

---

The stakeholder register is used as an input into a number of processes, including the Collect Requirements process, the Plan Quality Management process, the Plan Risk Management process, the Identify Risks process, the Plan Procurement Management process, and the Plan Stakeholder Management process. This shows how important the stakeholder register is to multiple parts of the project.

**Quick Check**

1. What is the main focus of the Identify Stakeholders process?

2. What is the best definition of a stakeholder?

3. What is your primary objective in identifying and managing stakeholders on your project?

4. How is the Identify Stakeholders process linked to other project management processes?

**Quick Check Answers**

1. The main focus of the Identify Stakeholders process is to carry out stakeholder analysis to develop your stakeholder register, which identifies stakeholders, their interest in the project, an assessment of the ways in which they can affect your project, and a consideration of the ways in which you can proactively manage and influence their engagement and expectations.

2. A stakeholder is any individual, group, or organization that can affect or be affected by your project.

3. Your primary objective when identifying and managing stakeholders on your project is to ensure that they stay engaged and their expectations are managed in order to ensure that they provide support to your project or, alternatively, do not oppose the project.

4. The output from the Identify Stakeholders process is the stakeholder register, which is used as an input into the Collect Requirements process, the Plan Quality Management process, the Plan Risk Management process, the Identify Risks process, and the Plan Procurement Management process, all of which are outside the stakeholder management area. It is also used as an input into the Plan Stakeholder Management process.

# Plan Stakeholder Management

▓ **More Info**   Plan Stakeholder Management

You can read more about the Plan Stakeholder Management process in the PMBOK Guide, 5th edition, in Chapter 13, section 13.2. Table 11-2 identifies the process inputs, tools and techniques, and outputs.

*Table 11-2.*  *Plan Stakeholder Management Process*

| Inputs ⇨ | Tools and Techniques ⇨ | Outputs |
|---|---|---|
| • Project management plan<br>• Stakeholder register<br>• Enterprise environmental factors<br>• Organizational process assets | • Expert judgment<br>• Meetings<br>• Analytical techniques | • Stakeholder management plan<br>• Project document updates |

The Plan Stakeholder Management process is a planning process that seeks to identify how the project will affect stakeholders, how stakeholders will affect the project, and how the team will proactively manage levels of stakeholder engagement, proactively influence stakeholder expectations, and ensure stakeholder support for the project, its objectives, and its deliverables.

The Plan Stakeholder Management process covers the following planning domain task:

- Task 13: Develop the stakeholder management plan by analyzing needs, interests, and potential impact, in order to effectively manage stakeholders' expectations and engage them in project decisions.

## REAL WORLD

A great deal of skill is required to be successful in proactively influencing stakeholder engagement and expectations. I strongly recommend that, as part of your professional development as a project manager, you focus on your ability to proactively influence stakeholders, because it is one of the key ways to ensure project success. Conversely, if it is done poorly, it is a surefire way to increase the chances of project failure.

# Inputs

The Plan Stakeholder Management process uses some or all of the following inputs.

## Project Management Plan

The project management plan is an input into the Plan Stakeholder Management process because it provides a wealth of information about different aspects of the project that is useful in developing a stakeholder management plan. Specific information that will be useful includes the project life cycle, the methodology selected to execute the project, the project's specific objectives and deliverables, and the forms of communication to be used. All this information can be found in different parts of the project management plan. The project management plan is an output from the Develop Project Management Plan process.

## Stakeholder Register

The stakeholder register is an extremely important input into the development of the stakeholder management plan because it outlines each of the stakeholders; their interest in the project; their power, interest, impact, and influence; and any particular identified ways of influencing both their engagement and expectations. The stakeholder register is an output from the Identify Stakeholders process.

## Enterprise Environmental Factors

The specific types of enterprise environmental factors that will be useful in the development of the stakeholder management plan are your particular organizational culture, structures, and internal and external political climate, because all of these will affect the method, frequency, and success or failure of your stakeholder management efforts.

## Organizational Process Assets

The specific types of organizational process assets that will assist in development of the stakeholder management plan include any lessons learned that your organization has gathered about stakeholder management activities from previous projects, any blank templates for the development of a stakeholder management plan, and any other relevant historical information.

# Tools and Techniques

The following tools and techniques are used on the inputs to deliver the Plan Stakeholder Management process outputs.

# Expert Judgment

Expert judgment is an excellent tool to use in the Plan Stakeholder Management process because it allows you to bring together people with experience and skills in the identification of stakeholders and in the development of specific ways in which to manage both their engagement and expectations. You may choose to draw on the expertise of the project sponsor, senior management, other identified key stakeholders, subject matter experts with experience in the area in which your project is operating, and any other relevant experts.

# Meetings

Meetings are an excellent tool for bringing together experts and members of the project team to carry out the process of developing and reassessing your stakeholder management plan throughout the life of your project.

A particularly effective meeting that can be useful in increasing levels of stakeholder engagement and proactively influencing stakeholder expectations is the kick-off meeting. The kick-off meeting is held after enough planning has been completed to enable the first project execution work to begin. It is used to bring stakeholders together face to face, to discuss the project and show everyone where the project is going.

# Analytical Techniques

You may choose to use a variety of analytical techniques to assess the level of engagement of individual stakeholders. There are several ways of assessing and documenting different stakeholders and the level of engagement they have with the project. Figure 11-3 shows a stakeholder engagement assessment matrix, which is a popular way of showing whether a stakeholder is unaware of the project, resistant to the project, neutral about the project, supportive of the project, or leading and actively engaged in ensuring that the project will be successful. The letter C (Current) shows where the stakeholder currently is, and the letter D (Desired) shows where you would like them to be; getting stakeholders to position D is the focus of your stakeholder management activities.

|  | Unaware | Resistant | Neutral | Supportive | Leading |
|---|---|---|---|---|---|
| Stakeholder A |  | C |  |  | D |
| Stakeholder B |  |  |  | C D |  |
| Stakeholder C |  |  | C | D |  |
| Stakeholder D |  |  |  | C | D |

*Figure 11-3.* *A matrix showing an assessment of stakeholder engagement both now and desired in the future*

# Outputs

The Plan Stakeholder Management process has the following outputs.

## Stakeholder Management Plan

The stakeholder management plan is the key output from the Plan Stakeholder Management process. The stakeholder management plan uses the information gathered from the stakeholder register to provide a plan that identifies stakeholder engagement and expectations and sets out a clear strategy for managing and influencing engagement and expectations to ensure that stakeholders are supportive of the project or at least do not oppose the project. The stakeholder management plan is used as an input into the Manage Stakeholder Engagement process.

---

▦ **Exam Tip**   Any question on the exam about your interaction with stakeholders will require you to take the position of continuously and proactively influencing their engagement and expectations. In order to do this, you will require a stakeholder management plan.

---

## Project Document Updates

The specific project documents that may be updated as a result of carrying out the Plan Stakeholder Management process include the communications plan, stakeholder register, and any other document that refers to or relies on stakeholder engagement.

### Quick Check

1. What is the main purpose of the Plan Stakeholder Management process?

2. What sort of information should a stakeholder management plan contain?

3. What does a stakeholder engagement assessment matrix show?

4. How do the activities contained in the Plan Stakeholder Management process interact with other project management knowledge areas?

### Quick Check Answers

1. The Plan Stakeholder Management process seeks to take the information gathered in the stakeholder register and use this to develop a coherent stakeholder management plan that proactively manages and influences stakeholder engagement and expectations to ensure stakeholder support of the project and its objectives.

2.  The stakeholder management plan should build on the information contained in the stakeholder register and contain information about the current and expected engagement levels of key stakeholders, the communications requirements and methods selected for the stakeholders, and the particular strategies to be employed in managing their engagement and expectations.

3.  The stakeholder engagement assessment matrix shows the level of engagement of individual stakeholders in the project.

4.  The project management plan, which refers to all other areas of the project, is used as an input into the Plan Stakeholder Management process, because any information about stakeholders' expectations, requirements, constraints, and engagement that may be included in the project management plan is essential in developing a robust stakeholder management plan.

# Manage Stakeholder Engagement

▒ **More Info**    Manage Stakeholder Engagement

You can read more about the Manage Stakeholder Engagement process in the PMBOK Guide, 5th edition, in Chapter 13, section 13.3. Table 11-3 identifies the process inputs, tools and techniques, and outputs.

*Table 11-3.* *Manage Stakeholder Engagement Process*

| Inputs ⇨ | Tools and Techniques ⇨ | Outputs |
|---|---|---|
| • Stakeholder management plan<br>• Communications management plan<br>• Change log<br>• Organizational process assets | • Communications methods<br>• Interpersonal skills<br>• Management skills | • Issue log<br>• Change requests<br>• Project management plan updates<br>• Project document updates<br>• Organizational process asset updates |

The Manage Stakeholder Engagement process is an executing process focused on the execution of the stakeholder management plan in order to ensure that stakeholder engagement and expectations are proactively influenced and managed.

---

▓ **Exam Tip**   By now you have seen the term *proactive* several times, particularly in the stakeholder management area. In relation to managing stakeholder engagement, being proactive means continuously engaging stakeholders in an appropriate manner to get their support for the project and ensure that you understand and can meet their individual expectations of the project. Being proactive also means being on constant alert for any concerns that may arise and dealing with them in a manner that stops them from arising or, if they do arise, minimizes the adverse impact.

---

The Manage Stakeholder Engagement process covers the following executing domain tasks:

- Task 6: Manage the flow of information by following the communications plan, in order to keep stakeholders engaged and informed.

- Task 7: Maintain stakeholder relationships by following the stakeholder management plan, in order to receive continued support and manage expectations.

# Inputs

The following inputs are used in the Manage Stakeholder Engagement process.

## Stakeholder Management Plan

The key input into the Manage Stakeholder Engagement processes is the stakeholder management plan, because it contains information about stakeholders, their ability to influence the project, their expectations, their level of engagement, and the documented strategies for proactively influencing all of these. The stakeholder management plan is an output from the Plan Stakeholder Management process.

## Communications Management Plan

The communications management plan is an essential input into the Manage Stakeholder Engagement process because it outlines individual stakeholders and the specific methods, frequency, and content of communication with them. Via the successful use of the information contained in the communications management plan, you can better execute the stakeholder management plan. The communications management plan is an output from the Plan Communications Management process.

## Change Log

The change log is an important input to have available because you want to be able to convey to stakeholders any changes that have occurred. The change log is an output from the Perform Integrated Change Control process.

## Organizational Process Assets

The specific organizational process assets that will be of use in the Manage Stakeholder Engagement process are any identified organizational communication methods, change control procedures, lessons learned, and historical information about similar previous projects and how they managed stakeholder engagement.

# Tools and Techniques

The following tools and techniques of this process can be used on the separate inputs to deliver the Manage Stakeholder Engagement process outputs.

## Communications Methods

The communications management plan outlines the specific methods and content of communication to be used for each stakeholder. As part of the communications model and methods discussed in Chapter 8, several methods of communication can assist you in managing stakeholder engagement. These methods include *interactive communication*, which means all parties to the communication are involved in the exchange of ideas and messages. This is the most common form of communication for influencing stakeholders, and it relies on all parties involved in the communication having strong interpersonal skills.

*Push communication* is a one-way, sender-driven communications method where one party, the sender, sends information to the other party, the receiver, without necessarily checking that it has been received and interpreted correctly. E-mail messages, letters, and press releases are all examples of push communication. As a communication method, it can be a very effective means of distributing information quickly and widely if care is taken to craft the message well.

*Pull communication* occurs when information is posted so that recipients can visit and draw down the information at their leisure. Company or project intranet sites are good examples of pull communication.

---

▓ **Exam Tip**    After reading this section on managing stakeholder engagement, you may want to read the communications management chapter (Chapter 8) again, because the two subjects are very closely linked.

---

# Interpersonal Skills

The process of managing stakeholders is based on building relationships, and the project manager's interpersonal skills are a key tool used in establishing relationships. The types of interpersonal skills you will want to use include leadership skills, decision-making skills, conflict-resolution skills, change management skills, and active listening.

---

▓ **Exam Tip**    Interpersonal skills are also used as a tool in the Develop Project Team and Manage Project Team processes described in Chapter 7.

---

# Management Skills

In addition to the interpersonal skills already mentioned, a range of *management skills* are more focused on directing and controlling stakeholders. These include presentation, negotiation, time management, and public speaking skills.

| REAL WORLD |
|:---:|

An artificial distinction is often made between management and leadership skills, somehow implying that they are separate and used individually. The reality is that as a project manager, you will need to develop both your leadership and management skills to high levels and use them concurrently, depending on the situation you are in and the outcomes you are seeking to achieve.

# Outputs

The outputs from the Manage Stakeholder Engagement process include the following.

# Issue Log

As you carry out the process of proactively managing stakeholder engagement, particular issues with individual stakeholders may arise that need to be documented so that they can be recorded and worked on. The best place to record these issues is the issue log. The issue log is used as an input into the Control Stakeholder Engagement process, the Manage Project Team process, and the Control Communications process.

# Change Requests

In addition to issues that may arise, there may also be change requests, including corrective or preventive actions, which need to be documented and assessed via the approved change-control process. Change requests are an input into the Perform Integrated Change Control process.

# Project Management Plan Updates

The specific parts of the project management plan that may be updated as a result of executing the Manage Stakeholder Engagement process include, obviously, the stakeholder management plan, as well as the communications management plan, the human resource management plan, and any other parts of the project management plan that are affected by stakeholder expectations and engagement.

# Project Document Updates

The specific project documents that may be updated are, obviously, the stakeholder register and any other documents specifically affected by stakeholder engagement issues.

# Organizational Process Asset Updates

As a result of carrying out the Manage Stakeholder Engagement process, you may want to update your organizational process assets: specifically, lessons learned, recording your experience in managing stakeholder engagement, and documents containing stakeholder feedback.

**Quick Check**

1.  What is the main purpose of the Manage Stakeholder Engagement process?

2.  What is the difference between push and pull forms of communication?

3.  Why is the issue log a main output from the Manage Stakeholder Engagement process?

4.  How does the Manage Stakeholder Engagement process interact with other project management knowledge areas?

**Quick Check Answers**

1.  The main purpose of the Manage Stakeholder Engagement process is the execution of the stakeholder management plan, in order to achieve stakeholder support for the project.

2. The difference between push and pull forms of communication is in whether the information is sent to specific recipients. In push communication, information is sent from a sender to a recipient; and in pull communication, recipients have to access the information themselves.

3. The issue log is a main output from the Manage Stakeholder Engagement process because, while executing the stakeholder management plan, you may identify particular issues with individual stakeholders that need to be recorded and documented in order to ensure that they are monitored and resolved.

4. The Manage Stakeholder Engagement process uses the change log from the Perform Integrated Change Control process and the communications management plan from the Plan Communications Management process.

# Control Stakeholder Engagement

▓ **More Info**    Control Stakeholder Engagement

You can read more about the Control Stakeholder Engagement process in the PMBOK Guide, 5th edition, in Chapter 13, section 13.4. Table 11-4 identifies the process inputs, tools and techniques, and outputs.

*Table 11-4. Control Stakeholder Engagement Process*

| Inputs ⇨ | Tools and Techniques ⇨ | Outputs |
|---|---|---|
| • Project management plan<br>• Issue log<br>• Work performance data<br>• Project documents | • Information management systems<br>• Expert judgment<br>• Meetings | • Work performance information<br>• Change requests<br>• Project management plan updates<br>• Project document updates<br>• Organizational process asset updates |

The Control Stakeholder Engagement process is a monitoring and controlling process focused on examining the execution of the stakeholder management plan to ensure that it is being executed correctly and appropriately, and to determine whether it needs changing.

The Control Stakeholder Engagement process covers the following monitoring and controlling domain task:

- Task 1: Measure project performance using appropriate tools and techniques, in order to identify and quantify any variances and corrective actions.

# Inputs

The following inputs are used in the Control Stakeholder Engagement process.

## Project Management Plan

The project management plan contains the stakeholder management plan and other plans and baselines useful for determining whether the stakeholder management plan is being executed correctly. The project management plan is an output from the Develop Project Management Plan process.

## Issue Log

The issue log describes all the issues raised by stakeholders; as such, it can be used to determine whether there are issues and, subsequently, whether expectations are being appropriately managed and dealt with. The issue log is an output from the Manage Stakeholder Engagement process.

## Work Performance Data

Work performance data is required to enable you to assess whether the work you have been doing according to the stakeholder management plan is being carried out as planned. Work performance data is an output from the Direct and Manage Project Work process.

## Project Documents

Several types of project documents are useful in determining whether you are controlling stakeholder engagement as per the stakeholder management plan. Examples of relevant project documents include the stakeholder register, change log, communications register, and project schedule.

# Tools and Techniques

The following tools and techniques of this process can be used on the separate inputs to deliver the Control Stakeholder Engagement process outputs.

## Information Management Systems

A stakeholder-focused information management system is a subset of the project management information system that allows for the documentation, distribution, and storage of information for and about stakeholders. The types of information that the information management system captures will reflect the particular interests of the stakeholders and may include information about any aspect of the project that can be measured and communicated, including information about project scope, cost, time, quality, risk, or any other relevant factor deemed of interest by stakeholders.

---

## REAL WORLD

I have often found that there is a huge disparity between stakeholders when it comes to the types of project information they are interested in. Some stakeholders are interested in the traditional cost and time progress of a project, whereas others have no interest in these and are more interested in quality measures or issues specific to their interests. It is very important that the project manager determine what parts of the project are important to individual stakeholders. You also may need to control the amount of information that goes out to certain stakeholders. We had a particular stakeholder on one project who we knew was distributing project information to the media; because this stakeholder was a senior member of the project control group, he expected to have access to whatever information he desired. We had to ensure that he was only given the information he wanted as a member of the project control group and the same information everyone else received.

---

## Expert Judgment

Expert judgment is a valuable tool that can be used in the Control Stakeholder Engagement process. You, as project manager, are one of these experts, as are members of your team. You may also choose to draw on the experience of senior management or experts with experience in effectively controlling stakeholder engagement. In addition, you may choose to draw on the expertise of key stakeholders themselves.

# Meetings

Meetings between the project manager, project team members, experts, and stakeholders are an excellent way of ensuring that stakeholder engagement levels are kept high. This will occur only if meetings are run appropriately and have the correct people attending for the right reasons. The types of information that may be exchanged at a meeting are status reports relating to project data that is of interest to the stakeholders.

# Outputs

The outputs from the Control Stakeholder Engagement process are the following.

## Work Performance Information

Given that work performance data is an input into this process, you can expect that work performance information is an output. It refines and analyzes the raw work performance data so that it can be presented in an appropriate format and used for decision-making.

## Change Requests

As a result of carrying out the Control Stakeholder Engagement process, you may discover a variance between what you planned to do and what is actually occurring, and that stakeholder engagement levels are not where you had planned for them to be. Thus, you may raise a change request, which could include changes to the stakeholder management plan or a recommendation for corrective or preventive actions.

## Project Management Plan Updates

As a result of carrying out stakeholder management activities, changes can be made to any other plan that forms part of the project management plan. This reflects the wide range of influences stakeholders have over the project.

## Project Document Updates

The specific project documents that may be updated as a result of carrying out the Control Stakeholder Engagement process include the stakeholder register and issue logs.

## Organizational Process Asset Updates

As a result of carrying out the Control Stakeholder Engagement process, you may learn information that requires you to update organizational process assets to ensure that they better reflect what you have discovered. Specific types of organizational process assets that may be updated include any templates or processes related to stakeholder engagement management, any project records collating feedback from stakeholders, and any lessons-learned documentation.

**Quick Check**

1. What is the main purpose of the Control Stakeholder Engagement process?

2. Why is the issue log an important input into the Control Stakeholder Engagement process?

3. What type of organizational process assets may be updated as a result of carrying out the Control Stakeholder Engagement process?

4. How does the Control Stakeholder Engagement process interact with other project management knowledge areas?

**Quick Check Answers**

1. The main purpose of the Control Stakeholder Engagement process is to monitor overall levels of stakeholder engagement against what is expected and make changes to the stakeholder management plan and the strategies around stakeholder engagement.

2. The issue log describes and documents individual issues raised by stakeholders. Therefore, using it as an input into the Control Stakeholder Engagement process allows you to view the number of issues, the complexity of issues, which stakeholders are raising issues, and whether the issues are being resolved to the satisfaction of stakeholders.

3. The types of organizational process assets that may be updated as a result of the Control Stakeholder Engagement process include any existing processes and templates, project records relating to your stakeholder engagement strategies and results, and, of course, your collection of lessons-learned documentation.

4. The Control Stakeholder Engagement process uses inputs from the Develop Project Management Plan process (the project management plan) and also the Direct and Manage Project Work process (work performance data).

# Chapter Summary

- The Stakeholder Management knowledge area is focused on the identification, management, and proactive influencing of stakeholders' interests, expectations, and engagement to ensure stakeholders' support for the project.

- The Identify Stakeholders process is an initiating process that produces a stakeholder register, which identifies stakeholders in the project.

- The Plan Stakeholder Management process is a planning process that produces a stakeholder management plan, which outlines how stakeholder expectations and engagement will be proactively influenced.

- The Manage Stakeholder Engagement process is an executing process that uses the stakeholder management plan to carry out the activities required to manage and influence stakeholder expectations and engagement.

- The Control Stakeholder Engagement process is a monitoring and control process that reviews the stakeholder management activities against what was planned and updates the stakeholder management plan as required.

# Exercises

The answers for these exercises are located in the "Answers" section at the end of this chapter.

1. Match the stakeholder management process on the left to a process key output on the right.

| Process | Key Output |
|---|---|
| 1. Identify Stakeholders | A. Stakeholder register |
| 2. Plan Stakeholder Management | B. Issue log |
| 3. Manage Stakeholder Engagement | C. Work performance information |
| 4. Control Stakeholder Engagement | D. Stakeholder management plan |

2. Categorize each item in the following list as an interactive, push, or pull method of communication.

A. Phone calls

B. Letters

C. Intranet sites

D. Video conferencing

E. Project reports

F. E-learning site

G. Meetings

H. Press releases

# Review Questions

Test your knowledge of the information in Chapter 11 by answering these questions. The answers to these questions and the explanation of why each answer choice is correct or incorrect are located in the "Answers" section at the end of this chapter.

1. Which of the following processes produces the stakeholder register?

   A. Identify Stakeholders

   B. Plan Stakeholder Management

   C. Manage Stakeholder Engagement

   D. Control Stakeholder Engagement

2. Which of the following is the best definition of a stakeholder?

   A. Your project team members, project sponsor, and client

   B. Any person or group who can affect or be affected by your project

   C. The client, the project sponsor, and external government agencies

   D. Any person or group

3. If you are using a Gardner grid to show the results of stakeholder analysis, what information about stakeholders are you showing?

   A. How much power, urgency, and legitimacy they have

   B. The amount of risk each stakeholder is willing to share

   C. The levels of power and interest of each stakeholder

   D. Their contact details and interest in the project

4. Which of the following documents will contain a description of stakeholder contact details and their requirements for the project?

   A. Stakeholder analysis

   B. Stakeholder register

   C. Gardner grid

   D. Stakeholder management plan

5. At what point in the project should you conduct the kick-off meeting?

    A. As soon as the project is initiated

    B. At the end of the project, to assist with project closure

    C. Only after all the planning work has been completed

    D. After enough planning work has been completed to begin execution

6. If you are assessing each stakeholder as either unaware, resistant, neutral, supportive, or leading, what technique are you using?

    A. Brainstorming

    B. Delphi technique

    C. Analytical technique

    D. Root cause analysis

7. If you are engaged in carrying out your project work and need to find out the planned timeframe and frequency for distribution of required information to stakeholders, where would be the best place to look?

    A. Project management plan

    B. Stakeholder management plan

    C. Stakeholder register

    D. Issue log

8. Which of the following is not an input into the Manage Stakeholder Engagement process?

    A. Stakeholder management plan

    B. Issue log

    C. Communications management plan

    D. Change log

9. You are sending out regular project updates to a list of stakeholders via e-mail. This is an example of what sort of communication method?

    A. Verbal

    B. Interactive

    C. Pull

    D. Push

10. Which of the following is not an example of a management skill a project manager may use while managing stakeholder engagement?

   A. Negotiation skills

   B. Public speaking skills

   C. Presentation skills

   D. Conflict resolution skills

11. What is the name of the document that lists any problems stakeholders may have and records what is being done about them?

   A. Change log

   B. Issue log

   C. Stakeholder register

   D. Stakeholder management plan

12. During which stakeholder management process is work performance data an input and work performance information an output?

   A. Identify Stakeholders

   B. Plan Stakeholder Management

   C. Manage Stakeholder Engagement

   D. Control Stakeholder Engagement

# Answers

This section contains the answers for the Exercises and Review Questions in this chapter.

## Exercises

1. Match the stakeholder management process on the left to a process key output on the right.

| Process | Key Output |
| --- | --- |
| 1. Identify Stakeholders | A. Stakeholder register |
| 2. Plan Stakeholder Management | D. Stakeholder management plan |
| 3. Manage Stakeholder Engagement | B. Issue log |
| 4. Control Stakeholder Engagement | C. Work performance information |

2   Categorize each item in the following list as an interactive, push, or pull method of communication:

| Interactive | Push | Pull |
|---|---|---|
| A. Phone calls | B. Letters | C. Intranet sites |
| D. Video conferencing | E. Project reports | F. E-learning site |
| G. Meetings | H. Press releases | |

# Chapter Review

1.  **Correct Answer: A**

    A.  **Correct:** The Identify Stakeholders process produces the stakeholder register.

    B.  **Incorrect:** The Plan Stakeholder Management process has the stakeholder management plan as its primary output.

    C.  **Incorrect**: Manage Stakeholder Engagement does not produce the stakeholder register.

    D.  **Incorrect**: Control Stakeholder Engagement does not produce the stakeholder register.

2.  **Correct Answer: B**

    A.  **Incorrect:** Your project team members, project sponsor, and client certainly are stakeholders, but they are a subset of all possible stakeholders and in this case not the best definition of stakeholders offered.

    B.  **Correct:** The best definition of a stakeholder is any person or group who can affect or be affected by your project.

    C.  **Incorrect**: The client, the project sponsor, and external government agencies may be stakeholders, but this is not the best definition of stakeholders.

    D.  **Incorrect**: In order to be considered a project stakeholder, any person or group must be affected by your project or be able to affect the project.

3. **Correct Answer: C**

   A. **Incorrect:** A diagram showing power, urgency, and legitimacy of stakeholders would use the salience model.

   B. **Incorrect:** The amount of risk stakeholders are willing to share would be shown in the stakeholder analysis.

   C. **Correct:** A Gardner grid shows the respective levels of power and interest of each stakeholder in order to classify them.

   D. **Incorrect:** Stakeholder contact details and interest in the project would be contained in the stakeholder register.

4. **Correct Answer: B**

   A. **Incorrect:** Stakeholder analysis is a technique used to gather information about stakeholders, but it is not a document.

   B. **Correct:** The stakeholder register contains information about stakeholders, including their contact details and their requirements for the project.

   C. **Incorrect:** A Gardner grid classifies stakeholders by their levels of power and interest.

   D. **Incorrect:** The stakeholder management plan sets out how stakeholder engagement will be managed.

5. **Correct Answer: D**

   A. **Incorrect:** The kick-off meeting does not occur as soon as the project is initiated.

   B. **Incorrect:** The kick-off meeting, as the name suggests, is not used to assist with project closure.

   C. **Incorrect:** You do not need to wait until all planning work has been completed to have a kick-off meeting.

   D. **Correct:** The kick-off meeting is held after enough planning work has been done to begin execution.

6. **Correct Answer: C**

   A. **Incorrect:** Brainstorming is an information-gathering technique.

   B. **Incorrect:** The Delphi technique is used to gather information anonymously from experts without peer pressure affecting the outcome.

   C. **Correct**: Categorizing stakeholders in this manner is a sign of using analytical techniques such as a stakeholder engagement assessment matrix.

   D. **Incorrect**: Root-cause analysis is used during quality management activities.

7. **Correct Answer: B**

   A. **Incorrect:** The project management plan includes the stakeholder management plan but is not the best answer presented.

   B. **Correct:** The stakeholder management plan contains a lot of information about the ways in which stakeholder engagement and expectations will be managed, including the planned timeframe and frequency for distribution of required information to stakeholders.

   C. **Incorrect**: The stakeholder register contains information identifying stakeholders and their requirements and is used as an input into the development of the stakeholder management plan.

   D. **Incorrect**: The issue log documents specific issues raised by stakeholders.

8. **Correct Answer: B**

   A. **Incorrect:** The stakeholder management plan is an essential input into the Manage Stakeholder Engagement process because it sets out how stakeholders' engagement and expectations will be managed.

   B. **Correct:** The issue log is an output from, not an input into, the Manage Stakeholder Engagement process.

   C. **Incorrect**: The communications management plan is an input into the Manage Stakeholders Engagement process because it records the communications methods and strategy to be used.

   D. **Incorrect**: The change log is used as an input into the Manage Stakeholders Engagement process because the impact of changes is communicated to stakeholders.

9. **Correct Answer: D**

   A. **Incorrect:** E-mail is not an example of verbal communication.

   B. **Incorrect:** Because there is no two-way communication occurring, this is not an example of an interactive communication method.

   C. **Incorrect:** The method, e-mail, is pushing information to stakeholders, not pulling it from them.

   D. **Correct:** Sending out information without checking whether the receiver understands it is an example of push communication.

10. **Correct Answer: D**

   A. **Incorrect:** Negotiation skills are an example of a project manager's management skills.

   B. **Incorrect:** Public speaking skills are an example of a project manager's management skills.

   C. **Incorrect:** Presentation skills are an example of a project manager's management skills.

   D. **Correct:** Conflict-resolution skills are an example of leadership, not management skills.

11. **Correct Answer: B**

   A. **Incorrect:** The change log records information about change requests and their status.

   B. **Correct:** The issue log records any issues that stakeholders may have and what is being done about them.

   C. **Incorrect:** The stakeholder register records specific information about each stakeholder but does not list any problems or issues they may have.

   D. **Incorrect:** The stakeholder management plan sets out how stakeholders' expectations and engagement will be proactively influenced and managed.

12. **Correct Answer: D**

A. **Incorrect:** The Identify Stakeholders process does not use either work performance data or work performance information.

B. **Incorrect:** The Plan Stakeholder Management process does not use either work performance data or work performance information.

C. **Incorrect**: The Management Stakeholder Engagement process does not use either work performance data or work performance information.

D. **Correct**: The Control Stakeholder Engagement process does use work performance data as an input and has work performance information as an output, as part of the monitoring and controlling activities.

# CHAPTER 12

■ ■ ■

# Ethics and Professional Conduct

This chapter focuses on the topic of ethics and professional conduct, which describes the way a professional project manager is expected to act in many different situations.

---

■ **Exam Tip** The expected and accepted behaviors described in this chapter may differ from your own experience. It is important to remember that, for the exam, the behaviors described here are considered the correct way to act in any situation.

---

No explicit domain tasks are reflected in this section. Several years ago, there were distinct questions about ethics and professional situations in the PMP® exam. However, these questions have now been incorporated into the main body of questions and may lie hidden in a question that appears to be about estimating, risk, quality, customer relations, or any other topic. Thus it is very important that you read the question carefully to determine whether it is presenting a situation that requires you to specify how you would act ethically and professionally.

Although there are no domain tasks for this topic, there is the Code of Ethics and Professional Conduct from the Project Management Institute (PMI). Both mandatory and aspirational standards are captured in the Code of Ethics and Professional Conduct. The Code of Ethics and Professional Conduct and the behavior of professional project management practitioners reflect the vales of responsibility, respect, fairness, and honesty.

The PMI Code of Ethics and Professional Conduct applies to all members of the Project Management Institute. Additionally, it applies to nonmembers who hold a PMI certification, those who apply to commence a PMI certification process, and nonmembers who serve PMI in a volunteer capacity. Beyond these people, whom it directly applies to, it also serves as a guideline for all professional project management practitioners.

A breach of this code can result in an ethics complaint to the PMI, which has the ability to consider the complaint and take action against anyone found to have breached the code.

© Sean Whitaker 2016
S. Whitaker, *Pass the PMP® Exam*, DOI 10.1007/978-1-4842-2074-0_12

```
┌─────────────────────────────────────────────────────────────────┐
│                         REAL WORLD                                │
└─────────────────────────────────────────────────────────────────┘
```

I have always found that the Code of Ethics and Professional Conduct serves as a very valuable reference to guide my decisions and behaviors in real-world situations where perhaps I might be tempted to act differently. It has also served as a guide to the behaviors I expect of other professional project managers. Keep in mind that sometimes the right course of action isn't the easiest course of action. When considering what is best to do in an ethical situation, one approach is to look at the impact a bad decision would have on your professional and personal reputation and credibility. Always select an answer that will enhance your credibility and reputation.

# Responsibility, Respect, Fairness, and Honesty

The four key foundational values for any project manager are responsibility, respect, fairness, and honesty. Although these may all seem to be fairly straightforward concepts that you think you both understand and apply consistently, you may not fully understand the implications and expected behaviors. Individually, they describe specific behaviors; collectively, they present a unified code by which any professional project manager can guide and assess their actions and the actions of others. Therefore, it is worth taking the time to investigate each one and review the specific actions and behaviors it demands of a professional project manager.

---

▓ **Exam Tip**  Take time when reading each question on the exam to determine whether it is presenting you with a technical situation or an ethical situation. If it is an ethical situation, then answer according to the Code of Ethics and Professional Conduct.

---

# Responsibility

---

▓ **More Info**  Responsibility

You can read more about responsibility in the Project Management Institute Code of Ethics and Professional Conduct.

---

*Responsibility* means being personally and professionally accountable for your own actions, being accountable for acting ethically and professionally at all times, and ensuring that others do the same. *Responsibility* also means you as the project manager are responsible for the actions of those on your team.

The mandatory standard of responsibility requires you to first make sure you know and uphold all the relevant policies, rules, regulations, and laws that govern your work, professional, and volunteer activities. If you disagree with any of these rules, you can seek to change them, but until they are changed you must abide by them.

Furthermore, you must always report unethical or illegal conduct to the appropriate people or body. This means whenever you discover or observe unethical or illegal behavior, you must report it to the appropriate authorities. If you discover someone on your project not dealing fairly or honestly with a stakeholder, you must report this to your project team or sponsor. Although your natural inclination may be to ignore the behavior if you regard it as minor, you must report it no matter how small it is. If the behavior is an ethical breach, you must report it to the PMI in accordance with the process on its web site. Make sure any complaints you file are substantiated by fact and documented appropriately.

You must also encourage people to do the same and neither retaliate yourself nor let others retaliate against any person who brings a breach of rules to the attention of the right person or body, or who files an ethical complaint. This is to encourage and support the role of the *whistleblower*.

## REAL WORLD

There will always be a temptation to avoid responsibility, but I have found that in addition to enhancing your professional reputation and credibility, the simple act of taking responsibility also contributes to your ongoing leadership development. Great leadership enhances the chances of project success, and being a great leader requires you to take responsibility and lead by example.

The aspirational standards of responsibility require you to make decisions and take subsequent actions based on the best interests of society, public safety, and the environment, not in your own best interests. The greater good of society, public safety, and the environment must always take precedence over self-interest. This means if a project you are working on conflicts with or adversely affects society, public safety, or the environment, you should reconsider whether the project is worth doing.

Taking responsibility also means accepting only project work that is consistent with your background, experience, technical and interpersonal skills, and qualifications. Don't be tempted to exaggerate you own ability; only take on work that you know you are competent to do. After the work is taken on, you must make sure you fulfill the commitments and see them through to completion.

If you make mistakes, errors, or omissions, you must take responsibility, take ownership, and make corrections as soon as possible. If you discover errors or omissions made by others, you must communicate them to the appropriate body as soon they are discovered. Knowingly acting in error or with information you know is false is considered a breach of this standard.

Finally, taking responsibility means protecting the intellectual property rights, copyright, and confidential information of any person or body. This means if you are in a situation where you have the opportunity to use intellectual property of a previous client, you should always seek their approval first. Additionally, you should not allow anyone to break any copyright rules, laws, or regulations.

▓ **Exam Tip**   If you discover anyone breaching these standards, you must report them to the relevant authority. So if you find someone breaking a company standard, you must report them within your organization. If you find someone breaking a PMI standard, you must report them to PMI; and if you find someone breaking the law, you must report them to the appropriate legal authorities.

### Quick Check

1. What role do you as project manager have in upholding the value of responsibility?

2. What must you do if you disagree with a particular policy that your organization has?

3. What must you do if you discover that a member of your team has made an error?

### Quick Check Answers

1. The project manager must lead by example and take personal and professional responsibility themselves and demand it from others.

2. If you disagree with a policy that your organization has, you must still follow it. You can seek to change it, but until it is changed, you must follow it.

3. Any errors, either by yourself or by another, must be recognized, reported, and acted on immediately.

# Respect

▓ **More Info**   Respect

You can read more about respect in the Project Management Institute Code of Ethics and Professional Conduct.

The value of *respect* means having appropriate regard for yourself and for others, personally and professionally. It requires you to negotiate agreements and contracts in good faith and not exercise the power of your expertise or position to influence the decisions or actions of others in order to benefit personally at their expense. This doesn't mean you can't influence people, because that is a key skill in stakeholder management and communications activities. It means you can't seek to benefit personally by taking advantage of others using your position of power.

Respect also means not acting in an abusive manner toward any other person. Keep in mind that abuse can take many forms, from outright verbal and physical abuse to the more insidious forms of gossip, slander, libel, and passive-aggressive behavior. Complying with this standard means observing the golden rule of treating others as you would like to be treated.

In addition, respect means you respect the property rights of others, which ties in nicely with the value of responsibility and protecting the intellectual property rights, copyright, and confidential information of any person or body. This means you must acknowledge the ownership and copyright that others hold on their work.

Demonstrating respect also means being aware of the norms and customs of others and avoiding engaging in behaviors they might consider disrespectful. This is increasingly important in an ever-more globalized economy, where projects are often done internationally. Many stakeholders may have different customs from your own, and effective communication and management of stakeholders requires you to understand their customs and treat them with respect. A key element in effective communications with and managing the expectations of stakeholders is the ability to listen to others' points of view and seek to understand them.

When it comes to resolving conflicts or disagreements, respect means dealing directly and in an open manner with those people with whom you have a conflict or disagreement. Seek to deal with the issue and not let personalities get in the way.

Whatever happens around you, and whatever the actions of others, respect also means you always conduct yourself in a professional manner, even when it is not reciprocated.

## REAL WORLD

I have always found that having respect for myself and for others is a significant personal asset. It improves my ability to build genuine relationships with others and understand their point of view. Keep in mind that people will know, either consciously or subconsciously, if you are faking respect, so make sure it is always genuine.

### Quick Check

1.  If you are given the opportunity to negotiate a contract that would place an undue burden on the other party, what should you do?

2.  If you are working in another country and it is a commonly accepted practice to pay bribes to get project work done, what should you do?

### Quick Check Answers

1. In any negotiations, you should seek to get an agreement that both parties can live with. You should not negotiate contracts if you have no intention of honoring them.

2. This is a tricky question. You know that you should always respect the culture and customs of others, but taking precedence over this is the requirement that you should always obey the laws of the country in which you are working. If bribery is illegal, it doesn't matter what the custom is—you simply do not participate in it.

# Fairness

---

▓ **More Info**   Fairness

You can read more about fairness in the Project Management Institute Code of Ethics and Professional Conduct.

---

The value of *fairness* deals with conflict of interest, favoritism, and discrimination.

A *conflict of interest* situation arises when your own personal interest may conflict with the interest of your employer, or you may derive personal benefit from an action undertaken on behalf of another person. Conflict of interest can be both real and perceived. Whether it is real or perceived, it should always be fully and openly disclosed as early as possible so that it can be dealt with in an appropriate manner. You should not participate in any process or project until the disclosure has been made and a decision has been made about the best way to move forward.

Conflict of interest situations can also arise as a result of the business dealings of family members or friends, when they have professional or business connections to your project. In this case, your relationship should always be fully disclosed.

---

## REAL WORLD

Many organizations keep a documented conflict-of-interest register where all employees must disclose and record any real or potential conflicts of interest. Often the level of conflict of interest is so small that it can be managed via simple disclosure; at other times, it may require those affected to be removed from a particular process or project. Always disclose any real or perceived conflict of interest quickly.

The value of fairness also extends to favoritism and discrimination. To display fairness, you must avoid both favoritism and discrimination, which means you neither hire nor fire, neither reward nor punish, and neither award nor deny contracts based on your own personal considerations, bias, or benefit. This means you should treat everyone equally and fairly, regardless of any preconceived notions you may have. It also means you must not discriminate against anyone based on gender, race, age, religion, disability, nationality, or sexual orientation.

In order to show and prove fairness, you must be able to demonstrate transparency and impartiality in your decision-making process and provide equal access to information to those who are authorized to have that information. This is particularly important in legal or contractual matters, because a lack of fairness could be grounds for a legal challenge to your decisions.

### Quick Check

1. What should you do if a family member works for a firm submitting a bid for contract work on your project?

2. What should you do if you are given the opportunity to provide extra information to a contractor to which you really want to award a contract?

### Quick Check Answers

1. If you, a friend, or a family member could benefit, or is perceived to benefit, from a commercial transaction in which you are involved, there is a real or potential conflict of interest. It must first be fully disclosed, and you should not take part in any process until it is resolved.

2. You should treat everyone involved in procurement negotiations fairly and equally. Everyone should receive exactly the same information at the same time.

# Honesty

---

▓ **More Info**   Honesty

You can read more about honesty in the Project Management Institute Code of Ethics and Professional Conduct.

---

*Honesty* seems like a self-evident term. We all know when we are being honest, and if we aren't being honest, then surely we are being dishonest. Or is there some grey area between honesty and dishonesty?

If you want to act in accordance with the value of honesty, there is no grey area; you are being either honest or dishonest. Telling half-truths or omitting key information is dishonest. In order to meet the standards required by this value, you must be 100% honest at all times. This means you, as a professional project manager, will not engage in or condone in others behavior that is designed to deceive anyone. This includes making misleading or false statements, telling half-truths, providing information out of context, or omitting information that, if known, would make your statements misleading or incomplete.

The value of honesty also ties in with the values of responsibility, respect, and fairness, and demands of you that you do not engage, condone, or participate in dishonest behavior with the intention of personal gain or at the expense of another.

---

▓ **Exam Tip**    If you are ever presented with a question that asks you what is best to do in a situation where you suspect dishonesty, the answer is always to disclose this and then investigate and rectify the situation with honesty.

---

Displaying honesty means being prepared to ensure that the information you are basing decisions on or providing to others is accurate, reliable, and timely. Being honest also means being prepared to share bad news even when it may be poorly received.

## REAL WORLD

Being honest will sometimes have repercussions that test your skill as a relationship builder and influencer. You may even lose some credibility in the short term. But over the long term, you will develop a reputation based on honesty, and this will serve you better than a reputation of being someone who isn't always honest.

Displaying the value of honesty also means you only make promises you can keep, and you keep the promises you make. By leading the way and acting honestly at all times, you will create a culture that encourages and expects honesty at all times. Ultimately, your reputation and credibility will be enhanced by sticking to this value at all times.

### Quick Check

1. If giving the truth about the status of your project to your project sponsor and client would result in the project being terminated when you are sure that the problem is short-lived and can be fixed, what should you do?

2. If you are halfway through a complex set of contractual negotiations with a potential vendor and your sponsor tells you that the project is likely to be cancelled, what should you do in relation to the contractual negotiations?

**Quick Check Answers**

1.  In order to be honest, you must openly share all information that you have. Communicating half-truths and omissions about the status of your project to buy time to fix the problems is dishonest.

2.  This question relates not only to the value of honesty, but also to responsibility, fairness, and respect. You have a duty to not continue the negotiations until the future of the project is decided, and to inform the vendor of the reasons.

# Chapter Summary

*   This chapter outlines the expected and accepted behaviors of a professional project manager. It outlines the four key values of responsibility, respect, fairness, and honesty, which define the behavior of a project manager and their behavior toward others.

*   The key value of responsibility requires a project manager to take personal and professional responsibility for their own actions, acting ethically and professionally at all times, and ensuring that others do the same.

*   The key value of respect requires professional project managers to display respect for themselves and others. It requires that they refrain from abusive behaviors and understand different customs and cultures.

*   The key value of fairness seeks to avoid either real or potential conflict-of-interest situations and avoid favoritism and discrimination by treating everyone equally and openly.

*   The key value of honesty requires a project manager to be completely truthful at all times and not engage in half-truths or omission of information.

# Exercise

The answers for this exercise are located in the "Answers" section at the end of this chapter.

1.  Categorize each statement from the PMI Code of Ethics and Professional Conduct in the following list as a value associated with responsibility, respect, fairness, or honesty.

    i.  We report unethical or illegal conduct to appropriate management and, if necessary, to those affected by the conduct.

    ii. We negotiate in good faith.

    iii.  We provide accurate information in a timely manner.

    iv.  We do not act in an abusive manner toward others.

    v.  We proactively and fully disclose any real or potential conflicts of interest to the appropriate stakeholders.

    vi.  We protect proprietary or confidential information that has been entrusted to us.

    vii.  We provide equal access to information to those who are authorized to have that information.

    viii.  We make opportunities equally available to qualified canaidates.

    ix.  We do not exercise the power of our expertise or position to influence the decisions or actions of others in order to benefit personally at their expense.

    x.  We do not engage in or condone behavior that is designed to deceive others.

    xi.  We inform ourselves and uphold the policies, rules, regulations, and laws that govern our work, professional, and volunteer activities.

    xii.  We do not engage in dishonest behavior with the intention of personal gain or at the expense of another.

# Review Questions

Test your knowledge of the information in Chapter 12 by answering these questions. The answers to these questions and the explanation of why each answer choice is correct or incorrect are located in the "Answers" section at the end of this chapter.

    1.  What are the four foundational values on which the PMI Code of Ethics and Professional Conduct is built?

       A.  Trust, honesty, respect, fairness

       B.  Honesty, respect, responsibility, fairness

       C.  Integrity, trust, respect, honesty

       D.  Respect, truthfulness, responsibility, transparency

2. You are the project manager on a project that is behind schedule and over budget. You have gathered your team together to think of ways you can make up time and save money. A team member who has recently joined your organization says that he has access to design drawings from his previous employer that are very similar to your current project, and using them would save both time and cost. What should you do?

   A. Use the drawings and acknowledge where they came from in your project reports.

   B. Refuse to use the drawings.

   C. Use the drawings without acknowledging where they came from.

   D. Refuse to use the drawings during the team meeting, then during a one-on-one conversation with your team member, encourage him to use them.

3. Your spouse is working for a company that is submitting a bid for a contract you are managing on your project. Your spouse's role in the company has nothing to do with the bid process. What should you do?

   A. You don't need to do anything because your spouse can have no impact, nor can they derive any benefit from the process.

   B. Refuse to allow your spouse's organization to participate in the bid process.

   C. Resign from the project.

   D. Disclose the potential conflict of interest to your project sponsor.

4. You are working on a project in a country where bribery is the norm, and the only way to get a permit you need processed is to pay a bribe to a local official. Your project cannot continue without this permit, and the amount of the bribe is relatively small. What should you do?

   A. Pay the bribe, but lodge a complaint with local officials.

   B. Pay the bribe.

   C. Do not pay the bribe.

   D. Do not pay the bribe, and continue your project without obtaining the permit.

5. You are about to walk into a meeting with your project sponsor and client to report progress on your project, and you notice that the financial figures you are about to present to them do not look correct and present an overly optimistic view of your project. What should you do?

   A. Go ahead with the meeting, and point out the mistakes.

   B. Tell your project sponsor and client that you can't proceed with the meeting until you are sure you have the correct information.

   C. Go ahead with the meeting, and hope they don't notice the error.

   D. Cancel the meeting without explanation.

6. You and several of your colleagues are studying to sit the Project Management Professional (PMP) examination when one of your colleagues admits that she has downloaded a copy of a copyrighted study book without paying for it, by using a peer-to-peer file sharing network. She offers a copy to you and recommends the text as a great way to help you pass the exam. What should you do?

   A. Gratefully accept the study aid.

   B. Offer to pay her for it.

   C. Refuse the offer, and report her to the author of the work.

   D. Use the book for your study, and delete it once you are finished.

7. Your project sponsor has asked you to lead a project and has given you a deadline of six months to deliver the product. After completing the time-estimating processes with your team, you discover that the fastest you can deliver the project is nine months. Your project sponsor asks you to start the project anyway and still try to deliver the project within six months. What should you do?

   A. Start working on the project, looking for ways to save three months.

   B. Start working on the project, knowing that it will take nine months regardless of what you do.

   C. Refuse to work on the project.

   D. Explain to your project sponsor that you cannot make a promise you can't keep, and that the project should not start without accurate and agreed timeframes.

8. You discover that a colleague of yours whom you have worked alongside for 12 years lied on his CV to get the job and does not have the engineering degree he claims to have. However, he has proven himself as more than competent to design and manage engineering projects over the 12 years you have worked with him. What should you do?

   A. Talk with your colleague, and encourage him to disclose this information to management.

   B. Report this information immediately to your employer.

   C. Do nothing, because he has proven himself competent.

   D. Refuse to work on projects with this person.

9. You are managing a project to build a new motorway next to land that your parents have owned for 50 years. As a result of the new motorway, the value of your parents' land will increase significantly. What should you do?

   A. Go ahead with the project because the land was there before the planned motorway.

   B. Keep your parents informed on project progress so they know the best time to sell.

   C. Disclose this to your project sponsor, and ask them what the best course of action is.

   D. Do nothing, because you will not personally benefit from this.

10. You are acting as a volunteer for the Project Management Institute. During a meeting in your capacity as a volunteer, the people you are meeting with discover that you are a skilled project management trainer and ask you to provide training services to them. What should you do?

    A. After you have spoken to them about PMI business, start discussing ways you can help them as a trainer.

    B. Explain to them that you are there on PMI business and it is not appropriate to discuss commercial possibilities at this time.

    C. Explain to them that you are there on PMI business, and then explain the situation to PMI and seek guidance on the best way forward.

    D. Try to get a contract for your training services signed before you leave.

11. You are the project manager on a project, and, during the business feasibility phase, you discover that your project will have large and irreversible effects on a natural wetlands area. Your project sponsor asks you to keep quiet about this because it will mean the project will not proceed. What should you do?

   A. Report the effects of the project to the local government agency responsible for the environment.

   B. Resign from the project.

   C. Keep managing the project because that is what you promised you would do.

   D. Manage the project, and try to minimize the impact on the environment.

12. You are preparing to give a talk to your team about how to improve your risk management planning and identification processes, and you plan to use an article you have downloaded for free from the Project Management Institute web site. The article is freely available to members for download and for their professional development. During the presentation, what should you do?

   A. Deliver a great presentation without making reference to the article.

   B. Acknowledge the article and attribute the authors' ideas during your presentation.

   C. Hand out a copy of the original article to all team members.

   D. Decide not to use the article because it would be a breach of copyright.

13. You have successfully managed a large, complex project for a client, and they are very happy with the results and your leadership. As a thank-you gift, they send you a brand new car with a note expressing their gratitude. What should you do?

   A. Make sure the ownership papers have been transferred into your name correctly.

   B. Refuse the gift because it does not align with your company's policy on receiving gifts.

   C. Sell the car and split the proceeds among all project team members.

   D. Have the car delivered to your home without telling anyone.

14. You are managing a large team whose members come from many different countries. Among your team members are several who observe a particular religious holiday at a time when your team is scheduled to be delivering part of the final deliverable. The team members have asked for time off to observe the holiday. What should you do?

   A. Allow the team members the time off, and use factors such as this as constraints in the resource calendar.

   B. Give all team members the time off so that everyone is treated equally.

   C. Do not approve the time off, because it will adversely affect your project.

   D. Do not approve the time off, because you are working in a country that does not recognize that particular holiday as a public holiday.

# Answers

This section contains the answers for the Exercise and Review Questions in this chapter.

## Exercise

1. Categorize each statement from the PMI Code of Ethics and Professional Conduct in the following list as a value associated with either responsibility, respect, fairness, or honesty.

   A. We report unethical or illegal conduct to appropriate management and, if necessary, to those affected by the conduct.

   RESPONSIBILITY

   B. We negotiate in good faith.

   RESPECT

   C. We provide accurate information in a timely manner.

   HONESTY

   D. We do not act in an abusive manner toward others.

   RESPECT

   E. We proactively and fully disclose any real or potential conflicts of interest to the appropriate stakeholders.

   FAIRNESS

F.  We protect proprietary or confidential information that
    has been entrusted to us.

    RESPONSIBILITY

G.  We provide equal access to information to those who are
    authorized to have that information.

    FAIRNESS

H.  We make opportunities equally available to qualified
    candidates.

    FAIRNESS

I.  We do not exercise the power of our expertise or position
    to influence the decisions or actions of others in order to
    benefit personally at their expense.

    RESPECT

J.  We do not engage in or condone behavior that is
    designed to deceive others.

    HONESTY

K.  We inform ourselves and uphold the policies, rules,
    regulations, and laws that govern our work, professional,
    and volunteer activities.

    RESPONSIBILITY

L.  We do not engage in dishonest behavior with the
    intention of personal gain or at the expense of another.

    HONESTY

## Review Questions

1.  **Correct Answer: B**

    A.  **Incorrect:** Trust is not one of the four foundational
        values of the Code of Ethics and Professional Conduct.

    B.  **Correct:** Honesty, respect, responsibility, and fairness
        are the four foundational values of the Code of Ethics and
        Professional Conduct.

    C.  **Incorrect:** Integrity is not one of the four foundational
        values of the Code of Ethics and Professional Conduct.
        Having integrity is an important value, though, because it
        means having a set of values and sticking to them.

    D.  **Incorrect:** Transparency and truthfulness are not part
        of the four foundational values of the Code of Ethics and
        Professional Conduct.

2.  **Correct Answer: B**

    A.  **Incorrect:** It would be unethical to use drawings that belong to someone else, even if you acknowledge where they came from. You should always seek permission and negotiate terms of use of someone else's intellectual property.

    B.  **Correct:** The best option in this instance is to refuse to use the drawings. You may also want to educate your new employee about expected ethical standards.

    C.  **Incorrect:** It would be unethical to use drawings that belong to someone else.

    D.  **Incorrect:** This answer displays a level of dishonesty and is not correct.

3.  **Correct Answer: D**

    A.  **Incorrect:** It doesn't matter whether there is an impact or not. What matters is whether there is a perceived or potential impact. So, in this case, you need to disclose your relationship.

    B.  **Incorrect:** This answer does not address the issue of potential conflict and puts your spouse's organization at a disadvantage.

    C.  **Incorrect:** Resigning from the project will not address the issue.

    D.  **Correct:** The first step is to disclose the potential conflict of interest and seek advice on how best to manage it.

4.  **Correct Answer: C**

    A.  **Incorrect:** You cannot pay the bribe because it is illegal, and lodging a complaint with officials will not make it okay to pay the bribe.

    B.  **Incorrect:** Paying the bribe is illegal, and thus you cannot do it.

    C.  **Correct:** Your only choice here is to not pay the bribe, because it is an illegal payment.

    D.  **Incorrect:** Not paying the bribe is correct, but proceeding without a legally required permit would be illegal and, as such, is not an option.

5.   **Correct Answer: B**

A.   **Incorrect:** You have an obligation to be honest at all times, and if you know or suspect that information is incorrect, you must address this; so, you cannot go ahead with the meeting.

B.   **Correct:** This answer presents the most honest approach to dealing with the situation.

C.   **Incorrect:** This would be dishonest.

D.   **Incorrect:** Cancelling the meeting without explanation is not the best option because you should be honest about the reason for the cancellation.

6.   **Correct Answer: C**

A.   **Incorrect:** She has downloaded a copy of a book without paying for it, and this is both illegal and dishonest, so this is not the correct answer.

B.   **Incorrect:** Paying her for it does not change the fact that it is an illegal copy.

C.   **Correct:** Your only option here is to refuse her offer and then report her illegal activity.

D.   **Incorrect:** You cannot use the book because it is an illegal copy.

7.   **Correct Answer: D**

A.   **Incorrect:** Starting to work on a project that you know can't be delivered is unethical.

B.   **Incorrect:** This option begins the project with dishonesty.

C.   **Incorrect:** Refusing to work on the project may be a last option, but it is not the best answer in resolving this dilemma.

D.   **Correct:** Being very honest about the situation is the best option.

8.   **Correct Answer: B**

A.   **Incorrect:** When you are aware of an unethical or illegal act, you must report it. You should not wait for him to disclose this.

B.   **Correct:** When you are aware of an unethical or illegal act, you must report it.

C. **Incorrect:** When you are aware of an unethical or illegal act, you must report it. Doing nothing is no longer an option.

D. **Incorrect:** Refusing to work with this person does not address the issue of fake credentials.

9. **Correct Answer: C**

A. **Incorrect:** This situation is an example of a real or potential conflict of interest; as such, it must first be disclosed before the project can proceed.

B. **Incorrect:** When the conflict of interest has been disclosed, you would not be able to give your parents any special information.

C. **Correct:** Because this is either a real or potential conflict of interest, you must disclose it first.

D. **Incorrect:** It doesn't matter whether you benefit from it directly; your actions could benefit a member of your family, and thus there is a conflict of interest.

10. **Correct Answer: C**

A. **Incorrect:** This situation requires you to be clear about the role you have. You would have to clearly separate your PMI activities from your commercial interests and explain that you are there on PMI business, not your own business.

B. **Incorrect:** This may be a good answer in the absence of answer C.

C. **Correct:** This is the best answer because it directs you to seek guidance on how to deal with this situation.

D. **Incorrect:** Mixing PMI interests and your commercial interest is not permissible because it is a clear conflict of interest.

11. **Correct Answer: A**

A. **Correct:** You have a responsibility to protect the natural environment, and thus this is the best answer.

B. **Incorrect:** Resigning from the project does not address the damage to the environment that the project will do. It may be a last-resort option, though.

C. **Incorrect:** You cannot be silent about this after you know about it.

D. **Incorrect:** This option requires you to be dishonest and, as such, is not a good choice.

12.  **Correct Answer: B**

   A.  **Incorrect:** You must acknowledge the authorship and ownership of the article during your presentation.

   B.  **Correct:** You must acknowledge the authorship and ownership of the article, and you should also check with PMI as to whether it is OK to use it this way.

   C.  **Incorrect:** Handing out a copy to your team members does not address the issues of ownership and authorship.

   D.  **Incorrect:** You can use the article as long as you follow the standard use of copyright articles such as acknowledging authorship and ownership.

13.  **Correct Answer: B**

   A.  **Incorrect:** You should first check your company's policy on receiving gifts. Many organizations have clear guidelines forbidding the acceptance of gifts, to ensure a lack of conflict of interest and promote fairness.

   B.  **Correct:** If the gift does not align with your organization's policy, then you must refuse it.

   C.  **Incorrect:** This does not address issues of honesty and fairness.

   D.  **Incorrect:** This does not address issues of honesty and fairness.

14.  **Correct Answer: A**

   A.  **Correct:** This is a common situation, and you should be prepared to allow for different customs among your team members.

   B.  **Incorrect:** This is not about treating everyone equally but about respecting the customs of everyone. Other team members may observe different holidays.

   C.  **Incorrect:** Not approving the time off shows disrespect for other people's customs.

   D.  **Incorrect:** Not approving the time off shows disrespect for other people's customs.

■ ■ ■

# CHAPTER 13

# Eligibility, Study, and Exam-Taking Tips

Here are some eligibility, study, and exam-taking tips you may find useful.

## Eligibility

Before studying for and taking the PMP' examination, you need to first check whether you are eligible to take it. Full eligibility criteria can be found at the PMI' web site (www.pmi.org); check this web site to ensure the following information is up to date.

### PMP Prerequisites

If you have a secondary degree (high school diploma, associate's degree, or the global equivalent):

- 7,500 hours leading and directing projects, spanning at least 5 years in total, within the last 8 years

- 35 hours of project management education

or, if you have a four-year degree (university degree or baccalaureate equivalent):

- 4,500 hours leading and directing projects, spanning at least 3 years in total, within the last 8 years

- 35 hours of project management education

## Study Tips

- Visit www.vark-learn.com to find out how you study best, and adapt your study techniques to suit.

- Set aside time each week to study.

© Sean Whitaker 2016
S. Whitaker, *Pass the PMP® Exam*, DOI 10.1007/978-1-4842-2074-0_13

- Plan your study so you know which sections you are studying.

- Complete all the Quick Check questions, chapter exercises, and review questions in this book.

- Figure out the areas you are weakest in, and focus extra attention on them.

- Ask someone to listen to you explain difficult concepts in your own words. If you can't explain it, you probably don't understand it.

- Form study groups with other candidates, and learn from each other.

- Ask for patience from workmates, family, and friends as you focus on your study. It does require a bit of effort, and you may strain some relationships.

- Use a commercial training provider that has courses specifically designed to help you pass the exam. We strongly recommend that you look for a PMI Registered Education Provider® (R.E.P.) to ensure you are getting a quality trainer.

- Lock in your exam date—nothing focuses your mind like having a deadline to meet.

# Exam-Taking Tips

- Visit the testing center before the day you have booked the exam so you know where it is and where you will park.

- Be early—allow enough time to relax.

- Take the required forms of identification as per the confirmation e-mail PMI sends you. If you don't do this, you will not be allowed into the exam testing center.

- Take some water and some easy-to-eat food. You will not be allowed to take this in to the test center, but you should be able to store it in a locker and access it during the 4 hours—remember, your exam time doesn't stop if you take a break.

- Don't panic! It's normal to feel some stress, but don't let it negatively affect your performance.

- Answer all the questions. No points are deducted for wrong answers.

- Use any remaining time to recheck answers—there are no points for leaving early.

- Check your progress throughout the exam. At the 1-hour mark, you should have answered about 40 questions. At the 2-hour mark, you should have answered about 90 questions. At the 3-hour mark, you should have answered about 150 questions.

# Question-Answering Tips

- Read each question fully.

- Reread the question! Seriously, many mistakes are made because people don't read the questions fully.

- Read all four answers before deciding which one is correct. Sometimes the first one looks really good, and you may be tempted to mark it as correct when a better answer is further down the list.

- Eliminate any obviously wrong answers.

- Place the answers on a spectrum of most right to most wrong, and choose the most-right one.

- Organize the answers in order of which would be done first to the one that would be done last, and choose the one you would do first.

- If all else fails, guess! Leave no question unanswered.

# CHAPTER 14

# Blank Mind Maps

Use the blank mind maps on the following pages as part of your study. Complete each mind map from memory, and check your answers against the chapters in this book.

© Sean Whitaker 2016
S. Whitaker, *Pass the PMP® Exam*, DOI 10.1007/978-1-4842-2074-0_14

Project Stakeholder Management

# CHAPTER 15

■ ■ ■

# Formulas to Remember

| | | |
|---|---|---|
| **Communications** | How many people in a communications network; n=number of people | $= n(n-1)/2 \dfrac{n(n-1)}{2}$ |
| **PERT** | Weighted average of three estimates (optimistic, realistic, and pessimistic) | $= (O+(4 \times R)+P)/6 \dfrac{(O+(4R)+P)}{6}$ |
| **Standard deviation (SD)** | A PMBOK® Guide heuristic for calculating standard deviation from the mean<br>1SD either side of the mean ≈ 68%<br>2SD either side of the mean ≈ 95%<br>3SD either side of the mean ≈ 99.7% | $= (P-O)/6 \dfrac{(P-O)}{6}$ |
| **Variance** | The standard deviation squared | $= \left((P-O)/6\right)^2 \left(\dfrac{(P-O)}{6}\right)^2$ |
| **Planned value (PV)** | How much you planned to spend on what you planned to have achieved. The total PV for the project is the budget at completion (BAC) | = planned % complete × BAC |
| **Earned value (EV)** | The value of the work performed expressed in dollars | = actual % complete × BAC |
| **Actual cost (AC)** | How much you actually spent on what you actually achieved | |

*(continued)*

© Sean Whitaker 2016
S. Whitaker, *Pass the PMP® Exam*, DOI 10.1007/978-1-4842-2074-0_15

| | | |
|---|---|---|
| **Budget at completion (BAC)** | How much you originally planned for the project to cost and the total planned value (PV) for the project | |
| **Cost variance (CV)** | The difference between what you have earned and what it cost at a certain point in time; positive is good; negative is bad | = EV – AC |
| **Cost performance index (CPI)** | Cost variance (CV) expressed as an index; above 1 is good, below 1 is bad | = EV/AC |
| **Schedule variance (SV)** | The difference between what you have earned and what you planned to have achieved at a certain point in time; positive is good; negative is bad | = EV – PV |
| **Schedule performance index (SPI)** | Schedule variance (SV) expressed as an index; above 1 is good, below 1 is bad | = EV/PV |
| **Estimate at completion (EAC)** | How much the project is forecast to cost at completion | = AC + ETC<br>= AC + (BAC – EV)<br>= BAC/CPI<br>= AC+[(BAC – EV)/(CPI × SPI)] |
| **Estimate to complete (ETC)** | How much more money it will cost to finish the project | = EAC – AC |
| **Variance at completion (VAC)** | Difference between what you thought the project would cost and what it actually ends up costing; positive is good; negative is bad | = BAC – EAC |
| **To complete performance index (TCPI)** | The rate at which you have to go to achieve the desired outcome of either BAC or EAC; above 1 is bad, below 1 is good | = (BAC – EV/(BAC – AC)<br>= (BAC – EV/(EAC – AC) |
| **Point of total assumption (PTA)** | The point in a form of fixed-price contract at which the seller assumes total responsibility for all cost increases | = target cost +((ceiling price – target price)/buyer's % share of cost overrun) |

■ ■ ■

# CHAPTER 16

# PMP® Examination Tasks Puzzle Game

Here is a great game to play to test your knowledge of the tasks you will be tested on during the actual exam. We have taken each of the domain tasks in the role-delineation study that defines the exam and put them into this puzzle game.

## Instructions

Cut out the following pages (or copy them), divide them into individual pieces by cutting along all the dotted lines, and then put them back in the correct order with each task in the correct domain area (initiating, planning, executing, monitoring and controlling, closing) and in the correct order. You can check your answer by downloading the PMP role-delineation study from PMI; a link is provided in Chapter 17.

© Sean Whitaker 2016
S. Whitaker, *Pass the PMP® Exam*, DOI 10.1007/978-1-4842-2074-0_16

**INITIATING THE PROJECT**

Perform stakeholder analysis using appropriate tools and techniques, in order to align expectations and gain support for the project.

Obtain project charter approval from the sponsor, in order to formalize the authority assigned to the project manager and gain commitment and acceptance for the project.

Perform project assessment based on available information, lessons learned from previous projects, and meetings with relevant stakeholders, in order to support the evaluation of the feasibility of new products or services within the given assumptions and/or constraints.

Identify high-level risks, assumptions, and constraints based on the current environment, organizational factors, historical data, and expert judgment, in order to propose an implementation strategy.

Conduct benefit analysis with stakeholders (including sponsor, customer, and subject matter experts), in order to validate project alignment with organizational strategy and expected business value.

Identify key deliverables based on the business requirements, in order to manage customer expectations and direct the achievement of project goals.

Participate in the development of the project charter by compiling and analyzing gathered information, in order to ensure that project stakeholders are in agreement on its elements.

Inform stakeholders of the approved project charter, in order to ensure common understanding of the key deliverables, milestones, and their roles and responsibilities.

**PLANNING THE PROJECT**

Review and assess detailed project requirements, constraints, and assumptions with stakeholders based on the project charter and lessons learned, and by using requirements-gathering techniques, in order to establish detailed project deliverables.

Develop a scope management plan, based on the approved project scope and using scope management techniques, in order to define, maintain, and manage the scope of the project.

Develop the cost management plan based on the project scope, schedule, resources, approved project charter, and other information, using estimating techniques, in order to manage project costs.

Develop the project schedule based on the approved project deliverables and milestones, scope, and resource management plans, in order to manage timely completion of the project.

Develop the human resource management plan by defining the roles and responsibilities of the project team members, in order to create a project organizational structure and provide guidance regarding how resources will be assigned and managed.

Develop the communications management plan based on the project organization structure and stakeholder requirements, in order to define and manage the flow of project information.

Develop the procurement management plan based on the project scope, budget, and schedule, in order to ensure that the required project resources will be available.

Develop the quality management plan and define the quality standards for the project and its products, based on the project scope, risks, and requirements, in order to prevent the occurrence of defects and control the cost of quality.

Develop the change management plan by defining how changes will be addressed and controlled, in order to track and manage change.

Develop the risk management plan by identifying, analyzing, and prioritizing project risks, and defining risk response strategies, in order to manage uncertainty and opportunity throughout the project life cycle.

Present the project management plan to the relevant stakeholders according to applicable policies and procedures, inw order to obtain approval to proceed with project execution.

Conduct a kick-off meeting, communicating the start of the project, key milestones, and other relevant information, in order to inform and engage stakeholders and gain commitment.

Develop the stakeholder management plan by analyzing needs, interests, and potential impact, in order to effectively manage stakeholders' expectations and engage them in project decisions.

*(continued)*

507

**EXECUTING THE PROJECT**

Acquire and manage project resources by following the human resource and procurement management plans, in order to meet project requirements.

Implement the quality management plan using the appropriate tools and techniques, in order to ensure that work is performed in accordance with required quality standards.

Implement approved changes and corrective actions by following the change management plan, in order to meet project requirements.

Implement approved actions by following the risk management plan, in order to minimize the impact of risks and take advantage of opportunities on the project.

Manage the flow of information by following the communications plan, in order to keep stakeholders engaged and informed.

Maintain stakeholder relationships by following the stakeholder management plan, in order to receive continued support and manage expectations.

Manage task execution based on the project management plan by leading and developing the project team, in order to achieve project deliverables.

**MONITORING AND CONTROLLING THE PROJECT**

Measure project performance using appropriate tools and techniques, in order to identify and quantify any variances and corrective actions.

Manage changes to the project by following the change management plan, in order to ensure that project goals remain aligned with business needs.

Verify that project deliverables conform to the quality standards established in the quality management plan by using appropriate tools and techniques, in order to meet project requirements and business needs.

Monitor and assess risk by determining whether exposure has changed and evaluating the effectiveness of response strategies, in order to manage the impact of risks and opportunities on the project.

Review the issue log, update it if necessary, and determine corrective actions by using appropriate tools and techniques, in order to minimize the impact on the project.

Capture, analyze, and manage lessons learned using lessons-learned management techniques, in order to enable continuous improvement.

Monitor procurement activities according to the procurement plan, in order to verify compliance with project objectives.

**CLOSING THE PROJECT**

Obtain final acceptance of the project deliverables from relevant stakeholders, in order to confirm that project scope and deliverables were achieved.

Transfer the ownership of deliverables to the assigned stakeholders in accordance with the project plan, in order to facilitate project closure.

Obtain financial, legal, and administrative closure using generally accepted practices and policies, in order to communicate formal project closure and ensure transfer of liability.

Prepare and share the final project report according to the communications management plan, in order to document and convey project performance and assist in project evaluation.

Collate lessons learned that were documented throughout the project, and conduct a comprehensive project review, in order to update the organization's knowledge base.

Archive project documents and materials using generally accepted practices, in order to comply with statutory requirements and for potential use in future projects and audits.

Obtain feedback from relevant stakeholders, using appropriate tools and techniques and based on the stakeholder management plan, in order to evaluate their satisfaction.

# CHAPTER 17

■ ■ ■

# PMP® Examination Role-Delineation Domain Tasks

It is important to remember that the PMP exam is not based up the PMBOK Guide, as many people think. It is based on the tasks captured in the regularly updated role-delineation study (RDS) undertaken by PMI.

We strongly recommend downloading the latest version of the PMP Examination Content outline from PMI and studying these tasks. You can download a copy from the PMI web site at www.pmi.org/certification/project-management-professional-pmp.aspx. This site also has the latest information about all aspects of the exam and eligibility.

© Sean Whitaker 2016
S. Whitaker, *Pass the PMP® Exam*, DOI 10.1007/978-1-4842-2074-0_17

# Glossary of Key Terms

**accept**   A risk response strategy for either positive or negative risks that involves simply accepting the consequences of risk occurring.

**accepted deliverable**   A project deliverable that has been through both validation and quality control to ensure that it meets the requirements and specifications.

**accuracy**   How close the measured value is to the actual value; compare with *precision*, which refers to how uniform measurements are.

**acquisition**   The tool of advertising externally for project team members.

**active listening**   A communications technique in which the listener takes active steps to ensure that the message was understood correctly.

**activity attributes**   Detail provided about activities on the activity list.

**activity cost estimates**   The cost estimates developed for each identified activity.

**activity duration estimate**   The estimate of the duration of a defined activity.

**activity list**   The list of identified activities developed as part of the schedule management processes.

**activity network diagram**   A tool used in quality planning to show relationships between interdependent activities and calculate the paths of activities and their durations. The generic term for all network diagrams, including those used in scheduling management.

**activity resource requirements**   The resources required to complete the work of identified activities.

**activity-on-arrow**   An arrow diagramming method that represents activities on arrows and uses dummy activities to represent multiple predecessor and successor relationships between activities.

**activity-on-node**   A precedence diagramming method that represents activity information on nodes and uses arrows to indicate the relationship between activities.

**actual cost**   The actual incurred cost of completing project work.

**additional quality planning tools**   In quality management, a generic referral to those quality tools not captured in the seven basic quality tools; includes the seven new quality tools.

© Sean Whitaker 2016
S. Whitaker, *Pass the PMP® Exam*, DOI 10.1007/978-1-4842-2074-0

**advertising**   A tool for promoting a project's procurement requirements to a particular audience.

**affinity diagram**   A graphical representation of ideas and similar concepts grouped by their relationship to each other. One of the seven new quality tools.

**agreements**   Any and all formal contracts that initiate a project.

**alternative analysis**   A consideration of all the possible different ways that a potential outcome may be achieved and making a decision about which method is best.

**alternatives generation**   A process tool that considers many potential alternatives in order to determine whether you have selected the most efficient and appropriate one.

**analogous estimating**   An estimating process that takes a similar activity and compares it to a planned activity to generate the estimate.

**analytical techniques**   A group of mainly mathematical techniques used to forecast potential outcomes based on known data.

**approved change request**   A change request that has been through the documented change-control process and received approval.

**approved change requests review**   A tool to determine whether approved change requests have been implemented as planned.

**assumptions analysis**   An analysis of the assumptions made when calculating estimates.

**audit**   A tool for carrying out an assessment of whether a defined process has been followed.

**avoid**   A risk response strategy for negative risk that involves putting in place measures to avoid the risk occurring.

**backward pass**   The process of calculating the late finishes and late starts in a network diagram. After calculating the backward pass, the amount of total float for each activity and the critical path can be identified.

**balanced matrix**   A type of matrix organizational structure in which power is equally shared between the functional manager and the project manager.

**basis of estimates**   Supporting documentation for activity cost estimates that provides additional information about assumptions, constraints, uncertainty, and estimating techniques used.

**benchmarking**   Comparing a project or parts of a project against other projects to judge how they compare.

**bidder conference**   A forum or meeting where all potential bidders on a procurement request can ask questions of the buyer for clarification.

**bottom-up estimating**   The process of aggregating individual activity estimates upward to arrive at a total cost.

**brainstorming**   A technique for gathering information that encourages creative and thorough thinking.

**budget at completion**   The original approved project budget to complete all the work.

**business case**   A document that examines the objectives, cost, benefits, strategic goals, constraints, and assumptions and provides s justification for an organization to approve a project.

**business value**   The sum of all tangible and intangible value in an organization.

**buyer**   The person or organization procuring external goods or services.

**cause-and-effect diagram**   Also called a Fishbone or Ishikawa diagram; a graphical representation of a known and identified effect and the potential causes of the effect. One of the seven basic quality tools.

**change log**   A log used to document change requests received and manage their status.

**change request**   A request made in response to new or amended requirements or as a result of variances discovered.

**change-control board**   A panel of people with experience to consider and make decisions on any requested changes as part of the change-control process.

**change-control meeting**   A meeting that is defined and scheduled by the documented change-control process. Change-control meetings typically occur at regular intervals, and attendees at the meetings have the necessary skills and authority to make decisions about change requests.

**change-control tool**   Any tool defined by the change-control process that can help define and manage the change requests received.

**checklist analysis**   A technique of having a predefined checklist of steps or activities that must be completed and ensuring that they are.

**checksheet**   One of the seven basic quality tools. Used to tally the number of times an event occurs during Quality Management activities. An effective tool used to quickly highlight defective areas of a process that need to be investigated.

**claims administration**   A tool for recording and assessing any claims made by either party to a contract.

**closed procurement**   A documented output that provides a formal record that a contract has been completed and closed.

**co-location**   Putting project team members in the same physical location so that they can see each other and work together more effectively.

**communications management plan**   The management plan that guides project communications.

**communications method**   A tool that recognizes that communications can be interactive, push, or pull.

**communications model**   A tool that describes how communications move from sender to receiver through a particular medium.

**communications requirements analysis**   A tool for gathering and documenting the communications requirements of project stakeholders.

**communications technology**   A tool that decides the particular form of technology to be used to disseminate information.

**conflict management**   The process of resolving conflict.

**conflict of interest**   A situation in which an individual may benefit personally from decisions or actions they undertake while acting in the best interests of another party.

**context diagram**   A method of graphically representing how users interact with a process.

**contingency plan**   A documented plan of contingent responses to a unplanned risk occurring.

**contingency reserves**   The reserve developed, usually as a result of quantitative risk analysis, for known unknowns for time or cost.

**contingent response strategy**   A risk response strategy for unplanned risk.

**continuous improvement**   An iterative process of always seeking to improve your overall approach to quality management and the specific results obtained from quality management processes.

**contract**   A formal agreement, usually in writing, between two or more parties, with obligations, roles, and responsibilities clearly defined.

**contract change-control system**   A technique for defining how the procurement process can be changed.

**control chart**   A graphical representation of data points mapped over time against an expected mean or average; upper and lower control limits are set three standard deviations either side of the mean, and beyond the control limits there are upper and lower specification limits. One of the seven basic quality tools.

**control limit**   A limit used on a control chart; set three standard deviations either side of the expected mean to get the upper and lower control limit.

**conversation**   A tool used to communicate with team members about their performance.

**corrective action**   An action that seeks to realign project performance with the project management plan.

**cost aggregation**   The technique of adding up lower-level cost estimates to arrive at a total cost estimate for higher-level deliverables.

**cost baseline**   The approved project cost over time.

**cost forecast**   A forecast that contains the project costs for a project or part of a project based on the available information.

**cost management plan**   The management plan outlining how you will plan, monitor, and control changes to your project costs.

**cost of quality**   A consideration of the impacts of manufacturing high quality or low quality over the life of the product.

**cost performance index**   A relative measure of cost performance calculated by dividing earned value by actual cost.

**cost variance**   A measure of variance between what was planned and what is occurring in relation to project cost performance, calculated by subtracting actual cost from earned value.

**cost-benefit analysis**   A tool for analyzing the expected costs to be incurred against the expected benefits to be gained. Benefits should outweigh costs.

**crashing**   A schedule-compression technique that involves allocating more resources to an activity to speed its completion. It usually involves additional cost.

**data-gathering and -representation techniques**   Techniques and methods of collecting and presenting data in graphical form for further analysis.

**decision tree**   A tool for making decisions about which option to select based on known probabilities and outcomes, to calculate the expected monetary value of each.

**decomposition**   The technique of breaking down high-level descriptions into their component parts. When used in the creation of a WBS, decomposition is used down to the work package level.

**defect repair**   A required activity to repair a discovered defect.

**deliverable**   A unique and verifiable product, service, or result produced by the project.

**Delphi technique**   An estimating technique that involves soliciting information from experts anonymously to avoid peer pressure.

**dependency determination**   The consideration given to whether activities represent mandatory, discretionary, external, or internal dependencies.

**design of experiments**   A tool for determining quality by using a known set of variables, designing an experiment, and being able to control different variables to determine the variable responsible, or most responsible, for quality issues.

**diagramming techniques**   A variety of techniques for using diagrams to show relationships between related activities, events, causes, and effects.

**document analysis**   A technique of analyzing existing documents to gather information.

**documentation reviews**   A technique of thoroughly examining documents that serve as inputs into processes to fully understand and review them.

**dummy activity**   A relationship, represented by a dotted line, between multiple activities in an activity-on-arrow (AOA) diagram.

**early finish**   The earliest an identified activity can finish. Calculated by adding the duration of the activity to the early start.

517

**early start**   The earliest an activity can start.

**earned value**   The value of the work completed.

**earned value management**   A technique for analyzing past performance and using formulas to forecast future performance based on planned value, earned value, and actual cost.

**effective listening**   Similar to active listening, a communications technique that also includes the listener or receiver monitoring nonverbal and physical communication.

**enhance**   A risk response strategy for positive risks that seeks to enhance the probability or impact of a risk occurring.

**enterprise environmental factor**   A factor that is external to a project and that can influence the success of a project.

**enterprise environmental factors update**   An update to the enterprise environmental factors as a result of completing processes.

**estimate at completion**   The formula for calculating what the forecast cost estimate at the completion of the project will be.

**estimate to complete**   The calculation to estimate how much more money there is to be spent on the project to reach the estimate at completion.

**expected monetary value analysis**   A mathematical technique, often using decision trees, of calculating the probability and impact of a particular decision in order to calculate expected monetary value.

**expert judgment**   Advice of and decisions made by people with specialist knowledge in a particular area.

**exploit**   A risk response strategy for positive risks that seeks to put in place strategies to ensure that if a positive risk occurs, you are ready to exploit it.

**exploratory study** An initial assessment and review of an issue to gain a preliminary understanding of potential ways to address it.

**facilitated workshop**   A workshop with a focus on a particular issue, directed by an independent facilitator.

**facilitation techniques**   A broad range of techniques designed to solicit information from groups of people with the objective of accomplishing project activities.

**fairness**   One of four key values underpinning the ethical and professional conduct expected of a project manager. It seeks to avoid conflict of interest, favoritism, and discrimination. See also *responsibility*, *respect*, and *honesty*.

**fallback plan** another name for a contingency plan developed to manage risks.

**fast tracking**   A schedule-compression technique that involves performing activities in parallel that were originally scheduled in sequence.

**feedback**   Cues from the receiver to the sender that indicate whether the message has been understood.

**Fielder's contingency theory**   A theory stating that leadership effectiveness is contingent on whether the situation is stressful or calm and whether the leader is task-oriented or relationship-oriented.

**final product, service, or result**   The deliverable, product, or service produced by the project and handed over to operations, or client.

**fishbone diagram**   Also called a cause-and-effect diagram or Ishikawa diagram; a graphical representation of a known and identified effect and the potential causes of the effect. One of the seven basic quality tools.

**flowchart**   A tool for showing in graphical form the steps in a process. One of the seven basic quality tools.

**focus group**   A gathering of a group of stakeholders or participants to address a particular issue or provide specific feedback.

**forecasting**   The technique of extrapolating from past performance what likely future performance will be.

**forward pass**   The calculation of early starts and early finishes in a network diagram that results in the project duration.

**free slack or free float**   The amount of time an activity can be delayed before it affects the next activity on the path.

**functional manager**   A general manager or team leader in charge of a functional area in an organization.

**functional organization**   An organization that is structured into its separate functional areas, each having its own technical specialty and manager or leader.

**funding limit reconciliation**   A technique for reconciling forecast funding requirements against actual funding limits.

**grade**   A measure of the number of features a product has. Low grade means the product has few features, whereas high grade means it has lots of features.

**ground rules**   Rules established by the project manager and project team members for accepted and expected behaviors for being part of the team.

**group creativity techniques**   A range of techniques used to get a group of people to generate and consider a wide range of possible options.

**group decision-making techniques**   A range of techniques to enable a group of people to reach a decision.

**grouping method** A particular method of deciding how results will be categorized for easy assessment and prioritization.

**Herzberg's motivation-hygiene theory**   A theory stating that hygiene factors do not motivate, but their absence will make staff unsatisfied, and that *will* motivate, but only if hygiene factors are in place.

**histogram**   Also called a bar chart; a tool for showing amount or frequency of a variable. One of the seven basic quality tools.

**historical relationships**   Any past information about interactions between variables used in an estimating process.

**honesty**   One of four key values underpinning the ethical and professional conduct expected of a project manager. See also *responsibility*, *respect*, and *fairness*.

**human resource management plan**   The management plan for planning, acquiring, developing, and controlling human resources on the project.

**independent estimate**   A technique that uses an independent professional to provide advice about what seller responses in relation to cost should reasonably be.

**influencing**   The technique of understanding, modifying, and changing the expectations and engagement of stakeholders to ensure that they support your project or do not oppose it.

**information management system**   A tool for the management, storage, and distribution of project information in either hard copy or electronic form.

**information-gathering techniques**   A variety of techniques for gathering information from project team members, subject matter experts, other stakeholders, and other sources of information.

**inspection**   The tool of physically checking work that has been done.

**interactive communication**   A form of communication where multiple parties communicate concurrently.

**interpersonal skills**   A range of technical, personal, and conceptual skills that a project manager should have and be able to display at appropriate times in order to increase the project manager's effectiveness.

**interrelationship digraph**   A tool for graphically showing the many relationships that exist among different variables or steps in a process. One of the seven new quality tools.

**interview**   A formal and structured meeting between small groups of people to solicit specialist information.

**Ishikawa diagram**   Also called a cause-and-effect diagram or a fishbone diagram; a graphical representation of a known and identified effect and the potential causes of the effect. One of the seven basic quality tools.

**issue log**   A document that lists and describes issues that have been identified and the status of those issues.

**just in time**   A tool for controlling inventory in which inventory is delivered just as it is needed. Can be used as a quality management tool, because lack of inventory in stock exposes mistakes very quickly and provides a reason to improve quality.

**kaizen**   The loose Japanese translation of *continuous improvement*, which means always seeking to improve your quality processes and products.

**kick-off meeting**   A meeting held before project execution activities start.

**lag**   The amount of time an activity must wait after its predecessor finishes before it can start.

**late finish**   The latest an activity can finish.

**late start**   The latest an activity can start.

**lead**   The amount of time before the finish of its predecessor that an activity can start.

**make-or-buy analysis**   A tool for assessing whether work should be done by the project team or procured from an external source.

**make-or-buy decision**   The output from the make–or-buy analysis that decides whether an organization will make the required goods or services or buy them from an external provider.

**management reserves**   A reserve of cost or time for unknown unknowns; under the control of management.

**management skills**   A set of skills a project manager should have that include presentation, negotiation, time management, and public speaking skills.

**market research**   As tool for examining and assessing current marketplace conditions in order to assess the impact on procurement decisions.

**Maslow's hierarchy of needs**   A theory stating that a person will always be motived by lower-order needs before being motivated by higher-order needs.

**matrix diagram**   A tool for graphically showing how one set of variables on a vertical axis interacts with other variables on a horizontal axis. One of the seven new quality tools.

**matrix organization**   A type of organizational structure in which projects are completed across functional lines and a project manager draws on different technical specialties from different functional areas.

**McClelland's human motivation, achievement, or three needs theory**   A theory stating that people will work not for more money, but instead for achievement, power, and affiliation.

**McGregor's theory X and theory Y**   A set of theories stating that managers view employees either as trustworthy and self-motivated (theory Y) or as untrustworthy and needing constant motivation (theory X).

**meeting**   A gathering of a group of people for a specific purpose or agenda.

**methodology**   A defined set of processes, tools, techniques, and templates for managing projects in a particular way.

**milestone list**   A high-level graphical representation of the milestones to be achieved on the project.

**mitigate**   A risk response strategy for negative risks that seeks to minimize the probability and impact of a particular risk.

**modeling techniques**   A variety of mathematical and computer-based techniques to forecast possible outcomes based on several different inputs.

**Monte Carlo analysis**   A complex statistical method of extrapolating from observed data what a likely future scenario or scenarios will be.

**multicriteria decision analysis**   A tool used to assess the different attributes of prospective team members and give each attribute a particular weight so that the overall ranking of the preferred team member can be assessed.

**negotiated settlement**   A technique for arriving at an agreed means of terminating and closing a contract between parties to the contract.

**negotiation**   A tool for interacting with another party and attempting to come to a mutually beneficial agreement.

**networking**   A tool used to build relationships between individuals and groups based on mutual benefit.

**nominal group technique**   A method of having group members vote on which ideas generated from a brainstorming session are most worthy of investigating or using further.

**nonverbal**   Communication in the form of body language, posture, and similar.

**observation**   A tool used to observe team members' performance so that performance appraisals can be completed; also, the technique of physically observing how people act in an environment and how they might use a particular product, service, or result.

**organizational chart**   A hierarchical and graphical representation of the way an organization is structured, identifying specific roles and their reporting lines.

**organizational process asset**   Any formal or informal process that the performing organization has in place to assist in delivery of the project.

**organizational process assets update**   Any update that will be made to existing organizational process assets as a result of information gathered or observations made during the execution of the project.

**organizational project management maturity**   A method of assessing the level of organizational maturity in relation to the use of portfolio, program, and project management processes, tools, templates, and methodologies.

**organizational theory**   A range of theories describing the way people and organizations interact.

**Ouchi theory Z**   A theory stating that employee loyalty and productivity can be increased by offering a job for life and providing full care.

**padding**   An unjustifiable increase in estimates of time or cost.

**paralingual**   Communication that is vocal but not verbal and includes tone of voice, inflection, and volume.

**parametric estimating**   An estimating technique that multiplies a known quantity by a known metric.

**Pareto diagram** A tool for showing the frequency of events individually and also cumulatively, so that the 20% of events responsible for 80% of the effects can be identified. One of the seven basic quality tools.

**payment system** A tool for ensuring that payments due under the terms of a contract are properly paid and recorded.

**performance reporting** A tool for collecting and disseminating appropriate reporting on project progress to stakeholders.

**performance reviews** The process of measuring, comparing, and analyzing actual project performance.

**personnel assessment** tools A range of tools and techniques that enable project managers and team members to assess individual and team performance, strengths, and weaknesses.

**phase** A defined part of a project marked by a milestone, stage gate, phase gate, or major decision point.

**plan-do-check-act (PDCA) cycle** An iterative cycle developed by Shewhart and Deming to describe continuous planning and checking processes.

**planned value** The value of work that should have been completed at a certain point in time; calculated by multiplying the budget at completion by percentage of time elapsed.

**PMBOK Guide** A collection of what is considered good practice in the profession of project management, providing a framework from which to draw appropriate processes, tools, and techniques for managing projects.

**point of total assumption** The price point in a contract at which the seller assumes total responsibility for all cost increases.

**portfolio** The range of projects being undertaken by an organization.

**portfolio manager** The person responsible for managing a portfolio of projects; the portfolio manager typically operates at strategic level.

**position description** A document that sets out the required responsibilities, skills, and experience for a particular role on the project team.

**preassignment** A tool that allocates project team members to a project based on their specific experience or contractual agreements.

**precedence diagramming method** A graphical representation of activities in the project with arrows indicating the relationship between them. The most common type of precedence diagram is the activity-on-arrow (AOA) diagram.

**precision** The degree to which measurements are clustered together rather than scattered. Compare to *accuracy*.

**predecessor** An activity that comes immediately before another activity.

**preventive action** An action to stop work that will cause the project to deviate from the project management plan.

**prioritization matrix**  A tool for prioritizing and weighting issues and events and displaying the results graphically. One of the seven new quality tools.

**probability and impact matrix**  A graphical means of displaying the combined probability and impact of risks in a standardized manner.

**process analysis**  A tool that follows steps in a process to determine whether they are appropriate and can be improved on.

**process decision program chart**  A tool that links ideas together and graphically represents them as a means to achieve a particular goal. One of the seven new quality tools.

**process improvement plan**  A plan that identifies the way in which project processes will be defined, analyzed, and improved. A subset of the project management plan.

**procurement audit**  A tool for auditing whether procurement processes and contracts are being carried out as per the approved documentation.

**procurement documents**  A range of documents produced by the procurement processes that provide additional advice or record decisions made about the procurement process.

**procurement management plan**  A management plan that provides guidance on how the procurement management processes will be carried out.

**procurement negotiation**  A technique of entering into negotiations with prospective sellers that results in an agreed contract.

**procurement performance review**  A technique for carrying out a structured review of a seller's performance and progress against an agreed contract.

**procurement statement of work**  A defined and documented description of the scope of work to be completed as part of the procurement process.

**product analysis**  The technique of breaking down a defined product into its component parts to fully understand it.

**program**  A number of projects that are interrelated in some way.

**Program evaluation and review technique (PERT)**  A graphical technique developed to evaluate the time and cost elements of a project and the relationship and interdependencies between them.

**program manager**  The person responsible for managing a program of projects.

**progressive elaboration**  A process of iteratively defining and planning work to be done on a project.

**project**  A temporary activity to deliver a unique product, service, or result.

**project calendars**  The times that activities on the project can and cannot be carried out in completing project deliverables.

**project charter**  The foundational document for the project; it provides political and financial support for the project.

**project communications**   The output from the Manage Communications process that includes all information created, stored, and disseminated by the project.

**project coordinator**   A person given a leadership role in managing a project with less power and authority than a project manager.

**project documents update**   An update to any project documents as a result of information gathered, or observations made during the execution of the project.

**project expeditor**   A person given a leadership role in managing a project with very little power and authority.

**project funding requirements**   The documented timing of when project funding will be required.

**project life cycle**   The defined stages of initiating, planning, executing, monitoring and controlling, and closing a project.

**project management**   The proactive application of professional project management practices to deliver a project.

**project management information system**   Any system the project uses to gather, store, record, and disseminate information about the project.

**project management office**   The center of excellence for project management in an organization.

**project management plan**   The collection of all planning documents used to guide project execution.

**project management plan update**   Any update to any part of the project management plan or its subsidiary plans.

**project management software**   Any software that provides monitoring and reporting capability for managing a project.

**project manager**   The person ultimately responsible for all aspects of the project.

**project performance appraisal**   A tool used to assess individual and team performance against expected performance, provide feedback to team members, identify individual training needs, and use this information to plan future team and individual performance.

**project schedule**   The expected timeframe the project will take.

**project schedule network diagram**   A graphical representation of all the activities to be completed on a project and the relationships between them.

**project scope statement**   The description of all the work to be done, and the work not to be done, as part of the project.

**project staff assignments**   A document outlining which project staff members are allocated to the project, their roles, and their contact details.

**project steering committee**   An oversight group made up of senior managers providing high-level advice, support, and governance to the project.

**projectized organization**   An organizational structure that reflects an organization that is divided and structured along project lines.

**proposal evaluation technique**   A technique for assessing and scoring all proposals received as part of a procurement process.

**prototype**   A technique of producing an example of the finished product, service, or result to seek feedback from stakeholders.

**published estimating data**   A database of known quantities or costs relating to completion of activities in the project. Such databases are usually available commercially.

**pull communication**   A form of communication where information is downloaded and accessed by the receivers when they want it.

**push communication**   A form of communication where information is sent to the receiver.

**qualitative risk analysis**   A variety of tools and techniques for analyzing risks qualitatively, or subjectively.

**quality**   The degree to which a set of inherent characteristics fulfills requirements.

**quality audit**   A tool for checking conformity to defined process to ensure that they are being followed.

**quality checklist**   An input/output that provides a standardized list of steps to be taken. Compare with *checksheets*, which are used as a quality tool.

**quality control measurement**   An input/output that describes the result of Control Quality activities.

**quality management plan**   A subset of the project management plan that describes how quality management will be defined, document, measured, and improved in a project.

**quality metric**   An input/output that describes a particular product or project attribute in detail and how the Quality Control process will measure it.

**quantitative risk analysis and modeling techniques**   A variety of tools and techniques for performing quantitative risk analysis.

**questionnaires and surveys**   Formal documented methods of asking for information and feedback from stakeholders.

**RACI chart**   A type of responsibility assignment matrix (RAM) that identifies particular team members and activities to be completed, and defines whether the team members are responsible, accountable, consulted, or informed.

**recognition**   A tool for acknowledging the performance of team members.

**records management system**   A tool used to record, store, and distribute information relating to procurement processes and decisions.

**reporting system**   A tool for gathering, storing, and distributing project information.

**requirements**   The attributes, condition, or capability that a stakeholder requires from a product, service, or result produced as part of the project.

**requirements documentation**   A document that describes individual requirements and their priority; developed in consultation with stakeholders.

**requirements management plan**   The document that sets out how you will define, document, and manage your project requirements.

**requirements traceability matrix**   A document that maps individual project requirements to specific business objectives and stakeholders.

**reserve analysis**   An analysis, usually using quantitative risk analysis, that results in the provision of either a contingency or management reserve for time and cost.

**resource breakdown structure**   A breakdown, using the process of decomposition, of the categories and types of resources required to complete the project.

**resource calendars**   The specific time periods that particular resources are available to be used on the project.

**resource leveling**   The process of optimizing and making most efficient use of resources over a given period of time.

**resource optimization techniques**   Any of the techniques that enable a more efficient use of resources on the project.

**resource smoothing**   A resource optimization technique that seeks to optimize the use of resources without extending the total float of any activity.

**respect**   One of four key values underpinning the ethical and professional conduct expected of a project manager. It seeks to ensure that respect is provided for. See also *responsibility, fairness*, and *honesty*.

**responsibility**   One of four key values underpinning the ethical and professional conduct expected of a project manager. It seeks to ensure that a project manager takes full personal and professional responsibility for all actions and decisions. See also *respect, fairness*, and *honesty*.

**responsibility assignment matrix**   A tool for displaying particular roles in a project and the responsibilities each role has.

**rewards**   A tool for compensating high performance.

**risk audit**   A technique for determining whether the processes outlined in the risk management plan for conducting risk management activities are being followed.

**risk breakdown structure (RBS)**   A graphical representation of different risk categories and subcategories.

**risk categorization**   A technique for assigning similar and interrelated risks into identified categories.

**risk data quality assessment**   A technique for examining the quality and certainty of data being used in risk analysis.

**risk management plan**   The particular management plan that outlines how you will approach the planning, monitoring, and controlling of risk management activities on your project. It is a subsidiary of the project management plan.

**risk probability and impact assessment**   A tool for assigning likely probability and impact to individual identified risks on the project.

**risk reassessment**   A technique for continually reassessing the information used to identify individual risks, their probability and impact, the prepared risk responses, and any new risks that may have arisen.

**risk register**   The documented list, analysis, and planned responses to identified risks on the project.

**risk tolerance**   The maximum level of risk that an organization is prepared to tolerate on a project.

**risk urgency assessment**   A technique for assessing those risks that are likely to occur in the short term, and prioritizing those over risks that will occur at a later point in time.

**rolling-wave planning**   A form of progressive elaboration that focuses on planning the immediate future in more detail than timeframes further off.

**rule of seven**   A guide for determining when a process may be out of control in a control chart. If seven consecutive data points appear above or below the mean and within the control limits, this may indicate that the process is out of control or is about to go out of control.

**scatter diagram**   A tool for graphically representing the results of two variables. One of the seven basic quality tools.

**schedule baseline**   The developed and approved project timeframe.

**schedule compression**   Any technique that reduces individual activity or the total project duration.

**schedule data**   The collection of information describing and controlling the schedule, including the schedule milestones, schedule activities, activity attributes, and any schedule contingency reserves.

**schedule forecast**   The estimated time the project, or parts of the project, will take, based on available information.

**schedule management plan**   The plan developed to guide the development, monitoring, and control of the project schedule. It forms part of the overall project management plan.

**schedule network templates**   Any templates that an organization has for assisting with developing a schedule network.

**schedule performance index**   A calculation measuring the time performance on the project. Calculated by dividing earned value by planned value.

**schedule variance**   The difference between what was planned and what is actually occurring in relation to the project schedule.

528

**scheduling tool**   Any manual or automated tool that focuses on the project schedule.

**scope baseline**   The scope statement, work breakdown structure (WBS), and WBS dictionary.

**scope management plan**   The document that sets out how you will define, document, and manage changes to your project scope statement.

**selected sellers**   The group of sellers chosen to participate in the procurement process either by being prequalified or by completing a stage in the procurement process.

**seller**   An individual or organization responsible for delivery of externally contracted goods or services.

**seller proposal**   A formal response to a procurement request from a prospective seller.

**sensitivity analysis**   A mathematical technique for determining which parts of the project are most sensitive to risk.

**seven basic quality tools**   Initially developed by Ishikawa; graphical ways of showing complex text-based or numerical information. They are cause-and-effect diagrams, flowcharts, checksheets, Pareto diagrams, histograms, control charts, and scatter diagrams.

**seven new quality tools**   A further seven ways to show information in graphical form. They are affinity diagrams, process decision program charts, interrelationship digraphs, tree diagrams, prioritization matrices, activity network diagrams, and matrix diagrams.

**share**   A risk response strategy for positive risks that seeks to increase the probability or impact of a risk occurring by sharing experience and capabilities with another organization.

**simple average**   A mathematical average obtained by adding a set of numbers and dividing the total by how many numbers are in the set.

**Six Sigma**   A proprietary approach to quality management that seeks to reduce defects and errors to as close to zero as possible. Named after six standard deviations, which includes 99.999% of a population.

**source-selection criteria**   A tool for developing a range of approved criteria for assessing seller responses to procurement requests.

**specification limit**   A limit used on a control chart outside the control limits set by the customer. Any product manufactured outside either the upper or lower specification limit will not be accepted by the customer.

**sponsor**   The person who provides financial and political support for the project, appoints the project manager, and authorizes the project charter.

**staffing management plan**   An important component of the human resource management plan that specifically addresses the skills required, the time people are able to work on the project, and how and when project team members will be obtained to work on the project.

**stakeholder**   Any person or group that can affect or be affected by your project.

**stakeholder analysis**    A technique for identifying and documenting stakeholders' interests, expectations, power, influence, and level of engagement in the project.

**stakeholder management plan**    The document that sets out how you will define, document, and manage stakeholders and their expectations.

**stakeholder register**    A register of all project stakeholders and information about their interest in the project, the power they have to influence the project, their expectations, and how their expectations will be managed.

**stakeholder risk profile analysis**    An assessment of individually identified stakeholders' attitudes toward risk on the project.

**standard deviation**    A measurement about how widespread a particular set of data is from the mean.

**statement of work**    A high-level narrative description of the work to be done on the project.

**statistical sampling**    A tool for sampling a small subset of a large population and extrapolating the result to the entire population. Used when testing the entire population is not possible or when destructive testing is involved.

**status meetings**    Regularly scheduled meetings that focus on a particular project status metric.

**strategies for negative risks or threats**    A range of suitable options for dealing with negative risks, including transfer, mitigate, avoid, and accept.

**strategies for positive risks or opportunities**    A range of suitable options for dealing with positive risks, including enhance, exploit, share, and accept.

**strong matrix**    A type of matrix organization in which the project manager has most of the power and authority, and the functional manager has little power and authority.

**successor**    An activity that comes immediately after another activity.

**SWOT analysis**    A technique that analyzes strengths, weaknesses, opportunities, and threats.

**tailoring**    The process of taking and using only those processes, tools, and techniques that provide benefit to managing your project.

**team performance assessment**    A tool used to develop a formal or informal assessment of a project team's effectiveness.

**team-building activities**    A wide range of activities designed to enhance team performance via the creation of team morale, culture, and ground rules.

**technical performance measurement**    A technique for checking whether predetermined parameters for initiating particular risk strategies have been met.

**template**    Any blank, preformed document that can be used to complete processes, documents, or forms on a project.

**three-point estimating**   A formula taken from the program evaluation and review technique (PERT) that calculates a weighted average of the optimistic, most likely, and pessimistic estimates. The formula is $(O + (4 \times M) + P)/6$.

**to-complete performance index**   The rate at which you must perform to achieve either the budget at completion or the estimate at completion.

**tornado diagram**   A tool for graphically representing the results of sensitivity analysis in hierarchal form to identify those parts of the project to be affected by risk, from most likely down to least likely.

**total quality management (TQM)**   A management-led philosophy and approach to quality that involves everyone in the organization and seeks to continuously improve all aspects of quality within an organization and a project.

**total slack or total float**   The amount of time an activity can be delayed before it affects the total project duration.

**training**   A tool used to increase the level of skills a team member has through formal learning.

**transfer**   A risk response strategy for negative risks, which involves making the probability and impact of the risk someone else's responsibility.

**tree diagram**   A tool for showing the systemic breakdown of concepts or issues. Used as a quality management tool. Also the generic term for breakdown structures such as the work breakdown structure and organizational breakdown structure.

**trend analysis**   A technique for identifying any trends and observed data and extrapolating from them a likely future outcome.

**Tuckman's five-stage model of team development**   A theory that describes the five stages a team goes through: forming, storming, norming, performing, and adjourning.

**validated change**   An approved change that has been acted on and checked for accuracy.

**validated deliverable**   A deliverable that has previously been verified and has been checked with stakeholders to ensure that it meets stakeholder requirements and expectations.

**variance**   The difference between what was planned and what is actually occurring.

**variance analysis**   The technique of checking what you planned to do against what you are actually doing and spotting any difference between the two.

**variance and trend analysis**   The technique of checking what you planned to do against what you are actually doing and using this information to forecast likely future trends.

**variance at completion**   The difference between the budget at completion and the estimate at completion.

**variance formula**   The formula used to determine the mathematical variance; calculated by multiplying the standard deviation by itself.

**vendor bid analysis**   The technique of getting an independent assessment of prices submitted by vendors to check for accuracy.

**verified deliverable**   A deliverable that has previously been verified and has been checked with stakeholders to ensure it meets stakeholder requirements and expectations.

**virtual team**   A tool that recognizes that project team members may come from different geographic locations but can still work together by using technology.

**Vroom's expectancy theory**   A theory stating that the expectation of receiving a reward for a certain accomplishment will motivate people to work harder, but that this works only if the accomplishment is perceived to be achievable.

**war room**   A specific form of co-location activity that places team members in the same room.

**weak matrix**   A type of matrix organization in which the functional manager has much more power and authority than a project manager.

**weighted average**   A mathematical average calculated by adding a set of numbers and prescribing different weights to each of them, and then dividing by the sum of the weights given; used to calculate three-point estimates.

**what-if scenario analysis**   A complex mathematical model that examines the probability of different scenarios.

**whistleblower**   Someone who reports illegal or unethical behavior in an organization.

**work breakdown structure (WBS)**   A hierarchical graphical representation of the work to be done on the project, broken down to work package level.

**work breakdown structure (WBS) dictionary**   A document providing additional information about each node in a WBS.

**work package**   An amount of work that can have time and cost accurately estimated; the lowest level of the WBS.

**work performance data**   The raw data gathered as part of observations and inspections.

**work performance information**   The refined work performance data presented in a relevant form.

**work performance reports**   The presentation of work performance information to stakeholders.

**workaround**   An acceptable response to unplanned risk, which involves creating a makeshift solution to allow work to continue.

# Index

## A

Acquire project team process
  input
    enterprise environmental
      factors, 293
    human resource management
      plan, 293
    organizational process assets, 293
  outputs
    project staff assignments, 295
    resource calendars, 295
  process plan, 292
  project management plan updates, 296
  tools and techniques
    acquisition, 294
    multicriteria decision analysis, 295
    negotiation, 294
    preassignment, 294
    virtual teams, 294
Activity duration estimates, 164
activity node, 171
Activity-on-arrow (AOA), 150
Activity-on-node (AON) network, 149, 192
Adaptive project life cycle, 16
Affinity diagram, 566

## B

Balanced matrix, 566
Benchmarking, 566
Benefit-cost ratio (BCR), 40
Bidder conference, 417–418
Budget determination
  inputs
    activity cost estimates, 215
    agreements, 216

    basis of estimates, 215
    cost management plan, 214
    organizational process assets, 216
    project schedule, 215
    resource calendars, 215
    risk register, 215
    scope baseline, 215
  outputs
    cost baseline, 218
    project documents updates, 219
    project funding requirements, 219
  planning domain task, 214
  process, 214
  tools and techniques
    cost aggregation, 216
    expert judgment, 217
    funding limit reconciliation, 217
    historical relationships, 217
    reserve analysis, 217

## C

Cause-and-effect diagram, 247, 567
Change-control tool, 567
Close procurements
  input
    procurement documents, 431
    project management plan, 431
  output, 433
  process outline, 430
  tools and techniques
    negotiations, 432
    procurement audits, 431
    records management system, 432
Close project/phase
  close procurements process, 76
  domain tasks, 75–76

Close project/phase (*cont.*)
 inputs
  accepted deliverables, 77
  organizational process assets, 77
  project management plan, 77
 outputs
  final product and service, 78
  organizational process asset
   updates, 79
 process, 75
 tools and techniques
  analytical techniques, 78
  expert judgment, 78
  meetings, 78
Collect requirements process, 99
Communications management
 blank mind maps, 499
 communication tool
  and definition, 345, 348
 description, 327
 input
  domain tasks, 329
  enterprise environmental factor, 330
  organizational process assets, 330
  project management, elements, 329
  stakeholder register, 329
 knowledge area, 327
 output
  plan communications
   management, 334
  project documents, 335
 stakeholders needs analysis, 329
 tools and techniques
  communications model, 331–333
  communications technology, 331
  interactive communication, 333
  meetings, 334
  pull communication, 333
  push communication, 333
  requirements analysis, 330–331
  types of communication, 334
Communications model, 567, 331–333
Communications requirements
  analysis, 330–331
Communications technology, 331
Conduct procurements
 input
  make-or-buy decisions, 416
  management plan, 415
  organizational process assets, 417
  procurement documents, 416

  project documents, 416
  seller proposals, 416
  source-selection criteria, 416
  statement of work, 416
 output
  agreement, 419–420, 422
  change requests, 422
  management plan updates, 422
  project documents updates, 423
  resource calendar, 422
  selected sellers, 419
 process overview, 415
 tools and techniques
  advertising, 418
  analytical techniques, 419
  bidder conference, 417–418
  expert judgment, 418
  independent estimates, 418
  negotiations, 419
  proposal evaluation techniques, 418
Conflict management, 304
Context diagram, 568
Contract change-control system, 426
Contracts types, 421, 435, 438
Control communications process
 input
  issues log, 341
  organizational process assets, 342
  project communications, 341
  project management plan, 341
  work performance data, 342
 monitor and control domain tasks, 341
 output
  change request, 343
  document update, 343
  organizational process assets, 344
  work performance information, 343
 process overview, 340
 tools and techniques
  expert judgment, 342
  meetings, 343
  reporting system, 342
Control costs
 inputs
  organizational process
   assets, 221
  project funding requirements, 221
  project management plan, 221
  work performance data, 221
 monitoring and controlling
   domain task, 220

outputs
    change requests, 229
    cost forecasts, 228
    organizational process assets
      updates, 229
    project documents updates, 229
    project management plan
      updates, 229
    work performance information, 228
process, 220
tools and techniques
    EVM (*see* Earned value
      management (EVM))
    forecasting, 225–227
    performance reviews, 228
    project management software, 228
    reserve analysis, 228
    TCPI, 227
Control procurements
  input
    agreements, 425
    approved change requests, 425
    procurement documents, 425
    project management plan, 425
    work performance data, 426
    work performance reports, 426
  output
    change requests, 429
    documentation updates, 429
    management plan updates, 429
    organizational process assets, 429
    work performance information, 428
  process plan, 424
  tools and techniques
    audits, 427
    claims administration, 427
    contract change-control system, 426
    payment systems, 427
    performance reporting, 427
    performance reviews, 426
    records management system, 428
Control quality
  inputs
    approved change requests, 264
    deliverables, 264
    organizational process assets, 264
    project documents, 264
    quality checklists, 264
    quality management plan, 263
    quality metrics, 264
    work performance, 264

monitoring and controlling domain
    task, 263
outputs
    change requests, 267
    organizational process assets
      updates, 267
    project documents updates, 267
    project management plan
      updates, 267
    quality control measurements, 266
    validated changes, 266
    verified deliverables, 267
    work performance information, 267
process, 263
tools and techniques
    approved change requests, 265
    inspection, 265
    seven basic quality tools, 265
    statistical sampling, 265
Control schedule process, 178–179
Control scope process
  domain, 119
  organizational process assets, 120
  project management plan, 119
  requirements documentation, 120
  requirements traceability matrix, 120
  work performance data, 120
Control stakeholder engagement
  domain task, 462
  inputs
    issue log, 462
    project documents, 462
    project management plan, 462
    work performance data, 462
  outputs
    change requests, 464
    organizational process assets
      updates, 464
    project documents updates, 464
    project management plan, 464
    work performance data, 464
  process, 461
  tools and techniques
    expert judgment, 463
    information management
      system, 463
    meetings, 464
Cost aggregation, 568
Cost management
  baseline development process flow, 200
  blank mind maps, 499

Cost management (*cont.*)
    control costs (*see* Control costs)
    definition, 199
    determine budget, 214–219
    estimate costs (*see* Costs estimation)
    plan cost management, 200–204
    processes, 199
Cost management plan, 204
Cost performance index, 569
Costs estimation
    direct costs, 206
    estimate ranges, 206
    fixed costs, 206
    indirect costs, 206
    inputs
        cost management plan, 207
        enterprise environmental
          factors, 208
        human resource management
          plan, 207
        organizational process assets, 208
        project schedule, 208
        risk register, 208
        scope baseline, 207
    outputs
        activity cost estimates, 212
        basis of estimates, 212–213
        project documents updates, 213
    planning domain task, 205
    process, 205
    tools and techniques
        analogous estimating, 209
        bottom-up estimating, 209
        cost of quality, 212
        expert judgment, 209
        group decision-making
          techniques, 212
        parametric estimating, 209
        project management software, 212
        reserve analysis, 211
        three-point estimating, 209–211
        vendor bid analysis, 212
    variable costs, 205
Critical chain method, 173
Critical path method, 169

### ▓ D

Decision-making skills, 303
Decision tree, 569
Decomposition, 112

Define activities process
    activity attributes, 142
    activity list, 141
    domain, 139
    enterprise environmental factors, 140
    expert judgment, 141
    inputs, 139
    organizational process assets, 140
    rolling- wave planning, 141
    schedule management plan, 139
    scope baseline, 140
    tools and techniques, 140
Define scope Process, 105
Delphi technique, 163
Develop project team process
    domain task, 297
    inputs
        human resource management
          plan, 297
        project staff assignments, 297
        resource calendars, 298
    output
        enterprise environmental
          factors, 309
        team performance
          assessments, 308
    team performance, 297
    tools and techniques
        co-location, 307
        ground rules, 307
        Interpersonal skills, 298
        personnel assessment tools, 308
        recognition and rewards, 307
Develop schedule process, 166
Direct and manage project work
    approved change requests, 57
    components, 56
    domain tasks, 56
    enterprise environmental factors, 57
    executing processes, 56
    organizational process assets, 57
    outputs
        change requests, 60
        deliverables, 59
        monitoring and controlling
          processes, 60
        project document updates, 60
        work performance data, 59
    process, 55
    project management plan, 57
    tools and techniques

expert judgment, 58
meetings, 58
project management information
system, 58
Discretionary dependencies, 147

## E

Earned value management (EVM)
actual cost (AC), 223
budget at completion (BAC), 222
cost performance index (CPI), 224
cost variance (CV), 224
earned value (EV), 223
planned value (PV), 222
project cost baseline, 222
schedule performance index (SPI), 224
schedule variance (SV), 224
Economic value add (EVA), 40
Effective performance reporting, 338
Enterprise environmental factors, 14, 44,
50, 281
Estimate activity durations process
activity list, 157
activity resource requirements, 157
analogous estimating, 159
domain, 156
enterprise environmental factors, 158
expert judgment, 159
inputs, 157
organizational process assets, 158
project risk register, 158
project scope statement, 158
resource breakdown structure, 158
resource calendars, 157
tools and techniques, 159
Estimate activity resources process, 151
activity list, 152
alternative analysis, 153
bottom-up estimating, 154
domain, 151
enterprise environmental factors, 153
expert judgment, 153
inputs, 152
organizational process assets, 153
published estimating data, 153
resource calendars, 152
Ethics and professional conduct, PMI code
fairness, 480
honesty, 481–482

respect, 478–479
responsibility, 476–477
EVM. See Earned value management
(EVM)
Expert judgment, 96
External dependencies, 148

## F

Failure mode and effect
analysis (FMEA), 66, 252
Fielder's contingency theory, 299, 571
Finish-to-finish (FF), 146
Finish-to-start (FS), 146, 149
Fixed-price incentive fee (FPIF), 422
FMEA. See Failure mode and effect
analysis (FMEA)
Focus groups, 101
Formulas, 504
Functional organizational structure, 288
Future value (FV), 41

## G

Gantt chart, 176
Group creativity techniques, 101
Group decision-making
techniques, 101, 162, 571

## H

Herzberg's motivation-hygiene
theory, 301, 316, 321
Histogram, 250
Human resource management
activity resource requirements, 281
blank mind maps, 499
definition, 280
outputs, 291
planning
activity resource requirements, 281
enterprise environmental
factors, 281
organizational process
assets, 282
process overview, 281
tools and techniques
expert judgment, 291
meetings, 291
networking, 287

Human resource management (*cont.*)
  organizational charts
    (*see* Organizational charts and
    position descriptions)
  organizational theory and impact
    (*see* Organizational theory)
Human resource management
    plan, 315, 572

## ▓ I, J, K

Information management systems, 338
Integration management, blank mind
    maps, 499
Interactive communication, 333
Internal dependencies, 148
Internal rate of return (IRR), 40
Interpersonal skills, 298
  build teams, 300
  coaching, 304
  communication skills, 302
  conflict management, 304
  decision-making skills, 303
  influencing, 302
  leadership, 299–300
  motivation, 300–302
  negotiation skills, 304
  political and cultural awareness, 303
  trust building, 304
  training, 304
Ishikawa diagram, 572

## ▓ L

Leadership, 298–300

## ▓ M

Make-or-buy analysis, 410, 413
Manage communications
  input
    communications management
    plan, 336
    enterprise environmental
    factor, 337
    organizational process assets, 337
    work performance reports, 337
  output
    document updates, 339
    management plan updates, 339

    organizational process
    assets, 339–340
    project communications, 339
  process outline, 336
  tools and techniques
    communications models, 338
    communication technology, 337
    information management
    systems, 338
    methods, 338
    performance reporting, 338
Manage project team
  input
    human resource management
    plan, 311
    issue log, 311
    organizational process assets, 312
    project staff assignments, 311
    team performance assessments, 311
    work performance reports, 311
  output
    change request, 314
    enterprise environmental
    factors, 314
    organizational process assets, 314
    project documents update, 314
    project management plan
    update, 314
  tools and techniques
    conflict management, 312–313
    interpersonal skills, 313
    observation and conversation, 312
    project performance
    appraisals, 312
Manage stakeholder engagement
  domain tasks, 457
  inputs
    change log, 458
    communications management
    plan, 457
    organizational process assets, 458
    stakeholder management plan, 457
  outputs
    change requests, 460
    issue log, 459
    organizational process assets
    updates, 460
    project documents updates, 460
    project management plan
    updates, 460

process, 456
tools and techniques
  communications model and
    methods, 458
  interpersonal skills, 459
  management skills, 459
Mandatory dependencies, 147
Market research, 411
Maslow's hierarchy of needs, 300, 316, 321
Matrix diagram, 573
Matrix organizational structure, 288–289
McClelland's human motivation,
  achievement, or three needs
  theory, 301, 316
McGregor's theory X and theory Y, 301,
  316, 320
Memorandum of understanding (MOU), 43
Modeling techniques, 174, 181
Monitor and control project work
  domain tasks, 62
  inputs
    cost forecasts, 63
    enterprise environmental factors, 65
    organizational process assets, 65
    project management plan, 63
    schedule forecasts, 63
    validated changes, 63
    work performance information, 64
  meetings, 67
  outputs
    change requests, 67
    project document updates, 68
    project management plan
      updates, 68
    work performance reports, 68
  process, 62
  project Integration knowledge area, 62
  project management information
    system, 67
  tools and techniques
    analytical techniques, 65–66
    expert judgment, 65
Monte Carlo analysis, 574
Multicriteria decision analysis, 295
Multiple-equation models, 66

▓ N

Negotiation skills, 294, 296, 304, 432
Net present value (NPV), 40
Networking, 287

▓ O

Organizational charts and position
    descriptions
  functional manager, 285
  part-time project team, 283
  program manager, 284
  project coordinator, 283
  project manager, 282
  project sponsor, 284
  project steering
    committee/group, 284–285
  project team, 283
  RACI chart, 286–287
  skills, project manager, 282
  text-based descriptions, 286
  virtual teams, 284
  WBS, 286
Organizational process assets, 14, 44, 96,
    106, 121, 330
Organizational project management
    maturity, 574
Organizational theory
  balanced matrix, 288
  functional organizational structure
    chart demonstration, 288
    shared services, 288
  matrix organization, 288
  organizational breakdown
    structure/organization chart, 287
  projectized organization, 289
  strong matrix organization, 288
  structures, authority, and power, 290
  weak matrix organization, 288
Ouchi's theory Z, 302

▓ P

Parametric estimating, 159
Pareto diagram, 249, 575
PDPC. See Process decision program chart
    (PDPC)
Performance reviews, 180
Perform integrated change control
  configuration identification, 71
  configuration verification and audit, 71
  decision-making process, 70
  gold plating, 70
  inputs
    change requests, 72
    enterprise environmental factor, 72

Perform integrated change control (*cont.*)
    organizational process assets, 72
    project management plan, 71
    work performance reports, 71
  monitoring and controlling
    domain task, 70
  outputs
    approved change requests, 73
    change log, 73
    project document updates, 74
    project management plan
      updates, 74
  process, 69
  tools and techniques
    change-control tools, 73
    expert judgment, 72
    meetings, 73
Perform quality assurance
  domain task, 255
  inputs
    process improvement plan, 256
    project documents, 257
    quality control measurements, 256
    quality management plan, 256
    quality metrics, 256
  outputs
    change requests, 262
    organizational process assets
      updates, 262
    project documents updates, 262
    project management plan
      updates, 262
  process, 255
  tools and techniques
    process analysis, 261
    quality audit, 261
    quality management and control
      tools, 257–260
Personnel assessment tools, 308
Plan cost management
  estimate costs and budget
    processes, 204
  inputs
    enterprise environmental
      factors, 202
    organizational process assets, 202
    project charter, 201
    project management plan, 201
  outputs, 204
  planning domain task, 201
  process, 201

  tools and techniques
    analytical techniques, 203
    expert judgment, 203
    meetings, 203
Plan-do-check-act (PDCA) cycle, 17, 575
Plan quality management
  domain task, 244
  inputs
    enterprise environmental
      factors, 245
    organizational process assets, 246
    project management plan, 244
    requirements documentation, 245
    risk register, 245
    stakeholder register, 245
  outputs
    process improvement plan, 253
    project documents updates, 254
    quality checklist, 254
    quality management plan, 253
    quality metrics, 254
  planning process, 244
  tools and techniques
    benchmarking, 252
    cost-benefit analysis, 246
    cost of quality, 246
    design of experiments, 252
    FMEA, 252
    meetings, 252
    quality planning tool, 252
    statistical sampling, 252
Plan schedule management process
  analytical techniques, 137
  domain, 135
  enterprise environmental
    factors, 136
  expert judgment, 136
  meetings, 137
  organizational process assets, 136
  outputs, 137
  project charter, 135
  schedule management plan, 137
  tools and techniques, 136
Plan stakeholder management
  inputs
    enterprise environmental
      factors, 453
    organizational process
      assets, 453
    project management plan, 453
    stakeholder register, 453

outputs
    project documents updates, 455
    stakeholder management plan, 455
  planning domain task, 452
  process, 452
  tools and techniques
    plan stakeholder management, 454
PMBOK Guide, 2–4, 18
PMP® examination
  eligibility, 495
  exam-taking tips, 496
  puzzle game, 505–509
  question-answering tips, 497
  role-delineation study (RDS), 511
  study tips, 495
Point of total assumption (PTA), 422
Portfolio management, 6
precedence diagramming
      method (PDM), 575
  dependency determination, 147
  FS, 146
  predecessor activity, 145
  predecessor and successors, 145
Present value (PV), 40
Process decision program
      chart (PDPC), 258
Procurement management
  input
    activity resource requirements,
      408
    cost estimates, 408
    enterprise environmental
      factors, 409
    organizational process assets, 409
    project management plan, 407
    project schedule, 408
    requirements documentation, 408
    risk register, 408
    stakeholder register, 408
  knowledge area, 405
  make-or-buy analysis, 406
  output
    make-or-buy analysis, 413–414
    management plans, 412
    procurement documents, 412
    project documents updates, 414
    source-selection criteria, 413
    statement of work, 412
  tools and techniques
    expert judgment, 411
    make-or-buy analysis, 410

    market research, 411
    meetings, 411
Program evaluation and review technique
    (PERT), 160, 576
Project calendar, 177
Project charter, development, 100, 106
  agreement, types, 43
  business case, 42–43
  domain task alignment, 37–38
  enterprise environmental factors, 44
  financial criteria, 40–41
  organizational process assets, 44
  outputs, 46
  planning processes, 47
  process, 37
  project-selection process, 38–39
  SOW, 42
  tools and techniques
    expert judgment, 45
    facilitation techniques, 45
Project closure, 77
Project integration management
  definition, 35
  project charter (*see* Project charter,
    development)
  tailoring, 36
Projectized organizational structure, 289
Project management
  competing constraints, 9
  environmental factors, 15
  groups and knowledge areas, 19
  life cycle, 15
  methodology, 16
  monitoring and controlling process, 25
  organizational influences, 13
  and organizational strategy, 12
  photographic memory, 4
  PMBOK® Guide, 2
  Project, program, and portfolio
    management, 6
  standardized terminology, 3
Project management institute (PMI), 475
Project management office (PMO), 7
Project management plan,
    development, 116
  component parts and subset plans,
    processes, 54
  enterprise environmental factors, 50
  iterative process, 48–49
  organizational process assets, 50–51
  outputs, 52–53

Project management plan,
        development (*cont.*)
    planning domain tasks, 48
    plans and baselines, 53
    process, 47
    project charter, 49
    successive iterations, output, 49
    tools and techniques
        expert judgment, 51
        facilitation techniques, 52
Project management software, 181
    activity resource requirements, 154
    outputs, 154
    project documents, 155
    resource breakdown structure, 155
Project performance appraisals, 312
Project quality management
    definition, 241
    just in time (JIT), 242
    precision and accuracy, 242
    processes, 241
    six sigma, 243
    total quality management (TQM), 243
Project schedule, 176
Project schedule network diagram, 149
Project scope management
    alternatives generation, 107
    benchmarking, 103
    context diagram, 103
    defining and documenting, 91, 93
    document analysis, 103
    environmental factors, 96
    expert judgment, 96
    knowledge, 91
    observations, 102
    organizational process assets, 96
    processes, 91
    process inputs, 94
    product analysis, 107
    project charter, 95
    prototypes, 102
    requirements
        documentation, 103–104
    tools and techniques, 96
Project scope statement, 107–108
Project-selection process, 39
Project staff assignments, 311
Project stakeholder management, 445
Project statement of work (SOW), 42
Pull communication, 333, 458, 578
Push communication, 333, 458, 578

▓ **Q**

Quality management and control tools
    activity network diagrams, 260
    activity-on-node (AON) diagrams, 260
    affinity diagrams, 257
    blank mind maps, 499
    interrelationship digraph, 259
    matrix diagrams, 260
    PDPC, 258
    prioritization matrices, 259, 260
    tree diagram, 259

▓ **R**

RACI chart, 286–287
Records management system, 578
Reporting system, 342
Requirements management plan, 98
Requirements traceability matrix, 104
Reserve analysis, 163
Resource breakdown structure, 154, 579
Resource calendars, 152, 295
Resource optimization techniques, 173
Responsibility assignment
        matrix (RAM), 286
Return on invested capital (ROIC), 41
Return on investment (ROI), 41
Risk breakdown structure (RBS), 579
Risk management knowledge area, 25
Risk register, 152, 158, 168, 208, 215, 245,
        367, 408
Risk urgency assessment, 580
Rolling-wave planning, 141

▓ **S**

Salience model, 449
Scatter diagram, 580
Schedule compression, 175
Schedule data, 177
Schedule forecasts, 183
Schedule network analysis, 169
Schedule performance index, 580
Scheduling tool, 175
Scope management, blank mind maps, 499
Sequence activities process
    activity attributes, 144
    activity list, 144
    domain, 143
    enterprise environmental factors, 145

inputs, 144
milestone list, 144
organizational process assets, 145
project scope statement, 144
schedule management plan, 144
Seven basic quality tools, plan quality
 management
 cause-and-effect diagram, 247
 checksheets, 248
 control charts, 250–251
 flowcharts, 247
 histograms, 249
 Ishikawa/fishbone diagram, 247
 Pareto diagram, 249
 scatter diagrams, 251
SOW. *See* Project statement of work (SOW)
Staffing management plan, 291
Stakeholder engagement assessment
 matrix, 454
Stakeholder management, blank mind
 maps, 499
Stakeholder management plan, 100
Stakeholder management process, 466
Stakeholder register, 100
Stakeholders identification
 domain tasks, 447
 inputs
  enterprise environmental
   factors, 447
  organizational process assets, 448
  procurement documents, 447
  project charter, 447
 process, 447
 stakeholder register, 450
 tools and techniques
  expert judgment, 449
  meetings, 450
  salience model, 449
  stakeholder analysis, 448–449
Standard deviation (SD) calculation,
 160–161
Start-to-start (SS), 146
SWOT analysis, 582

## ▓ T, U

TCPI. *See* To-complete performance index
 (TCPI)
Team-building activities, 305–306

Team performance assessments, 311
Time management
 blank mind maps, 499
 control schedule process, 134
 development process, 134
 knowledge area, 133
To-complete performance index (TCPI), 227
Total quality management (TQM), 583, 243
Tree diagram, 583
Tuckman's five-stage model of team
 development, 305, 316, 320, 583

## ▓ V

Validate scope process, 115
 accepted deliverables, 117
 change request, 117
 inputs, 115
 project documents, 118
 project management plan, 116
 requirements documentation, 116
 verified deliverables, 116
 work performance data, 117
Variance analysis, 120
Virtual teams, 284, 294
Vroom's expectancy theory, 301, 316, 321

## ▓ W, X, Y, Z

WBS. *See* Work breakdown structure
 (WBS)
WBS process, 110
 decomposition, 111
 dictionary, 113
 enterprise environmental
  factors, 111
 expert judgment, 112
 graphical representation, 111
 inputs, 110
 numbering system, 113
 organizational process assets, 111
 project document updates, 114
 project scope statement, 110
 scope baseline, 112
 validate scope, 115
Work breakdown structure (WBS), 109,
 113, 155, 286, 584
Work performance data, 121, 342
Work performance reports, 311

# Get the eBook for only $5!

Why limit yourself?

Now you can take the weightless companion with you wherever you go and access your content on your PC, phone, tablet, or reader.

Since you've purchased this print book, we're happy to offer you the eBook in all 3 formats for just $5.

Convenient and fully searchable, the PDF version enables you to easily find and copy code—or perform examples by quickly toggling between instructions and applications. The MOBI format is ideal for your Kindle, while the ePUB can be utilized on a variety of mobile devices.

To learn more, go to www.apress.com/companion or contact support@apress.com.

Printed in the United States
By Bookmasters